Jacket illustrations

Front: detail of a head of Zeus, from a temple at Lo
Scasato, Falerii Veteres. Rome, Museo di Villa
Giulia
Back: cemetery, Sutri

Overleaf
Tomba dei Rilievi, cemetery of Cerveteri

Frontispiece
Wrestlers, from the Tomba degli Auguri, Tarquinia

Jacket illustrations

Front: detail of a head of Zeus, from a temple at Lo
Scasato, Falerii Veteres. Rome, Museo di Villa
Giulia
Back: cemetery, Sutri

Overleaf
Tomba dei Rilievi, cemetery of Cerveteri

Frontispiece
Wrestlers, from the Tomba degli Auguri, Tarquinia

Francesca Boitani

Maria Cataldi

Marinella Pasquinucci

Etruscan Cities

with an Introduction by Mario Torelli

General Editor: Filippo Coarelli

Cassell · London

Editorial Manager
Orlando Bernardi

Assistant Editors
Fernando Solinas
Salvatore Canni

Design
Daniele Baroni

Layout
Floriana Sciarpa

Maps and Plans
Marina Bighellini

Photography
Marcella Pedone
Mauro Pucciarelli

English Translation
Catherine Atthill
Elisabeth Evans
Simon Pleasance
Pamela Swinglehurst

CASSELL & COMPANY LTD
an imprint of
Cassell & Collier Macmillan Publishers Ltd
35 Red Lion Square, London WC1R 4SG
and at Sydney, Auckland, Toronto, Johannesburg
*and an affiliate of The Macmillan Publishing Company
Inc, New York*

Originally published in Italian as
LE CITTÀ ETRUSCHE
Copyright © 1973, 1974 by Arnoldo Mondadori
CEAM Milan
English translation copyright © 1975 by
Cassell & Company Ltd

Filmset by BAS Printers Limited, Wallop,
Hampshire
Printed in Italy by A Mondadori Editore, Verona

ISBN 0 304 29602 3

Contents

Sources of illustrations

Introduction

Pistoia

Lucca

Quinto Fiorentino

Comeana

Fiesole (Faesulae)

Pisa

Artimino

Florence

Arno

Livorno

P Sócana

Castiglioncello

Castellina in Chianti

Arezzo (Arretium)

Volterra (Volaterrae)

Cecina-Vada

Siena (Saena)

Cortona

Asciano

Murlo

Perugia (Perusia)

Massa Marittima

L. Trasimene

Montepulciano

Chiusi (Clusium)

Populonia

Vetulonia

Roselle

Ombrone

Orvieto

Tiber

Elba (Ilva)

Grosseto

Saturnia

Sovana

Sorano

Bolsena

Magliano

Montemerano

Pitigliano

Volsinii

Poggio Buco

Bisenzio

Talamone

Marsiliana

L. Bolsena

Ferento

Orte

Vulci

Tuscania

Acquarossa

Montecristo (Oglasa?)

Orbetello

Viterbo

Cosa

Civita Castellana (Falerii Veteres)

Giglio (Igilium)

Vetralla

L. Vico

Tarquinia

Giannutri (Dianium)

Blera

Sutri

Nepi

Capena

Monti della Tolfa

Mignone

Civitavecchia (Centumcellae)

L. Bracciano

S. Marinella

Cerveteri (Caere)

Tiber

Santa Severa **(Pyrgi)**

Veio (Veii)

Palo

Rome

Fregenae

Both ancient and modern authorities have expressly recognized that the Etruscans should be credited with the beginnings of civilization in the whole of central Italy, between the area under the direct political control or influence of the Greek colonies in southern Italy and the northern boundary of ancient Italy, traditionally drawn between the rivers Magra and Rubicon. According to the Augustan administrative division of Italy, Etruria, where the historic Etruscan cities were situated, was the area bordered by the Arno to the north and the Apennines and the Tiber to the east and south, an area corresponding to modern Tuscany, the western part of Umbria and northern Latium. But Etruscan political control extended beyond their homeland. There were Etruscan colonies in central Campania and much of the plain of the Po by the Archaic period, probably from late prehistoric times and certainly from the 7th century B.C.; these survived in one instance until the end of the 5th century B.C. and in another until the end of the 4th century B.C. Direct rule was extended, according to our sources, by the traditional means of confederations of city-states in groups of twelve (each known as a dodecapolis). This implies that there must also have been some kind of indirect political control over the scattered population of the areas in between, to give some unity to the territories under Etruscan rule. For example, Rome, lying between Etruria and the Etruscan colonies of Campania, at a point where the Tiber could easily be crossed, was ruled for more than a century by a dynasty of Etruscan kings, traditionally from 616 to 509 B.C.

The twelve cities of Etruria proper included the great coastal cities of Cerveteri, Veii, Tarquinia, Vulci, Vetulonia, Roselle and Populonia, and the cities of Volsinii, Chiusi, Perugia, Arezzo and Volterra in northern and central Etruria. With the downfall of some of these, other cities—initially of lesser importance—were added, for instance Cortona and Fiesole. In Roman times, with the Augustan religious revival, the *duodecim populi* became fifteen, with the further addition of cities such as Pisa which had been insignificant or even outside the boundaries of Etruria at the time of Etruscan independence.

While it is not easy to identify the original twelve cities of Etruria, it is impossible to reconstruct completely the dodecapolis of Campania and that of the Po valley. The names of some of the cities are known, and in modern times other cities have been discovered which could also have been members, although we do not know their names; for example, the sizeable city discovered near the small town of Marzabotto in Emilia. The most important city in Campania was certainly Capua, then called Volturnum. Other Etruscan centres were Nola, Acerra, Nocera and the important but nameless centre near Pontecagnano (Salerno); coins give the names of other cities which have not yet been identified: Irnthi (there is a river Irno in the Salerno region), Velsu, Urina, Velcha. In the Po valley the most important city was Félsina (Bologna), and other towns almost certainly founded by the Etruscans are Ravenna, Cesena, Mantua, Rimini, Spina, Parma, Piacenza, Modena and Melpum (Milan).

Populonia. Cemetery of Porcareccia: exterior view
of the Tomba dei Flabelli

This organization of the city-states into confederations was not meant to unite them in a single organic structure. The system derived from a prehistoric custom of religious association which was revived again in the Archaic period under the influence of the Greek leagues (particularly the Ionian League). The only assemblies were the festivals held periodically in Etruria at the great sanctuary near Volsinii, the *Fanum Voltumnae*. Most probably similar sanctuaries existed for the colonies in Campania and the Po valley; the temple of Diana Tifatina near Capua has been suggested in modern times as the probable sanctuary of the Campanian confederation.

Besides their land empire, the Etruscans exercised considerable sea power; indeed, the Tyrrhenian Sea, the part of the Mediterranean that washes the west coast of Italy, is called by their name (in its Greek form Tyrsenoi or Tyrrhenoi). Etruscan thalassocracy (mastery of the seas), dated, as we shall see, between the 8th and 5th centuries B.C., brought Corsica under Etruscan control: there is clear evidence of their presence in the former Phocaean colony Alalia (modern Aléria). However, except for Populonia, no important Etruscan city was actually built on the coast; the so-called coastal cities—including such prominent towns of southern Etruria as Cerveteri, Tarquinia, Vulci, Vetulonia and Roselle —are in fact some distance inland, though they often had ports on the coast which were politically and administratively dependent on them. Cerveteri, for example, had three outlets, the main one at Pyrgi and the other two at Punicum (Santa Marinella) and Alsium (Palo). Tarquinia's port was Gravisca. The landing-places on the *Lacus Prelius* (by mediaeval times the marshes of Castiglione, near Grosseto) served Vetulonia and Roselle, while Vulci's port was near Montalto di Castro, on a site identified with the mythical Regisvilla.

The cities of Etruria proper, at least, generally have certain geographical and topographical features in common. The oldest settlements, whether they subsequently became important cities or remained small villages, were usually set on top of hills rising from the surrounding farmland. Usually there were steep slopes on three or four sides, with one or more watercourses providing a reliable water supply and an easy means of communication. Around the main cities was a network of small centres. These gradually decreased in number between the 7th and 4th centuries B.C. and changed in function: from being ordinary small rural settlements they became strongholds (*castella*, *oppida*) for border defence and control. In Roman times some of these *oppida* won political and administrative independence, as a result of their changed status after the decline of the city-states, now reduced to the level of an ordinary Roman *municipium*. Typical of these changes are the smaller towns round Tarquinia—Tuscania, Blera and Castel d'Asso—which became comparatively important mediaeval towns.

Origins

The problem of Etruscan origins was posed by the earliest Ionian historians. Whereas the origins of other peoples of ancient Italy were not considered a problem, the national consciousness of the Etruscans, which made them seem a people set apart from the others, and the high level of culture which they reached at such an early date raised the questions of their origin. Classical authors themselves were unable to agree on the question. It was the historian Dionysius of Halicarnassus (I, 25–30) in the 1st century B.C. who first discussed all the alternative theories; he rejected the hypotheses that the Etruscans were either pre-Greek Pelasgians from the Aegean area or Lydians from Asia Minor and instead suggested that they were an indigenous people called the Rasenna, a theory which he claimed came from the Etruscans themselves.

The oldest theory and the one most favoured in the ancient world was that of an Etruscan migration from Lydia in legendary times; the fullest version of the story appears in Herodotus (5th century B.C.). It was widely accepted amongst Greeks and Romans, so that in their texts the ethnic terms 'Lydian' and 'Etruscan' are synonymous. A variation on Herodotus is to be found in his contemporary Hellanicus, who identified the Etruscans as the nomad Pelasgians. This theory is combined with the other 'Lydian' theory by Anticlides (3rd century B.C.; quoted by Strabo), who refers to a Pelasgian migration led by Tyrrhenos (the name of the Lydian king in Herodotus's story) after colonizing the Aegean islands of Lemnos and Imbros.

Modern scholars have continued to work on these two theories of Eastern or indigenous origin, attempting to place either the migration or the moment when the Etruscans emerged as a people in ancient Italy in a precise historical, linguistic or cultural context.

Eastern sources (primarily Egyptian) speak of an invasion taking place at the time of the pharaohs Amenhotep and Rameses III (1230–1170 B.C.), which was repulsed by Rameses. The invaders were a group of 'peoples of the sea', including, as well as Achaeans, Philistines, Lycians and Dardanians, the *Trš.w*. While there is general agreement in identifying the Egyptian names of the first four as peoples well known in other contexts, uncertainty about the transliteration of the Egyptian texts makes it impossible confidently to identify the *Trš.w* with the Tyrsenoi or Etruscans, although many modern historians have wished to do so. The theory is an inviting one, as it would make it possible to date the Etruscan migration to the west at the same time as the upheaval of the Eastern world at the end of the 2nd millennium B.C., but it cannot yet be adequately proved. However, the slight but significant evidence for the language which the natives of Lemnos used before the Athenian conquest in the 6th century and their subsequent assimilation, shows that the pre-Hellenic dialect of Lemnos and the Etruscan language were closely related.

Linguistic evidence shows that Etruscan was isolated from the other languages of ancient Italy, which were mainly of Indo-European origin, although obviously over the centuries contact between the Italic dialects (of the proto-Latin and Umbro-Sabellic groups) and Etruscan influenced the linguistic structure and vocabulary of both.

Archaeological evidence, however, provides a unified and coherent picture of the cultural development of Italy between the end of the 2nd millennium and the early centuries of the 1st millennium B.C. The dominant culture of the peninsula during the 2nd millennium B.C. was the Bronze Age Apennine culture, which extended from the southern part of the Po plain to Calabria and was quite distinct from the Terramara culture of northern Italy. Towards the end of the 2nd millennium B.C. Apennine culture by a gradual process developed into the Sub-Apennine culture, under strong north Italian influence. Within the Sub-Apennine culture there are signs—although they lack geographical continuity— of evolution towards a new culture, the proto-Villanovan, source of the Villanovan culture which spread through the protohistoric age over the area of the peninsula that was occupied in historical times by the Etruscans.

On the basis of the evidence provided by literature, history, linguistics and archaeology, modern scholars have put forward a number of reconstructions of Etruscan origins, based in part on the old theories breaking new ground. The theory of Eastern origin has, in part been widely upheld, both because it was so generally accepted by the ancients, and because of the powerful linguistic evidence of the similarities between Etruscan and the dialect of Lemnos. While one may not now agree with some scholars who postulate a migration in the 7th century B.C. to explain the great flowering of Etruscan culture during the Orientalizing period, nonetheless the Eastern theory is the one which best takes account of the available data. Of course the arrival of the Etruscans would not have occurred in the way described by classical historians, as a single mass migration. Instead we should think in terms of the establishment of small groups which could be defined as proto-Etruscan in terms of language, but which were not yet Etruscan in terms of culture, since Etruscan culture and national identity developed gradually in historical times, on Italian soil.

The theory that the Etruscans were a native race is one which appeals mainly to certain linguists and is supported chiefly by Dionysius's statements. Etruscan is seen as an isolated relic of an earlier 'Mediterranean' linguistic substratum. However, this hypothesis con-

Top: hut-shaped bronze cinerary urn, from Vulci (?). Rome, Museo di Villa Giulia

Above: boat-shaped nuraghic lamp, from Porto Clementino (Gravisca). Tarquinia, Museo Nazionale

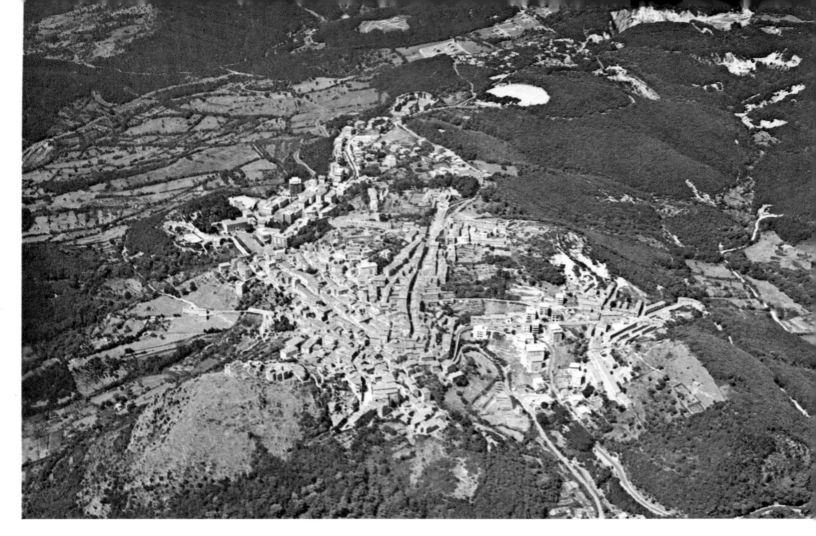

Tolfa, on the northeastern slopes of the Monti della
Tolfa, 24 km from Civitavecchia

flicts both with the well-documented reconstruction of the evolution of the Aegean world
in the 2nd millennium B.C. which is now possible, and with the linguistic situation in
ancient Italy, in which successive waves of Indo-European linguistic deposits overlaid
pre-Indo-European strata which cannot easily be related to Etruscan; the dynamic of
this process, again, conflicts with the theory of indigenous origin. The known archaeological
situation also appears to be at odds with this reconstruction; it does not easily admit of
different migratory movements bringing new linguistic elements (in this instance Indo-
European).

These two ancient theories have now been joined by a third modern reconstruction of
the origins of the Etruscans, according to which the Etruscans invaded from the north;
this is based on a controversial passage in Livy (V,33,11) about the origin of the Rhaetians,
whom he believed to be barbarized Etruscans, and on the undeniable similarities between
the Danubian and Italic cultures of the beginnings of the 1st millennium B.C. But this
hypothesis again disregards some of the evidence and, in the standard positivist fashion,
confuses ethnographic with historical and cultural data. Apart from anything else, the
similarities between Etruscan and the dialect of Lemnos mean that to uphold this theory
one must imagine complex movements of the proto-Etruscans on two fronts, in both the
Italian and the Balkan peninsulas, and these movements do not tally with the ethnic and
linguistic situation of the areas involved.

To conclude this brief survey, it should be emphasized that the problem of Etruscan origins has to be seen in the context of a complex process of cultural formation, of which we can see only the end results. The question, then, is not so much where the Etruscans came from, as how they became what they were, and it is obvious that Eastern influences played a dominant part in this.

History

Although the first signs of the formation of an Etruscan people can be seen in the development of Villanovan civilization, it is more difficult to make a judgement about the proto-Villanovan stage. There are several proto-Villanovan centres known outside the area the Etruscans were to occupy—Tímmari in Lucania, Pianello della Genga in the Marches, and Bismantova and Fontanella Mantovana in Emilia. In Etruria itself important proto-Villanovan sites have been discovered in the Monti della Tolfa (near modern Allumiere), at Luni sul Mignone and along the upper reaches of the river Fiora. Characteristic of the proto-Villanovan culture are fortified settlements of huts built on the tops of high hills, cremation cemeteries with burials which on the whole consist of roughly-made biconical urns of impasto (unpurified fired clay), placed in stone holders, and a fairly simple range of pottery drawing only in part on Sub-Apennine tradition, decorated with comb-incised patterns of primitive geometric motifs and grooves. At a later stage elements appeared which were to flourish subsequently—for example the hut-urn and a range of different types of fibula (a kind of brooch or safety pin of Eastern origin), including the simple bow and violin-bow. It has been suggested that the proto-Villanovan culture was an isolated local variant of the more widespread and important Villanovan culture. But even though the later phases of proto-Villanovan may have overlapped the earliest Villanovan period, the style of the fibulae and the general character of proto-Villanovan culture bear marked 'early' characteristics. Unfortunately the two cultures are not related stratigraphically, but the various Villanovan sequences presuppose, from the point of view of both culture and topography, the existence of a preliminary proto-Villanovan period.

Unlike proto-Villanovan, Villanovan culture (so called after Villanova near Bologna, where the first discoveries were made during the 19th century) has a more even geographical spread, covering the area round Bologna, the bordering areas of Romagna, the whole of Etruria and Etruscan Campania, and it is generally more coherent in character and structure. The fact that the geographical distribution of Villanovan culture more or less coincides with the ancient historical sites of the Etruscans, and the cultural continuity from this protohistoric stage into the historical era, have generally led people to consider Villanovan culture as a preliminary stage to Etruscan culture.

Unfortunately Villanovan culture is known more from its cemeteries than from systematic exploration of its settlements. This is partly because modern archaeologists prefer to excavate the richer and more homogeneous sites, and partly because many of the Villanovan dwellings are in fact underneath other dwellings dating from the historical era, some of them still standing. The cemeteries, however, always stand alone on high ground surrounding the inhabited area, or at any rate beyond the edge of the town, a custom which survived through the centuries down to the Middle Ages.

Although there is little to go on, it can be said that the earliest Villanovan settlements were mostly built on low but easily defensible hills; later they also appeared on the plains and along the coast. The settlements consisted of a small number of huts. There is no definite evidence of fortifications from this period, but it seems probable that they were defended by palisades or earthworks with small ditches. An interesting question concerns the settlements situated in places where the great historical Etruscan cities were to develop

(unfortunately only cursorily explored): was the later urban area completely covered with huts (and thus a kind of proto-city), or were the huts split up into independent nuclei, not actually linked together? The distribution of cemeteries around these areas is also relevant to this question. There may be four or five separate cemeteries in the vicinity, and it seems to fit existing documentation and evidence from sources for the history of Rome better to assume that these villages were nuclei of a tribal nature, with primitive political links between them, but each having a degree of autonomy. The number of cemeteries would support this.

The Villanovan cemeteries were really urnfields, similar in structure to those of central Europe: the tombs are pit-tombs dug deep into the soft tufaceous rock, and containing the biconical cinerary urn, richly decorated with incised swastikas and meanders, covered with a bowl in the case of a woman's burial, or a high-crested pottery helmet for a man. The remains were accompanied by a few personal ornaments—fibulae, bracelets, necklaces, weapons (swords, spearheads and horses' bits), symbolic objects (spindle whorls and spindles) and a few small vases, mainly for ritual purposes. The picture of Villanovan economic and social structure to be drawn from this archaeological evidence is of a society organized along tribal lines, with a primitive division of labour according to sex, but still fairly egalitarian, with artisan activities which were only marginal, except for the comparatively well-developed metal-work influenced by the advanced metallurgy of central Europe and the Danube. The basis of the economy was certainly agriculture, as is shown by both the distribution of population and the implements for milling grain which have been found; animal husbandry, mainly of smaller breeds, appears to have been a permanent feature.

At the beginning of the 8th century B.C., with the first visits from Greek and Phoenician seafarers, we find a gradual change in the Villanovan social structure, as it changes from a broadly egalitarian society into one divided into classes. An easily recognizable richer class emerges, with increasing means at its disposal; this can be deduced from the growing richness of some tombs compared with the others. The practice of inhumation of the dead spread. It is significant that in the later cremations, contemporary with the first inhumations, the cinerary urns are less decorated or even unadorned, and the use of hut-urns disappears; these were common particularly in southern Etruria and Latium (as part of the 'Latial' culture of the proto-Latin peoples) at the beginning of the Iron Age. The designs of fibulae become markedly more varied: as well as the disc-footed and enlarged-bow fibulae of the early Villanovan period, we find serpentine, elbow and leech-shaped fibulae, while the catch-plate gradually becomes longer, perhaps influenced by a Greek fashion seen in the oldest tombs of Pithecusa (Ischia), founded about 770 B.C.

Just as the early Villanovan cultural unity became fragmented, so apparently did its territorial unity. Compared with the uniformity of Apennine and Sub-Apennine culture in the Bronze Age, the variety of cultures in the Iron Age of prehistoric Italy indicates the emergence of different ethnic groups; similarly the territorial fragmentation of Villanovan culture shows that urbanization was already taking place as a result of the division of society into classes.

The coastal regions of southern Etruria were by far the most advanced economically, with Tarquinia in the lead, followed by Veii and Vulci; Capua also became important. On the other hand, the Po valley and central and northern Etruria remained culturally isolated, developing more slowly and gaining nothing from outside contacts. The first signs of the Etruscan urban civilization of the historical period appeared in the coastal towns, the region of Campania most in contact with the Greek colonies of Ischia and Cumae (740 B.C.) and in the non-Etruscan area between Etruria proper and Campania, that is to say at Rome and Praeneste (Palestrina).

By the last decades of the 8th century B.C. the centres which had undergone the process of urbanization and social diversification had acquired some of the status of cities. Classes of nobles emerged, though certainly prehistoric monarchical institutions survived

Vulci. Ponte and Castello della Badia

Three-lobed oinochoe with Subgeometric decoration. Tarquinia, Museo Nazionale

too. With precious Eastern and Orientalizing objects increasingly available, the nobles vied with one another in pomp and splendour in their everyday life and burial ceremonies. Cerveteri became increasingly powerful, at the expense of nearby Tarquinia and also perhaps neighbouring Veii. At that time Cerveteri gained control of the Monti della Tolfa with their mineral deposits, which may have been known from the Mycenaean age, as is suggested by the fragments of Mycenaean pottery found in the Apennine and Sub-Apennine strata at Luni sul Mignone. It should not be forgotten that while the economic foundations of Villanovan and Archaic Etruscan society were primarily agricultural, much of Etruscan economic expansion was due to the vast mineral deposits of iron, copper, silver and alum to be found in the Monti della Tolfa, the Colline Metallifere, Monte Argentario, Monte Amiata and Elba, all firmly in the control of one or another Etruscan *polis*. Moreover, the earliest Greek colony, Ischia, was apparently established to trade, primarily in metals, with Etruria.

The noble tombs of the Orientalizing period, often treasure troves of gold, silver, amber and bronze objects, are monumental and architecturally complex chamber-tombs built under tumuli: for example, the *tholoi* or false vaults of central and northern Etruria, or the magnificent imitations of house interiors discovered in the Cerveteri cemeteries. Tomb furnishings of this first Orientalizing phase include the treasure, worthy of a Pharaoh, buried with a member of the Larth family in the Tomba Regolini-Galassi at Cerveteri, or the riches of Vetus, the Etruscan lord of Latin Praeneste, buried in the Tomba Bernardini. During the 7th century B.C. the changes which had occurred earlier in southern Etruria spread to the central and northern cities. While some cities continued to develop only slowly, others revealed rich economic potential, with an active aristocratic class in process of becoming thoroughly Hellenized. In the second half of the century, with the decline of Vetulonia, Vulci became more powerful.

At the same time there was more rapid development in what had previously been fringe areas: for example Populonia, or round the upper reaches of the Arno (Quinto Fiorentino, Comeana, Artimino), doubtless because that area controlled the natural route to the Po valley and Emilia.

Etruscan mastery of the sea or thalassocracy dates from the same period. Evidence of it comes mainly from Greek sources, but it is illustrated too by some important Etruscan monuments: for example, the Tomba della Nave at Cerveteri, or the vase showing a naval battle between Greeks and Etruscans, painted by the Greek painter Aristonothos who emigrated to Cerveteri about the middle of the 7th century. The Etruscans' ruthless and systematic rule over the Tyrrhenian Sea involved piracy; although this meant that for the Greeks 'Etruscans' and 'pirates' were synonymous, their activity must be seen in the context of an economic system which made no clear distinction between piracy and trade. Indeed, the most enterprising Greeks, the Ionians, and more particularly the Phocaeans, had a similar reputation. Etruscan privateering (and therefore trade) was in direct competition with Greek seafaring activities, whether based on the Greek cities of the eastern Mediterranean or on the Greek colonies in the west. Thus it is possible to date to this period the beginnings of the rivalry between Greeks and Etruscans, a rivalry which later brought Greek warships to the Etruscan coast, Etruscan raids on the coast of southern Italy and Sicily, and a number of battles: between Cumaean and Etruscan hoplites beneath the walls of Ariccia; between the allied Carthaginian and Etruscan fleets and the Phocaean fleet off Sardinia; and between the Etruscan ships and those of Hieron of Syracuse off Cumae.

This growth of sea power may have begun as early as the 8th century if Ephorus (4th century B.C.) is correct in maintaining that the first colonists of Naxos (the oldest Greek colony in Sicily, founded traditionally in 736 B.C.) encountered Etruscan 'pirates' off the Sicilian coast. It was matched by vigorous expansion on land. The Etruscans needed to control the routes to Campania through Latin territory, and so already in the first half of the 7th century we find Etruscan princes at Praeneste and, traditionally from 616 B.C., Etruscan kings at Rome.

However, this expansion did not proceed altogether smoothly. At first, during the last half of the 7th century and the first quarter of the 6th century the urban structure of the southern Etruscan cities was still 'open' and the cities were capable of absorbing alien elements. This is illustrated by the legend (historically quite plausible) of the arrival in Tarquinia of the exile Demaratos from Corinth, or by the Etruscan inscriptions found at Tarquinia and Cerveteri showing that people of Greek origin were admitted into the Etruscan social structure. However, from the first decades of the 6th century B.C. such incidents become rarer and then disappear altogether. Instead, areas were established outside the cities for trading, which was the chief point of contact with foreigners; an example is the Greek sanctuary which developed during the early 6th century B.C. at Gravisca, outside Tarquinia. The aim was twofold: to keep out the floating population of foreigners and to facilitate fiscal control, that is the levying of dues, a long-standing feature of Mediterranean ports. In this context must also be placed the achievements of Servius Tullius, one of the Etruscan kings of Rome, who created an organization for the city, building boundary walls, giving it a political structure and establishing a monetary system. The city thus acquired a definite character, becoming 'closed' instead of 'open' and more or less obviously different in nature from the countryside. Significantly Servius Tullius was held to be 'democratic', and his actions point to the social divisions that were developing in the Etruscan cities and were to erupt at the end of the 6th century with the direct seizure of power by the aristocracy and the setting up of republican regimes.

The 6th century was marked not only by the first signs of bitter social division. It was also a time of internal hostilities between Etruscan cities and international conflict between Etruscans and Greeks. The Etruscan legend about Servius Tullius, recorded by the learned emperor Claudius and depicted in the frescoes of the Tomba François at Vulci, is not the same as the Roman story; instead it describes Servius Tullius as an Etruscan military leader from Vulci, at odds with the Tarquin dynasty from Tarquinia. Once Rome was free of the Etruscan kings, it found itself in conflict with a king from Chiusi; eventually the two made common cause against the Tarquins' attempt to regain the city. Aristodemos, ruler of Cumae, in 504 B.C. defeated the Etruscan forces in a great battle fought under the walls of Ariccia, involving two huge coalitions of people from the whole of central Italy. On the other hand, when refugees from Phocaea, the great Ionian city destroyed by the Persians about 540 B.C., settled at Aléria in Corsica, the Etruscans from Cerveteri had to join up with the Carthaginians and fight the Phocaean fleet off Sardinia, probably near Aléria itself. The Phocaeans were defeated and forced to abandon Corsica to the Etruscans and Sardinia to the Carthaginians.

The unsettled internal and international situation, together with a series of dramatic events in the eastern Mediterranean, including the Ionian revolt (494 B.C.) and the Graeco-Persian wars, caused a series of economic and political setbacks in Etruria. Greek imports into Etruria were sharply reduced as a result of the collapse of Ionia. Trade was also affected by the emergence of a trading centre at Spina on the Po delta, intended to supply the new expanding market of the Po valley and nearer to the important outlets of the major communication routes to central Europe. In the south, the decline was already apparent in the early 5th century B.C. and became rapid in the second half of the century, wheras at this same period we find an unprecedented increase in the quantity and quality of pottery at Spina and Bologna. Meanwhile in 474 B.C. Etruscan sea power suffered a major blow when Hieron of Syracuse destroyed an Etruscan fleet off Cumae; by setting up a garrison on Ischia, which the Cumaeans had given him as a reward, he blocked the Etruscans' passage to the south. The loss of control over Latium at about the same time cut off their direct route to the colonies of Campania which, once isolated, were easy prey for the peoples of the Samnite hills fifty years later.

And so the 5th century B.C. was a time of withdrawal for the Etruscans, with their internal difficulties provoked by the rapid expansion and urbanization of the previous century, and international difficulties caused by the changed political and economic trends in the Mediterranean. Their plight is reflected by cultural stagnation all over the Etruscan territory and surrounding areas like the Faliscan and Latin regions. Rome was involved in bitter domestic struggles and local conflicts over a small area, very different from the theatre of events in the late 6th and early 5th centuries B.C. Its main opponents were Veii, Fidenae and the small Sabine and Latin cities, while the Volsci and the Aequi also acquired increasing strategic importance; these were mountain peoples attracted to the Latin plains by the more fertile soil, and by the power vacuum left after the collapse of Etruscan hegemony. This situation was perhaps the price which had to be paid for the rapid urbanization and the rivalry in expansion of the Etruscan cities (we should remember that about 500 B.C. the small towns of Acquarossa and Murlo were razed to the ground and abandoned); perhaps even more it was the result of the cities' rigid social system, exemplified by the clash between plebeians and patricians in Rome.

But at the close of the 5th century there are signs of renewal. Etruria seemed again to take the initiative in relation to the Greek colonies, with its participation under a Tarquinian *zilath* (praetor), Velthur Spurinna, in the ill-fated Athenian expedition against Syracuse (413 B.C.); retaliation followed thirty years later when Dionysios of Syracuse raided the Etruscan coastal cities (Pyrgi, 384 B.C.). There was also a definite cultural revival, with renewed building activity and the spread of new artistic products to all southern, central and northern Etruscan cities, after the stagnation of the second half of the 5th century. The revival was encouraged by the emergence of a new aristocracy: not the aristocracy which had appeared in the 7th century, developed during the 6th century and both flourished and declined during the 5th century, but a new, landed nobility, proud of itself and of its traditions; by analogy with Rome, it could be defined as patricio-plebeian.

At Cerveteri, Tarquinia, Volterra and Volsinii and most other Etruscan cities new boundary walls were built round the extensive inhabited area. This revealed an enthusiasm for building which could not be explained solely by fear of invaders. After all, the new invaders, the Gauls, were forced to abandon Etruria after being repulsed by Chiusi and defeated by Cerveteri. They then, with greater success, attacked Latium and Rome (390

B.C.). Hostilities between Etruscan cities were not yet finished: Rome took over Veii with the tacit consent of the other Etruscan cities, particularly Cerveteri, which had a pact of political and military alliance with Rome; this pact was scrupulously honoured for many years and saved Rome's sacred objects during the Gallic invasion. From epigraphic and literary documents we learn that the 'kings' of Cerveteri were dispossessed by a Tarquinian praetor; that Tarquinia intervened in the internal affairs of Arezzo during a slave revolt; that there were violent struggles for supremacy in the league of Etruscan cities.

These events appear from our sources to have culminated in the struggle between Rome, scarcely recovered from the Gallic disaster, and Tarquinia and Falerii, with the acquiescence of Cerveteri, in 358–353 B.C. Roman sources describe this as an episode which finished well for Rome, but other evidence and the small body of information from non-Roman sources suggest that the outcome was not total victory. However, events did favour Rome. Expansion towards Campania, at the expense of the Samnites who had settled there with the collapse of Etruscan rule in 424 B.C., gave Rome an economic and military potential which the divided Etruscans could not match. There was a series of clashes with various Etruscan cities in the last decades of the 4th century B.C., culminating in the decisive battle of Sentinum (295 B.C.) between Romans and a great coalition of Etruscans, Samnites, Umbrians and Gauls. Rome was able to bring the Etruscan cities to their knees, one after another, from Cerveteri (292 or 273 B.C.) and Vulci (280) to Volsinii (265), right into the heart of the Etruscan territory.

The outcome of these clashes was that the coastal stretches of the territory of Cerveteri, Tarquinia and Vulci were confiscated and used to found Roman and Latin *coloniae*—at Alsium, Fregenae, Pyrgi, Castrum Novum (S. Marinella), Gravisca and Cosa—near the sites of the ports of the Etruscan cities; a series of treaties was concluded with the rest of the Etruscan cities, committing them to supplying military aid to Rome if required (as was done for Scipio's expedition to Africa in 205 B.C.), in exchange for implicit recognition of their political independence. However, this so-called independence was a mere formality, in accordance with the wishes not only of the Romans, but of the Etruscans themselves. This is shown by events at Volsinii in 265–264 B.C. There, perhaps as an outcome of the social upheaval which inevitably follows war, the *servi* or slaves had infiltrated the ruling classes, as a result of the increasing use of the *manumissio* procedure for freeing slaves, and had taken power; the *domini*, the dispossessed rulers, requested Roman intervention. When it came it was ruthless, ending with the destruction of the city, which stood where Orvieto now is (according to one interpretation of the literary and archaeological evidence), and the removal of the population to a new site at Volsinii Novi (Bolsena). This terrible episode, which is barely mentioned by the rather sketchy literary sources, is recalled by a great monument erected by the victor M. Fulvius Flaccus at Rome in the temple of Fortuna and Mater Matuta (the so-called sacred area of S. Omobono), with traces of the bronze statues, two thousand of which were taken as loot during the sack of the city, or more probably of the federal sanctuary, the *Fanum Voltumnae*. Similar events occurred earlier at Arezzo, in 302 B.C., when an internal revolt against the powerful clan of the Cilnii was crushed by Roman military intervention.

In the late 4th century and the first half of the 3rd Etruria was thus again in a critical state of social unrest. Despite the renewal at the end of the 5th and the beginning of the 4th century, the aristocratic structure had proved incapable of dealing with social tension and change. Without a solid commercial base as time went on, it simply chose to rely on the imperialist might of Rome. In the centuries which followed, especially in the southern cities, the surviving aristocrats sought ways of integrating themselves into the Roman ruling class, abandoning their cities of origin. Later, Rome's imperialist wars in the Mediterranean destroyed the traditional system of production in Italy, based on small agricultural holdings. The labour market was flooded with increasing numbers of slaves, bought in the market-places of the East or looted in the conquests of the West. This sealed the fate of the agricultural economy of central and northern Etruria. Tiberius Gracchus, to support the proposed measures of his agrarian reform, took the plight of the Etruscan countryside as an example of land to be reclaimed, since he described it as populated only by a scanty slave work force of barbarian origin. This may have been true of southern Etruria, where the Etruscan nobles must have followed Cato's precepts in his treatise on farming, thus laying the foundations for the famous *Tusca ergastula*, the large slave farms found in Etruria in the early days of the Empire. But the land around Chiusi, Volterra and Perugia must still have been farmed by many small landowners, the farmers who in 91 B.C., threatened by the agrarian laws of Livius Drusus, organized a protest march on the capital to demonstrate their opposition to the tribune's proposed reforms. In vain did the Etruscans turn to their favourite brand of propaganda—prophecy, proclaimed in written form (a small fragment has survived, apocalyptic in tone, which was placed in the mouth of the Etruscan nymph Vegoia), or in the Etruscan haruspices' interpretations of prodigies (unnatural occurrences on earth or in the heavens), an activity which was, symptomatically, much on the increase at this time.

The fate of Etruria was settled. The Social War (the revolt of Rome's Italian *socii* or allies), started by the equally desperate Samnites, failed, and the survivors of this protest joined Marius's faction in its bitter struggle against the oligarchical groups of the Roman senate. The Etruscans instinctively sided with Marius and in revenge Sulla dealt harshly with the rebel cities, settling *coloniae* of his own veterans there. The last signs of life came in the middle of the 1st century B.C. The revolts against Sulla's colonists, swiftly crushed by Rome, the support for Catiline, the dramatic last attempt at revolt at Perugia, drowned in blood by the cynical Octavian, mark the final stages in the destruction of the Etruscans as a people. The surviving aristocrats, at first hesitantly, then, with the restoration under Augustus (Octavian's eventual title), eagerly took refuge in the Roman senate. There they gradually stagnated, smugly proud of their ancient lineage, in an assembly increasingly made up of ex-centurions and provincials. Pointlessly and pathetically they defended their old customs, but in the changed climate of Imperial autocracy they were utterly ignored, as was to be expected.

Religion

The extensive Hellenization of Etruscan culture from the 8th century B.C. gave Greek forms to Etruscan deities, myths and ritual. This largely obliterated its origins in primitive agriculture religion, aspects and figures which can only occasionally be traced. The bronze lid of a cinerary urn from the Bisenzio cemetery (Museo di Villa Giulia) is thus particularly important, since it antedates the representation of the native deities in human form; it depicts a ritual dance of armed men round a monstrous creature, which should be interpreted as a non-anthropomorphic Etruscan underworld deity, like, for instance, the fearful infernal *larvae* of Roman tradition.

By the late 7th century the process by which the Etruscan pantheon was assimilated to the Greek one appears complete. All over Etruria there appear representations of Greek myths according to Greek iconographic conventions. By the 6th century each important Etruscan deity had his or her equivalent among the Greeks: Tinia is Zeus, Uni Hera, Menerva Athene, Turan Aphrodite, Turms Hermes, Nethuns Poseidon, and so on. Other deities were imported directly from Greece: for example Apulu/Apollo, Aritimi/ Artemis and Hercle/Heracles. However, there were some who seem to have been assimilated to Greek figures only superficially, if at all: for example the obscure Voltumna (Vertumnus in Latin), the god of the federal sanctuary at Volsinii, who was perhaps a god of the earth; or the mysterious semi-divine female Lasae, roughly equivalent to the Greek nymphs, who were able to interpret local myths and also figured in the complicated Etruscan afterlife; they were often depicted on mirrors. But on the whole the Archaic Etruscan religious world was extensively Hellenized, to judge from the Greek or Graecizing appearance of most religious sculpture and painting. At this time, however, the foundations were laid for a ritual which was a peculiar heritage of the Etruscans and was developed and perfected after the 4th century: the grouping of deities into triads, or groups of three, introduced into Rome by the Etruscan dynasty (with the Capitoline triad of Jupiter, Juno and Minerva). Although perhaps affected by influences from Magna Graecia, the triads certainly developed in Etruria on a large scale and explain one of the most typical features of Etruscan religion— the temple with three cellae (it is a mistake to suppose that this feature was not Etruscan). Also in the Archaic period, the complex Etruscan science of divination developed. This involved augury, the observation of the flight of birds, and haruspicy, the examination of the entrails (especially the liver) of sacrificial animals. These doctrines, which were to make the Etruscans famous all over Italy, were founded on the ancient belief, fundamental to native religious thought from the earliest times, that there was a hidden correspondence between macrocosm and microcosm; and on the division of the sky into favourable and unfavourable quarters. It became customary in Rome to call on Etruscan haruspices whenever particularly weird prodigies occurred: as the haruspices were of aristocratic extraction, their reactionary responses represented the official voice of Etruscan opinion about various political situations.

The Athena di Arezzo. Florence, Museo Archeologico

As a result of the upheavals of the early 4th century the Hellenized religion of the 7th to 5th centuries B.C. gave way to a new religious spirit, more adapted to popular needs. Native legends, such as the story of the divine boy Tages or the story of Cacus/Cacu, play a greater part, or merge with old Greek myths through the addition of local heroes or Lasae. This change, which came with the transfer of power to new social classes, is clearly apparent in the new concepts of the after life. The old traditional *funus*, with funeral banquet, gladiatorial games and dancing, expressing an oligarchical view of the world, were replaced by fearful and tormented visions of the demons from Hades (Charun and the Lasae). The only reassuring note is the continuation of class distinctions, emphasized by the journey to the underworld in the style of a magistrate's procession. This dramatic vision of the afterlife, with its elements of Orphism and Neo-Pythagoreanism drawn from the Greek world of southern Italy, also figured in an extensive religious literature, collected in the *Libri Acherontici*. Then there were other religious books: the *Libri Rituales*, which recorded in detail the rites to be performed during public ceremonies, from the founding of cities to the conduct of a magistrate's duties; the *Libri Fatales*, which attempted to explain the hidden will of the gods, particularly the most mysterious and obscure; the *Libri Fulgurales* and *Aruspicini*, which described practices of divination from lightning or the liver of sacrificed animals. Fragments of these documents have reached us indirectly through Latin authors. Original Etruscan texts which have survived are the ritual calendar of the mummy of Zagreb (2nd or 1st century B.C.), a text written on linen which was cut up and used to wrap an Egyptian mummy—the text is thought to be part of the *Libri Rituales*; and the Capua tile (5th century B.C.), a long inscription on a tile found at Capua which perhaps gives a series of instructions for funeral rites and can thus be compared to the *Libri Acherontici*.

This account of Etruscan religion suggests a ritualistic religious mentality, obsessively seeking to grasp the hidden will of the gods. It clearly expresses the pessimism of the Etruscan ruling class in the 3rd and 2nd centuries B.C. But this fatalism inevitably also gave rise to expectations of salvation, particularly among the lower classes. These popular hopes seem to have found expression in what has been described as a 'healing mania': great quantities of clay models of limbs and other parts of the body were placed in all the Etruscan (and Latin) sanctuaries for the gods to heal. Then too there was the Dionysiac theology and practices, which promised a happy life free from the constraints of the class system. In fact when there was an outbreak of secret Bacchic worship at Rome, closely connected with extensive slave revolts, it was discovered that the signal for the rebellions came from Etruria, on the initiative of Etruscan priests, described by Livy as a people unequalled in their devotion to religious rituals. Cato's advice that slaves should be forbidden to consult *harioli*, wandering soothsayers, usually Etruscans, was thus obviously prudent and well-founded.

Cippus of Sostratos, from Gravisca. Tarquinia, Museo Nazionale

Language

One of the most prevalent misconceptions about the Etruscans is that their language is indecipherable. In fact Etruscan, written in a simple variant of the Greek alphabet introduced via Cumae at the beginning of the 7th century B.C., can easily be read by anyone even slightly familiar with the Greek alphabet. It is understanding Etruscan which presents problems, since it is of unknown origin and cannot with certainty be related to any groups of known languages.

However, a century or more of linguistic study has had some remarkable successes. Because of the nature of Etruscan, the etymological method of the 19th century—the attempt to identify Etruscan words with words known in other languages—was not very fruitful. The late 19th- and early 20th-century method of 'combining' different texts and cross-checking the translations proposed has been more rewarding. We now have a long list of correspondences of vocabulary, some more certain than others, and a rudimentary idea of grammar. For example, we know that *clan* means 'son', *avil* 'year', *zilath* 'praetor' and so on; and that *al, ale, alce, aliqu, alice* are verbal forms of a root meaning 'to give'. But only a small body of written Etruscan survives. There are about 6,000 inscriptions, either funerary texts (giving name, age and any public offices held) or brief sacred dedications (giving the names of the dedicator and the deity and the words of consecration); and a dozen or so texts of more than twenty words. This has meant that the method of combining texts has not been able to make any notable advance on the results already produced during the 1920s.

A third approach, borrowed from historical method around the time of World War II, is the bilingual method. This assumes, justifiably, that the geographical and cultural proximity of Etruscan and other languages of ancient Italy must have led to mutual influence on their respective religious and legal formulae. Starting from complex texts in known languages (Latin, Osco–Umbrian, Greek), it is possible to work out the substance and structure of an Etruscan text which was intended for the same purpose.

This method has considerably increased our understanding of Etruscan. To cite only one find out of many, we can now positively identify the text of the Zagreb mummy as a sacred calendar; it contains instructions, preceded by the date (apparently September), for sacred offices to be celebrated in honour of various gods (mainly Nethuns/Neptune, though others figure too), on behalf of a sanctuary and city.

However, three gold plaques have recently been discovered at Pyrgi; these record the consecration of a shrine and a statue of Uni in that important sanctuary by the tyrant (ruler) of Cerveteri, Thefarie Velianas. Written in Etruscan and Phoenician, the plaques show the limitations of the bilingual approach, since a comparison of the texts shows that the bilingualism of such ancient texts was always approximate. Religious formulae were expressed in a traditional, set way, so that without a thorough grasp of the structure of a language exact translation is practically impossible.

And so, in the light of modern structural linguistics, a general re-examination of Etruscan phonology is being undertaken. The aim is to reconstruct the morphological, grammatical and syntactic structure of Etruscan, in order to understand how the language actually worked, without fruitless attempts at 'translation' often by totally unscholarly short cuts. Among recent successes has been the discovery of a phonological contrast between the verbal suffixes *-ce* and *-che* which are used in the perfect, indicating respectively the active perfect and the passive perfect: previously these two were confused.

These brief examples show both the progress that has been made and the work that remains to be done if we are to build up an adequate picture of the Etruscan language. Etruscan is not the mystery so many romantic writers would still have us believe. It is a scientific problem to be solved scientifically.

Terracotta sarcophagus from Cerveteri (Sarcofago degli Sposi). Rome, Museo di Villa Giulia

Detail of the Apollo di Veio, terracotta statue from the sanctuary of Portonaccio, outside Veii. Rome, Museo di Villa Giulia

Art

The atmosphere of mystery which quite needlessly and irrationally surrounded Etruscan culture in European circles during the interwar years—notions about the 'vanished race', the 'undecipherable language' and so on—soon gave place, when it came to art, to a fit of overenthusiasm: Etruscan figurative art was favourably compared with the classical Greek style. Luckily a more scholarly approach has ended such deliberate mystification, reassessing Etruscan art as a provincial culture, with certain distinct characteristics of its own, but part of the larger and more cultured Greek world.

The originality of Etruscan art was a classic middlebrow discussion point in the 1920s and 1930s. In fact the question is irrelevant if the nature of artistic production in the ancient world is correctly understood. Artists then did not try to be original and the system of production by craftsmen in workshops, perpetuating existing models, explicitly excludes, almost by definition, the pursuit of originality.

Once these misconceptions are cleared up, one can make a calm and objective assessment of Etruscan art as a marginal activity intended to express the artistic needs of a society which was certainly Hellenized but structurally very different from Greek society, and which in the first place depended on imported works of art and artists. Against the Greek concept of the *polis* the Etruscans set the ideal of the noble family; against the Greek humanist individualist spirit of the 4th and 3rd centuries B.C. they exalted the status of the individual as guarantee and promise of fortune and honour for future generations of the family. Apart from their fundamentally different social structures and related ideals, the forms and traditions of artistic production in the two cultures were also different. Greece had a solid, lasting tradition of workshops and craftsmen (equalled only by the Italian Renaissance). In Etruria, however, modes of expression were less consistent, depending to a large degree on the changing demands of the aristocratic class which provided most of the custom, and on the mobility and turnover of craftsmen. These features are already apparent in the early stages of Etruscan art. In spite of the lasting local preferences for certain forms (wall painting appears mainly at Tarquinia, bronze work and monumental sculpture at Vulci, major architectural works at Cerveteri and so on), identifiable workshops were remarkably short-lived.

In the middle and late Villanovan period, following the fashion for simple abstract geometric forms in vase decoration, the first attempts at representative art developed. Stylized small figures made of impasto or bronze were used to decorate functional and ritual objects. It is argued that some of these objects, for example the beautiful bronze sword from Vulci (in the Museo di Villa Giulia) show the influence of Greek Geometric modelling, but generally speaking the objects were made independently as part of the developing local Geometric culture.

During the Orientalizing period which followed, a complex and monumental style of architecture appeared. Although the traditional prehistoric hut still provided the typical basic structure (seen in the Tomba della Capanna at Cerveteri), its elaboration shows the effect of Eastern Mediterranean influence coinciding with the flood of precious artistic products from all over the East—from Phoenicia, Syria, Cyprus and Greece. Halfway through the 7th century local schools of vase painting were formed, first by Greek artists who had arrived singly, like Aristonothos, then by whole groups of Corinthian painters who arrived together; we know for example that the Corinthian exile Demaratos came to Tarquinia with a small group of artists. At the same time new architectural styles spread, including the layout (familiar from domestic architecture in Anatolia and the East) which developed a few decades later into the typical temple plan, with three cellae or a cella and alae, the standard pattern for Etrusco–Italic temples. At this time too we find at Acquarossa the first architectural decorations made in terracotta, derived from contemporary Greek tradition, apparently via the Greek colonies.

The late 7th and early 6th centuries B.C. were thus the formative period of Etruscan culture, flourishing then in the cities of southern Etruria. At Vulci we find the first Etruscan sculptures (the Centauro di Vulci, now in the Museo di Villa Giulia), and the first major school of Etrusco–Corinthian vase painting, later copied in other southern cities—Cerveteri, Tarquinia and Veii. Cerveteri first produced bucchero, a type of pottery invented in Etruria as an elegant, cheaper substitute for metal ware, and its great tumuli achieve an impressive monumental architectural style. Veii provides the first important example of wall painting in the Tomba Campana. In the northern cities, Vetulonia, Populonia, Volterra and in the Arno valley, as well as extensive imports from the southern cities, we find the germs of a local architectural style: the large *tholoi*, though similar in layout to the monumental tombs of the south, are distinguished structurally by their false vaults.

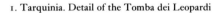

1. Tarquinia. Detail of the Tomba dei Leopardi

2. Caeretan hydria with Heracles, Cerberus and Eurystheus. Rome, Museo di Villa Giulia

3. Pyxides in bucchero, from Cerveteri, Sorbo cemetery. Rome, Musei Vaticani

26

Cerveteri. Tomba della Capanna

Between 570 and 470 B.C. Ionian influence prevailed, stimulated by the diaspora of Greeks from the eastern Mediterranean. Imports of Greek vases (now almost a monopoly of Athens) increased fantastically, and in places local demand led to the setting up of schools of decorators, potters, stone-cutters and painters. At Cerveteri the architectural forms which had developed during the previous period were now enhanced by graceful Archaic Ionian elements. A great artist from East Greece (known as the Master of the Caeretan Hydriai) set up a small, short-lived school of potters there too. Anonymous modellers brought the flowing lines and gently modelled forms of the Ionian style to the smooth oval countenances and softly folded draperies of their sarcophagi (for example the Sarcofago degli Sposi, Museo di Villa Giulia). At Vulci the schools of sculpture adopted the new conventions of the Ionian schools (e.g. the youth riding a sea monster). A different style, but again of Ionian origin, appears in the school of Vulca of Veii, called after the artist responsible for the decoration of the temple of Jupiter Capitolinus, the only Etruscan artist whose name is known to us, to whom the great statues of the temple of Apollo are attributed. Tomb paintings appeared at Tarquinia, the first of a series which from the mid-6th century, through its peak at the end of the century, until 470 B.C., displayed the triumphs of line and colour achieved by the thriving East Greek painters. Provincial versions of the styles prevalent in the southern cities now developed in the central and northern cities; the small cippi and Archaic urns of Chiusi, the bucchero with miniaturistic decoration of Orvieto, the stelae of Volterra and Fiesole, express, each in its own way, different aspects of the Ionian style developed in the south by Greek artists or artists trained in a Greek cultural setting. The vase painter active in Cerveteri and known as the Master of the Caeretan Hydriai is just one example of those Greek artists.

The crisis of the second quarter of the 5th century inevitably affected figurative art, which lapsed into dull and mechanical reproduction of the late Ionian style, only occasionally (for example in the Pyrgi relief) enlivened by elements of the Greek severe style. The great Etruscan bronze-work of the previous century, exemplified in the beautiful bronzes from Vulci and much appreciated in Greece itself, continued in a lifeless way, but one by one the workshops of each Etruscan city closed down. Building activity ceased.

Not until the early 4th century, with the political, economic and cultural revival of Etruria and Italy in general, did artistic schools and workshops thrive again. Inspiration came not from Greece itself but from the Greek colonies of southern Italy and Sicily which had now, after all their difficulties in the late 5th century, reached the height of their importance with the Neo-Pythagorean regimes of Tarentum and the tyrannies of Syracuse, which attracted philosophers of the standing of Plato. Schools sprang into being again, shaking off their torpor—sculptors at Vulci, painters at Tarquinia, decorators of cinerary urns and sarcophagi at Chiusi. New local traditions and workshops appeared too. At Falerii a school of vase painters was set up by painters in the Atticizing style who may have come from the colony of Thurii, in southern Italy; this school was active throughout the 4th century, at Falerii, Cerveteri or Rome, showing the increasing influence of Campania and Apulia. At Tarquinia there was a school of sculptors engaged in producing sarcophagi, at first with enthusiasm but then in a more and more uninspired and unskilful way (3rd and early 2nd centuries). The great bronzes of Arezzo revived the splendours of the Archaic tradition. There were thriving schools of modellers in various cities, Falerii, Cerveteri, Tarquinia and Volsinii, making terracotta sculptures of a high standard of workmanship. At Volterra alabaster urns were produced, an activity which was to increase in the late 3rd and 2nd centuries. And the list could go on.

This 4th-century revival was slow and uneven at the start. In the first half of the century artistic production was on the whole of a fairly high level, but it seemed the result of episodic and uncoordinated activity. But by 350 B.C. most of the workshops had established clear traditions of technique and form. Production, however, was halted by the establishment of Roman hegemony in the first half of the 3rd century B.C. Some activities ceased altogether, especially in the southern cities most directly affected by Roman expansion; the workshops which survived produced only mediocre, if not positively barbarized work, as is shown, with a few exceptions, by the paintings and sarcophagi of Tarquinia or the sculptures of Vulci or Chiusi. In the north—at Perugia, Volterra and Arezzo—the more favourable economic climate and social structure offered more scope for independent artistic production, to satisfy the needs of a fairly large clientele, of a type which had not existed in the southern cities for some time. Thus in the 2nd century these cities were centres of lively cultural activity, though not to the same degree of intensity as Rome or cities which had benefited by Rome's imperialist expansion. Their flourishing artistic production in the late Hellenistic style and their building activity explain the dramatic and desperate commitment of their anti-Roman struggle at the beginning of the 1st century.

The 'peace' of Augustus came to a devastated and crisis-torn land. Only the potters of Arezzo were still flourishing and they were the exception in a scene of economic and cultural disarray. The southern cities, which had been worn down over the centuries by the big landowners, were depopulated by the early Middle Ages. The other towns became small, remote provincial centres, carrying on a little building, but almost totally dependent on the capital culturally and artistically.

Mario Torelli

1. Alabaster urn depicting the Seven Against Thebes, with the story of Capaneus. Volterra, Museo Guarnacci

2. Terracotta cinerary urn with the legend of Eteocles and Polynices. Chiusi, Museo Archeologico

3. Detail of the sarcophagus of Laris Pulenas (Sarcofago del Magistrato). Tarquinia, Museo Nazionale

Northern Etruria

Fiesole

Among the Etruscan settlements north of the Arno—documented by the discovery of Villanovan material in the centre of Florence and in various places nearby, by the Orientalizing tombs at Quinto, Comeana and Artimino, and by small centres and cemeteries scattered through the various valleys, which flourished over a long span of time, at least until the end of the Hellenistic age—Fiesole is of particular importance.

The ancient settlement was built, like the present one, on the top of the hill, in a naturally defended position. Archaeological excavations have revealed that the summit must have been inhabited as long ago as the early Iron Age, and that additional dwellings were established on the slopes during the following centuries. It is generally believed that there must have been a city proper as early as the 6th or at latest the 5th century B.C., when a wall may have been built round the top of the hill, corresponding to the hillock on which stand the convent and church of S. Francesco, but there is no archaeological evidence to confirm the existence of the city at such an early date.

We can be certain only that an organized centre existed from the beginning of the 3rd century B.C. The encircling wall, the oldest buildings excavated inside it and the oldest tombs discovered outside have in fact been dated to this time.

The city wall has an irregular perimeter, following the natural lie of the terrain; it is about 2,500 metres in circumference and is built of large blocks of stone, coursed, random-coursed and irregular; long stretches of it are still to be seen, being in a particularly good state of preservation along the northern and eastern sides, and they give us an impressive example of the defences of Etruscan cities at that time.

Fiesole. Excavated ruins of the Etruscan and Roman temples

View of the town from the south

Within the circuit, several buildings have been uncovered in the northern area, and others have been located close to the southern boundary; all too little has been excavated in the centre of the city, where the ancient buildings have been continually overlaid by modern.

Among the buildings uncovered by excavation in the northern area, one of the oldest and most important is the Etruscan temple, which can be dated to the 4th or early 3rd century B.C. As part of the elevation is preserved, it is possible to reconstruct the plan with certainty: it was a temple with a central cella flanked by two alae or wings, open at the front, whose side walls extended forward to the porch of the building and terminated in antae or piers. Between the two antae stood two characteristic 'Etruscan'-type columns of *pietra serena* (a bluish sandstone), which we can position precisely, since the base of one of them has been found *in situ*. The walls of the building were rendered, on the inside at least, with red plaster, fragments of which can be seen in the museum adjoining the archaeological site. As for the frontal elevation, excavation uncovered various pieces of the terracotta decoration, including a series of antefixes. At the foot of the flight of steps leading up to the temple, and in alignment with the temple, stood the altar, later incorporated in the foundations of a new temple and now no longer visible, since the trench dug in the course of excavation was subsequentally filled in again to protect the remains from the effects of exposure to the atmosphere.

This building is of particular interest because, unlike the majority of Etrusco–Italic temples—which had, as is well known, a stone podium or base, but walls of perishable material faced with terracotta—it has stone walls which are still preserved to quite a considerable height.

The votive deposit of the temple contained small objects of the usual kind: bronze feet, legs, heads and statuettes, offerings to the god or goddess (probably a healing deity) to whom the temple was dedicated, in either propitiation or thanksgiving. Possibly the deity in this case might have been Menrva (Minerva), for among the votive offerings is a small bronze owl, the creature sacred to the goddess, which is now to be seen in the museum.

During the early decades of the 1st century B.C., the temple and the adjoining buildings were destroyed by fire, traces of which were found in the course of excavation, and were rebuilt within a short time at a higher level and with more impressive dimensions. This destruction can be connected with the troubles of Fiesole at the beginning of the 1st century B.C.: we know that the city was involved in the Social War against Rome; that it was conquered and half destroyed by L. Cato in 90 B.C.; and that during the civil strife it sided with Marius, and was subsequently punished by the victorious Sulla, who settled there a *colonia* of his veterans, against whom there was a violent revolt in 78 B.C. A new temple arose on the site of the earlier temple, reproducing many features of the original and following the same plan, but built on a larger scale; at some distance in front of the temple stood the altar, of the type associated with the Republican period, which can still be seen today.

Flanking the temple was a large rectangular open colonnade, accessible through two doorways and evidently connected with the place of worship. This is thought to have been analogous to the *stoa* of Greek sanctuaries, a place built as a lodging for pilgrims.

These two buildings are now part of Roman Fiesole. We have only partial knowledge of the layout of this city: the outer wall was unaltered; the forum probably corresponded to the present Piazza Mino, around which various remains of buildings, sculptures and inscriptions have been uncovered. The principal public buildings were erected in the 1st century B.C., more precisely in the Augustan age, in the northern sector of the city, in the same area as the temple, and were sited picturesquely on terraces at different levels, in accordance with a well-conceived plan. On the top terrace, at the same level as the forum, stood a building which afforded access to the theatre.

The theatre backs on to the hill and dates from the early Imperial age, a stout retaining wall of masonry being built into the hillside above the auditorium to protect the building

from the weight of earth behind. Passing through the *vomitorium*, which originally had double-leafed doors fastened with bars, traces of which have been found, we come to a gallery with a vaulted roof, and then to the *cavea* or auditorium, divided into four sections by three narrow tiers of steps. The two flights of steps that run the length of either end of the *cavea* facilitated the movement of spectators, who could have numbered as many as 3,000. The semicircular area of the *orchestra* includes the first three rows of steps, with marble seats for persons of high rank; other specially important seats were above the vaulted side passages leading to the *orchestra*. Facing the *cavea* is the *proscenium*, the long rectangular stage on which the plays were performed; the front wall had a series of niches and was in all probability ornamented with a marble frieze now to be seen in the museum, depicting Dionysus with his panther and other motifs associated with the god and his *thiasos* (band of revellers), such as satyrs and cupids. The *proscenium* was enclosed at the back by a wall which is only partially preserved, the *frons scaenae*, decorated with columns, pilasters and marble facings, and with three doorways through which the actors would enter and exit. At the back, small rooms have been uncovered which probably served as dressing rooms and storerooms. Excavation has also brought to light the equipment for the drop-curtain, which was housed in an open trench running the length of the front wall of the stage and could be raised or lowered, with the help of a system of weights, by machines at each side of the stage.

The floor of the *orchestra* is on a level with the middle terrace of this area of Roman Fiesole; symmetrically positioned to one of the entrances leading on to the stage, there may have stood a triumphal arch, the base of which survives. The lowest terrace extends between the temple, the northern stretch of the wall and a complex of baths built to the northeast of the theatre in the early Imperial age. The baths provided a series of rooms designed to give clients opportunities to take a hot, a cold or a steam bath, exercise, stroll, read or gossip. Particularly well preserved are the *caldarium*, the room for baths heated by air brought to a high temperature by a system of furnaces and circulated between the hypocaust pillars which supported the floor, and the public lavatory, with marble seats and a small water cistern.

The buildings investigated were repeatedly restored and altered during the first centuries of Imperial Rome up to the time of Septimius Severus; in the late Roman age this area was reached by a paved road which skirted the theatre and may have followed the route of a more ancient road. The progressive raising of the ground level in the lower terrace caused the area in front of the temple to become buried, and the Republican altar, fallen into disuse, was enclosed between two rough walls surmounted by the paving slabs of the Imperial road which ran at that level.

Little by little Fiesole was supplanted in importance by Florence, a Roman *colonia* founded shortly after the mid-1st century B.C. whose prosperity steadily increased during the early centuries of the Empire; the inhabited area gradually shrank to the highest and most easily defended part of the hill, as seems to be attested by the fact that the northern slope, to the edges of the upper terrace, was used by the barbarians as a burial ground; and this situation persisted throughout the entire Middle Ages.

In the museum can be seen the objects uncovered by the excavations at Fiesole: the votive deposit and architectural elements from the temple, marble sculptures which decorated the theatre and other public buildings and places, and stelae (slabs) and cippi (pillars) in *pietra serena*, characteristic of the Fiesole area.

The museum also contains cinerary urns in alabaster and terracotta from Chiusi and Volterra, Archaic and Hellenistic pottery, mostly from northern Etruria, Etruscan and Roman lamps, missiles or projectiles of lead and terracotta, and a bronze cinerary urn dating from the 2nd–3rd centuries A.D.

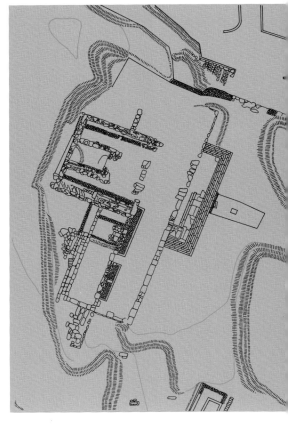

Plan of the temple at Fiesole

Funerary stele depicting a funeral banquet, dancing figures and fighting animals. Museo di Fiesole

34

Quinto Fiorentino

Quinto Fiorentino. *Dromos* leading into the tomb called La Montagnola

Tomb finds have been the most usual indication of other Etruscan settlements north of the Arno. Quinto Fiorentino lies a short distance from Florence, north of the Arno, and its name derives from its position five (*quinto*, 'fifth') miles along the Roman road that ran along the right bank of the Arno. Here, on the left bank of the river Zambra, three great corbelled-dome tombs have been found close together.

The northernmost tomb is called La Montagnola because from the outside it looks like a hillock; it is a fairly massive construction about 70 metres in diameter, with a plinth of roughly rectangular limestone slabs running round the base. The tomb itself consists of a *dromos* or entrance passage that leads into a long rectangular antechamber; this is surrounded by rectangular side rooms, while the one at the very rear of the antechamber leads into the main burial chamber. This is a circular room with a massive tapering pillar support in the centre constructed from blocks of tufa.

The *dromos* is at present exposed, but in the course of many burials it was blocked with deposits of earth and stones. Notches in the stones of the *dromos* walls show that access was provided by four steps that then led through a portal of monolithic antae and architraves, which could be blocked by a great stone slab, and into the antechamber. The roofs of the antechamber and burial chambers are constructed from corbelled (progressively overlapping) courses of stones: an ancient Mediterranean building method that was much used in Etruria, especially in the north.

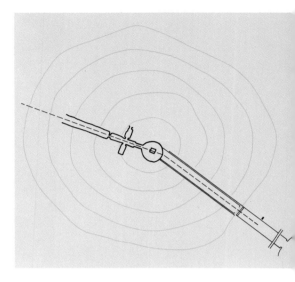

The walls of the tomb chamber are made up of blocks of the local *alberese* and other forms of limestone from the immediate vicinity. The surface of these walls and the central pillar was covered with a thin layer of clay and then a final layer of plaster. There are also clear traces of painting in a colour resembling burnt sienna and in dark blue on the antae of the entrance to the right side room, with engraved designs including a horse, a boar, and five-pointed and schematic stars.

The tomb clearly belonged to a very important family and its furnishings must have been of a sumptuous quality, judging by its imposing size and the few objects found inside during the official excavations carried out in 1959 after tomb robbers had been at work.

Quinto Fiorentino. Cross-section and plan of La Montagnola

Below, the vault, and right, interior of La Montagnola

These were in bone and ivory (the leg of a folding stool complete with joint pin; discs decorated with friezes of fantastic animals and geometric patterns; plaquettes with perforated decorations of sphinxes, a stag and stylized plant motifs, originally designed to cover cylindrical surfaces; decorative plates for caskets, ornamented with rows of friezes of fantastic animals alternating with palmettes and geometric motifs; a miniature griffin head; two figurines of cloaked women); in alabaster (little elongated vases for perfume or unguents, consequently called *alabastra*); and in bucchero. Other objects found in the tomb included an imitation shell, obviously acquired because of the fashion for the great tridacna shells with Orientalizing incised decorations that were widely exported by Greek merchants who obtained them in the East; a little blue glass vase, a sword, a knife and an *obelos* or spit in iron, a little bronze head of a lion; a gold fibula and a gold ribbon with appliqued four-petalled gold rosettes, little discs with gold plating on silver, embossed with stylized roses, and pieces of ostrich egg.

These rich tomb furnishings, typical of the current Orientalizing style, show the presence of a wealthy ruling class north of the Arno, and date these burials between the 7th and 6th centuries B.C.

Southeast of La Montagnola is the Tomba della Mula, known since the 15th century and now part of the cellar of the Villa Shokley; access to it is at present down a modern staircase that corresponds in part to the ancient *dromos*. The structure of the burial chamber dates it to the last quarter of the 7th century B.C.: it is a circular room with a corbelled vault of overlapping stone blocks. The absence of any central support is a particularly impressive feature of this tomb. Modern alterations have been made to the original structure: the top of the roof was partially dismantled to make an opening to bring light and air into the cellar, and a shelf for barrels was built round the wall.

In 1820 a third tomb with a tumulus similar to the others was discovered near the Villa Carter, to the east of the Tomba della Mula. No trace of it remains, but it is said that a quantity of gold objects was also discovered.

The three Quinto Fiorentino tombs were built almost contemporaneously, and belonged to wealthy and powerful families. So far no traces of any settlement that they belonged to have been discovered.

The only Etruscan settlement that has been identified in that area is at Poggio al Giro. It is surrounded by a dry wall of uncertain age, and has so far yielded nothing to date it any earlier than the 3rd century B.C.

However, the existence of another Archaic cemetery at Palastreto may be seen as proof that small settlements were scattered on the spurs of land that form the ridge of hills to the northeast of the Florentine plain, and controlled the lines of communication between Etruria proper and its extension to the Po valley.

Artimino

Other settlements have been found on the hills to the southwest of the Florentine plain, more precisely the foothills of Monte Albano. Of these, Artimino has recently become well known; it lies at a strategic point controlling the Arno and its tributaries the Pistoian Ombrone and the Bisenzio—all important lines of communication to the north. The Etruscan settlement crowned a hill that divides into three ridges connected by three saddles. Finds of fragments of pottery and architectural terracottas indicate that it extended from the hill where the Villa Medicea now stands to that on which the modern village of Artimino is built, and was inhabited from the 7th to the 2nd century B.C. The cemeteries were situated along the southeastern slope running down from the Villa Medicea towards the Arno, with tombs constructed as tumuli or excavated in the sandstone of the mountain itself, and also to the north and northeast of the Villa Medicea. Excavations have so far revealed that the Etruscan centre at Artimino was culturally influenced by Fiesole and Volterra, which underlines the importance of this area along the lines of communication between northern Etruria and the Po valley.

Comeana

Not far from Artimino two tombs were discovered at Comeana, on the slopes going down to the Pistoian Ombrone. One of these is a tumulus situated at Boschetti, near the modern cemetery of Comeana: the top of the mound has been destroyed over the years by agricultural work. The *dromos* is entered from the southwest and is marked by low walls of *alberese* and yellow sandstone blocks on either side. A large stone slab was fixed in the entrance as a door, and behind it lay the rectangular vestibule with a floor of local grey sandstone, while the sides consisted of two great slabs of sandstone fixed vertically in the ground. A passage that could be blocked off in the same way as the entrance led to the burial chamber itself: its sides are monolithic slabs of stone and meet the rear wall at right angles, with proper fixed joints. The floor consists of slabs of *pietra serena* carefully laid to fit perfectly together; in roughly the centre of the rear wall three narrow pieces of stone are fixed vertically to mark the little rectangular opening, less than one metre square, that was probably designed to take a cinerary urn. Among the tomb furnishings found inside this tomb were impasto vases, fragments of ivory with decorations in relief and in the

Comeana. Entrance to the Tumulo di Montefortini

round, a cylindrical ivory box decorated with two friezes of fantastic animals carved in low relief, separated by linear, spiral and herringbone patterns, and finally fragments of bucchero and of a bronze vase that date the tomb to the end of the 7th century B.C.

Not far from the Tomba dei Boschetti, at the edge of the village of Comeana, is the Tumulo di Montefortini, a tumulus that has a maximum diameter of 70 metres and lies on the southern side of the road to Signa. An oak wood now covers the tumulus and has had the effect of preserving its original form. The plinth that forms its base is built of vertical slabs surmounted by three course of stones, the bottom course projecting slightly over the edge of the plinth, and the top two courses progressively tapering in.

Only one tomb has been found inside the tumulus: its *dromos* is entered from the west-northwest and is exceptionally large, measuring about 13 metres in length and more than 2·50 metres across. The walls are built of blocks of local sandstone and limestone, and have been crudely smoothed on the outside only; they were originally rendered with a type of clay-based plaster. The *dromos* leads to a vestibule with monolithic antae and architraves, originally blocked by another monolithic slab, which in turn leads to a rectangular antechamber. From there a similar doorway leads to the rectangular burial chamber itself. Both these chambers have domes made from progressively projecting courses of stone following the same method of corbelling used in the great tombs of nearby Quinto Fiorentino. In the burial chamber a broad stone ledge runs along the side and rear walls just below the eaves, and was probably used to display the tomb furnishings. Only fragments of these original furnishings remain: they consisted of impasto and bucchero vases, objects of sheet bronze, iron, glass paste, ivory and bone, and decorated sheet gold.

In short, the furnishings were typical of a princely tomb of the Orientalizing period, which shows that the Tumulo di Montefortini was in use between the mid-7th and the early part of the 6th century B.C.

Fighting elks. From the tomb furnishings of La Montagnola, Quinto Fiorentino

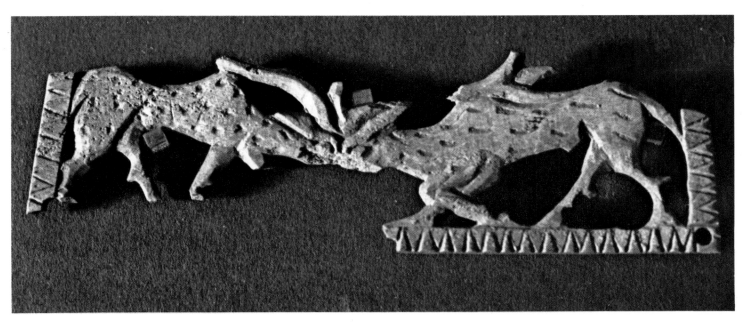

Arezzo was one of the most important Etruscan centres of the Val di Chiana, indeed of the whole of northern Etruria, as is clearly indicated by the frequent references to it in historical sources, especially from the time of its first contacts with Rome. The Etruscan settlement was built on a hill overlooking the northern end of the valley, superbly sited strategically to control the lower reaches of the river Chiana. The settlement must originally have covered only the upper part of the modern city, where the cathedral and the citadel now are, but only very sparse remains are left, because of the continuous existence of the city up to the present day. There are stretches of a city wall made of large rectangular stone blocks, but its date is uncertain and some even consider it to be mediaeval—some of the restoration work certainly dates from the early Middle Ages. One special feature of Etruscan Arezzo was its walls of unfired brick, which are singled out for mention by two authoritative Latin writers, Pliny (*Natural History*, 35, 170–173) and Vitruvius (II, 8, 9). After lengthy research and debate, a partially collapsed section of this wall was discovered in 1918 in the Catona district, and other stretches subsequently turned up in various parts of the city. Stratigraphic excavation has made it possible to establish that the brick walls were built after black Hellenistic pottery had come into use, in other words after the late 4th century; and that they were destroyed before the emergence of another type of pottery, the coral-red so-called *terra sigillata*, about the mid-1st century B.C.

Some remains of Etruscan buildings have been discovered in the vicinity of the citadel, but on the whole traces of the buildings of Etruscan Arezzo are to be found in the numerous

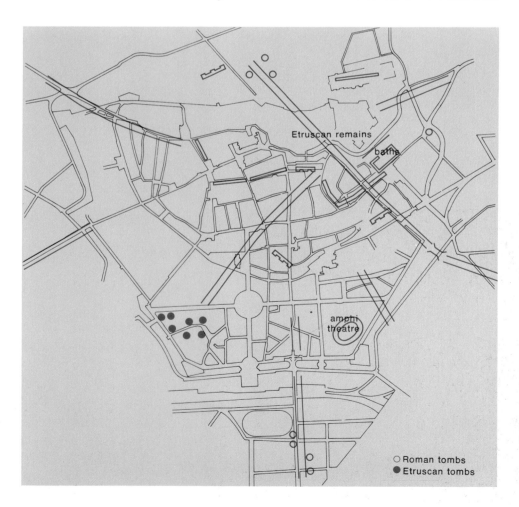

Arezzo. Plan of the archaeological zone

architectural terracottas, unearthed in various parts of the city, which originally decorated public and private buildings of particular importance. Thanks to the discovery of its terracotta decoration, we can state that a temple of fairly impressive size, decorated with, among other things, antefixes depicting battle scenes, was constructed in Arezzo in the first half of the 5th century B.C.; similar material, though of a later date, has been found in the Via Guido Monaco, near the Piazza S. Francesco, in a well by the cathedral, below S. Croce, and in the Quarata and Catona areas. It was at Catona in particular that numerous architectural terracottas were found heaped together underneath the brick walls; in all probability the remains of several temples built inside the city were piled up on the outskirts of the built-up area after violent destruction which may have had something to do with the war waged against Sulla by the inhabitants of Arezzo, who sided with Marius. Especially interesting are a carefully modelled head of a young man in a Phrygian cap, where the oval face is caught in an attitude of some pathos, probably dating from the mid-3rd century; a small helmeted female head, probably representing the goddess Athene, which is quite similar in dimension and style to the above and may be attributed to the same artist; and a half-life-size male head, belonging to the emotional and dynamic movement in art which started with Scopas in Greece and culminated in the Hellenistic school of Pergamum, dating from about the mid-2nd century B.C. Another female head may perhaps also be attributed to the same artist; here the head is sharply inclined towards the left shoulder, the facial expression betrays some strong agony, the brow is deeply lined, with mouth open; it may depict either one of the daughters of Niobe or a wounded Amazon.

It is clear that Etruscan Arezzo was the seat of at least one and probably more highly thought-of schools of sculptors in clay, influenced by the culture and tastes of contemporary Greek art.

Terracotta decoration of the pediment of a temple.
Arezzo, Museo Archeologico

The Chimera di Arezzo, bronze sculpture. Florence, Museo Archeologico

Side by side with these schools, a highly developed school of bronze-working also flourished, as is attested by the discovery of small Archaic bronzes, and in particular the famous bronze chimaera, found in the upper part of the city in the 16th century, restored by Benvenuto Cellini, and now in the Museo Archeologico in Florence. This piece is of considerable interest, and probably dates from the end of the 5th century B.C. With one foot wounded, the monster looks up at the enemy who has inflicted the wound; because of this stance it is considered to have formed part of a group with Bellerophon on Pegasus, following a design similar to that depicted on an engraved mirror from Praeneste in the Museo di Villa Giulia. The large bronze statue of Minerva (the Athena di Arezzo) now displayed in the Museo Archeologico in Florence was also found within the Etruscan city-limits.

Arezzo's importance as a centre for metal-working, henceforward organized on what might be called an industrial scale, is confirmed by the fact that in the 3rd century B.C. it supplied grain, weapons and tools for the expedition against Carthage mounted by Scipio Africanus during the Second Punic War. According to Livy's report (XXVIII, 45) of the various Etruscan cities which gave contributions, Arezzo was the only city to supply metal products, clearly manufactured in its own workshops.

In the 3rd century B.C. Arezzo entered peacefully and permanently into the Roman orbit. During this period it briefly issued its own currency; in fact the *aes grave* series with a wheel on the obverse and an amphora or a krater on the reverse, quite frequently found in the area, may be attributed to Arezzo.

There is no doubt that in the Hellenistic period the city enjoyed considerable prosperity, as evidenced by the discoveries of architectural terracottas and the flourishing workshops

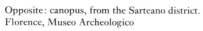

Opposite: canopus, from the Sarteano district. Florence, Museo Archeologico

1. Funerary cippus, from Chiusi. Arezzo, Museo Archeologico

2 and 3. Architectural terracottas, from Arezzo. Florence, Museo Archeologico

4. Arretine vase. Arezzo, Museo Archeologico

producing black-gloss pottery and bronze and iron weapons. So much so, it would appear, that a sanctuary was built on the Colle di S. Cornelio, where the remains of a large terrace wall built of rectangular blocks are to be seen.

During the civil wars Arezzo sided with Marius; as a punishment, Sulla settled colonists called *Arretini fidentiores*, who remained side by side with the other inhabitants, the *Arretini veteres*; later on more colonists, the *Arretini Iulienses*, were settled there by Caesar. The city did not move, but was simply enlarged, and continued to prosper throughout the 1st century B.C., greatly helped by its agricultural and industrial wealth, and by the fact that the Via Cassia passed right though it. In the final decades of the century there developed large-scale production of the characteristic—hence 'Arretine'—red pottery, in various workshops producing the two varieties: one smooth-surfaced, the other decorated in low relief with various designs; this pottery was widely exported up to the first decades of the 1st century A.D.

In the 1st century A.D. the city continued to expand: public and private buildings were constructed outside the city wall, in areas previously occupied by potters' workshops and cemeteries, though for the latter we have only isolated evidence. The forum was probably in the upper part of the city, near the cathedral, but it is impossible to reconstruct the complete plan of the settlement because of the fragmentary nature of the various discoveries. The most noteworthy building of which remains survive is the amphitheatre, built at the beginning of the 2nd century A.D., with its longer external axis measuring 122 metres. Although it has been partly destroyed by time and events, it is an impressive reminder of the city's prosperity during this period.

Later periods, however, saw the beginning of a process of deterioration, contributed to by the diversion of the Via Cassia and the declining activity of the pottery workshops,

Arezzo. Roman amphitheatre

which were gradually replaced by provincial ones. It was not until the early Middle Ages that the city became important again.

Many of the archaeological finds from Arezzo and thereabouts are on display in the Museo Archeologico Mecenate. The museum, which was founded by the Fraternità dei Laici and was enriched by private donations, including the Gamurrini collection, has recently been moved to the former monastery built on the ruins of the Roman amphitheatre; it is named after Augustus' adviser Maecenas, a descendant of the *gens Cilnia*, the most influential clan in Etruscan Arezzo from the 4th century B.C. onwards, which produced in the course of time its share of senators who were at the heart of the political life of Rome.

The rooms of the former monastery contain numerous architectural terracottas found locally, cinerary urns in alabaster, stone and terracotta, of various origins, Roman inscriptions and portraits. The collection of Arretine vases is especially noteworthy: some of these pieces display exceptional technical refinement. They are largely the product of the major workshops, whose names are known to us from stamps impressed in the clay: Perennius, Cornelius, Ateius, Rasinius, all with long periods of activity in the city.

From nearby Marciano in Val di Chiana there is a male torso in stone, covered by a small loincloth the ends of which are crossed at the front and hang down over the thighs in two points. This statue belongs to the Chiusine style and shows certain Athenian influences in its sober and restrained design; it probably dates from the beginning of the 5th century B.C.

Other notable collections are those of Athenian pottery, Etruscan vases, small Etruscan and Roman bronzes, engraved Etruscan mirrors, glass, gold work, and Etruscan and Roman coins.

Two typical examples of Arretine vases: they depict, respectively, the slaughtering of a pig and girls dancing. Arezzo, Museo Archeologico

47

Pieve Sócana

To the north of Arezzo, on the right bank of the Arno, along the road to Pontassieve and Florence, an impressive Etruscan altar has recently been discovered at Pieve Sócana. Originally it stood in front of a temple, but it has been possible to identify only the wide entrance stairway of the latter, as the remainder of the building lies beneath the Romanesque church of S. Antonino. The temple steps are below the apses of the church. This is a striking example of continuity of worship in the same place, and of the conservative force of religious tradition, which deters the faithful from abandoning places where they are used to praying.

Pieve Sócana. The Etruscan temple as excavated

Cortona is situated on a hill dominating the Val di Chiana, about half-way between Arezzo and Lake Trasimene. It has been continuously inhabited down to modern times, so that its historical remains have been absorbed and destroyed, as is the case with the majority of these northern centres of Etruscan culture. A network of roads approximately corresponding to its modern counterpart led to the Etruscan city with its imposing wall, probably built in the 5th century B.C. and originally more than 2 kilometres in length, of which long stretches still remain. It follows the contours of the hill in an unbroken line of roughly-squared stones laid in irregular courses, occasionally filled in with smaller stones. It now includes a Medicean fort—the Fortezza del Girifalco—that was probably built on the site of the ancient acropolis at the highest and best protected point of the city. The stretch of this wall left round the Piazza del Mercato contains traces of a double-arched doorway that may be a later construction. The Etruscan wall continued to defend the city for many centuries, and remained substantially unchanged until in the Middle Ages it was built up further in the characteristic mediaeval fashion with rectangular blocks cemented together with lime. Of the Etruscan settlement, and the Roman city that succeeded it, there remain only scattered fragments—stretches of walls and sewers, mosaic pavements—which do not provide sufficient information to reconstruct the plan of the city.

Cortona. Position of the principal Etruscan tombs

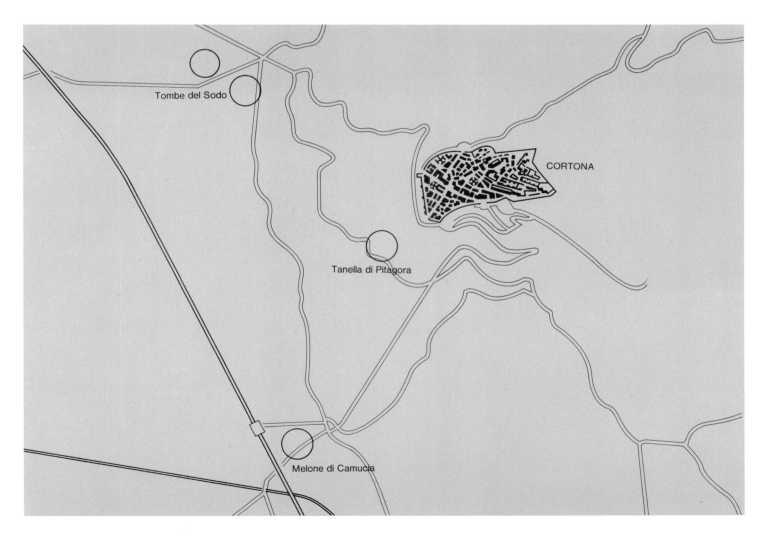

It is clear, however, that Etruscan Cortona was a centre of decorative bronze work; the most famous and impressive example is the lamp now in the Museo dell'Accademia Etrusca. It was found near the city, and consists of a plate-like circular base with sixteen spouts; it is remarkably richly decorated, on the lower surface only, as it was designed to be seen from below. In the centre is a gorgon's head in relief surrounded by a frieze of animals in combat; round this runs a wave design supporting alternating figures of a harpy and Silenus that act as caryatids or supports for the spouts, and between these on a higher level are heads of Acheloüs. This lamp is unique of its kind, and dates from about the end of the 5th century B.C. Later artefacts include the little votive bronzes representing divinities, suppliants and animals, originating in Cortona and dating from the 4th century B.C. and the Hellenistic period, which are now in the Museo dell'Accademia Etrusca or in various museums in Italy and elsewhere.

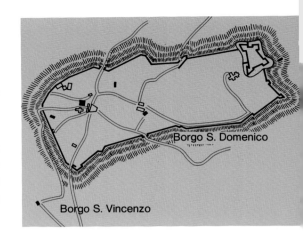

Along the slopes and at the foot of the hill of Cortona tombs have been discovered that are of particular interest from an architectural point of view. The oldest were at the foot of the hill at Sodo and Camucia; because of their distance from the city there is some doubt whether they actually belonged to Cortona itself or to some hitherto unidentified smaller settlement nearby. These Archaic tumuli are called *meloni* ('melons') by local people: the Melone di Camucia is the largest of the three, about 200 metres in circumference and 14 metres high. The layout is fairly complex, with two entrances in the lateral walls of the antechamber leading into two little side rooms that were probably for the remains of less important people. Two other doors in the rear wall of the vestibule each lead into two axial chambers. The roof is built according to the normal method of corbelled courses of progressively overlapping stones, but differs in that the space at the top is covered by a stone slab resting on the two final courses. Furnishings found in the tomb include bronze and gold objects, impasto and bucchero vases, and painted Etruscan and imported Greek pottery that dates the period during which the tomb was in use to the 7th–6th centuries B.C. The stone side of a funeral couch, decorated in low relief with figures of mourning women, was also found and is now in the Museo Archeologico in Florence with the rest of the tomb furnishings. It is worth noting that the excavation of this tomb was carried out by Alessandro François, whose name is linked with many important discoveries in several places in Etruria in the 19th century.

There are two similar tumuli at Sodo, not far from Camucia. The first *melone* is, as usual, covered with earth; the *dromos*, entered from the south-southwest, leads easily to an antechamber on an axis with two central rooms and the burial chamber at the rear, while two small rooms open off each side. The corbelled roof is constructed from overlapping courses of stone; the gap between the topmost courses is filled with wedge-shaped stones. There is a three-line inscription engraved on the architrave of the entrance linking

the two left-hand side rooms that reads: *tusthi thui hupninethi arnt mefanates veliak hapisnei*
—'In this tomb [lie buried] Arnt Mefanates [a man's first name and clan name] and Velia Hapisnei [a woman named in the same way]'. The second Melone del Sodo is similar to this, but is in a much worse state of preservation.

Two tombs situated close together on the outskirts of Cortona near the Cinque Vie crossroads are later constructions, dating from the 4th century B.C. or the Hellenistic period. One has long been known, and is called the Tanella or Grotta di Pitagora ('Pythagoras's Den' or 'Cave'), since a legend has it that the philosopher lived at Cortona (this is, however, a confusion between Croton in southern Italy, where Pythagoras did in fact live, and the Etruscan name of Cortona). It consists of a circular plinth about 1·70 metres high, surmounted by a false barrel vault of large blocks of stone. Inside is only one quite small room, with six niches for cinerary urns.

The other tomb of this type, called Tanella Angori, has only recently been discovered; it is very similar, but all that is left is the circular plinth and the stone-slab floor of the inner chamber, built on the Greek-cross plan.

In the 18th century Cortona was the centre of intense activity in the field of Etruscan studies, culminating in the founding of the Accademia Etrusca as a meeting-place for local experts and students of Etruscology, and to encourage further historical research and archaeological work. Meetings were held in members' homes, presided over by an officer called the *lucumo*, and records were kept of all their discussions and activities. The Accademia Etrusca gradually acquired a fine library and various precious objects of different periods that formed the nucleus of the Biblioteca Etrusca and the Museo Etrusco at Cortona.

3 2

The museum shares the Palazzo Casali with the Accademia Etrusca, and houses among other things a rich collection of Etruscan and Roman bronzes, Athenian and Etruscan pottery, and a large coin collection. The most famous items in the museum are, however, the bronze lamp that has become almost the emblem of Etruscan Cortona, and a painting on slate of the Muse Polyhymnia that was originally considered Roman but is in fact probably a late 17th-century work.

One curious item from the museum is the square base (for a statuette) inscribed with the Etruscan word *curtun*, which may well have been the ancient name of Cortona itself.

Opposite:
1. Plan of the Melone di Camucia
2. Plan of Melone del Sodo II
3. Interior of Melone del Sodo I

Above: Cortona. The Tanella or Grotta di Pitagora

Right: bronze Etruscan lamp. Cortona, Museo dell'Accademia

Chiusi

Chiusi, Poggio Renzo. Interior of the Tomba della Scimmia

Of Etruscan Chiusi there survive a few remains of the city and the vast cemeteries that were built over the centuries on the surrounding hills. The first urban settlement dates from the 8th–7th centuries B.C. This settlement, for which we have two ancient names, Clevsin (Clusium in Latin) and Camars, grew in time to become one of the most important cities in the Etruscan league; a solid agricultural-based economy guaranteed its prosperity and it dominated from the south the Val di Chiana and the lines of communication between inland southern Etruria and the north. The area was already fairly densely inhabited in the Bronze Age; one of the most important prehistoric settlements in central Italy has been discovered on nearby Monte Cetona, where the plateau of Belverde has revealed a proper fortified village of huts and caves whose inhabitants built a system of artificial terraces as a base for their dwellings.

There is little to see of the Etruscan city of Chiusi except a few stretches of the stone-block walls that encircled the summit of the hill; the Roman town that succeeded it is much more in evidence, despite the fact that Chiusi has been continuously inhabited down to the present day. The oldest part of the town still retains the rectangular grid system typical of Roman settlements: the chief north–south street (the *cardo maximus*) corresponds to the first stretch of the present-day Via Porsenna, as far as the Porta Lavinia, and the chief east–west street (the *decumanus maximus*) is covered by the second stretch of Via Porsenna, from the cathedral to Piazza Graziano, and by Via Arunte.

There is also a large 1st-century B.C. cistern under the Piazza del Duomo that can be entered by the door leading into the mediaeval campanile. It consists of a rock-cut chamber with two naves; its walls have been carefully plastered to make them waterproof, while the roof has two vaults made from large blocks of tufa with two openings to let in the water from above. On one side is the entrance to an ancient *cuniculus* (underground passage), which is one of many found under the city, probably forming the drainage system.

It is clear that the flourishing economy of Chiusi and its territory was based on agriculture: the minor Etruscan settlements at Città della Pieve, Cetona, Sarteano, Chianciano, Montepulciano and Castiglion del Lago had a material culture similar to that of Chiusi, which proves that this whole area was densely populated with rural settlements closely associated with the chief city.

There is little doubt that the period of greatest prosperity for Chiusi was from the end of the 6th century to the 4th century B.C., as is attested by finds in the cemeteries and the legends relating to Lars Porsenna, the king of Chiusi, who attacked Rome, and according to some sources even conquered it. Porsenna's expedition has been linked in literature with the expulsion of Tarquin the Proud from Rome and the heroism of Horatius Cocles, who alone defended the Sublician bridge from the Etruscan army, stories that prove the expanding power of Chiusi at the end of the 6th century B.C.

Later, between the 4th and 3rd centuries B.C., the city peacefully became subject to Rome and preserved its institutions and cultural independence until the 1st century B.C., when Sulla established a military *colonia* there.

The oldest cemetery is at Poggio Renzo, to the northeast of Chiusi: it was in use from the Villanovan period to the late Hellenistic age; the tombs then extended to Pania and Fonte Rotella, and later to Colle Casuccini, Poggio Gaiella and Vigna Grande.

The Villanovan tombs follow the usual pattern of pits containing a cinerary urn and some tomb furnishings. However, by the second quarter of the 7th century B.C., in the cemetery of Poggio Renzo itself, the first tombs appeared with fair-sized jars containing cinerary urns that came to be called *canopi*. This name derives from the Egyptian vases for containing entrails of mummified corpses, which have a superficial similarity to the Etruscan cinerary urns. The Etruscan canopi had an egg-shaped body which held the ashes of the deceased and was closed by a lid resembling a human head: the oldest types are simple spherical lids with two small depressions to indicate eyes, but they became increasingly anthropomorphic, first with the addition of a bronze mask, then with facial features shaped directly in the clay, and finally with heads properly modelled in the round. The heads of 'female' canopi have pierced ear-lobes, and some have kept the original gold earrings that went in them.

The canopi are made to look more human in many cases by the addition of two short arms, in a variety of positions, attached to the main body of the urn. These urns can be of impasto, bucchero or bronze, while the head-shaped lid is usually impasto, and rests on a type of high-backed stand in embossed bronze or terracotta. It is interesting to observe that the terracotta stands copied the bronze ones, with little applied studs and fillets.

The canopi are a special feature of Chiusi and the surrounding area, and their anthropomorphic tendency obviously expresses particular beliefs about death and the afterlife; the beliefs are largely unknown to us, since our only sources of information are the tombs and their furnishings. During the earliest period, from the end of the 8th to the first half of the 7th century, the same anthropomorphic tendency was also visible in some cinerary urns from Vulci, Saturnia, Marsiliana and Bisenzio—a very well-defined and homogeneous part of Etruria from many aspects besides the purely artistic one. Chiusi itself kept cremation as its form of burial for a very long period, and developed at a later date highly characteristic and interesting cinerary statues, urns and sarcophagi.

Jar-tombs still continued in the cemeteries until the end of the 6th century B.C., but at the same time the first rock-cut chamber-tombs appeared from the end of the 7th century B.C. The oldest of these are extremely small, and some contained canopi, including the famous Dolciano canopus (called after the place where it was found). Gradually these tombs became larger and more complex in plan. By the end of the 7th century and the beginning of the 6th century B.C. wall painting began to be used; two tombs (now lost) were found at Pania and Poggio Renzo decorated with the fantastic animals typical of the Orientalizing period. However, a school of painting flourished at Chiusi only during the first half of the 5th century, and noteworthy examples of its work survive; it is now possible to visit the Tomba della Scimmia ('Tomb of the Monkey') at Poggio Renzo and the Tomba del Colle at Colle Casuccini, dating respectively from the first and second quarters of the 5th century B.C. The former is so called because a little crouching monkey is painted (among other subjects) on the wall opposite the entrance to the tomb. The plan of this tomb is complex, with a central chamber which has an entrance door and a door in each of the other three walls, leading into smaller side rooms.

The central chamber has wall paintings enclosed between two cornices. Close study of the walls shows the technique used by the ancient painter (or painters) commissioned to decorate the tomb of one of the richest and most powerful families in the city. The outline of the various scenes and the individual figures was traced with a pointed instrument in the wet plaster, and some of the artist's corrections are still visible; the colour was then applied, and has remained substantially unaltered for centuries, although unfortunately it has begun to deteriorate more seriously in recent decades. Starting from the wall on the right of the entrance, the paintings are: the lady for whom the tomb was probably built, identifiable by the parasol she is holding, which in this case signifies isolation, and hence

Above: the Paolozzi pottery cinerary urn

Below: head of a female canopus with gold earrings. Chiusi, Museo Archeologico

Opposite: Chiusi, Poggio Renzo. Interior of the Tomba della Pellegrina

death; she is seated on a magnificent chair, and completely wrapped in a dark cloak, with the typical Etruscan *tutulus* (conical cap) on her head. In front of her a male figure in a broad-brimmed hat is playing on a double flute, and a little farther on a young woman dressed in a short tunic is dancing with a kind of large candelabrum balanced on her head; farther to the left are two clowns, a horseman, two more clowns, a warrior, two boxers, a man and a boy playing or competing in a game with a sort of bag, the monkey tied to a tree, wrestlers, horsemen and a chariot race. The deceased lady is thus shown watching the entertainments and the athletic and equestrian competitions organized in her honour.

The ceiling is decorated with the same carved coffering as are those in the side rooms, and with painted gorgon's heads, while the rear chamber has a particularly striking ceiling with a coloured rosette supported by four harpies.

The Tomba del Colle Casuccini is slightly later than the Tomba della Scimmia: it still has its original door, made of two well-smoothed slabs of travertine hanging on hinges. Inside are two chambers; the first is painted with racing chariots and athletic and banquet scenes, while the second shows male and female figures dancing among young trees.

The Tomba di Orfeo ed Euridice, with scenes of dancing, and the Tomba Paolozzi, with its scenes of battle, must have been painted at about the same period; they are now both lost. Other painted tombs are known only from drawings and watercolours that do not give enough details to identify the style of the work, and thus its date.

It is clear that painting flourished in Chiusi during a time of great prosperity; the scenes showing athletic competitions, entertainments, banquets and music are themes found in the great period of Tarquinian painting, but their execution is generally less skilful and varied, and seems almost provincial in comparison.

Chamber-tombs were used throughout the Hellenistic period; some of them were certainly painted, for example, the Tomba della Tassinaia, now difficult to visit. The single, almost square burial chamber, containing terracotta sarcophagi of the Tius family which are now in the museum at Chiusi, has an interesting barrel-vaulted ceiling; the walls were originally decorated with garlands, discs, paterae and birds, and pictures of the two people for whom the tomb was made. From the stylistic aspect, the use of chiaroscuro is interesting; it is cleverly employed to give an added depth and dimension to the work.

The Tomba della Pellegrina at Poggio Renzo has a long *dromos* entered from the north-east and several little rooms in the walls to the right and left big enough to contain a cinerary urn. These urns, still *in situ*, are decorated with the usual low relief on the front; one has a rosette between shields, others show the death of Hippolytus, and Achilles and Ajax as suppliants at an altar. A fairly large side room goes off at an angle to the left, just before

Left: polychrome terracotta cinerary urn

Below: cinerary statue of seated woman. Chiusi, Museo Archeologico

Opposite page. Above: detail of the alabaster sarcophagus of Laris Sentinate Larcna. Chiusi, Museo Archeologico

Below: polychrome sarcophagus of Larthia Seianti, from Chiusi. Florence, Museo Archeologico

the end of the entrance passage, and contains benches and an urn decorated with a low-relief scene of the sack of the sanctuary of Delphi by the Gauls—a fairly common subject for this type of urn.

Right at the end of the entrance passage is the main burial chamber, also with benches running round the sides; these supported three large polished sarcophagi in a niche opposite the entrance, three urns along each of the side walls, and a smaller urn by the wall near the entrance.

The top of one of these sarcophagi is propped open with the lid of an urn, just as it was left by thieves who broke into the tomb in the 19th century, removing nearly all the furnishings except the urns and the sarcophagi, which they opened and searched for jewellery, coins and any other valuables that might have been buried with the dead. The urns are variously decorated: with garlands, mythological scenes and scenes of battle.

The construction of the Tomba della Pellegrina marks an interesting stage in the progression from chamber-tombs to tombs where the most important area is not the central or rear chamber, but the passage containing niches or *loculi* for remains.

Another important group of Hellenistic cemeteries near Chiusi is at Poggio Gaiella, the northernmost of the hills surrounding the city. Numerous underground passages and tombs were built on three different levels in the hillsides, making a somewhat complex maze; they are now almost completely inaccessible because of subsidence in the tufa. This burial ground has been wrongly identified with the tomb of Porsenna, described by Pliny (*Natural History*, 36, 19, 4) as a 'labyrinth'. Pliny, however, was probably describing a religious or funerary building of the Hellenistic period consisting of a base and five pyramidal storeys surmounted by a disc, as can be seen in a tomb in Albano, in reliefs and in pictures of buildings of this type.

The structure of other Hellenistic tombs such as the Vigna Grande and Granduca tombs is also of interest. The latter was discovered in 1818 on a farm belonging to the Grand Duke of Tuscany—hence its name. Its entrance faces east and was originally closed by a double door; traces of its hinges are still visible on the door-jambs. The burial chamber is cut into the tufa, but also has walls and a barrel vault made of squared and accurately fitted blocks of stone. A bench runs along the walls holding eight urns decorated in relief with gorgons, sea gods—an obvious reference to the journey by sea to the underworld—and Dionysus on his sacred beast, the panther. Inscriptions on the urns show that the tomb, built towards the end of the 3rd century B.C., belonged to the Pulflua Peris family, whose members were in turn buried there.

The cemeteries at Chiusi have been known for centuries; continuous habitation and intensive agriculture in the area led first to chance discovery of more or less rich and interesting tombs, then to a systematic search for further antiquities. As long ago as the first half of the 19th century unsystematic amateur excavations carried out in the cemeteries of Chiusi led to the formation of local collections of antiquities, which were then partially described in a publication called the *Etrusco Museo Chiusino*, which came out in two volumes in 1833–34. The richest of these collections, belonging to the Casuccini family, was acquired by the museum at Palermo in 1863; other collections were dispersed among museums in Italy and abroad, dealers and other collectors. Thus the connections between individual objects and their origins in particular tombs and cemeteries were largely lost, since the individual object was then the subject of interest.

In spite of this dispersal, however, we still have enough information to give a fairly clear picture of the artistic culture of Chiusi. Besides a school of painting, the city produced one or more workshops of sculptors and bronze-workers. The canopi of the 7th–6th centuries B.C. were the predecessors in the area of other works of funerary art; towards the end of the 6th century B.C. there begin to be stone cippi, urns and sarcophagi with very low-relief decorations showing banquets, funeral games, dances, sacrifices and farewells, that link up with designs widely current in Etruria during this period, and especially well known from tomb painting. In style, the craftsmen of Chiusi were also strongly influenced by Ionian art, which dominated the artistic culture of central Italy from the mid-6th century to the beginning of the 5th century B.C. with its fluidity of form and line and elegance of style.

Other characteristic products of the funerary art of Chiusi are free-standing statues in local stone, particularly female figures with long hair and hands flat on their breasts, and seated sphinxes reminiscent of Oriental models and influenced by Greek sculpture. It should be noted that there are very few examples of Etruscan stone sculpture compared with contemporary Greek sculpture, and figures of animals and monsters, standing guard over tombs, are more common than human figures; it is a funerary art, intended only for tombs.

There is a direct link between the canopi and the stone cinerary statues that were produced in the workshops of Chiusi from the late 6th century B.C. to the early Hellenistic age. They represent seated male or female figures with movable heads and containing a cavity in the thorax for the ashes of the deceased; the oldest are made of two or three stone blocks, one on top of the other. A single example of these statues is known where the figure is standing, not seated; it comes from Chianciano but was certainly made in Chiusi in the 5th century B.C.

These works reflect Greek sculpture, whose innovations and characteristic forms influenced the sculptors of Chiusi; late Archaic, early classical and Phidian influences met in the workshops there, although they affected only individual works and did not combine in a unified artistic culture. Many cinerary statues have proved to be fakes or at least of doubtful authenticity, and can be attributed to restorers working at Chiusi in the 19th century, who also produced copies of ancient terracottas and pottery that found their way to museums and collections in Italy and abroad.

Sculptors were still active in Chiusi in the Hellenistic age, producing a large number of funerary objects: these include some very expressive statuettes, urns, and stone and terracotta sarcophagi. Their little stone urns can easily be distinguished from those of the same period from Volterra and Perugia, by the style of their decoration and the use of a white alabaster with dark veins and various other types of stone from the Chiusi area. Another local feature is the widespread use of terracotta, first with incised and later with mould-impressed decorations. In this case also the urn itself was decorated with ornamental motifs, figures or mythological scenes, and the figure of the deceased was shown, usually semi-recumbent, on the lid; his name was written along the upper edge of the urn. The series of little mould-impressed urns depict two constantly recurring themes: the duel between Oedipus's sons Eteocles and Polynices, and a battle scene showing, in the centre, a god called Echetlos armed with a huge plough. There are groups of reliefs from the same mould, which becomes increasingly worn; most of these reliefs still have traces of their original bright colours, principally yellow, red and blue.

Besides locally produced artefacts, the cemeteries of Chiusi have produced many other objects of varying interest and value, including a quantity of imported Athenian red- and black-figure vases. The cemetery of Fonte Rotella, in particular, contained a magnificent volute krater signed by the painter Kleitias and the potter Ergotimos that is called the François Vase in honour of its discoverer: it is now in the Museo Archeologico in Florence. These vases were probably imported into the Val di Chiana by way of Vulci, and then transported by river via Poggio Buco and Sovana to Chiusi and beyond. Many artefacts from Vulci have also been found at Chiusi, such as the Pania casket, so called after the place where it was found; it has bands of low-relief decoration, one above the other, showing different scenes including the Homeric stories of Scylla and the escape of Ulysses and his companions from Polyphemus's cave by clinging to the bellies of rams. Gold work and other precious objects from southern Etruria, perhaps from Cerveteri, have also been found at Chiusi.

Products of the workshops of Chiusi were exported to the surrounding area, especially the 'heavy' buccheri with cylinder-impressed decorations. The earliest were vases and foculi in the characteristic black, almost shiny pottery with its very rich relief and free-standing decoration. The most common decorative motifs were real and fantastic animals, human and gorgon busts, and palmettes, which all derive from Greek art. The cylinder-decorated buccheri were impressed with bands of decoration while they were still soft. There was a wide market for them from Florence via Murlo, Roselle, Vetulonia and Orvieto down to Vulci. Since they were produced between the 7th century and the first half of the

5th century B.C. (approximately), they confirm Chiusi's prosperity and expansion during the reign of Porsenna, who traditionally launched the famous attack on Rome.

An archaeological commission was set up in 1870 in Chiusi to prevent further dispersal of Etruscan antiquities from the cemeteries round about, and to organize research, hitherto unofficial and unsystematic. It also initiated a series of excavations, and the finds formed the nucleus of the present Museo Civico, with the later addition of Count G. Paolozzi's collection of antiquities from the Chiusi area, and the Mieli Servadio collection, consisting mainly of material found in the Castelluccio di Pienza area, which includes outstanding prehistoric, Corinthian and Etrusco-Corinthian pottery.

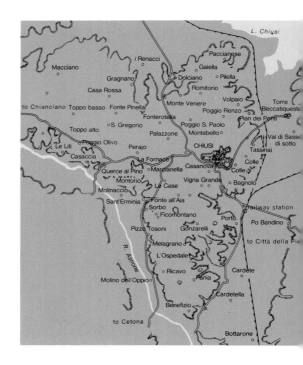

Chiusi and the surrounding area

The Gualandi cinerary urn is one of the most interesting items in the Museo Civico. It is a large impasto vase with a lid surmounted by a free-standing female figure with almond-shaped eyes and a network robe; she is wrapped in a cloak that hangs from her shoulders. Below her a row of roughly-formed figurines with long robes and hands raised to their breasts runs round the vase; still lower down, the same figurines alternate in couples with two griffin heads with gaping jaws. Similar to this is the Paolozzi cinerary urn, with a lid of the same type decorated with large griffin heads in imitation of the griffins on the Oriental-type bronze cauldrons that have been found in many rich tombs of the high Orientalizing period. Both these cinerary urns date from about 600 B.C. and are typical of the Chiusi region.

A series of canopi with stands shows clearly the development of these cinerary urns, from the earliest forms with their almost spherical lids, via those where anthropomorphization consisted of a bronze mask attached by metal wires running through holes in the clay, the later ones where the face was modelled in the clay but was still independent of the rest of the head, to the final ones with a head properly modelled in the round. It is interesting to note that the back of the head is in many cases quite roughly modelled, or even left completely smooth, probably because these heads were covered with material, of which traces may be found on a well-preserved canopus coming from a tomb where humidity has remained extremely low; vegetable fibres and organic material have survived only very occasionally, as a result of unusual ground conditions.

The rich collection of buccheri includes vases of different shapes with cylinder-impressed decorations, important examples of 'heavy' buccheri, and foculi (trays) containing little vases, spatulas and a little writing tablet, making up a complete set of domestic utensils.

Examples of Archaic sculpture consist of free-standing statues and cippi, little urns and stands with low-relief decoration. A tufa sphinx, dating from the late 7th–early 6th centuries B.C., has great curled-up wings on its back with traces of the original red paint on its feathers; there is also a typically Chiusine statue of a female figure in *pietra fetida* (a local sandstone) with hands pressed to its breast and long hair, reminiscent of Archaic Greek models.

A representative selection of cippi and their stands and Archaic urns show the variety of themes which were chosen to decorate these funerary objects and which had some symbolic connection with Etruscan beliefs about death and the afterlife.

In many cases, traces are preserved of the original paint, predominantly red, used to decorate the reliefs. The standard of craftsmanship and modelling is notably high, for example in the minutely detailed rendering of clothing, which sometimes appears to be the merest veil covering the body, and the details of faces, hair and objects.

The Hellenistic pieces include, in particular, a uniform series of little terracotta urns with moulded decoration and painted in bright colours, and little alabaster cinerary urns, with the urn itself carved in low relief and the lid carved with the reclining figure of the deceased. One outstanding lid is from the Tomba della Pellegrina and depicts Aule Seiante, whose name is written from right to left across the edge; it is one of the finest examples of Etruscan portrait sculpture.

The museum also contains a collection of Etruscan and imported pottery: biconical cinerary urns and impasto vases of the Villanovan period, Corinthian vases, Athenian

Pietra fetida cippus depicting a funerary dance.
Chiusi, Museo Archeologico

black- and red-figure vases decorated with mythological or general scenes, Etrusco-Corinthian pottery and Etruscan black- and red-figure vases. It is easy to tell Etruscan from Greek vases by the colour of the clay and the style of the decoration, always more careless and inexpert compared with Greek examples, and frequently displaying a taste for heavier and less restrained ornamentation. From Roman Chiusi there are a marble head of Augustus and a headless draped female statue, dating from the 2nd century B.C., that probably stood in the forum or in some other important public place, a head of Dionysus and other minor items.

Montepulciano

The larger towns of the ancient territory of Chiusi preserve traces of the Etruscan settlements from which they grew. Montepulciano, for example, has a small collection of objects found locally, exhibited in the Palazzo Tarugi, and one of its finest buildings, the Palazzo Bucelli, situated almost at the head of the Via Roma, has the whole lower part of its façade decorated with Etruscan cinerary urns of the Hellenistic period and stone slabs with Etruscan and Latin inscriptions. The urns, decorated with rosettes, paterae, monsters and various other motifs, are typical of the Chiusi area.

Chianciano, Pienza and Città del Pieve also have small collections of Etruscan and Roman antiquities that have escaped dispersal. At Sarteano the chamber-tombs of the Colle di Solaia, Bel Riguardo and Le Tombe can be seen, and remains of Etruscan and Roman buildings that are incorporated in the church of S. Lorenzo.

Opposite: the hills of Montepulciano

Etruscan urns in the façade of the Palazzo Bucelli

Below: detail of the façade of the Palazzo Bucelli

Perugia

From the 4th century B.C. Perugia was the most powerful Etruscan centre in the upper
Tiber valley. For the preceding period we have sparse evidence that does not permit us
to construct a clear organic plan of the settlement. The 4th–3rd-century city crowned an
uneven hill that dominates the Umbrian plain and the valley of the Tiber. Long stretches
of the original wall surrounding the city can be seen; it is built of great square blocks of
travertine and follows the terrain in and out for about 3 kilometres. The original perimeter
can be traced with precision: it ran from the Porta Marzia to the church of S. Ercolano,
to the Porta Sole, up to the Arco di Augusto, to the Porta della Mandorla and the Torre
dei Donati. About 2·5 metres thick, this wall protected the city throughout the Middle
Ages until the 13th century, when it had to be extended.

The Porta della Mandorla is Etruscan, but was substantially remodelled during the Middle Ages. The Porta Marzia nearby is better preserved: in the 16th century the architect Antonio da Sangallo, who was responsible for the Rocca Paolina, incorporated in the eastern tower the door-jambs of the gate that previously existed at that point in the Etruscan wall, and reconstructed the upper part stone by stone to include it in the exterior of the new tower. Although the Porta Marzia still faces in the original direction, it is about 4 metres outside the line of the Etruscan wall; it is, however, as imposing as it ever was in ancient times. Two heads, possibly of tutelary gods of the city, were built into the wall either side of the arch, and the now formless stone that surmounts it may also have been a head. The coping is a kind of loggia, closed below by *transennae* (pierced screens) and supported by fluted Corinthian pilasters, in between which are the carved high-relief busts of three gods and, at the end, two horses' heads. Two Roman inscriptions, of which one can be acribed to Octavian, run along the slabs of stone that enclose the top and bottom of the loggia.

The Arco Etrusco, or Arco di Augusto, is another monumental gate in the northern part of the ancient city wall. It is flanked by two large trapezoid towers and surmounted by an arch with two rows of ashlar masonry with the inscription *Augusta Perusia*, above which is a frieze of five round shields alternating with little Ionic pilasters. Above is an arch between two further Ionic pilasters. A small balcony dating from the 16th century runs around the top of the left tower.

Little remains of Etruscan and Roman Perugia, as much has been destroyed in the course of constant rebuilding in mediaeval and modern times. Worth mentioning is the great mosaic to be seen in Viale Pascoli, a remnant of the baths built in the 2nd century A.D.; it is a huge pavement of black and white tesserae showing Orpheus taming wild beasts with his sweet music.

Left: Perugia. Porta Marzia

Right: Perugia. Arco Etrusco or Arco di Augusto

Below: archaeological plan of Perugia

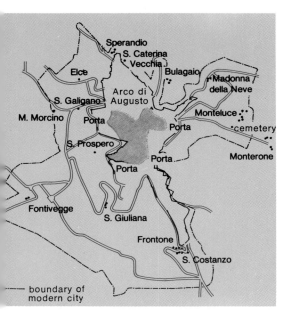

Vast cemeteries have been excavated on the hills that surround the city, especially during the 19th century when Perugia was very active as a centre of Etruscan studies.

One of the largest burial grounds is at Palazzone, where one can visit the great Ipogeo dei Volumni. This is a tomb belonging to a noble family of the late Hellenistic age; it has a central chamber with a burial chamber beyond the rear wall, and eight side rooms. The roof of the central chamber imitates the structure of a real gabled roof, from which used to hang a terracotta cupid holding a bronze lamp, which has since been destroyed. The triangular space above the entrance is also decorated in relief with a shield between two dolphins, and the opposite wall is decorated with a shield between two swords and two male busts. The rear chamber has a ceiling decorated in relief with a large gorgon's head, and contains seven cinerary urns; one is the marble urn of Arnth Velimna, one of the finest Etruscan urns known. The dead man is shown in a semi-recumbent position on a bed covered with drapery and cushions, leaning on a raised support with two female demons of the underworld, called Vanth by the Etruscans and depicted with torches in their hands; in the centre is an arched doorway that symbolizes the door to the afterlife, with a figure which has partially disappeared.

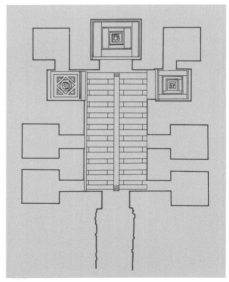

Above left: interior of the Ipogeo di S. Manno, near Perugia

Below left: Perugia. Plan of the Ipogeo dei Volumni, with details of roofs

Above: urn from the cemetery of Palazzone. Perugia, Museo Archeologico

Below: Ipogeo dei Volumni

The Ipogeo dei Volumni is a fine example of a princely tomb built in the late Hellenistic age and used right up to the 1st century A.D. Nearby is a little museum displaying objects found in the tomb and in other tombs in the Palazzone cemetery. These are mostly travertine and terracotta urns, with a simple lid shaped like a gabled roof and a polished container either inscribed or decorated in relief with scenes from mythology or other subjects. One of the most interesting items found in the Ipogeo dei Volumni is a large column-krater manufactured in Volterra and exported to Perugia; it is decorated with a scene showing Jason struggling with the sea monster, whose enormous gaping jaws can be seen, and is now in the museum at Perugia. Also found in this same tomb were a fragment of a shield, a spherical bronze helmet, two shin-guards, bronze vessels and a *kottabos* (a little stand used at banquets for resting a goblet into which everyone tossed some wine in turn, deriving omens from the outcome of the game).

Another well-known tomb in the Perugia area forms part of the crypt of the Romanesque church of S. Manno at Ferro di Cavallo. The tomb, with a barrel vault, is rectangular and made of carefully laid blocks of travertine; the two side rooms also have vaulted roofs. There is a three-line Etruscan inscription on the arch leading into the left side room (which contained the cinerary urns, on two little benches) a rather obscure text referring to two members of the Precu family, for whom the tomb was built.

It is also possible to visit the Ipogeo di Villa Sperandio, consisting of a burial chamber cut into the tufa with a vaulted roof; a travertine sarcophagus contained the skeleton of a woman and the tomb furnishings mostly lay on the floor. These were typical of a wealthy woman's possessions and included bronze vessels and a bronze mirror decorated with the engraved figure of a winged spirit (a Lasa) and Adonis, with a bone handle decorated with two winged figures. Since the woman also had gold earrings and a diadem in sheet gold in the form of lanceolate leaves worked in relief, she was obviously a member of a particularly wealthy family, and some scholars even think she may have been a priestess.

The Museo Archeologico Nazionale dell'Umbria is at Perugia, and contains one of the leading prehistoric and Etruscan collections in Italy, built up from private collections and various other acquisitions. It is housed in the former convent of S. Domenico; in the cloisters on the ground floor are displayed Etruscan urns, a sarcophagus depicting the story of Meleager, architectural fragments, Roman cippi and stelae, a puteal (well-head) with a battle scene between Greeks and Amazons—all products of Perugian culture in the Hellenistic and Roman period. On the first floor is a large collection of urns, mostly from the area around Perugia, which are grouped according to the tombs in which they were found. Many have relief decorations showing mythological scenes, while others have rosettes or funereal scenes such as the journey to the afterlife, or leave-taking from the family. The cover may be gabled, and then the urn assumes the appearance of a model house where the ashes have found their last resting-place, while others are decorated with the semi-recumbent figure of the deceased. Most have inscriptions naming the deceased, his family, and sometimes also his father and mother. Obviously urns coming from one single tomb all belong to members of the same family. Many still bear traces of the colours used to heighten the relief decorations and make the inscriptions clearer; it is interesting to note the stylistic uniformity of these urns, which are clearly distinguishable from those produced at Chiusi or Volterra during the same period by their material, technique and subject-matter. Hellenistic and other influences current in Etruria at the time were a source of inspiration for the craftsmen of Perugia, but they worked according to their own taste and that of their clients.

The museum also displays a famous example of the Etruscan language, the Perugia cippus, which has a long inscription on two sides mentioning two families called Velthina and Afuna, plots of land and burial-grounds; it was probably used as a boundary stone.

In Archaic times the territory round Perugia must have been populated with small settlements scattered on the hillsides between Lake Trasimene and the upper course of the Tiber, with a mainly agricultural economy. Each of these little settlements had its own burial-ground, which has preserved a record of its existence down to modern times; some of the most interesting objects found in them are displayed in the museum.

The Monte Gualandro stele, for example, shows a duel between two warriors and dates from the beginning of the 6th century B.C.; the Sarcofago dello Sperandio, named after the cemetery at Sperandio where it was found, shows clear Chiusine influence in the relief decorations on the coffer, depicting the return of a war-party and banquet scenes. Some statues in bronze and embossed sheet bronze come from Castel S. Mariano and date from about the middle of the 6th century B.C.; they are probably decorations for a chariot or a piece of furniture, and are undoubtedly among the most important examples of metal-work of the time, influenced by Ionian motifs and style.

Other items in the museum come from the Perugia area and include rich tomb furnishings from the cemeteries of Monteluce, Frontone, S. Caterina and Sperandio, such as bronze vases, imported Athenian pottery, red-figure Etruscan kraters from Volterra, beautifully worked weapons, mirrors, carved bone and jewels.

One large room contains a rich collection of buccheri, Athenian and Etruscan pottery, bronzes, mirrors and weapons belonging to different periods. It leads into the coin room and treasury, which contains a large collection of coins of Republican and Imperial Rome, and Etruscan and Roman gold-work.

The prehistoric collection includes an interesting series of stone implements from the Palaeolithic and Neolithic Ages, including hand-axes, scrapers, arrow-heads, axes and long blades skilfully chipped from flint core, using another flint as a tool.

Next to this on the upper floor is the protohistoric collection, which comprises Bronze and Iron Age finds from cemeteries and settlements in Umbria, the Marches and the Abruzzi. The most interesting are those from the caves of Belverde di Cetona, including vases of different shapes and sizes, some with incised decoration, bone tools and weapons, and ornamental objects such as a set of deer-antler hairpins beautifully decorated with circles and other markings. The daily life of these early times is recalled by containers still holding wheat, beans, acorns and millet and the millstones for grinding cereals, on display in the centre of the room.

The prehistoric and protohistoric collections make up the Museo Preistorico dell'Italia Centrale, which is one of the most important in Europe; it was formed originally from the Bellucci collection and then enriched by excavations and private donations.

Above: the so-called Perugian cippus

Left: Etruscan sarcophagus depicting a ritual scene. Perugia, Museo Archeologico

Volterra

Volterra, like the majority of Etruscan cities, stands in a naturally defended position on the summit of a hill. The city dominates the valleys of the Cecina and the Era, and is also, by way of a series of mountain gorges and narrow valleys, within easy reach of the Valdelsa. Its geographical situation determined the directions of the territorial and commercial expansion of Volterra, which was one of the most powerful states of Etruria. The ancient road system must have roughly corresponded to the present one, being in fact determined by the nature of the terrain.

Volterra. The Balze, and the Volterran countryside

Proof that the area was already inhabited in Villanovan times is given by the cemeteries that surround the hill, and in particular by those of Badia and Guerruccia; the pit- and trench-tombs show persistence to a late date compared with the Villanovan cities of the coast, so that in the later period we find Villanovan cremation burials and inhumation burials in small chamber-tombs. There was no break in the continuity of life through the Orientalizing and Archaic periods, but the evidence that has come down to us is rather fragmentary, although significant. For instance, in a jar-tomb a biconical cinerary urn of the Villanovan type was found together with a bucchero lid of the late Orientalizing period, which proves the persistence of traditional Villanovan rites and materials throughout the 7th century B.C. Later, in the 6th and 5th centuries, burials also took place at the

Volterra. Etruscan walls at S. Chiara

Portone, where an Athenian black-figure vase was found. But on the whole evidence of life in Volterra prior to the 4th century B.C. is limited and fragmentary; this may well be the result of landslides which have carried away parts of the western slopes of the hill and may have destroyed the Archaic cemeteries, leaving only the sheer cliffs of the Balze.

We have much fuller evidence, for both the city and the cemeteries, for the period from the 4th century B.C. to the early Imperial age. The city was defended by a wall of which considerable stretches are preserved, which was built and extended in successive periods. The acropolis had a circuit of walls which were, as far as we can tell, extended between the end of the 6th and the beginning of the 5th century B.C. to a circumference of 1,800 metres; later, in the first half of the 4th century B.C. or shortly afterwards, the great walls, extending for more than 7,200 metres, were built, of large roughly-squared blocks of local stone. These follow the entire perimeter of the hill, enclosing the Archaic cemetery of the Guerruccia plateau, near the cliffs of S. Giusto. The walls are of a later period than the tombs, because ancient burial places were never inside a city.

Two of the gates in the city walls are still well preserved. In the northern sector is the Porta Diana or Portone, slightly outside the present city on the Via di Porta Diana. The strong tower on the right, a truncated pyramid, supports the blocks of the Etruscan pier; the other ancient pier leans against the hillside. Above is a mediaeval arch.

The Porta all'Arco, in the southern sector, still has the original piers and imposts, though the arch is apparently to be attributed to rebuilding in the 1st century B.C., following a fierce fire which destroyed a great part of Volterra during the war against Sulla. Set in the arch are three carved stone heads, badly worn; these have been thought to represent famous persons or, alternatively, to commemorate the practice of beheading

Volterra. Porta all'Arco

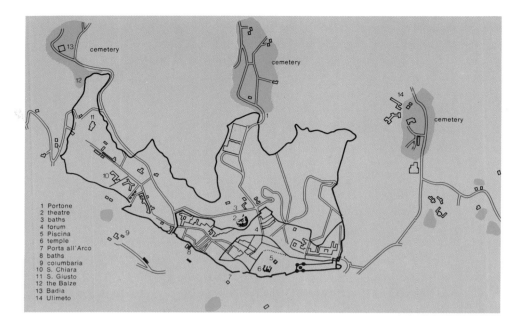

1 Portone
2 theatre
3 baths
4 forum
5 Piscina
6 temple
7 Porta all'Arco
8 baths
9 columbaria
10 S. Chiara
11 S. Giusto
12 the Balze
13 Badia
14 Ulimeto

the vanquished and displaying the heads as a trophy and a warning to the enemy, but they are most probably to be interpreted as the tutelary deities of the city.

In the Hellenistic period, Volterra grew to its greatest size; we know only isolated elements of the city, but these are sufficient to give us a picture of the prosperity and the building activity of the time. On the acropolis, corresponding to the Piano di Castello, stood a temple orientated northeast–southwest; part of the podium survives, with a section of moulding and an incomplete course of blocks from the wall above; around it, on three sides, ran a well-preserved terrace paved with large slabs alternating with blocks inserted in a wedge formation. In the mid-Hellenistic period, alongside this temple on the side where a pit now opens, a second temple was built; it appears to have been surrounded by pillars, with a double row of four columns on the façade. Both these buildings were originally decorated with polychrome architectural terracottas, as was usual at that time. The plateau of the acropolis was further covered, on the western and southern sides, by buildings of the same period as the older temple or slightly earlier, and by several cisterns for collecting rain-water.

Other remains of Etruscan buildings have been identified in the area of S. Michele and S. Francesco, and in the northern part of the city, under the Roman theatre, near which has also recently been uncovered the base of an Etruscan temple of the Hellenistic period, easily recognizable by the construction of its podium in huge squared blocks of local stone.

The Hellenistic cemeteries are outside the walls, covering the same area as the Archaic ones and extending farther towards the plain at Badia, Montebradoni, the Portone, Marmini, Ulimeto and Poggio alle Croci. The tombs are chamber-tombs, cut in the soft *panchina* (brownish local stone) of the slopes, surmounted by a cippus; the chamber, which is reached by a short corridor, may be rectangular in plan, sometimes with small side rooms, or else circular, with a central pillar. Along the walls there are generally benches for the burials, these too being cut out of the rock.

One of the most famous of these Hellenistic tombs is the one known as the Tomba Inghirami, after one of the oldest families in Volterra, which owns the land on which the tomb was found and numbers among its forebears a celebrated 19th-century Etruscologist. It is a large, roughly circular tomb with a thick central pillar, and has been reconstructed

Krater with scene of dancing, and krater with portrait. Volterra, Museo Guarnacci

in the garden of the Museo Archeologico in Florence; along the walls runs a low bench on which stood the urns, of the usual type with a chest decorated with scenes in relief, covered by a slab on which the deceased is represented in a reclining position.

A short distance outside Volterra, several chamber-tombs are visible in the embankment which flanks the road leading down to the level ground at the Porta Diana; these were discovered by chance in the course of road-widening work, and provide a series of tombs typical of the Volterran region.

During the Hellenistic period a few stone-cutters' workshops were active in Volterra, producing numerous series of tufa and alabaster urns, and one or two potters' workshops, to which are to be attributed column-kraters, stamnoi, red-figure cups, skyphoi decorated with a large swan overpainted in red, black-gloss vases finely and richly decorated in relief, and black-gloss pottery for more general use. Alongside these there were probably also small workshops of bronze-workers, who met local requirements for dishes, weapons and objects of everyday use.

These typically Volterran products are found not only in the cemeteries of the city itself but also in the cemeteries of the centres of population in the surrounding region directly dependent on the city, and they were exported as far as the Val di Chiana and Umbria, Populonia and Roselle, and, to the north, Bologna, Spina and Adria.

This is proof of the expanding trade and prosperity of Volterra during the period from the late 4th century to the 1st century B.C., confirmed by the extent of building activity within the city precincts and derived primarily from an organized economy firmly based on agriculture. Among the Etruscan cities which in 205 B.C. furnished aid to Rome for Scipio's expedition against Carthage, Volterra is mentioned as providing wood for the keels, fittings for the ships, and a large quantity of grain, as did Perugia, Roselle, Chiusi and Cerveteri, whilst Tarquinia furnished flax for the sails, Populonia provided iron, and Arezzo a total of 50,000 helmets, javelins and spears of various types, tools and utensils, timber and wheat. This confirms the evidence provided by archaeological finds, which show all around the city a dense network of clearly agricultural settlements, closely dependent on the metropolis. Volterra also struck its own coins.

In the 3rd century B.C. the city peacefully entered the Roman political alliance, and continued to hold a prominent position among the cities of northern Etruria until the first decades of the 1st century B.C.; during the civil wars Volterra sided with Marius, as did the other Etruscan cities, and was besieged for a long time by Sulla, who took it only after two years. On the acropolis, the Hellenistic remains to the southwest of the temple show clear traces of a fire which has been connected with this incident, and it is also thought that the Porta all'Arco underwent a certain amount of reconstruction at about the same time, after being damaged.

In the 1st century B.C. Volterra was still prosperous, though the inhabitants were fewer in number than when the city was at the height of its greatness. In the second half of the 1st century B.C. considerable construction work was in progress, and more public buildings were erected: just outside the second circuit of walls, the one dated to the 6th–5th centuries B.C., a new area of public buildings was created on the remains of earlier dwellings; it comprised the forum, a temple, a bath complex and a theatre. On the acropolis was built a great cistern with cemented walls and floor, the so-called Piscina ('swimming bath'), divided into three sections by two rows of *panchina* pillars and covered by an imposing vaulted roof.

The most remarkable evidence of this building activity is the theatre, in the Vallebuona area, with its *cavea* or auditorium backing on to the hillside and surmounted by the mediaeval (13th-century) walls. When these walls, which show very clearly the contraction of the urban area as compared with the Etruscan and Roman periods, were built, the highest part of the theatre, including what remained of the monumental entrance to the *cavea*, was left inside, while the steps and the stage were outside. The monuments inside the walls were buried or else re-used as building material in the mediaeval period, whilst those outside the walls were not much damaged. The theatre in particular, which had already been completely abandoned at the end of the 3rd century A.D., became a dump for refuse, which gradually buried it and thereby saved it from destruction.

The building was constructed in accordance with the canons of the classical Roman theatre as expounded by Vitruvius, the architect of the Augustan age: it stands on a north-facing slope, sheltered from the southerly winds, and in the afternoon the seats are in shade. The stage is twice as long as the *orchestra*; the height of the front wall of the stage is less than 1.50 metres, so that the spectators seated in the lower rows could have a clear view of the actors on the stage, as recommended by Vitruvius. The main entrance was at the height of the gallery which ran around the top of the building and opened on to the north side of the forum. The *cavea* was divided into two tiers of steps by a single

Volterra. Remains of Etruscan walls, and portico near the Roman theatre

passage or *praecinctio*. On the steps were inscribed the names of the most important clans of Volterra: the Caecinae, the Persii, the Laelii, the Petronii; those which occur most frequently are the Persii and the Laelii, who evidently patronized the theatre more than did the high aristocracy of the city, who by now no longer resided permanently in Volterra, having interests and duties in Rome. In front of the first row of seats there is a semicircular channel to draw off rain-water from the *cavea* into the drains below; lacking from the edge of the *orchestra* are the two rows of seats for the most honoured patrons which are found in other Roman theatres. The floor of the *orchestra* was paved with marble of various colours; in fact, no expense was spared in the decoration of the theatre: marble, especially Carrara marble, was widely used in the facing of the stage and the decoration of the *scaenae frons* (the back wall of the stage), and doubtless also in other parts of the building, for example the monumental entrance. Particularly rich was the decoration of the *scaenae frons*; it was divided into two storeys, together reaching 15.50 metres above the stage, with Corinthian columns and capitals, architraves and cornices. Here an inscription testified that the Caecinae wanted to demonstrate their devotion to Augustus by building the theatre in his honour. Excavations brought to light two heads of Octavian (Augustus as a young man), now exhibited in the Museo Guarnacci.

Of the Roman city there also remains a bath building close to S. Felice; the ruins bear witness that it was of considerable size, and a mosaic pavement shows that here too was a building of luxury and refinement.

The Museo Guarnacci in Volterra contains one of the best-known and most important collections of Etruscan material. It was founded in 1732 when Canon P. Franceschini presented the municipality with a group of forty urns from the Portone cemetery. The collection was enriched by the excavations carried out in the Badia and Ulimeto districts, and by the gift of Monsignore Guarnacci, who in 1761 bequeathed to the city his library and archaeological collection, at the same time leaving an annuity for the upkeep and expansion of the museum. Later the museum acquired the Topi collection and the Museo Pagnini, to which was added material from gifts and from excavations carried out in the environs of the city.

The museum is in three sections: the prehistoric and protohistoric section is on the ground floor, to the left of the entrance; the Roman section is also on the ground floor, to the right, whilst the Etruscan section occupies all the rest of this floor as well as the floor above.

The prehistoric and protohistoric section contains a representative and rich selection of material from Volterra and its immediate surroundings. Of particular interest are the reconstructions of Villanovan pit- and jar-tombs, containing the typical biconical urns decorated with incised geometric designs and covered with a bowl, and the usual grave goods, such as crescent-shaped bronze razors, bronze fibulae, small vases in impasto or sheet bronze, flasks in sheet bronze with embossed decoration, pendants on chains.

Here can also be seen a famous bucchero vase, a single-handled cup on a tall inscribed stem, which comes from Monteriggioni, a place in the Valdelsa which came under strong Volterran influence. The vase is highly interesting for its inscription and its shape, which is identical with that of other buccheri found in several places in northern Etruria.

Also in the museum is the famous stele of Aule Tite, named after the dead man whose tomb it marked; his name can be read in the inscription which runs along the left edge of the slab. The stele is rounded at the top and decorated in low relief with the figure of a warrior, facing to the left, wearing a close-fitting tunic with short sleeves. He is armed with a long spear and a knife that hangs by his side, and has an elaborate hairstyle of the type that has been called a 'multi-layered wig'.

Funerary stelae of this type, which can be dated to the 6th century B.C., have been found not only at Volterra and in the surrounding region but also at Roselle and in the Arno valley, and show close similarities to Syro-Hittite and Aramaic stelae. In them can thus be seen the influence of Eastern models, received and adapted by Etruria.

Etruscan coin with the inscription *Velathri*. Volterra, Museo Guarnacci

The sculpture of Volterra in the Archaic period is also represented by a male head,
called the Lorenzini head after its first owner, which shows the influence of Greek sculpture
of the late 6th–early 5th centuries B.C. but is certainly of Etruscan workmanship, as is
clear from the heaviness of the features and ridging of the eyebrows, which call to mind
Etruscan bronzes. The marble used for this head is possibly local: certainly the use of
marble in Etruscan sculpture is exceptional, and confined to a very few pieces. It is quite
possible that this sculpture was a religious statue; in further support of this theory may be
cited its larger-than-life size, its elaborate hairstyle and the garland of leaves, possibly
myrtle, around its temples.

The Museo Guarnacci contains the largest collection in the world of Volterran urns;
there are pieces in tufa, in terracotta and above all in alabaster, which is the characteristic
material of Volterran urns and is still worked today, in craftsmen's workshops scattered
throughout the city, with tools similar to those used in ancient times.

The urns are arranged according to the subjects which decorate the front of the chest;
the covering lid is not always the right one. We should in fact not forget that the majority
of these pieces came to light in the 18th and 19th centuries, when there was no interest in
the association of objects in a single burial, but only in collecting pieces that might furnish
antiquarian information or that were worth studying for the mythological scenes depicted
on them. The system of their classification therefore took account solely of the individual
classes of objects and their decoration; the chronological clues furnished by the association
of different objects in a single tomb were thus lost to us. As a result, many pieces can be
only broadly dated to the Hellenistic period, since it is impossible to establish their dates
with precision on the basis of stylistic data alone.

1. Urn lid in alabaster with a female figure
2. Cinerary urn in alabaster with a male figure
3. Stele of Aule Tite
4. Lid of terracotta urn, the Urna dei Coniugi.
Volterra, Museo Guarnacci

Tufa was used exclusively for the small urns up to about the mid-3rd century B.C.,
after which it continued in use alongside alabaster, which came into use at that time and
was most popular during the 2nd and the early years of the 1st century B.C. Some series
of urns are decorated with general motifs such as large rosettes, or with motifs painted
on the smooth surface of the chest; others have griffins, sea monsters, dolphins, sea-
demons (Scyllas), cupids with flowers and paterae, which allude to the underworld and
the sea journey which, according to some beliefs, souls had to make before reaching their
resting-place. In other cases the funerary symbolism is more obvious: the dead person
is shown journeying to the next world on horseback, on a sea monster, or in a chariot,
sometimes accompanied by a slave or by Charun himself, a god of the dead, bearing a
heavy hammer; or else they depict a farewell scene in which the deceased is taking leave
of his relatives, who are grouped about him in attitudes of grief and mourning, or magistrates accompanied by a line of people carrying the insignia of their rank or objects relating
to the duties of the office they held in life. In other cases a married couple travel together
to the next world in a two-wheeled covered carriage (in Latin *carpentum*) drawn by mules
or horses.

Other series of urns are decorated with episodes from Greek mythology, depicted in a
vivid and lively style, often with the inclusion of an Etruscan demon of death (a Charun
or a female Vanth) in those which depict or imply an act of bloodshed. The subjects are
drawn from the Trojan and Theban cycles, and show, for example, Helen being carried
off by Paris, who is leading her on board a ship ready to weigh anchor; the sacrifice of
Iphigenia to induce the gods to favour the Greeks in their expedition against Troy. Or
else they show Ulysses and Polyphemus, Ulysses and Circe, Ulysses lashed to the mast
of his ship so as not to be lured by the sweet singing of the Sirens; the duel between
Eteocles and Polynices below the walls of Thebes; the death of Capaneus, who fell from
the walls of Thebes struck by the lightning-bolt of Zeus; Actaeon torn to pieces by his
hounds in punishment for having come upon the goddess Artemis while she was bathing
in a stream; and many other more or less familiar scenes.

Alongside these, we also find Etruscan figures and myths that are unknown to us:
one of the most interesting shows a huge chained wolf half emerging from a well, sur-

2

4

rounded by figures in various attitudes and sometimes by demons, who suggest a connection with beliefs concerning death that escape our knowledge.

Many urns still bear traces of the original polychrome and gilt decoration that embellished them and made the reliefs more striking; but it is of particular interest to note the disparity of workmanship between one relief and another, the greater or lesser skill of the artisan to whom the work was entrusted, and his more or less direct knowledge of the designs and forms of Greek art of the Hellenistic age.

Amongst the other material of Volterran manufacture can be seen a series of red-figure vases, especially column-kraters decorated with human heads in profile, grotesque figures, a centaur, a winged figure astride a dolphin. In many cases these vases had been used in the tombs as cinerary urns, and the subjects chosen to decorate them allude to their funerary use: the human heads, for example, some of which show elements of portraiture, are clearly intended to represent the deceased.

The production of the pottery workshops active in Volterra from the 4th to the 1st century B.C. is also represented by numerous black-gloss vases, kraters, shallow dishes, jugs, cups of various shapes, often decorated with small heads or bunches of grapes made in a mould and applied to the surface of the freshly-made vase. Beside these, there is the vast production of uncoloured pottery for everyday use.

The museum also contains fragments of architectural terracottas which once covered the temples of the acropolis, and near these can be seen the very famous terracotta urn lid depicting a married couple (the Urna dei Coniugi). There is also a rich collection of coins, small bronzes, gold ornaments and glass-ware, all of local origin. One of the bronzes is very elongated, of a type also found in other areas of Etruria, and probably has some ritual significance.

The Roman section of the museum contains, in particular, material uncovered during the excavation of the theatre, one of the most striking pieces being a head of Octavian.

Urn in alabaster depicting a departure for the underworld. Volterra, Museo Guarnacci

In the Etruscan period Siena was probably a small agricultural settlement, one of many scattered in the Valdelsa and the side valleys, all strongly influenced by the material culture of Volterra.

A small cemetery has recently been excavated at Malignano, a few kilometres west of Siena, and can be taken as typical of the Hellenistic cemeteries in the area, of which that at Monteriggioni is the best known. The tombs at Malignano are easily accessible; they are cut into the soft rock of the southern slope of a hillside, and are of various shapes: roughly circular in plan, with or without a central supporting pillar, or rectangular. Tomb finds consisted mainly of uncoloured or black-gloss pottery, and red-figure vases from Volterra.

The Museo Etrusco in Siena has a collection of archaeological material, of local origin and also from Chiusi and the surrounding area. It was formed out of three large private collections: the Bonci Casuccini (objects from Chiusi), the Bargagli Petrucci (principally objects from Sarteano) and the Chigi Zondadari (objects of varied origin).

The Bonci Casuccini collection comprises Archaic sculpture, typical canopi and cinerary urns from Chiusi, Athenian red- and black-figure pottery, a fine series of buccheri, Etruscan and Apulian vases, bronze vessels and personal ornaments.

The Bargagli Petrucci collection contains, besides the usual objects typical of Chiusi, a magnificent collection of terracotta and travertine urns. Fourteen of these urns were found in a chamber-tomb the entrance to which was closed by a huge roof tile with the word *cumere* scratched on it; this was the name of the family to which the tomb belonged, and is repeated in the inscriptions on the urns.

The Chigi Zondadari collection comprises items from Chiusi and Casole d'Elsa, Athenian black- and red-figure pottery, buccheri, Etruscan black- and red-figure vases, and vases from Apulia, Lucania and Campania.

One room in the museum contains terracottas from Etruria and southern Italy, notably some antefixes, two Archaic heads of deities, and heads of a satyr and a maenad that were originally part of a single group.

The numismatic section of the museum has a fine collection of Etruscan and Roman coins, among which the Etruscan and Italic cast coinage is particularly worthy of note.

Detail of a travertine sarcophagus. Siena, Museo Etrusco

Typical objects from the Chiusi area
1. Canopus with male head
2. Biconical bronze cinerary urn of the Villanovan period
3. Pottery cinerary urn with human figures and animal heads on the lid
4. Canopus with female head
5. Bucchero vessels forming part of the furnishings of a tomb
6. Pottery head. Siena, Museo Etrusco

2

5

3

4

6

Asciano

An Etruscan cemetery was found in the upper valley of the Ombrone, between Siena and the Val di Chiana, about five kilometres west of Asciano. It probably belonged to a small but fairly prosperous agricultural settlement, judging from the richness of the tomb furnishings found there.

The cemetery consists entirely of chamber-tombs, cut into a hillside at Poggio Pinci, and all the furnishings found there are displayed in topographical order in the Museo Etrusco at Asciano.

The first tomb contained two deposits with a few funerary vases, including an Arretine cup dating from the end of the 1st century B.C. The second tomb, the richest and most interesting, has a central burial chamber and three side rooms, and was in use from the end of the 5th century B.C. to the beginning of the 1st century A.D. The dead were either placed on the floor, or cremated and the ashes placed in small travertine cinerary urns stored one on top of the other. The most interesting point, however, is the inscription incised on the front of most of these urns, giving the deceased person's first name, family name and parents' names, according to the Etruscan custom of the time. We thus know that the tomb belonged to the Hepni family, who Latinized their name to Hepenius when the influence of Roman institutions and language spread to northern Etruria. The tomb also contained a tufa urn with the chest decorated in relief with the scene of a funeral procession, a terracotta urn, and some later burials in inscribed vases of coarse ware. Along with the ashes, the urns contained coins, gold, bronze and iron trinkets and some precious stones. The most noteworthy tomb furnishings are an imported Athenian cup, and two Etruscan vases decorated by overpainting, a technique in which the figures are not left in the natural colour of the clay on a black background, but painted in red over the black gloss that covered the whole surface of the vase. The Hellenistic black-gloss vases are from a later period, and the red-gloss plates date from the 1st century B.C. to the beginning of the 1st century A.D.

The third tomb at Poggio Pinci, with a single burial chamber, belonged to a branch of the Hepni family; the name is scratched on two of the cinerary urns. This tomb also was used for many burials, and red-figure column-kraters were in some cases used as cinerary urns; they were made in Volterra, and have been found from there to the Val di Chiana and beyond.

The fourth tomb has a single burial chamber; two bodies were laid out on the floor, perhaps a husband and wife, as one had objects typical of a male burial, such as an iron spearhead and two bronze strigils, placed beside it, while the other had a bronze mirror laid upon it and gold earrings, identifying it as a woman. Several vases stood around the bodies, including a skyphos with an overpainted red swan that was certainly made in Volterra and confirms the close connections between Volterra and this Etruscan settlement on the route to the Val di Chiana.

The fifth tomb is very similar to the last and was used for the same form of burial.

It is likely that the Etruscan settlement was on the same site as the modern village of Asciano; this has been continuously inhabited at least since Roman times, as is attested by a fine mosaic still *in situ* near the chemist's shop.

Murlo-Poggio Civitate

Poggio Civitate is a wooded hill forming part of the eastern spurs of the Colline Metallifere that rise between central Tuscany and the coast, not far from the river Ombrone. There is a sanctuary at the eastern end of Poggio Civitate, on the Piano del Tesoro; although its history is something of a mystery, two distinct phases of building have been identified. The building on top is a great rectangular complex consisting of four wings, more than 60 metres long, enclosing a central court. The foundations in rough stone survive of the porticos that ran along the northern, eastern and southern sides of this court; on the western side, however, there is a small rectangular building, the most important part of the whole complex, possibly a sacred area (a *templum* in the original sense of the word). Behind it in the wing of the sanctuary is a room without a front wall, but probably originally covered by a roof; this room must be closely associated with the sacred area, perhaps with the religious ceremonies performed there.

Entrance to the court is provided by two openings in the eastern and western wings. Little now remains of the sanctuary besides the foundations, but we must picture the four wings and the inner porticos covered by a roof and decorated with architectural terracottas. A large number of the facing plaques have been reconstructed; they are made in moulds and perforated for hanging on the walls, and are decorated with banquet scenes, deities seated on folding stools, horse races, and a couple in a carriage attended by two servants leading the horses and others carrying various objects such as fans, a vase and a stool. Numerous tiles of various shapes have also been found with single Etruscan letters incised on them, probably to indicate their position on the roof; similar letters have in fact been found elsewhere incised on facing plaques, being used instead of numerals to indicate where the plaques should be affixed to the building.

However, the most astonishing decoration of the sanctuary consisted of almost life-sized terracotta statues of figures seated on thrones, wearing long cloaks and hats with broad turned-up brims, with long, thin, rather Oriental-looking beards. These were fixed in place on large curved tiles, probably at the top of the gabled sanctuary roof.

From the style of the architectural terracottas and the pottery found during excavation, it is possible to date the sanctuary to about 575 B.C. Its life was certainly very short, since it was deliberately destroyed during the last quarter of the 6th century B.C., strange as this may seem. The building was razed to the ground and the terracottas buried in existing trenches or specially dug pits, and a rampart was built up around the sanctuary as a symbolic barrier to desecrating or entering it. An older sanctuary, dating back to the 7th century B.C., existed on the same spot and was burnt during the first quarter of the 6th century B.C.; a few traces of it were found under the 6th-century building. The reason why this great building was intentionally destroyed so that no trace of it remained is still obscure. It may have been the religious and political centre for several cities, and demolished by a more powerful enemy; or else its destruction may be connected with the crisis that affected numerous settlements in southern and central Etruria at the end of the 6th century B.C. It has also been suggested that nearby Chiusi was to blame for the act, since by the end of the 6th century its power and its expansion were considerable. Clearly the intention was to preclude any further use of the sanctuary, and the site was then totally abandoned.

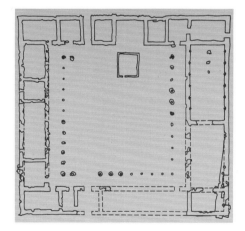

Poggio Civitate. Plan of the sanctuary at Piano del Tesoro (top of plan = west)

Castellina in Chianti

There was an Etruscan settlement on the hill of Castellina Vecchia, near Castellina in Chianti, that was continuously inhabited from Archaic to Roman times. It occupied a particularly favourable position, since the natural lines of communication following the rivers Pesa and Greve linked it with the Arno valley at Florence, and a road running through Monteriggioni gave access to Volterra in ancient times.

North of the village is a small cemetery where a little head carved in *pietra serena* was found that shows the influence of Volterran art. Of greater interest is the Montecalvario tumulus, near Castellina. The tomb is a large construction covered with the usual earth mound; inside are four tombs built of roughly-squared blocks of the local *alberese* on a cruciform plan, each facing a cardinal point of the compass. In both the south- and the west-facing tombs the *dromos* leads to an antechamber which has an entrance in the rear wall leading to the burial chamber, and two small rooms opening off the side walls. The eastern tomb has only the two side rooms, and the northern one has a single burial chamber.

The tomb, robbed many years ago, produced only a few fragments of the furnishings; these probably consisted of ivory, bone, bronze and iron objects like those found in other tombs of the 7th–6th centuries belonging to the wealthiest families. In the right side room of the south-facing tomb, a lion's head in *pietra serena* was found, with gaping jaws and tongue hanging out; apparently this was originally built into the wall, half-way up beside the left door-jamb, probably to ward off evil spirits and protect the dead.

View of Montecalvario, near Castellina in Chianti

Interior of the Montecalvario tumulus

Plan of the tombs (top of plan = west)

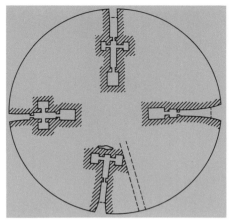

Luni

The city of Luni (the ancient Luna) lies on the boundary between Liguria and Etruria, on the left bank of the river Magra, but in territory originally Ligurian (Polybius, who gives the earliest reliable reference to the city, puts it in Liguria). Under the Augustan reorganization of Italy it was included in region VII (Etruria). However, nothing Etruscan remains at Luni, which was established as a *colonia* of Roman citizens in order to keep at bay the dangerous Ligurian tribes, defeated several times during the early years of the 2nd century B.C. Although the port was already in use at the beginning of the century, the *colonia* was founded only in 177 B.C. This marked the arrival of urban civilization in this farthest region of ancient Italy; Strabo records in his *Geography* that the Ligurians were still living in a tribal society at the time.

The town owed its importance first to its fine port, and later to the quarries that produced a marble called *lunense* after the town, the modern Carrara marble. This was used locally occasionally from the 2nd century B.C., and became famous in the time of Caesar; after that it was increasingly popular, especially during the reign of Augustus when marble from Luni was used in many of the public buildings built at that time in Rome and practically everywhere else in Italy.

The ancient city has been excavated at various dates but only in a really scientific way in modern times. It has an irregular rectangular plan, measuring about 488 metres by 450 metres, and covering an area of about 250 hectares. The road system follows the normal pattern of Roman *coloniae*, based on two main axes that are a continuation of the roads

Luni. Detail of the Roman amphitheatre

leading into the city, the main one (*cardo*) running from north to south, and the lesser one (*decumanus*) running from west to east. A wall built of blocks of local stone encircled the city; a few remains are visible today.

The forum, recently identified, was situated at the intersection of the two main roads. Here were discovered the foundations of the *capitolium* (temple of Jupiter, Juno and Minerva), built of polygonal blocks of local stone, obviously at the time the *colonia* was founded. The modern building that houses the museum of Luni has been built, somewhat unfortunately, on the same spot. In the northwestern part of the city, remains are clearly visible of another temple, earlier wrongly identified as the *capitolium*. These monumental remains, built in rubble concrete, belong to a rebuilding of the temple in the Flavian period. Below them traces of an older building have been found, and its original plan can be reconstructed: it was an Italic-style temple with a double colonnade in front and the rear part divided into three sections, which is fairly close to the model described by Vitruvius in the Augustan era. This tripartite cella caused the speculation about its being the *capitolium*, but it probably had a single cella with alae either side. Moreover, the later temple had only a single cella. A few fragments of a large marble cult statue were found here, and, even more interesting, the terracotta pedimental decorations, two-thirds life-size, representing various myths including that of Niobe, now in the museum at Florence. These were probably made during the early years of the Roman *colonia* (the second quarter of the 2nd century B.C.), clearly under the influence of the neo-Attic sculptors who were active in Rome at that time. The temple was probably dedicated to Diana/Luna, the tutelary goddess of the city (hence the name Luna).

In the northeast of the city a Roman theatre has been found, although little of it remains. The rather more impressive amphitheatre, probably dating from the time of Augustus, was found outside the city, to the east. Nothing is visible today of the baths, excavated in 1880, near the north gate. The sculptures and mosaics that were found there are now in the Museo Fabbricotti at Carrara.

Other remains include some late Republican and Imperial tombs.

Archaeological finds made during recent excavations are now in the Antiquarium Lunense, built in the centre of the ancient city (others are dispersed in various museums in Florence, Genoa, La Spezia and Carrara). These include a plinth with an inscription of Manius Acilius Glabrio, consul in 191 B.C. and victor over Antiochus III and the Aetolians, and the capital of a pillar (clearly once supporting a statue) with a dedication to Marcus Claudius Marcellus, consul for the second time in 155 and victor over the Apuan Ligurians in the same year. This is the oldest instance known of the use of Luni marble. The museum also has an inscription, of white tesserae set in an *opus signinum* pavement, coming from the same temple as the pedimental terracottas. This inscription names a certain L[ucius] Folcinius, son of Lucius, and a C. [Gaius] Fabrius, *duumviri* (the most important magistrates) of the city, who assigned the contract for making the pavement and then gave it their final approval. The characters are extremely archaic; so it is probably the original temple floor, dating from shortly after 177 B.C.

Castiglioncello

Archaeological finds in the area of the old tower, at Caletta and Cotone and in various parts of Castiglioncello itself indicate that the promontory of Castiglioncello was inhabited in ancient times.

However, these finds have been too fragmentary to give any clear idea of the plan of the ancient settlement. A few remains of a Hellenistic or Roman building were discovered under the Poggetto citadel, where the museum now is; parts of a terracotta water-pipe can be seen, preserved *in situ* in the basement.

Judging from the furnishings of the tombs found during the construction of roads and the railway in the area, the Etruscan settlement flourished from the 4th to the 1st century B.C., and especially from the 3rd century B.C., when the region came under Roman control. In the 1st century B.C. some rich families built villas along the coast and at Castiglioncello itself.

This was obviously a small commercial centre that attracted some of the seaborne trade of the western Mediterranean; the tombs in fact contained black-gloss pottery from southern Italy that was exported as far afield as Liguria, Provence and Spain, imported Iberian vases, and objects from Gaul and the North. Close contacts with the hinterland are proved by the discovery of Volterran black-gloss vases and an alabaster urn.

The Museo di Castiglioncello was built between 1912 and 1914 and is based on the design of a small cinerary urn in the museum at Florence; it is in course of rearrangement. Among the most interesting finds there is a jar-tomb preserved exactly as it was found; it was a small pit in which was buried a large jar containing ashes, remains of cremated bones and a little funerary urn, with a cup and three small vases around it. The cover of the jar, a large bowl, was kept in place by a stone. The cippi and stelae that were stuck into the earth above the tomb to mark its position are typical of Castiglioncello.

Cremation was the principal burial rite in the cemetery of Castiglioncello; besides jars, cylindrical or truncated-cone vases were also used to contain the ashes. Inhumation was practised in a very few tombs; these consist of trenches lined and covered with stone slabs or flat tiles.

Tomb furnishings consist mainly of vases, only rarely decorated, generally of coarse or black-gloss ware; some tombs contained jewellery in gold and silver or in amber, ivory ornaments, or small glass vases, but these are always of comparatively little value. The fine alabaster cinerary urn decorated on the front with a scene showing the abduction of Helen by Paris is from Volterra, and was apparently found in a chamber-tomb. The lid depicts the bejewelled figure of the deceased, Velia Carinei, in a semi-recumbent position, holding a magnificent fan in her right hand.

The same material culture is exemplified by the objects in the Museo di Rosignano Marittimo; these were found at Castiglioncello Alto and various places in the area of Rosignano, such as Paggipaoli, Villana, Casaguanti, S. Gaetano di Vada, Castellina Marittima and Belora.

Vada

Vada was the port of Volterra, at least from the late Republican period. Several classical authors and the itineraries or road-books of the Roman empire call it Vada Volaterrana; the *Itinerarium Maritimum* situates the *Vadis Portus* 30 miles from Populonia. Rutilius Namatianus, who put in there in November, A.D. 415, describes the entrance to the port, through a tricky channel marked by stakes to which branches were lashed. The old port is identical with the modern anchorage, whose access channel follows the course of the original one, but there is no conclusive evidence that the site dates back to Etruscan times. The remains of ancient Vada, which was also a posting-station on the Via Aurelia, consist of late Hellenistic buildings and tombs.

Valley of the Cecina

Cecina

Cecina is situated near the mouth and on the left bank of the river of the same name; the Cecina valley leads inland to the foot of the hill on which Volterra stands. The name (ancient Caecina) is typically Etruscan, with its *-na* ending, and is also the name of a famous Volterran clan often mentioned in inscriptions and literary sources. For centuries Cecina must have given Volterra its direct access to the sea; the nearby cemetery at Belora has yielded fairly lavish funeral objects which show that, in Etruscan times, this town was under the direct influence of the nearby metropolis and enjoyed comparative prosperity, possibly because of the mining activities in the area and the trade associated with them. Life carried on without interruption into the Roman period, during which various impressive buildings were erected, notably a large swimming-pool.

The Museo Civico contains a display of recently collected objects of local origin, and others found in other Etruscan sites in the vicinity. In addition to the tomb furnishings of various dates, there is a monument of special interest which has been dismantled and reconstructed in the museum grounds. This is the corbelled tomb from Casaglia, a site on the right bank of the river Cecina half-way between Volterra and the sea. The roof of the tomb consists of superimposed courses of stones which overlap one another, thereby forming a kind of stepped dome.

This type of funerary architecture also occurs in the area immediately inland of Cecina, still in the Volterra region, in another tomb, from Casale Marittimo; this tomb has been known for some time and is now reconstructed in the grounds of the Museo Archeologico in Florence.

Cecina. Ruins of an Etruscan tomb

Populonia

Populonia was the only major Etruscan city to be built actually on the coast, on the promontory opposite the island of Elba. In the Villanovan period the area was inhabited by two separate groups of people; these later merged to form a single city, called Pupluna or Fufluna by the Etruscans, divided into two districts. The upper part, corresponding to the acropolis, stood on top of the two hillocks known as Poggio del Molino and Poggio del Castello, on the site of the modern village. The lower part, in other words the port and industrial area, extended down the slope between the acropolis and the bay of Baratti.

Populonia had a complex defensive system: the upper part was surrounded by a wall, 2,500 metres long, of roughly-squared stone blocks, dating from the 6th–5th centuries B.C.; at I Massi, near Cala Buia, one stretch of the wall in good condition is still visible. The blocks come in a variety of sizes and are laid one on top of the other in fairly irregular courses. It seems likely that some stretches of the wall, built with smaller stones more regularly aligned, are the result of more recent restoration.

The lower city had its own defences. Judging from the construction, these were built at the end of the 4th and beginning of the 3rd century B.C. and consist of a wall which

Populonia. Plan of the archaeological zone

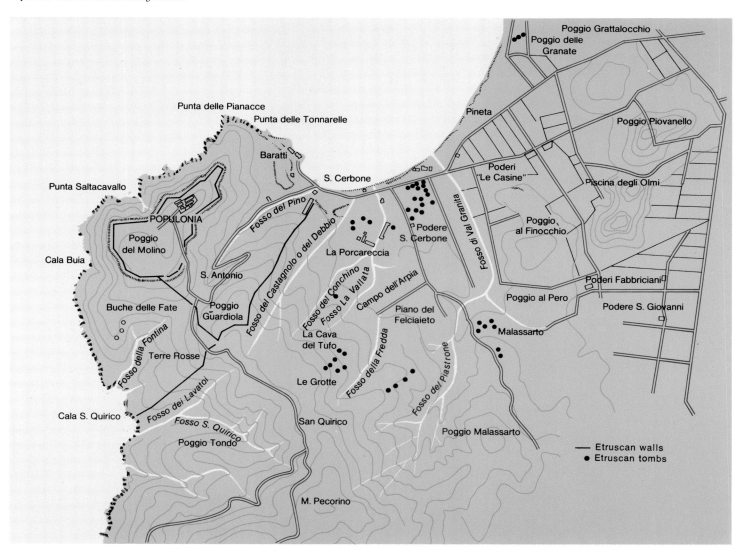

Populonia. Bay of Baratti, and the Tomba dei Letti Funebri in the S. Cerbone cemetery

Populonia. Poggio della Porcareccia, Tomba della Spirale d'Oro per Capelli

94

originally ran from the bay of Baratti to the Poggio Guardiola, just below the crest of the ridge, with rectangular towers projecting from it. From the Poggio Guardiola a second stretch linked the first with the wall around the acropolis, and a third stretch ran down towards the bay of S. Quirico, terminating in a tower which is now in ruins. The whole system thus hinged on the Poggio Guardiola, and the security of all Populonia depended upon occupation of that hill.

A stretch of roadway, part of the original road system, has been found on the Poggio della Porcareccia, heading from the southeast towards the lower city, across the Fosso del Castagnolo. It passed through a gateway in the wall and there crossed another road which ran up from the bay to the Poggio Guardiola, along the inside of the walls. Another street, in the lower city, climbed the hill alongside the present-day road.

Information about the buildings within the urban area is fragmentary and incomplete. Not a trace remains of the upper city, although there are a few remains of the industrial zone: traces have been discovered on the Poggio della Porcareccia and at the farm called Podere S. Cerbone of buildings connected with the processing of the iron ore brought here from Elba. Remains of some buildings of the Etrusco-Roman and Roman city have also been identified in the area of modern Baratti, the site of the ancient port, and outside the walls.

In ancient times Populonia was famous for its iron industry; the city was associated from the start with mining in the region, and because of its favourable geographical position it was able to develop an industrial and commercial activity that formed the basis of its long-lasting prosperity and its renown.

At first, Populonia was an important trading-centre for copper and bronze; these came in from Elba and above all from the area around Campiglia, where one can still see signs of the shafts and tunnels used in ancient times to extract tin and tin ore; here too the remains of some extremely old smelting furnaces were found (8th century B.C.).

The opportunity of acquiring ores and metals in exchange for various other goods attracted the first Greek traders, and in this way a commercial activity began that lasted for centuries; the most obvious evidence of this is to be found in the tomb furnishings themselves, abounding as they do in objects imported from Greece and the Near East.

Later on Populonia became the centre for working the iron extracted from the mines on Elba. Smelting furnaces were installed around the southern end of the bay, and evidence of their intensive and long-standing use is provided by the huge slag-heaps thrown up as a result. These gradually encroached upon the area occupied by the Archaic cemetery; they have been re-sifted in modern times to extract the residual metal by more advanced processing methods. There can be no doubt that the iron industry in Populonia thrived from the Archaic period right up to Roman times.

During the Imperial period luxurious seaside villas were built at either end of the bay, on the Poggio del Molino, Poggio di S. Leonardo and Poggio di Villa del Barone.

The ancient port was the hub of Populonian life and prosperity. It was situated between the Baratti tower and the chapel of S. Cerbone, and protected by a mole of roughly-squared sandstone blocks, on the same site as the modern mole. The harbour was located in the area now occupied by the village of Baratti and was gradually silted up by the action of wind and currents; it included warehouses, silos and similar buildings. The cemeteries extended from the promontory to the northern end of the bay.

The Villanovan burials were in the vicinity of the Podere S. Cerbone and the Casone and, farther north, on the Piano and the Poggio delle Granate: the tombs were shaft- or simple pit-type, with biconical or hut-shaped urns, or else trench-type.

In the Orientalizing period the cemeteries were first established in the same areas as the Villanovan ones and later extended progressively to surrounding areas. Inhumation is the rule, with very few exceptions, and there are two distinct types of tomb: chamber-tombs and trench-tombs. The former are the more numerous, and can be divided into two groups, the one comprising chamber-tombs beneath a tumulus with a cylindrical plinth, the other having no plinth and being commonly known as 'high-tumulus tombs'. The first have at their base a cylindrical plinth, built of slabs of *panchina* laid in random courses, and the earth is piled up on top of this. Inside is the funeral chamber, usually rectangular, access to which is through a corridor or *dromos* of varying size, roofed with slabs set horizontally; in some cases smaller chambers to house the funerary objects open off this corridor.

The walls of the chamber are built with regular courses of blocks; at each corner a connecting corbel is used as a base for the false dome of the roof, with courses of slabs progressively overlapping inwards up to the centre of the vault, which is closed by a single large slab.

In the oldest and most precisely constructed tumuli, inside the chamber, there are

Populonia. Poggio della Porcareccia, Tomba dei Flabelli

funerary couches made of large flat slabs of *panchina* and small moulded columns, in imitation of wooden or metal originals. In later times the layout of the chamber was in some cases subdivided by stone slabs placed vertically.

The plinth, a low structure without any moulding, unlike plinths in the tumuli of southern Etruria, is usually surrounded on the outside by an outward-sloping paved surface, broken at the entrance of the *dromos*. The topmost section consists of a series of downward-sloping slabs projecting outwards (the *grundarium*), supported by other less projecting slabs (the *suggrundarium*), the purpose of which was to prevent the continual dripping of rain-water from damaging the surface of the plinth. Above, a row of blocks bounded the tumulus and reinforced the *grundarium*.

Access to the chamber and to the *dromos* was blocked off by a squared stone slab; in the interval between two burials, the corridor was blocked with large stones to keep out thieves attracted by the costly funerary objects.

To this group of tombs belong, in the S. Cerbone cemetery, the Tomba dei Letti Funebri ('Tomb of the Funeral Couches'), so called because it contains the traces of six stone couches, and the Tomba dei Carri ('Tomb of the Chariots'). In the latter, which dates from the mid-7th century B.C., two two-wheeled war or ceremonial chariots were found; they were covered with thin sheets of bronze with embossed decoration of figures of felines and hunting scenes, inlaid with iron.

In the Porcareccia cemetery, the Tomba dei Flabelli and the Tomba delle Oreficiere belong to this group. The former had a wealth of funerary objects, now in the Museo Archeologico in Florence, as is most of the material from Populonia, including pottery, gold-work, four bronze helmets and four fans (*flabelli*), also in bronze. Near this tomb, in the 3rd century B.C., a foundry was set up; an indication of this is the extremely reddened earth, and there are also remains of the flue.

The Tomba delle Oreficiere ('Tomb of the Jewellery'), which is noteworthy for its still intact ceiling, is so called after the costly gold-work found among the funerary objects, including *a baule* (horizontal cylinder) earrings, acorn-shaped pendants with granulated decoration, and so on.

A variant of this type are the tombs with a vestibule before the entrance to the *dromos*; this projects more than a metre from the plinth and has in front of it a rectangular paved area bordered by stone slabs driven vertically into the ground. Among those belonging to this group are the Tomba delle Pissidi Cilindriche in the S. Cerbone cemetery, dating from the last third of the 7th century B.C., and the Tomba della Tazza con i Satiri Cercatori di Tracce, near the Casone, dating from the early decades of the 6th century B.C.

The so-called 'high-tumulus tombs' do not have the stone surround about the base. The earth covering, made waterproof by a fairly thick inner layer of clay, rests directly on the ground. Around the outside is a row of limestone slabs with pointed ends driven into the earth. The chamber within is rectangular, with a passage in the centre and two burial niches at the sides; in some cases a third niche is added in the end wall. In these tombs, too, the ceiling is built of courses of progressively projecting blocks.

Tumuli of this type date from between the end of the 7th and the first half of the 6th century B.C.; examples of them are the Tomba dei Colatoi and the Tomba con Porta Chiusa in the Campo del Casone, and the Tomba degli Aryballoi and the Tomba della Spirale d'Oro per Capelli on the Poggio della Porcareccia.

Topographical study of the cemeteries shows that the oldest monumental tombs, those with the cylindrical plinth, are to be found at S. Cerbone, dating from about the mid-7th century B.C.; thereafter burials spread progressively to the nearby areas: Poggio della Porcareccia, Conchino, Costone della Fredda, Campo dell'Arpia and Felciaieto, Poggio

Populonia. Tombs in the S. Cerbone cemetery

del Malassarto, Casone and Poggio al Finocchio, reaching their greatest extent during the late Orientalizing period.

A study of the tombs and the funerary objects in them has shown that Populonia reached its peak of splendour between the mid-7th and the first half of the 6th century B.C. During this period, thanks to the imported objects, it can be shown that the city had direct contact with nearby Vetulonia and other centres in northern Etruria, as well as with southern Etruria; and the presence of Corinthian and East Greek pottery indicates that Populonia did business on a large scale with Greek traders, drawn there by the ores of Campiglia and Elba.

In the 6th and 5th centuries B.C. the burial-grounds extended still farther, to the district known as La Sughera della Capra, and in this same period the Piano and the Pioggio

Populonia. Tomba del Bronzetto di Offerente in the S. Cerbone cemetery

delle Granate were abandoned; the tombs were mainly for inhumation, though there are a few instances of cremation tombs. The ashes at this time were usually placed in cinerary urns carved from a single block of *panchina*; these urns were rectangular, hollowed out inside and covered by a stone lid, either of the ridged type or semi-cylindrical. A noteworthy exception is a cremation tomb which consists of a terracotta tiled box containing an Athenian red-figure vase which was used as an urn and covered with a bronze patera.

The 6th-century inhumation tombs, on the other hand, are of the trench type, surmounted by a stone stele or cippus; either there was a smooth-surfaced sarcophagus carved from one or two hollowed-out blocks, or there were four large flat slabs fitted closely together. A third type is the shrine-tomb, built on a rectangular plan and covered by a ridged roof, with an internal chamber. A well-preserved example of this type is the Tomba del Bronzetto di Offerente ('Tomb of the Bronze Statuette of a Person Offering'), so called after one of the few funerary objects left behind by robbers who forced their way into the tomb in ancient times. Towards the beginning of the 3rd century B.C., a workshop for processing iron ore was set up here, and both the tomb and the sarcophagi placed outside it were plundered; the funerary objects were taken away, and the bones of the bodies lying in the tomb were put in the sarcophagi outside.

Similar events occurred throughout the area occupied by the Archaic cemetery, which from the 4th century B.C. onwards was covered by factories for processing iron, clearly an expanding activity. Many tombs were broken into and plundered, and then covered by the slag from the foundries. At the same time, however, other cemeteries appeared on the Poggio del Malassarto, Le Grotte and Le Buche delle Fate, where burials were still carried out in the 3rd century B.C. The tombs here are of the trench and the chamber types. At Le Grotte, in particular, two interesting tombs have been discovered with painted chambers, the first of this type to be found at Populonia. One of these is called the Tomba del Corridietro because the walls are painted in red with a wave motif (*corridietro*); on the benches are painted *klinai* in imitation of real couches, and 15 iron nails for hanging up funerary objects were hammered into the walls. The other tomb, known as the Tomba dei Delfini ('Tomb of the Dolphins'), shows two dolphins on the left-hand door-jamb and a ram's head on the bench at the rear, as well as red stripes on the walls.

At a later date the Roman cemetery was established in the industrial area around the bay; the tombs are easily identifiable, being of the *cappucina* type, covered by ridged tiles, or of the coffin-and-trench type, or of the type where the body is deposited in a large amphora. The cremated bodies, on the other hand, were buried inside terracotta or bronze vases, or in small urns of local *panchina*.

The Museo di Populonia, in the centre of the village, contains a display of material found locally that gives a systematic portrait of the life and culture of the ancient city. Many of the objects found in the cemeteries are, however, in the Museo Archeologico in Florence.

Massa Marittima

With its palaces and mediaeval churches which make it one of the most striking small towns in the whole of Tuscany, Massa Marittima stands on top of a hill which is in the centre of an important mining region. There is no doubt that the mines in the surrounding area were exploited by the Etruscans, and in all probability the two most powerful nearby cities, Populonia and Vetulonia, played an active part in the smelting and marketing of the copper, iron, silver and alum that were extracted from the hillsides round about.

In the Museo Civico at Massa Marittima there is a display of finds from the Lake Accesa cemetery, which provide proof of a Chalcolithic settlement in a zone rich in mineral deposits situated a few kilometres south of Massa.

Bronze bit, from Lake Accesa. Massa Marittima, Museo Civico

Lake Accesa

A view of the Colline Metallifere near Massa Marittima, showing a stretch of the river Merse

Vetulonia

The Etruscan city known variously as Vatluna, Vetluna and Vetalu, which the Romans called Vetulonia or Vetulonii, has been identified, after much controversy, with the settlement on the Poggio Colonna.

The heights on which it stood originally overlooked the *Lacus Prelius*, a large expanse of water which became gradually silted up and is now part of the plain of Grosseto. The place was densely populated from the early Villanovan period; in the 8th century B.C. there were certainly two centres of habitation, corresponding respectively to the cemeteries of Poggio alla Guardia, Poggio alle Birbe and Poggio al Bello to the east, and of Colle Baroncio and Le Dupiane to the west.

The earliest tombs were pit-type and contained the typical biconical urn and a few funerary objects; the later ones were trench- and pit-type. These last were called 'foreigners' hoards' by their discoverer because compared with the older tombs they had richer furnishings, which were believed to have been imported by foreigners who had settled at Vetulonia. It is however clear that the objects in question are the same as those in the trench-type tombs.

Lower down, around the edges of the Villanovan burial-grounds, 'interrupted-circle' tombs have been found, dating from the end of the 8th century B.C.; these are made of rough-cut stones driven into the ground some distance from each other, surrounding groups of pit- and, less often, trench-tombs. The objects found in these tombs show that we are now in a phase of transition from the Villanovan to the Orientalizing period. It is worth noting that the circular tombs were found in topographical and chronological succession to the older Villanovan tombs.

In the 7th century B.C. the inhabited centre became a single unit, and life there carried on into the 6th century, when, it would appear, the city wall was built; some stretches of the wall are still to be seen, made of large rectangular blocks filled in with smaller stones. This wall enclosed a very wide area—some 120 hectares—which testifies to the prosperity and influence that the city enjoyed in the Archaic period.

Countryside around the heights of Vetulonia

The acropolis, in all probability, was situated on the uppermost part of the hill, where life was concentrated in the Middle Ages and where a long stretch of the old fortified wall can still be seen on the eastern side of the village.

After this, for reasons which are still quite unclear, life stopped almost completely. Vetulonia did not revive until after northern Etruria came under the sway of Rome, i.e. from the 3rd century B.C. onwards. In this period the inhabited districts spread on to the slopes of the hill, with areas of special interest for their buildings at Costa Murata, the convent and Le Banditelle. In the first of these areas, recent excavations have brought to light the remains of terracing, buildings and paved roads.

There were probably two main streets, one on the northeastern ridge of the city, the other along the northern ridge. A long stretch of the first can still be seen, with secondary roads leading off it visible in the area of the so-called 'city' excavations. The second was connected with a road coming from the walls and another that ran along the southern side of Costa Murata.

The layout of the city thus followed the terrain, and a regular system is apparent only in individual regions.

The forum of the Roman city must have been in the region of the Convento Nuovo di Sestinga, as seems proved by an inscription with the name of Caracalla, set into a window of the convent, and by other inscriptions found in the immediate vicinity.

A Roman quarter built over a Hellenistic one has been discovered to the north of the present-day village, at Costia dei Lippi; here a paved Roman road, running from east to west and flanked by pavements and gutters, runs between impressive retaining walls.

Vetulonia. Archaeological plan

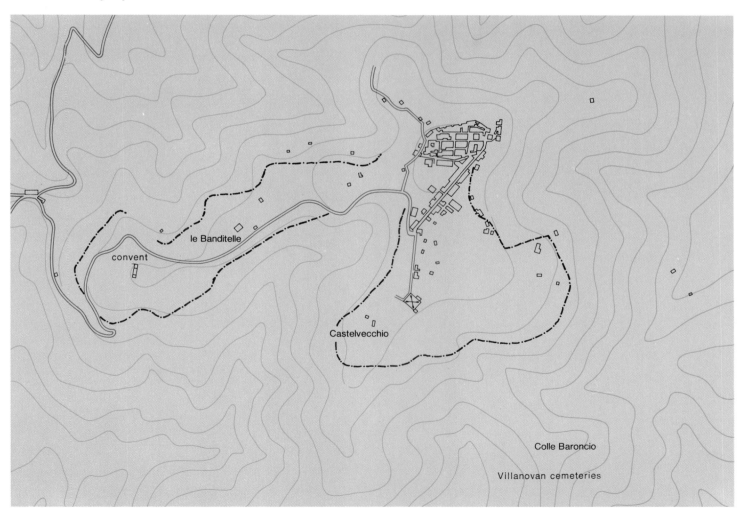

le Banditelle

convent

Castelvecchio

Colle Baroncio

Villanovan cemeteries

The cemeteries provide clear proof that life was interrupted between the end of the Archaic period and the beginning of the Hellenistic. The tombs which correspond to the 7th-century city are the 'continuous-circle' or 'white-stone circle' tombs, which succeeded the earlier 'interrupted-circle' ones.

These later tombs consist of slabs of local stone driven vertically into the ground, often slightly outward-sloping, marking off a circular space some 15–20 metres in diameter, occasionally as large as 30 metres, inside which there were one or more trenches, frequently lined with stone slabs.

These tombs have yielded a wealth of costly funerary objects, including pieces in bronze, gold, silver and amber. The bronzes are mainly locally manufactured, comprising

large plated globular vases with tall stems in the shape of truncated cones and cast handles, often decorated with animal heads and stylized lotus flowers; tripods with hemispherical bowls and feet made of flat strips of metal, decorated with small stylized horses or warriors on horseback; cylindrical objects known as 'censers', with slightly concave pierced sides and a lid surmounted by a hinged handle; so-called 'candelabra', slender rods with a human figurine at the top and small brackets, used for hanging cups and small jugs.

Vetulonian gold-work is characteristic, in the Etruscan context, because its decoration is generally by granulation or by dusting, in other words with tiny specks of gold affixed to the surface of the piece. There is thus a prevalent taste for surface design, whereas in the gold-work of southern Etruria applied moulded decoration tends to prevail; the latter is so rich that it often obscures the lines of the object itself.

Extensive use is also made of filigree at Vetulonia; typical examples are the bracelets

Vetulonia. Interior of the Pietrera tumulus

Following pages: Vetulonia. Tomba del Diavolino 2

made of thin strips of sheet gold joined by a zigzag gold wire, in which the central, longer part formed the clasp. Also quite common is a kind of gold-plated disc embossed with female heads; these discs were possibly pendants for necklaces. The 7th-century tombs also frequently yield cornelian or faience scarabs, which were used as amulets or personal ornaments.

Vetulonia. Interior of the Tomba del Diavolino 2

In the first half of the 7th century B.C. the richest circle-tombs were the Tomba dei Monili and the Secondo Circolo della Sagrona; in the second half of the century the Circolo dei Lebeti ('Circle of the Cauldrons') is particularly noteworthy, so called because it contained several large bronze cauldrons, imported from a city with a flourishing metal-working industry, together with a cart decorated with small ducks in the round; likewise the Circolo del Tridente, the two Circoli delle Pellicce and the Tomba del Littore ('Tomb of the Lictor'). This last is so called because in it was found an object made up of several very rusted small iron rods, in which Falchi, the first man to undertake large-scale systematic excavations at Vetulonia, at the end of the 19th century, recognized a lictor's fasces, made up of several thin rods and a double axe. Even though some doubts have been expressed, it is likely that this object is a scaled-down model for funerary use of the lictorial fasces that symbolized the union of military and judicial power, the invention of which is attributed by our sources precisely to the people of Vetulonia. The double axe, in particular, is confirmed as coming from Vetulonia by the famous stele of Avile Feluske, upon which there is engraved a warrior armed with a helmet and round shield, raising in his right hand a double axe.

Other especially rich 7th-century tombs are the Circolo dei Leoncini d'Argento and the Tomba del Duce ('Tomb of the Leader'), so called because, judging from the furnishings, it must have belonged to a very influential figure; this tomb contained, among other things, bronze and bucchero objects, a silver-plated urn with embossed decorations,

Gold fibula with granulated decoration, from Vetulonia, Tomba del Littore. Florence, Museo Archeologico

and a small bronze boat imported from Sardinia. This, together with others found in the Tomba delle Tre Navicelle ('Tomb of the Three Small Boats') and the Tomba della Costiaccia Bambagini, provides archaeological evidence for the relations between Etruria and Sardinia which are also mentioned in the literary sources. It is interesting to note that these contacts were largely with northern Etruria, both for practical navigational reasons and because of the mines of the region of which Populonia and Vetulonia were the major centres.

The circle-tombs are succeeded by the tumulus-tombs of the so-called late Orientalizing period. At the present time it is possible to visit the most famous of these, the Tomba della Pietrera, which consists of an artificial mound with a circular plinth, more than 60 metres in diameter; inside it there are two chambers, one on top of the other; the older chamber is the lower, circular one. Shortly after it was built it would appear that this chamber collapsed and was replaced by another one above it, rectangular in plan, covered by a false dome made of courses of projecting, overlapping blocks connected to the walls by corner corbels.

Outside, alongside the tumulus, numerous trench-type tombs were constructed, the fifth of which appears to be contemporary with the chamber-tomb, the others dating from the end of the 7th and beginning of the 6th century B.C.

The older chamber contained the stone sculptures now on display in the museum at Florence, dating to the end of the 7th century B.C. These are some of the oldest examples of stone sculpture from Etruria and from Italy, and depict male and female figures. The best-preserved piece is a female bust with the hair gathered into tresses down the sides of the face; the lips are protruding and compressed and the arms pressed against the breast, which points to the strong influence of Oriental models.

Not far away, to the left of the Via dei Sepolcri on the way out of Vetulonia, is the Tomba del Diavolino 2, so called to distinguish it from the Tomba del Diavolino 1, which has been moved and reconstructed in the grounds of the museum at Florence. This is a large tomb surrounded at the base by a plinth made of three courses of the local stone called *sassoforte*; inside there is a square chamber with corner corbels supporting the false dome, supported at the centre by a rectangular pillar made of blocks laid on top of one another.

Not far from this is the Tomba della Fibula d'Oro, another example of a chamber-tomb with a central pillar. Most of the tumuli that have come to light during excavations undertaken in these cemeteries are no longer visible.

Among the furnishings from Vetulonian tombs large vases made of fairly crude impasto have frequently been discovered; these have thick sides and impressed or incised decoration, and can probably be attributed to a local workshop. Subsequently the sides are made thinner, the surface looks polished and is decorated with bean-shaped motifs or impressed or incised designs, enriched by small studs in relief. The bucchero vases are rather crude. The small number of Protocorinthian and Athenian vases among the imported pottery is striking.

In 1965 a slab of local sandstone, now in the museum at Florence, was discovered, on which is inscribed a complete alphabet of the 3rd century B.C. Because it was found quite by chance during agricultural work, it is not possible to establish its purpose and function.

The Antiquarium at Vetulonia contains various local objects, though most of the finds from the city's cemeteries are in the Museo Archeologico in Florence. Among the most significant pieces on display at Vetulonia one should mention some rather coarse large bucchero kantharoi, decorated with stamped animal figurines or rosettes in a sunken rectangular field, which certainly come from some local northern Etrurian workshop. In addition there is a rich series of personal ornaments, including fibulae and faience, and a small collection of Hellenistic pottery and architectural terracottas.

Roselle

Roselle (in Latin Rusellae) stood on the southern edge of the ancient *Lacus Prelius*, a lagoon formed by a former bay which gradually became silted up and is now the plain which stretches between Grosseto and Castiglione della Pescaia. From its site on top of a hill, the city overlooked the point where the river Ombrone was crossed by the coast road which ran from Marsiliana and Saturnia to Vetulonia, at the northern end of the lagoon.

The earliest evidence of a settlement goes back to the late Villanovan period; Roselle gradually grew in importance and finally became one of the most powerful cities in Etruria. Ancient historians mention it among those cities which, along with Chiusi, Arezzo, Volterra and Vetulonia, promised to assist the Latins against Tarquinius Priscus; later, Roselle waged a long-drawn-out struggle against Rome. Unlike other northern Etrurian cities, in fact, it did not enter peacefully into the Roman political organization, but was finally subdued after a long and bloody siege, during which, according to Livy, two thousand citizens died and as many again were taken prisoner.

We also know that its economy was predominantly an agricultural one, because in the year 205 B.C. it supplied grain and timber for Scipio's expedition against Carthage. Later, although the date is uncertain, a Roman *colonia* was founded there; during the Imperial period the city went through a process of progressive decline, while the importance of the coastal centres along the Via Aurelia increased, to the extent that in the 5th century A.D. Rutilius Namatianus (*De Reditu*, I, 220) describes it as half-abandoned. Life continued there, nevertheless, until the beginning of the 12th century.

The ancient city occupied the summit of a smallish hill which is the last spur of the Monteleone range towards the coast; it has two higher points separated by a small valley which opens out towards the west into a fairly wide plateau.

The defence of the city was provided by a strong wall, still almost entirely standing, measuring some three kilometres. The oldest part dates from the 6th century B.C.; it is

Roselle. Archaeological plan

Roselle. Ruins of the Roman baths

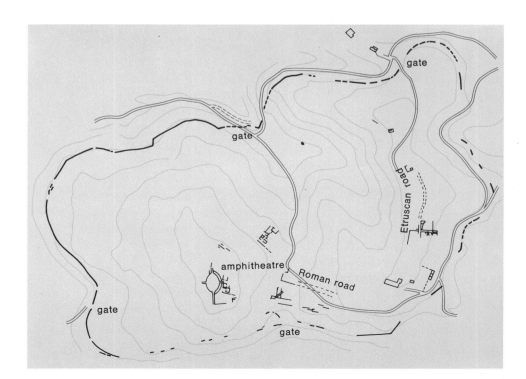

built of polygonal stonework, and is preserved on the eastern, northern and northeastern sides. In some places it reaches a height of 7 metres; it is 2.30 metres thick at the base and 1.90 at the top. Other stretches are built of different-sized rectangular blocks laid in frequently irregular courses. The more regular walls are almost certainly the product of more recent reconstruction work, and some of the restoration is Roman, as is shown by the use of concrete.

A specific problem is raised by one stretch of wall, with stone foundations and upper parts of unfired brick, which has been unearthed below the 6th-century wall and dates from the 7th century B.C. Because of its remarkable thickness, and because it would certainly appear to be a section of the city wall, it may be deduced that, at least in the northern sector, the city had a fortified wall as early as the 7th century B.C., the course of which was covered by the later walls.

There were probably five gates in the walls, situated at the points where access to the city was easiest because of the lie of the land; the north gate can be identified with certainty by the presence of the entrance and the drain running under the road. The original road system must have corresponded to the present-day paths which climb up the hill following the natural contours.

Inside the walls, the city never covered the whole of the enclosed area, except perhaps in certain districts, and then only in the Hellenistic period. The public buildings were concentrated in the small central valley throughout the life of Roselle; the residential areas were situated on the northern and southern hills; in the open area to the north and east can be seen stone-quarries which were probably used for the walls and the houses.

In the 7th and the first half of the 6th century B.C. there were buildings made entirely of unfired brick in Roselle; later on, in the 5th and 4th centuries B.C., construction was usually in stone or in unfired brick with a low stone plinth.

Some of these unfired-brick buildings have been discovered in the central valley, preserved in some places to a height of more than two metres, thanks to the formation of deep silt in this region through the centuries. More or less at the centre of the natural depression, there is a wide enclosure with two stretches of brick wall still standing, running east–west and north–south. The first of these stretches is flanked, along the outer side, by a footpath of beaten clay beside which runs a small gutter for drainage; near the western end of this wall there is a gate which shows, in its western jamb, the cavity left within the thickness of the bricks by the wooden upright, and on the sill, which is embedded in the clay ground, part of the beam into which was fixed the bolt for closing the two sides of the gate.

Inside this enclosure, about half-way along the longer side, there is a partially preserved building, circular in plan, five metres in diameter, with an east-facing entrance indicated by a doorstep made of small stones; along the wall opposite the entrance, a row of small slabs formed a kind of bench. The ceiling may have been corbelled, with courses of bricks jutting out progressively towards the central point; or there might have been a thatched roof, or a wooden roofing-frame covered with tiles. Inside, the walls are 'plastered' with a fine pale yellow clay. Finds here include a spherical earthenware pot made of reddish polished ware, two large weights, and fragments of impasto and bucchero vases.

Farther to the east, a building has been unearthed with two rectangular rooms with rough stone walls preserved to a height of more than two metres, rendered inside with a thick layer of clay and 'plastered' with paler clay; the rooms are divided by a wall of un-fired brick. Since clay fragments have been discovered with impressions of twigs, together with pieces of tiles, it is likely that the building had a wooden roof structure covered with tiles, and that wattle and daub was used to protect the walls from the elements. The purpose of these two extremely ancient buildings is unclear, but they were very possibly public buildings.

Similar remains have come to light beneath the northern wing of the Roman basilica and under the paved roadway; the orientation of these buildings was east–west and re-mained unchanged in later periods. This leads one to suppose that the course of the roads likewise remained virtually unaltered, and consequently that the roads that climbed the hill followed an irregular route inside the gates.

Buildings in stone and unfired-brick walls with stone plinths have also been identified on the northern and southeastern hills. Here the alignment of the Archaic inhabited area was undoubtedly preserved in the Hellenistic period; in addition, the Hellenistic road is on the line of its predecessor, there being a well-preserved pebbled stretch of the later road still visible today.

On the southern terrace, protected by the walls, there was once an Archaic temple; the terracing walls remains, as do several architectural terracottas and votive deposits containing bucchero vases and fragments of Athenian black-figure ware.

On the northern hill, among other things, a two-roomed Archaic house has been dis-

Opposite: Roselle. The Etruscan walls

Below: detail of the Roman city

covered. Its foundations are of stone and its walls of unfired brick; it dates from the 6th century B.C., to judge from the objects found in the stone and mortar which formed its floor and other objects which were found outside the walls.

The bricks used in building these houses are between 37 and 50 cm long and between 8 and 12 cm thick, and were dried under shelter for a long time.

The Archaic inhabited area presents a cultural aspect similar to that of the cemeteries of nearby Vetulonia. Besides the ordinary and the decorated pottery produced locally, fragments have also been found of bucchero vases of a type made in north-central Etruria, some of which are mould-decorated, with sphinxes and other designs on a rectangular field. Certain bronze objects, such as a 'censer' and a 'candelabrum', might have been imported directly from Vetulonia. Among the imported pottery, mention should be made of Subgeometric, Proto- and mid-Corinthian vases and Ionian cups; Athenian black- and red-figure pottery started to appear towards the end of the 6th century B.C. and con- tinued throughout the 5th century. The architectural terracottas were mostly produced in local workshops.

Towards the end of the 4th century B.C. Roselle was conquered by the Romans and largely destroyed. After an immediate reconstruction, it attained its greatest size in the Hellenistic period; in this period there was a cobbled road on the southeastern hill, following the ridge in a wide sweep; on both sides of it, along the low pavements, stood houses built on the sites of older dwellings. These houses were constructed on wide terraces supported by thick walls; they have stone walls, *opus signinum* and stone and mortar floors, and cisterns cut into the rock or else made of stone and plastered to make them watertight. On the northern hill, too, remains have been found of elegant mansions built over the ruins of earlier houses.

In the central valley there was probably, as in the earlier period, a concentration of public buildings, signs of which are a drainage and water system connected to a tank and a series of architectural terracottas discovered in the archaeological level.

In Roman times, the city was smaller than in the preceding period, and concentrated around the forum, which is situated in the centre of the small valley. The flattened area was extended towards the west by large terracing walls in stone and in concrete with reticular-faced cement work; these walls supported the buildings on the western side.

The main road, possibly corresponding to the *cardo maximus*, runs alongside the eastern edge of the forum in a north–south direction; it takes a sharp turn towards the east at the point where the remains of a fountain have been found, and descends in a wide curve

Roselle. Etruscan buildings of unfired brick in the forum area

towards the walls, possibly towards the eastern gate.

Another stretch of roadway heads northeast from the central point of this curve; moreover, a *decumanus* (main cross-street) has been located on the slopes of the southern hill.

Among the buildings which faced on to the forum, one of the most important is the basilica; on the inside can be seen the foundation wall of the colonnade which subdivided it, supporting the roof, and fragments of the column bases have also been found. Beneath the paving there is the opening of a rock-cut cistern, bottle-shaped and plastered to make the walls watertight; the circular opening is closed by a large irregular-shaped stone and is related to a layer of *opus signinum* which is possibly the flooring of a building older than the basilica.

The southern side of the forum was possibly closed in by a portico; at the western end there is a huge building, access to which was not through the portico but through an opening farther to the west. This building contains a large rectangular room, the walls of which are in part faced with marble slabs, in part decorated with painted vertical stripes and panels imitating marble facing. It was here that an important group of statues was found, from the Julio-Claudian period, depicting the imperial family: Claudius, Livia, Tiberius, Drusus and Antonia the younger.

It would appear that the southern hill was not inhabited in Roman times; on the northern hill, however, remains of several buildings showing reticular facing have been found. Here too, on the summit of the high ground, there was a small amphitheatre, built evidently in proportion to the not very numerous population of the city. This amphitheatre has a longer axis measuring 38 metres and two uncovered entrance-ways at the ends, and a shorter axis of 27 metres and two covered entrance-ways with barrel vaults at each end. The steps are only partially preserved, because the building was later robbed for construction material. In the Middle Ages a small triple-aisled church was built on top of a Roman building decorated with mosaics, in the east-central part of the city; only a few walls remain of other buildings of that time.

The cemeteries were situated outside the city walls on the slopes of the hill, but they have not been systematically explored. The Villanovan tombs are of the usual sort, either pit- or trench-type; at a later date the use of chamber-tombs became widespread. Some of these, rectangular in plan and roofed with corbelled vaults, may be seen along the road that leads off the main Siena–Grosseto road to Roselle, on the eastern slope of the hill. The finds from these tombs are in the Museo Archeologico at Grosseto.

Lower down, on the coast, stood the port of Roselle; originally on the *Lacus Prelius*, the harbour must have been continually shifted on account of the progressive silting-up of the lagoon.

On high ground which rises up to the south of Roselle stands the Moscona fort; it consists of an elliptical enclosure, 101 by 88 metres, with limestone-block walls two metres thick, surrounding an area where foundations of huts of the 8th century B.C. have been identified. Outside, towards the east, the wall was reinforced by three curved walls, concentric with the main wall, and regularly spaced. In the mediaeval period, in the 10th century to be exact, a circular building was erected at the west end; it had a diameter of 30 metres and walls two metres thick, built of stone blocks taken from the old fort.

Grosseto

The Civico Museo Archeologico at Grosseto owes its existence to donations, excavations and acquisitions from 1860 onwards. It is arranged topographically, with the aim of making immediately clear the features of the artistic and material culture of the individual sites displayed.

Numerous important objects from Roselle are on display, among them being several Villanovan impasto urns, decorated with incised and engraved geometric designs; a horse's bit in bronze from about the mid-8th century B.C., consisting of two double-plated segments ending in two rings, each with a loop in the form of a small stylized horse; a bronze axe decorated with groups of concentric circles and thin engraved lines, probably used for ritual purposes, judging from the small, slender blade. In addition there is a rich series of vases: bucchero-type impasto vases and bucchero vases, often decorated with moulded sphinxes, prancing horses or other relief designs on an impressed square field; and Athenian and Etruscan black- and red-figure pottery, all of it imported. There are also several architectural terracottas from Roselle: antefixes in the form of human heads; panels decorated with geometric and plant designs, one of which still retains three of the original bronze nails needed to affix it to the wooden structure of the building; and small fragments of pedimental decoration, one of the most interesting being the figure of a warrior. Besides these exhibits, there are bronze figurines, mirrors decorated with engraved figures, and a fragment of a stone stele of the Archaic Volterran type.

From Vetulonia there is a series of Villanovan urns, each with its bowl as lid, mainly decorated with the usual engraved geometric designs; also several large clasps in cast bronze, consisting of two rectangular frames to which are fixed, respectively, two or three hooks ending in human or animal heads, and two or three loops into which the hooks were inserted. These large belt-clasps are typical of north-central Etruria and were widespread in the Orientalizing period. There are also bronze tools and various objects, such as strigils and furniture ornaments surmounted by figurines in the round.

Great importance attaches to the evidence for the centres in the Albegna and Fiora valleys, notably Marsiliana, Saturnia, Poggio Buco, Pitigliano and Sovana, with pots and urns decorated with characteristic concentric ribbing and projections in relief, Etrusco-Corinthian pottery imported from southern Etruria, and personal ornaments, all of which are typical of this area with its prevalent Vulcian cultural influence.

From Vulci there is a man's bust in *nenfro* (a kind of tufa), possibly a rider on a sea-horse, which is an interesting example of the local Archaic sculpture in stone, and an instance of the influence of Peloponnesian sculpture; also a ram's head with long curved horns, likewise in *nenfro* and dating from the 6th century B.C., undoubtedly for funerary purposes. There is also imported Greek and Etrusco-Corinthian pottery. From Castro, in the Vulci district, there are heavy bucchero vases and some Etrusco-Corinthian pottery.

In addition the Grosseto museum has, in its prehistoric section, a group of axes with hammered lateral blades, a spear-head, a chisel, a torque (open neck-ring) and an armilla (bracelet), fibulae and pendants, all in bronze, coming from the Campese hoard on the island of Giglio, and datable between the end of the 9th and the beginning of the 7th century B.C.

Ram's head in *nenfro*, from Vulci. Grosseto, Civico Museo Archeologico

Below: vase from Poggio Buco. Grosseto, Civico Museo Archeologico

Opposite, above: Euboean krater, 8th century B.C., from Pescia Romana

Below: proto-Villanovan burial-urn. Grosseto, Civico Museo Archeologico

Talamone

Talamone lies on the coast between the mouths of the Ombrone and the Albegna, and retains a form of its Etruscan name Tlamu (Latin Telamon). The modern town dates from the late Middle Ages and occupies a good defensive position on the little promontory that closes the bay at its northern end. According to legend the ancient city was founded by the Argonauts and named after one of them; it has in fact been located on the hill of Talamonaccio that descends steeply to the sea a little to the south of the modern town. Here, on the southeastern part of the hill, a small temple was discovered; its foundations and a good many of its architectural terracottas have survived.

The panels that made up the pediment were particularly interesting and are now in the Museo Archeologico in Florence; although each piece is a different shape and size, they were all made to fit together perfectly in the overall design; they have applied high-relief decoration. It has therefore been assumed that they were made out of one great terracotta slab which was then cut into pieces, each of which shows the holes for the pins which held it to the wooden structure of the building.

The relief decorations show episodes from the Theban cycle of myths: the flight of Adrastus, the chariot of Amphiaraüs falling into the chasm opened by Zeus to save the hero from the pursuing enemy, and Oedipus between his two dying sons. The figures show a fine sense of movement and are clearly influenced by Greek figurative art. Vivid polychromy renders the whole scene even more animated and dynamic. The temple was built after the battle fought near Talamone between the retreating Gauls and the Roman troops led by the consuls Lucius Aemilius Papus and Gaius Atilius Regulus.

A mass burial was found on the left bank of the river Osa at Camporegio, containing skeletons of men and horses covered with quicklime; this has been connected with the battle, which took place in 225 B.C., but there is no certain proof of this identification.

Near the temple, deposits including many bronze and iron objects were found, among them little models of agricultural implements and weapons, now in the Museo Archeologico at Florence; these were probably votive offerings.

Further evidence of Etruscan life was provided by architectural terracottas dating from the end of the 6th–beginning of the 5th century B.C., found on the Colle di Bengodi.

In the cemetery, tombs of the 3rd century B.C. have been found, with furnishings that include black-gloss and uncoloured ware, balsam pots, askoi and skyphoi.

Talamone had a fairly important port; the ancient coastline followed the present route of the Via Aurelia, and the landing-place used in Etruscan and Roman times lay in the area between the modern port and the Pineta della Vergine, where the bay made a long sweep inland. Marius landed here in 87 B.C., returning from Africa. In 82 B.C. Talamone was devastated by Sulla's troops, but life continued there and the port remained active.

The most striking remains dating from Roman times are the ruins of a four-arched bridge carrying the Via Aurelia, still visible in the bed of the river Osa, and the ruins at S. Francesca, near the cemetery of Talamone. The latter consist of walls of *opus reticulatum* and *opus spicatum*, portions of mosaic pavements in white and black tesserae, huge cisterns, remains of swimming-pools and water-tanks, all part of a magnificent villa with baths attached, dating from the 2nd century A.D. and obviously belonging to wealthy local land-owners. The building methods and the use of tufa alternating with courses of bricks are typical of the Cosa area and the neighbouring islands of Giglio and Giannutri.

Orbetello

Modern Orbetello occupies the same strategic position as the ancient city, at the end of a narrow peninsula extending into a lagoon that is cut off from the sea by the sandbars of Feniglia to the south and Giannella to the northwest; hence its importance as a port and a military base in both ancient and modern times.

A settlement existed as early as the 8th century B.C. and was continuously inhabited down to the Hellenistic and Roman period, as is proved by finds made in the cemetery extending along the isthmus connecting Orbetello to the mainland. The city obviously became very prosperous, thanks to its coastal position and its rich and densely populated hinterland.

A few stretches of the walls of polygonal stones that protected the city are still visible; although these are no earlier than the mid- or late 4th century B.C., it has been thought that they followed the line of an older fortification. The perimeter wall is slightly less than two kilometres long and is built on two rows of oak and pine piles, with another row of piles in front on the seaward side to protect it from the sea and the currents. These walls now survive on three sides only, since the landward section disappeared some time ago, being absorbed and destroyed by the modern fortifications. The best-preserved stretch is near the breakwater, opposite Monte Argentario; here there must have been a gate and a landing-place.

No trace of the ancient city remains; it is not certain whether a building discovered under the cathedral is a Hellenistic temple, and the Latin inscriptions built into the walls of the town hall come from Cosa. One of particular interest is the dedication to Caracalla by the *curator* of Cosa, Marcus Porcius Severinus, that may have belonged to the base of a statue of the 3rd century A.D.

The Etruscans built a port in the lagoon of Orbetello, which at that time was separated from the sea by the Feniglia sandbar alone, along which ran the road linking Cosa with Porto Ercole; the Giannella sandbar was only just emerging. There were three channels leading to the sea: a northern channel that went as far as the mouth of the Albegna, and two southern channels that cut across the Feniglia sandbar at Monte Argentario and at the hill of Cosa. The coast and the three ports of Cosa, Porto Ercole and Orbetello are described by Strabo (V, 225), who adds that near the promontory there was a place in the gulf for tunny fishing.

At nearby La Parrina there are remains of a large Roman building that may have been a villa with its own baths, since one room with hypocaust pillars is still visible.

The cemeteries were situated on the isthmus and in the immediate neighbourhood of the city; the oldest tombs contained typical Villanovan vases. There were also later tombs with two or three chambers either cut into the rock or built of blocks of local stone. Tomb furnishings included a series of bucchero vases, Italo-Geometric and Etrusco-Corinthian vases imported from southern Etruria, Athenian and Etruscan black- and red-figure pottery, and several bronze vases.

Objects found locally are displayed in the Antiquarium of Orbetello, following their chronological and topographical order as closely as possible. These include cinerary urns from the Archaic cemetery of Orbetello, some noteworthy examples of which are in the form of jars on tall stands, not unlike some from Bisenzio.

From Poggio alla Campana, on the estate of S. Donato, come two fragmentary sarcophagi, an incomplete sphinx in *nenfro* and a limestone head, found with Athenian black-figure pottery near a large tumulus that had already been broken into. A tufa sphinx from I Poggetti shows clear influence of Vulci. As well as the pottery found in cemeteries in and around Orbetello, there are also series of small Etruscan bronzes and personal ornaments, and a collection of Roman marble sculptures and inscriptions.

Above, left: central panel of a bronze shield with animal decorations. Orbetello, Antiquarium

Left: Orbetello

Right: bronze belt-clasp with three animal heads. Orbetello, Antiquarium

Cosa

Cosa is situated on a rocky promontory, about 100 metres above sea-level, seven kilometres southeast of Orbetello.

For a long time it was thought to be an Etruscan city and linked with the Etruscan cemetery at neighbouring Orbetello, but recent excavations carried out by the American Academy in the area of the ancient city have proved conclusively that Cosa began life as a Roman city. Its oldest remains are those of the Latin *colonia* founded in 273 B.C. in the territory of Vulci after that ancient and powerful city came completely under Roman influence.

Cosa was defended by an impressive surrounding wall about 1.50 kilometres long, with three gates facing respectively northwest, northeast and southeast, called the Porta Fiorentina, Porta Romana and Porta Marina. Three roads led down from the gates to the Feniglia sandbar, the Via Aurelia and the port respectively. The upper sections of the two northern roads are still clearly visible; they are 4.45 metres or 15 Roman feet wide, and lead to the Via Aurelia, which skirted the foot of the hill.

The walls are still quite well preserved and are built of polygonal stones very accurately fitted together; they are strengthened by eighteen towers placed at irregular intervals, according to a clear strategic plan. This is based on the nature of the terrain under the walls and is designed to eliminate any dead ground at points where access to the walls is relatively easy. On the outside the walls are 8–10 metres high, and on the inside 1–2 metres, though in a few places they are 4–5 metres high. The three gates are all of the so-called

Cosa (Ansedonia). Part of the Roman walls

propylon or inner-court type—that is, with the gateway projecting inwards from the line of the walls.

The circuit is largely uniform in construction, and can be dated to the second quarter of the 3rd century B.C.; it follows the contours of the hill, utilizing the unevenness of the terrain and enclosing an area that includes the twin summits of the hill and the saddle that lies between them, and also a part of the northern slope that is sheltered from the prevailing winds.

On the southern summit is the fortress or *arx*; the forum is situated on the saddle. The city follows a regular pattern in relation to these two central points and the three gates, based on the original plan of the *colonia*: the streets intersect at right angles, enclosing rectangular blocks of houses 32.50–37 metres wide and usually 82 metres long. Thus Cosa is an important example of a city that follows a rectangular plan of house blocks (*strigae*), which proves that a regular town plan was not limited to cities built on level ground but could be used even on a less favourable terrain.

The three principal streets inside the city are the two streets, six metres wide, leading from the northeast and southeast gates, crossing at the approximate centre of the city and running along two sides of the forum, and the one coming from the northwest gate and leading to the northwestern corner of the forum. A street 4.45 metres wide ran round the city about 6–7 metres from the inside of the walls, creating a defensive area. All the streets, even the smaller ones, were paved with local limestone.

The *arx* or acropolis of the city was protected by the outer city wall and was separated from the rest of the city by two stretches of walls in polygonal stone and natural rock that may have had some symbolic and ritual significance as a boundary to the acropolis.

This formed a sacred area containing at least three temples: the smaller two date approximately from the foundation of the *colonia*, the third being built in between them at the beginning of the 2nd century B.C. This is a *capitolium* of quite considerable size, visible from miles out to sea. The Via Sacra, an extension of the street linking the *arx* and the forum, led to the centre of the sacred area.

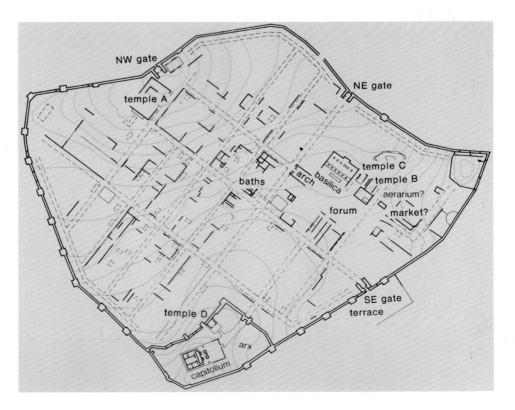

Cosa. Archaeological plan

Left: Cosa: the citadel or *arx*

Below: the forum

Cosa. The *arx* seen from the *capitolium*

Below: Cosa. Plan of the *arx*

The *capitolium* is called Palazzo della Regina ('The Queen's Palace') locally because of its impressive walls that rise to a height of 6–7 metres from a high podium facing east-northeast, reached by stairs almost as broad as the temple itself. It is divided into two parts of almost equal length: the pronaos and the three cellae, with the central cella broader than the two side ones. The pronaos had a row of four columns in front and two behind, aligned with the walls of the central cella.

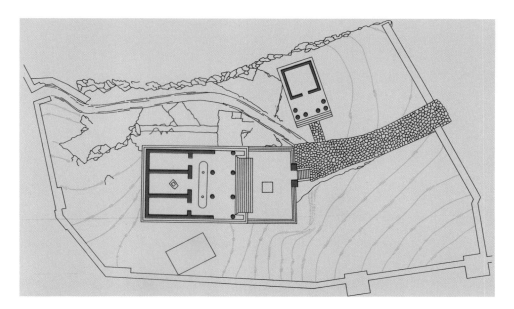

Left: the Porta Romana in the walls of Cosa

Below: chamber-tomb

Impressive in its dimensions, the building must have been even more striking in its original covering of polychrome terracotta. There was also a terrace in front, reached from the Via Sacra by a central stair that led up to a sacrificial altar, on the same axis as the temple. The *capitolium* was in use, visited and restored, until about the middle of the 3rd century A.D.; in the 10th century a church was built on the site, and it was incorporated into the Castello di Ansedonia in the 13th century.

Opposite the northern corner of the terrace in front of the *capitolium* is temple D, orientated northwest–southeast and overlooking the city. It has a low podium of polygonal work, a single square cella and a deep pronaos, with four columns in front and one on each side behind, in line with the side walls of the cella. The altar was in front, on the polygonal paving visible between the entrance stair and the Via Sacra.

The third temple on the *arx* was built on the crest of the hill, between the southern side of the *capitolium* and the walls, and faced northeast. It was destroyed by a fire (cause unknown) half-way through the 1st century B.C. and never rebuilt. Only traces of walls and fragments of terracotta decorations remain.

The *arx* reached its architectural peak at the beginning of the 2nd century B.C. when the *capitolium* was built: the temples, and possibly also other buildings now lost, dominated the city and were visible far out to sea in the richness of their bright polychrome terracotta decorations. The area continued to be used for worship until the 3rd century A.D., long after the decline of the city, as is proved by marble statues, inscriptions and stamped tiles found there.

Sacred buildings at Cosa were not confined to the *arx*; a large temple, called temple A, existed in the northwestern part of the city near the walls, on the right coming from the

Porta Fiorentina. It was orientated in the same way as the axial roads within the city and was about the same size as the *capitolium*; part of the podium and the cella survives, and it seems probable that the temple faced southwest.

There was another temple in the eastern corner of the city, reached by a long processional way from the forum.

The forum, centre of public life in the city, covered an area of about 30 metres by 90 metres, orientated northwest–southeast. The northwestern part had a monumental entrance, a triple arch that opened directly on to the street leading to the northeast gate; there was a corresponding monument at the opposite end of the forum, as yet unidentified.

The buildings that run along the northeastern side are fairly well preserved and consist of a basilica, two temples and the *aerarium* (treasury); on the southwestern side, however,

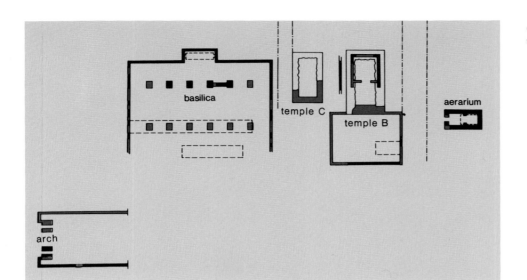

Cosa. Plan of the forum, with the basilica, the two temples and the *aerarium*

there are only a few unidentifiable remains. The basilica is a large rectangular building subdivided by a double row of six piers and with a shallow *tribunal* in the centre of the rear wall, which was pierced by a high window, perhaps arched. The walls have partially survived, to a height of about five metres. The original plan of the basilica included a double row of columns rather than piers; the latter were constructed during a later phase of rebuilding and supported a series of arches. During the earliest phase a row of shops was situated along the façade that looks on to the forum.

Next to and aligned with the basilica were two small temples. Their heavy podia, of polygonal or irregular stonework, survive, and a little farther on can be seen the remains of a small rectangular building with exceptionally thick walls, evidently designed to support a vault; this may have been the *aerarium*.

At the approximate centre of the city, near the arch that leads to the forum, on the right coming from the northeast gate, is a complex of bath buildings. The most important rooms were originally barrel-vaulted. The *caldarium* may have occupied the western corner of the building, since a fragmentary bath or *labrum* in white limestone was found beside it. In the southern corner the water tank is visible, and near this is a circular room that was probably the *frigidarium* and had walls originally decorated with sixteen flat pilasters.

The water supply for the baths was ensured by a system of exceptionally large cisterns, partially carved out of the ground under the building itself, and consisting of a principal compartment 3.75–3.57 metres by 15–18 metres, with a vaulted roof and a right-angled projection on each side.

Within the built-up area of the city remains of houses have been identified, with rather rough walls built on concrete and *opus incertum*. The uniformity of these houses is remarkable; the walls are fairly thin, since they were probably only single-storey buildings; there is no large *domus* with an atrium, and one can tell that the houses were grouped in uniform blocks, since it is still possible to distinguish each individual unit just from the position of the cisterns.

As in the majority of ancient settlements, water-supply was quite a problem in Cosa, since there are no springs on top of the limestone hill and rain-water is rapidly absorbed by the porous rock, so that wells and springs are found only at the foot of the hill, where some, probably the same as the ancient ones that provided water for animals and the public washing-places, are still in use today. Rain-water had to be collected for everyday use. Thus all public buildings and private houses in the ancient *colonia* must have had at least one cistern to collect rain-water; this was partly cut into the rock and partly built

Opposite: Cosa. The so-called Tagliata Etrusca, a work of Roman engineering

up, and plastered with a waterproof lining of lime mixed into *opus signinum*. These cisterns had vaulted roofs and were built in various forms on L-, T-, H-shaped or rectangular plans. They were fed by conduits that opened into the cistern at the level of the base of the vault; the water was obtained through circular openings in the roof of the cistern. Public supplies were provided by three great open reservoirs situated in various parts of the city that collected rain-water off the roads that ran beside them.

The port, called *Portus Cosanus* in ancient times, was at the foot of the hill, at the western end of a lagoon well sheltered from the winds. Ships could reach the inner basin, now long since silted up, by way of a channel cut through the dunes at the foot of the hill. It was a perfect port: well protected from westerly and southerly winds, dominated by the city and no more than 500 metres from the nearest city gate.

On the northern side of the port, facing the sea, was a little temple dedicated to the tutelary god of the port and its maritime trade. A little farther on, the streets of the Succosa harbour district are still visible.

One of the most incredible features is the channel leading into the inner basin of the harbour and its entrance: the channel was dug right at the foot of the rocky cliff that forms its western side for about 140 metres, cutting through the coastal dunes at the point where they joined the eastern spur of the hill. Since the entrance was in constant danger of silting up with sand brought by currents, two narrow channels were dug to make an artificial current that would constantly move the sand and prevent the silting of the deep channel. The earlier of these canals, the Spacco della Regina, is 260 metres long and between one and six metres broad; it runs from the open sea to the mouth of the harbour channel, and is a natural cleft in the rock that was artificially widened and levelled to the required size. Later it was damaged by rock-falls and cracks and replaced by another channel, the Tagliata, that was completely artificial; this runs roughly parallel to the promontory wall, separated from the sea by only a thin wall of rock. For better protection against silting-up of the harbour mouth, the entrance was enclosed between two parallel jetties about 90 metres long, with huge foundations of rough stone underwater and great concrete blocks that appeared above the water and may have been connected by arches.

During the Empire the harbour began to decline, as can be seen by the fact that a large villa was built on the dunes that flank the ancient channel and on part of the basin, then silted up. The Tagliata was of no further use and was blocked to make fish tanks or boat sheds.

Cosa was abandoned by the 1st century A.D. and its inhabitants established themselves near the port and the Via Aurelia, founding the posting-station of Succosa on the road; gradually the ancient *colonia* became an isolated and impressive ruin, as described by Rutilius Namatianus (*De Reditu*, I, 285) in the 5th century A.D.

A little way from the city, along the northeastern and northwestern roads that led to the harbour, remains of these settlers' tombs can be seen; they are mostly small tombs of shrine form, uniform in type, and very few have any monumental pretensions.

Magliano

North of the Albegna, on the right bank of the Patrignone stream, stand the ruins of Heba, a city which was first Etruscan, then Roman. Life was continued down to modern times, not far from the ancient settlement, at the mediaeval town of Magliano in Toscana, with its walls dating mainly from the Renaissance.

The tombs in the neighbouring cemeteries show that the Etruscan city was first inhabited at the end of the 7th or the beginning of the 6th century B.C. and was occupied continuously until it became the Roman *municipium* of Heba. The discovery of a travertine cippus bearing the inscription *genio coloniae Hebae* near the convent of S. Maria in Borraccia has made it possible to identify the Roman ruins in the valley to the east of the walls of Magliano as the city of Heba mentioned in Latin sources. Furthermore, at Le Sassaie a very important inscription known as the *tabula Hebana* was found: this is a bronze tablet which is a copy of a resolution made in A.D. 20 concerning special honours in memory of Germanicus, nephew of the emperor Tiberius.

The city's economy must have been based on agriculture and mining. Its territory is rich in sulphur, antimony and mercuric ores, and it is well placed geographically on the route between the Albegna valley and the port of Talamone.

Round the inhabited area are the cemeteries, which show how long the Etruscan city was inhabited. Underground tombs cut into the tufa have been discovered at S. Maria in Borraccia, S. Bruzio, Banditella and Le Sassaie. The tombs are reached by a *dromos* sloping gently down to a vestibule which leads to the rectangular chamber proper.

Above: the Magliano lead plate. Florence, Museo Archeologico

Right: the Colle d'Albegna

Sometimes the chambers are partially divided into two by a partition built out from the wall facing the entrance; sometimes there is a central pillar, which may end in a carved capital. As a rule, rock-cut benches run along the walls; the remains of the dead were placed on these with some of the burial treasures, the rest being left on the floor.

The most important Etruscan find at Magliano is an inscribed lead plate, now in the Museo Archeologico at Florence; the text, written on both sides in a spiral starting at the edge and working towards the centre, contains at least seventy recognizable words. Names of gods, such as *cauthas*, *aiseras*, *marisl*, *tins* and *calus*, alternate with instructions, apparently for a funeral ritual.

Marsiliana

Northeast of Cosa, in the middle Albegna valley, stands Marsiliana d'Albegna, on the site of a once prosperous Etruscan city. From its position on a hill, near where the Elsa joins the Albegna, the city commanded a view over an important route leading towards Monte Amiata and the Val di Chiana. Its ancient name is believed to have been Caletra, since that was the most important city in the area between the rivers Fiora and Albegna, which was therefore known as the *Ager Caletranus*. The modern name is later, and is probably derived from a Roman surname. The city's economy must have been based on agriculture and trade, but there is not as yet any evidence to show for certain whether Marsiliana was active in maritime trade, and in particular whether there was a port at the mouth of the Albegna before the 3rd century B.C.

There are no visible traces of the Etruscan city, but the cemeteries are known, and indicate that the site was inhabited from shortly before the beginning of the 7th century B.C. until the beginning of the 6th. Occupation ceased at a time when Marsiliana was thriving; in fact the richest tombs are among the most recent.

The reason why the town was abandoned is not known. It has been suggested that it may have had something to do with the emergence in the early 6th century B.C. of a settlement a few kilometres north of the Albegna, at present-day Magliano; the inhabitants may have moved there to work the mines of the area. What is known is that other nearby cities, such as Poggio Buco and Sovana, underwent a similar crisis, for reasons still undiscovered.

The most important cemeteries at Marsiliana are those of Banditella and Perazzeta, on either side of the Camarrone. Between the Camarrone valley and the hills which slope down towards the Elsa is the Poggio Volpaio burial-ground, which has chamber-tombs cut into the tufa, and the Macchiabuia site, where tumulus-tombs have been found.

There are a large number of circle-tombs—trench-tombs surrounded by a circle of travertine slabs set vertically in the ground. These are the richest graves, normally consisting of two trenches, the central one for the remains, the other for the funerary objects.

The river Fiora, the ancient Arminium

The most sumptuous tombs have been found in the Banditella cemetery, the so-called Circolo degli Avori and Circolo della Fibula. The first contained—in addition to three skeletons buried side by side in the trench, with three spears, a shield and a chariot—a rectangular block of stone, hollowed out on top to hold a cauldron in which had been placed precious objects and a selection of particularly interesting ivory pieces (hence the name 'Circle of the Ivories'). They consist of a comb decorated with fantastic animals in low relief and in the round, a casket, again decorated with scenes of figures and fantastic motifs, fragments of human figures, and lions—all items for personal and domestic use, probably belonging to a woman. A further find was a writing-tablet inscribed along one edge with the Greek (Euboean) alphabet which the Etruscans took as the model for their script, stylus handles and spatula-shaped erasers, making up a complete set of writing equipment.

The Circolo della Fibula is called after an ornate gold serpentine fibula with a long catchplate which was found during the excavations carried out by Prince Corsini at the beginning of this century. It has granulated geometric decoration, enriched by small figures of ducks and lions on the upper part of the catchplate and the bow; there are also two balls attached inside the bow, with triangular granulated decoration on their surfaces.

Besides the circle-tombs, the Marsiliana cemeteries contain trench-, pit- and chamber-tombs. Study of the objects found in the tombs show that the local culture had much in common with that of Vetulonia, as well as with the artistic civilization of southern Etruria, particularly Vulci and its hinterland.

Below: the Corsini gold fibula, from Marsiliana. Florence, Museo Archeologico

Right: Marsiliana. Etruscan chamber-tomb

Saturnia

Saturnia stands on a travertine eminence, overlooking the point where the Stellata joins the Albegna, in a commanding position at the centre of a network of communication routes.

The site was first inhabited in the 8th century B.C. as is shown by the late Villanovan pit- and trench-tombs which have been found, and was occupied until the beginning of the 5th century B.C.; there was then a long break until after the Roman occupation. The evidence for these dates comes almost entirely from the cemeteries and the objects found there; little is known about the Etruscan city itself because its site has been occupied continuously down to the present day.

All that remains of the Etruscan city are some stretches of its walls, built of polygonal travertine blocks; gates interrupted the walls at points where the nature of the rocky slope made access easier. The roads which climbed half-way up the hill continued inside the gates, often at an angle to the course of the walls. Very little is known about public or private buildings.

We know more about the Roman city which was built over the Etruscan one, established first as the *praefectura* (assize-town) of Saturnia, later as a Roman *colonia* (183 B.C.).

Saturnia. The road network outside the city, and the cemeteries

Inset: plan of the city (top of inset=south)

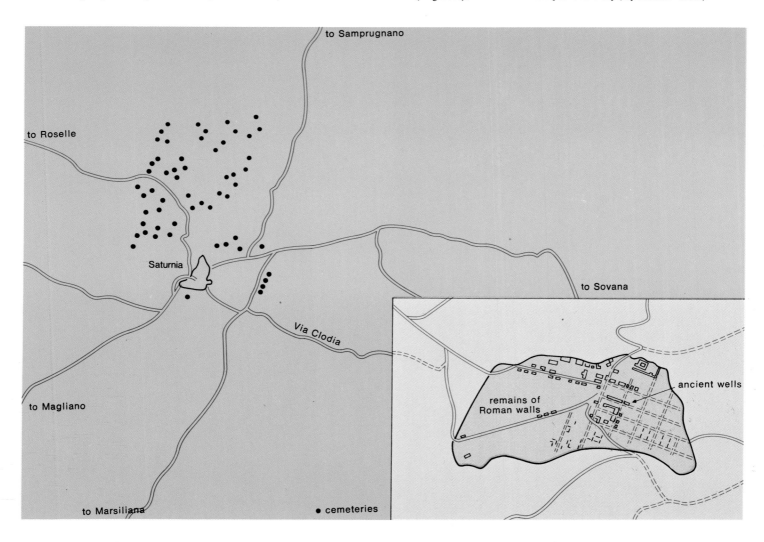

to Samprugnano

to Roselle

Saturnia

to Sovana

Via Clodia

to Magliano

to Marsiliana

• cemeteries

ancient wells

remains of Roman walls

In the western part of the present inhabited area, air photography, taking still identifiable remains as its point of reference, has revealed a grid system with blocks two *actus* (=240 Roman feet=71.04 metres) long and about an *actus* and a half wide; but as there are signs of an axis running between the southwest and northeast gates, the city must originally have had another orientation, now unknown.

The Porta Romana, a water-tower and some stretches of paved road are what remain of the Saturnia of the period. One section of road may be part of the Via Clodia, built in the first half of the 3rd century B.C. to consolidate Roman power in central Etruria, which was densely populated but difficult to reach; the road entered Saturnia from the south through the Porta Romana of today. Other sections of paved road leave from the Porta Fiorentina, going north towards Monte Amiata and east towards the water-tower at Murella, following a similar course to the mule-track which today still leads to Sovana.

The city was destroyed by Sulla as a reprisal in 82 B.C., but life went on and the city flourished until the 6th century A.D.

The Etruscan cemeteries are scattered on the outskirts of the city. The Villanovan pit-tombs often contained biconical cinerary urns with spherical lids resembling a human head, following a tendency towards anthropomorphic urns that is also typical of Marsiliana and Chiusi. Later tombs are chamber-tombs. They are occasionally dug into the ground, but more often built up, with stone slabs laid on top to form a kind of tumulus; sometimes they are cut into the ground to two-thirds of their height, the remaining third being built up with the usual slabs.

In the Castello di Saturnia there is an Antiquarium, housing a collection of local finds.

Saturnia. Remains of the Etruscan and Roman city near the Castello

Below: Porta Romana

Poggio Buco

Farther up the Fiora valley, between Manciano and Pitigliano, was an Etruscan city of some importance, situated in a position which made it a natural stronghold. The Bavoso and Rubbiano, tributaries flowing into the Fiora on its right side, mark off a plateau, known as Le Sparne, which is protected to the north, east and south by the three watercourses and their valleys. To safeguard the west side a trench was dug and the earth from it piled up to make a little fortified hill. The acropolis, overlooking the point where the Rubbiano joins the Fiora, was defended to the north by an artificial trench and its own walls. During the Middle Ages the Knights of Rhodes built a small church there, now in

Poggio Buco. Plan

Two views of the Poggio Buco cemetery

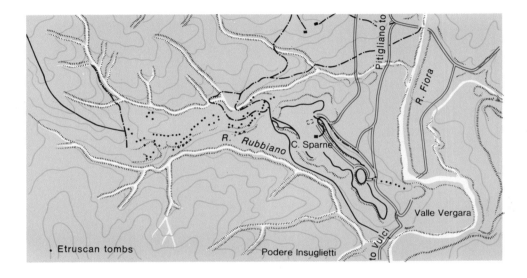

ruins. Along the brow of the plateau stretches of wall have been discovered, built of rectangular tufa blocks; so it would seem that only the most exposed and accessible sections were fortified.

The ancient road network can fairly clearly be identified. The eastern side of the city is flanked by a road which runs along the Fiora from Vulci. A road branches off it up to the acropolis, while another leads more to the north to a paved area where the remains of a temple have been discovered, together with three buildings of uncertain purpose, perhaps houses. Another road leads from the west, passing through the Poggio Buco cemetery, to the south side of the earthwork.

In the inhabited area some remains of buildings have been found. Near the eastern edge of the level ground remnants of a temple, badly damaged by agricultural work, have been uncovered. Fragments of tufa blocks, bricks, architectural terracottas, votive offerings and coins have been found scattered all over the area, and in a number of pits cut into the rock. The architectural terracottas are all Archaic and are among the oldest found in Etruria. Dating from the beginning of the 6th century B.C., they consist of ridge tiles and openings shaped like panthers' heads, an acroterion in the form of a horse's head and three series of facing plaques decorated in low relief with Orientalizing motifs: processions of animals, columns of chariots and warriors, and ranks of horsemen. The votive offerings, however, are mainly from the Hellenistic period.

Poggio Buco is generally identified with the Etruscan Statnes or Staties and the Roman Statonia, which was made a *praefectura* after the Romans conquered Vulci in 278 B.C. Near the walls some lead sling bullets or missiles, of a type common in ancient times, have in fact been found, bearing the Etruscan inscription *statnes* or *staties*. As some of

Poggio Buco. Left: entrance to an Etruscan tomb

Above: an ancient road across the cemetery

these seem not to have been used in battle, and since it was customary to write the name of the city or its inhabitants on such missiles, it is likely that the inscriptions do in fact give the name of the Etruscan city. Moreover, not far away is Lake Mezzano, the ancient *Lacus Statoniensis*.

The cemeteries extend round the city. The largest is Poggio Buco; the Italian name ('hill of holes') is a fair description of the locality, which is riddled with tombs. The other cemeteries are at Valle Vergara, Selva Miccia and Podere Insuglietti. The oldest tombs are simple trench-tombs, the later ones chamber-tombs and trench-tombs with one or two side niches (*loculi*) for the burial objects. Study of the objects found shows that the city was notably prosperous in the 7th and 6th centuries B.C. There was then a break, until the city revived in the 3rd–1st centuries B.C., after the Roman conquest of the territory of Vulci.

Pitigliano

At Pitigliano life has continued to the present day, gradually absorbing and destroying any signs of the Etruscan settlement which first developed on this spur of tufa, protected by rocky cliffs and not far from that important inland communications route, the river Fiora.

Near the gate called Porta di Sovana a section of the Etruscan walls survives. Built in very regular *opus quadratum*, this wall was later incorporated into the mediaeval fortifications.

Groups of tombs have been discovered in the faces of the cliffs below the town, particularly on the south side, along the Meleta watercourse, at Valle della Fontanelle, Marmicelli and so on. Commonest are the chest-type, but there are also many chamber-tombs and tombs of an intermediate type, as at Poggio Buco. The furnishings also closely resemble those of Poggio Buco. Obviously Pitigliano was culturally within Vulci's zone of influence, situated on the trade-route leading from Vulci via Poggio Buco, Pitigliano and Sovana to the Val di Chiana, linking the northernmost city of southern coastal Etruria with the interior.

From the objects found in the tombs it would appear that the town was abandoned at the end of the 6th or beginning of the 5th century B.C.; it revived rather feebly in the Hellenistic age, continuing into Roman times. Chest-tombs and *columbaria* have been found which can be dated to the first centuries of the Empire. The Roman occupation also left its mark in the village's present name, which apparently comes from a *gens Petilia*, probably local landowners.

General view of Pitigliano

Above: Pitigliano. Group of Etruscan tombs cut into the rock face below the town

Left: Etruscan road cut into the tufa

Sovana

Not far from Pitigliano is Sovana, another important Etruscan city. It occupied the same site as the mediaeval town and modern village, on a spur of tufa between the rivers Calesine and Folonia, cut off on its eastern side from the rest of the plateau by a natural depression which was probably deepened by artificial means; there are similar trenches at Poggio Buco, Blera and S. Giuliano. The city was walled only where the natural defences seemed inadequate; some stretches of the walls are still visible. One section, consisting of five courses of rectangular blocks, is built into the Rocca Aldobrandesca, another can be seen below the modern washing-place on the hillside facing the Folonia, and there are further sections near the cathedral. These remains show that the plateau on which the city stood was enclosed by walls of local tufa blocks, from the church of S. Vito all along the eastern edge, the southeast and the south. On the southwestern side the wall must have swung back sharply beside the natural rise on which the cathedral now stands.

In the inhabited area several tunnels cut into the tufa have been discovered. They are of a type found in a number of places in central and southern Etruria, roughly 1.70 metres high and 0.60 metres wide, with vertical shafts, and were perhaps used for drainage.

Sovana. Plan of the archaeological zone

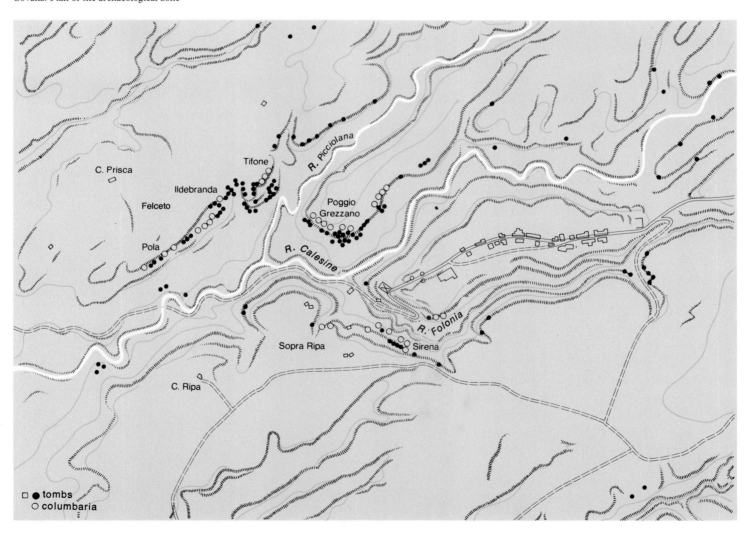

There is also known to have been a small temple just outside the walls. Its base was built of large tufa blocks; some tufa column-drums have been discovered, as well as part of the terracotta decoration, now in the Museo Archeologico at Florence. These consist of facing slabs decorated with plant and geometric motifs, antefixes, and some figures in high relief, including a number of men dressed in skins and short cloaks who are perhaps engaged in combat; these can be dated to the end of the 3rd century B.C.

The ancient road system was much the same as the one existing today. The city could be approached from the southwest and the northeast, along two roads following the lie of the land and roughly corresponding to the modern ones.

Near the city are two ancient roads, sunk deep into the tufa. The tufaceous rock wears away quickly and the passage of people, animals and vehicles, together with the draining-away of water, soon lowers the road level. In central-southern Etruria there are many such sunken roads, worn 10–15 metres or more down into the tufa, while vegetation often forms a natural vault above. Although the depth of these roads may be a sign of age, the only certain proof that they date from Etruscan times is the presence of tombs along the way or inscriptions carved on the rock faces.

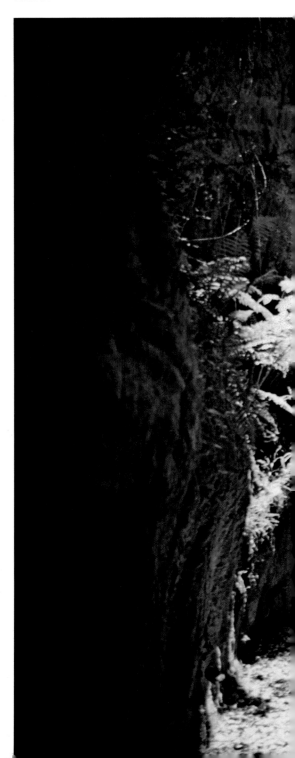

Sovana. An important Etruscan road, the Cavone, northwest of the city, between Felceto and Poggio Stanziale

At the Cava di S. Bastiano, southwest of Sovana, a series of tombs high up in the rock face shows the level of the ancient road. This could have been the continuation of the road which led into the city from the west and climbed the hillside opposite, leading on to the clusters of dwellings which groups of isolated tombs show to have existed at Tollena, Pian Costanzi and Fosso S. Pietro.

The Cavone, northwest of Sovana, between Felceto and Poggio Stanziale, is one of the most impressive of these roads. The tombs and inscriptions found in its sheer walls show that it was already cut deep into the rock in ancient times. It runs in a straight line for about a kilometre to the top of Poggio Stanziale, and then disappears into the Pianetto di Sovana. Going towards the city, it joined a road, at the Picciolana, which ran alongside the part of the cemetery richest in monuments and continued perhaps all the way to Saturnia.

The Etruscan road to Pitigliano and Sorano followed the Calesine valley and can still be identified today by the series of tombs which flanked it.

There are cemeteries all around the city. The tombs are cut into the sides of the ravines, preferably facing the sun, and chest-tombs can easily be identified on the edges of the plateaux. Some of the chamber-tombs are simple, others have architectural façades cut in the living rock. Originally these façades seem to have been covered with a thin layer of stucco of which traces remain on many late tombs. Under the façade, roughly in the centre, a corridor leads to the burial chamber, which was generally cut at the bottom of the seam of tufa where it met an easily-worked layer of sand and gravel. Compared with the façades, the chambers are roughly cut and become even more so in the later tombs.

A number of different basic types can be distinguished: cube-tombs, temple- and shrine-tombs, tombs with pediment and portico, and niche-tombs.

Cube-tombs (a dado), widespread in the cemeteries of the Viterbo area and in Sovana and its environs, are probably the commonest type of tombs with architectural façades. Over the chamber is a kind of cube more or less detached from the tufa cliff face, decorated on its upper part with three architectural mouldings, the hawksbeak, torus and fasces; the style of these makes dating possible. In the centre of the flat top is a rectangular block; one or more cippi were set on top of this, which may therefore be thought of as an altar designed for that purpose. The top of the cube thus became a small sacred area, and in some cases narrow steps leading up to it were cut alongside the cube.

The temple-tombs are the most characteristic and impressive type in the cemetery; in these the monument carved above the funeral chamber is a scale model, of varying accuracy, of the façade of a temple, with columns and friezes in relief.

One example is the Grotta Pola, standing in the southwestern part of the cemetery, on the hillside of Poggio Prisca. Damaged long ago, it originally had eight fluted columns in front. Capitals surmounted these, decorated with human heads among volutes and foliage, and supporting an entablature of which the triglyphs can be seen. Behind the façade, jutting out from the cliff face, are two slightly projecting antae, in imitation of real buildings. The entrance to the burial chamber is aligned with the centre of the colonnade. The chamber must have contained a good many burials.

Not far from this tomb, which dates from the 3rd century B.C., is the slightly later Tomba Ildebranda, named after Hildebrand, a high-born native of Sovana who became Pope Gregory VII. A flat rectangular area has been cut out of the rock face and the monument is carved at the back of it. A podium with mouldings, flanked by two stairways for access, supports a façade with six fluted, very tapered columns, surmounted by heavy voluted capitals decorated with acanthus leaves among which are carved heads of young and

bearded men. On either side are three columns. Above, there was a cornice and a frieze with griffins carved in relief among plant motifs, surmounted by a second frieze of prominent plant volutes. The final element was a series of dentils and large rosettes at regular intervals, perhaps in imitation of antefixes. The wall at the back is cut to form a central section jutting out from the two wings which terminate the colonnade. In the centre of the front is a projecting slab decorated with lozenges in low relief, perhaps in imitation of the lattice screen of a door. The burial chamber below is interesting for its cruciform shape and its ceiling which slopes down from the central beam. It has a single bench along the back wall, with two recesses. The tomb's façade must have been particularly striking not only because of its monumental scale, but also because of the brilliantly coloured stucco—white, red, yellow, green and blue—which covered it and of which traces have been found.

At Poggio Stanziale there are two examples of tombs with pediment and portico, imitating the façade of a small gabled building. Under the pediment two antae are built out at the sides, forming a small portico at the back of which an imitation door is carved. This type is very similar to the shrine-tombs which developed, particularly in the Hellenistic age, in many cemeteries in the Mediterranean basin. There are two noteworthy examples at Sovana. The Tomba del Tifone at Poggio Stanziale has two fluted antae supporting a pediment at the centre of which is a head in the tragic style, worked in high relief, which can be dated to the 2nd century B.C. The other tomb, known as the Tomba della Sirena, is west of the city on the Sopraripa hillside. It has a central recess with a couch inside, on which is carved the reclining figure of the dead man; on the sides are two winged spirits in high relief. Over the recess is an entablature and a pediment, originally triangular,

decorated with a sea-demon (Scylla) enfolding two young men in her coils. The rich façade contrasts with the burial chamber below, which is small and roughly cut, set at an angle to the axis of the monument.

The Tomba Siena, on the bank of the Folonia south of the city, is an example of a shrine-tomb with two simple pilaster strips in low relief.

The most impressive section of the cemetery lies between Poggio Prisca and Poggio Stanziale, northwest of Sovana. It is here that we find the two temple-tombs, a row of cube-tombs, the tombs with pediment and portico, and the shrine-type Tomba del Tifone. In other parts of the cemetery only isolated groups of monuments have been discovered.

Moving on to the techniques employed, it is clear that the façade was carved first and the chamber made later; in some cases there is no trace of an actual tomb below the monument. The tools used were a mason's hammer, with a blade on one side and a point on the other, and a wide-bladed chisel, which has left its mark more or less everywhere. Often there are holes in the rock face which perhaps show where wooden scaffolding was used for working high up.

From the evidence provided by the cemeteries, it appears that Sovana flourished in the 7th–6th centuries B.C., but was then deserted until the end of the 4th century B.C., when it once again began to prosper. Here we find yet again the same crisis which affected the other cities of the Fiora valley, for reasons now unknown. Culturally, Sovana certainly came within the territory of Vulci. After the Romans defeated Vulci in 278 B.C. it became a *municipium*; its name, Suana, is also known. During the Hellenistic period it became the area's most important and prosperous city, as is shown by the cemeteries of that period, which are more extensive and richer than those of the same date at Poggio Buco and other smaller towns.

Around Sorano a number of scattered Etruscan tombs have been found, cut into the steep banks of the Calesine ravine, containing objects closely resembling those of the Archaic tombs of Sovana. However, these tombs were attached to some small agricultural community rather than to any sizeable settlement. There are similar groups farther away to the northeast, at Case Rocchi and Montepalaro, probably marking a communication route linking the towns of the Fiora valley to Chiusi, via Proceno, Trevinano, Poggio Corno, S. Casciano and Cetona.

Only in Roman times can Sorano have been an inhabited centre, producing the many fine *columbaria* which can be seen in the lower part of the present-day village and in the ravines around it, at Colombarie, Rocchette, Castelvecchio and S. Rocco. Generally the tombs are reached from a little vestibule. Two rectangular chambers lead off it to either side, with openings to let in light in the upper part of the front. Cut into the walls of the two chambers are staggered rows of niches, square at the bottom, rounded at the top, arranged at regular intervals, separated by spaces a little narrower than the niches themselves. Other *columbaria* are more complex, remarkably high and with several chambers. Some, at Colombarie, show such careful workmanship that they bear comparison with *columbaria* of the Augustan age at Rome.

Sovana also provides some notable if untypical examples of tombs of this style; on the whole, they date from the 1st century A.D. At present many of the *columbaria* cannot be visited because of landslides, but even in antiquity some of them can only have been reached by temporary steps.

Picturesque Sorano

The Islands

The islands of the Tuscan archipelago still show signs of their occupation in ancient times in their names and their archaeological remains. The northernmost island, Gorgona, is the ancient Urgon; it was probably inhabited by the Etruscans, and there was certainly a settlement there in Roman times, as is proved by the ruins of the Pian dei Morti.

Capraia is the Roman Capraria; it was visited by Greeks and Romans, and in the 4th century A.D. became a refuge for religious communities.

Elba was densely populated from prehistoric times and apparently already known to Mycenaean seafarers heading west in search of ores and metals. The Greek name for it was Aithalia ('smoky'), the Latin name being Ilva. Its open-cast iron mines were certainly intensively exploited by the Etruscans, who transported the crude ore to Populonia, on the mainland opposite, where it was processed.

The mineral wealth of Elba was always a great attraction to the various powers of the ancient world; in the 5th century B.C. the Syracusans mounted a naval expedition to seize it. Later the island came under the sway of Rome, and Sextus Pompeius made it a naval base around 40 B.C. On Monte Serra are the ruins of an Etruscan temple dedicated to Tin (Jupiter), and in several places there are visible remains of Roman buildings, including a particularly sumptuous villa.

The coastal waters of the island are littered with traces of ancient seafaring: anchor stocks have been found at Punta Fetovaia and Scoglio della Triglia; at Capo S. Andrea is the wreck of a Roman cargo ship, laden with wine-jars.

On Pianosa (ancient Planasia, so called after its comparatively flat profile) there are traces of Neolithic settlements and Roman occupation; of particular interest are the natural caves which were used as catacombs, because the outcrops of hard rock made it impossible to dig deep tombs in the ground.

The island of Montecristo is possibly the Roman Oglasa. On Giglio there is evidence of prehistoric settlement from the Neolithic period onwards; Etruscan occupation is probable, but no traces remain. The Romans called Giglio Igilium, the island 'of goats' or 'inaccessible to goats', on account of its precipitous cliffs. It was owned by the extremely powerful family of the Domitii Ahenobarbi, who had a villa built near the port, at Bagno del Saraceno, with a fish-pond fed by sea-water. Another Roman villa was built in the

second half of the 1st century A.D. at Punta Castellare, on the hillock overlooking the south of the port: its construction, with diagonal brick facing, is typical of the villas in the area around Cosa. In ancient times Giglio exported wine and granite.

Giannutri, called Dianium by the Romans, has traces of buildings dating from ancient times: at Cala dello Spalmatoio there are remains of the Roman port, consisting of a massive breakwater made of large blocks, *horrea* (warehouses) and cisterns. A magnificent villa was built near Cala Maestra towards the end of the 1st century A.D., and was lived in until about the mid-3rd century. This is a complex of buildings which covers an area of about five hectares, built on terraces stepping down towards the sea; it had a large water-tank which served the needs of the island, consisting of five large, carefully plastered cisterns; there are also storehouse, masters' and servants' quarters, and a bath complex where it is possible to see the *praefurnium* and the *caldarium*, with its floor decorated with dolphins. There was also a landing-place for the owners; the building was embellished with columns of Giglio granite, mosaic and painted decoration, and marble cornices.

At the foot of the cliff on which the ruins of the villa stand is a wreck dating from the 2nd century B.C.: the hull lies on the seabed, with its anchors of lead and iron; it was laden with black-gloss pottery.

Florence, Museo Archeologico

Left: Artemis. Detail of the François Vase. Florence, Museo Archeologico

Below: the boar-hunt of Meleager. Detail of the François Vase. Florence, Museo Archeologico

The original nucleus of the Museo Archeologico in Florence—one of the most important archaeological museums in the world—was the Egyptian collection, to which the Museo Etrusco was added after 1870. This latter comprised the Etruscan material from the Medici and Lorena collections, including such famous works as the François Vase and the bronze statues of the Chimera, the Arringatore and the Athena di Arezzo, which had for a long time been kept in the Galleria degli Uffizi.

In 1880 the two museums were transferred to their present site, occupying the Palazzo della Crocetta and part of the Palazzo degli Innocenti, which are linked by a series of rooms along one side of the garden.

The garden is an integral part of the museum because it houses tombs and funerary monuments from various sites in Etruria, which have been dismantled at the place of excavation and rebuilt in the museum grounds, following the original orientation exactly; only two of the tombs, the Tomba Inghirami from Volterra and the Tomba Golini from Orvieto, are modern reconstructions. The door of the former is the original one and the urns standing on the benches are some of the forty such urns found when the tomb was opened; only one was leaning against the central pillar, and on the floor there were fragments of lids which had fallen off and broken; the tomb clearly belonged to a rich and powerful *gens* (clan), whose name, *Atia*, is known from its recurrence in the inscriptions on the urns.

From Vetulonia there are several conical shields made of local stone, which were placed in the form of coping on tumulus tombs of the Orientalizing period, and various tombs: the Tomba del Diavolino, named after the site where it was found, has an access corridor closed off by a door and a rectangular chamber with corner corbels joining the walls and the false-dome ceiling. Another tomb, dating from the 7th–6th centuries B.C., has a rectangular cella and an architrave, which is a copy of the original, with the inscription *husl hufnithui*. Also from Vetulonia are pit-tombs containing biconical or hut-type cinerary urns, and covered by a stone shield.

Other tombs come from Picenum: one contains the skeleton of a warrior laid out beneath the chariot he used either in battle or on ceremonial occasions, with funerary objects (weapons and bronze and impasto vases) nearby.

In the region of Volterra, at Casale Marittimo to be precise, a circular tomb was found with a central pillar propping up the corbelled ceiling, dating from the 7th–6th centuries B.C.; the floor consists of stone slabs, and the *dromos* still has the original doors. A similar structure, but with the faces of the courses of stones forming the ceiling cut to make two uniform sloping surfaces on the inside, is found in a tomb from the Crocifisso del Tufo cemetery at Orvieto.

Among the many monuments gathered in the museum grounds, a fine example of a Hellenistic tomb is the Tlesnei family tomb, which was found near Chianciano: the rectangular chamber, with a barrel-vault, contains a sarcophagus of the 3rd century B.C.; a niche on the left of the chamber, access to which is along the tomb corridor, contains cinerary urns belonging to the same family; the niche is closed off by a tile bearing the words *thana thlesnei nute*, the name of a deceased woman.

The ground floor of the museum, which housed the topographical section, was seriously damaged, as was the garden, by the floods of 1966; water and mud invaded the rooms and underground basements, reducing everything there to fragments. Thanks to patient

1. The Mater Matuta, Archaic sculpture from Chiusi
2. Urn with drip spouts, from Chiusi, depicting a banqueting scene
3. Bronze statuette depicting a warrior-god (origin unknown)
4. Montescudaio cinerary urn, detail of the lid
5. Globular vase with geometric decoration, from Bisenzio
6. Detail of the so-called Pania casket, from Chiusi. Florence, Museo Archeologico

5

6

rescue work and a long and painstaking programme of restoration, conducted by the most modern methods in the laboratories and workshops of the Soprintendenza, the sculptures, bronzes, pottery and ivories of the Museo Topografico have been totally restored and, in many cases, freed from older restoration work which had partially misrepresented them.

This whole section of the museum is therefore in the process of being reorganized, until such time as the restoration is completed of all the material which comes from southern and north-central Etruria. From Fiesole there are typical trapezoid and drop-shaped stelae and cippi of the 6th–5th centuries B.C. in *pietra serena*; from the region of Florence there are the finds from the tomb at Quinto Fiorentino and from the Villanovan tombs discovered in the centre of Florence. From Arezzo there are red-gloss vases and the corresponding moulds, showing in negative the decoration to be produced in relief on the outer surface of the vase; from Cortona there is the stone funerary couch decorated in low relief with eight female figures, which was found in the Melone di Camucia. From Brolio in the Val di Chiana there is a votive deposit of early bronze figurines in a very archaic style; from Chiusi a series of canopi, the typical ossuaries with lids in the shape of human heads, the Pania casket, a collection of urns made of local stone, and one of funerary objects. From the area around Chiusi there is an alabaster urn with two compartments, dating from the 5th century B.C. and found at Città della Pieve; it is shaped like a couch, with the two deceased sitting on it. The interior box has two compartments for the ashes, and the entire surface shows traces of the original polychrome decoration. Another important example of the Archaic sculpture of Chiusi is the so-called Mater Matuta, a statue-urn depicting a woman holding a child on her lap, sitting on a throne with arms in the shape of crouching sphinxes with spread wings; the head is removable, to enable the ashes to be deposited in the cavity within, and it is not certain whether or not it is the right head. Recent restoration work has revealed that the statue is carved from a single block of stone, and that during the 19th century it was extensively and rather arbitrarily restored and completed with new pieces.

From Perugia, among other things, there is a series of bronzes and the golden crown from the Ipogeo dello Sperandio; from Orvieto there is a warrior's head of *nenfro*, dated to the 5th century B.C. (p. 273).

The Archaic sculpture of Volterra is exemplified by the round-topped stele of Larth Atharnie found at Pomarance, not far from the city, and the stele from Laiatico. Also from the region of Volterra is the famous 7th-century urn from Montescudaio, reminiscent in shape of the Villanovan urns, but decorated with large swastikas in relief; on its lid is a figurine in the round of the deceased, wearing a short-sleeved tunic and sitting at a circular three-legged table laden with cakes, loaves of bread and offerings. Standing beside it is a servant and beyond him a large vase, possibly for mixing wine. Two figurines identical with that of the deceased are on top of the handles, on the body of the vase.

From Valdelsa there are the Barberino and Monteriggioni alabaster urns of the Hellenistic period, including an urn with two compartments, which was protected by a large tile from being damaged by dripping water. Here too are the few objects found in the great tumulus of Castellina in Chianti, which illustrate the typical funerary objects of the Orientalizing period.

The objects discovered in the vast and rich cemetery at Populonia are mostly in the museum at Florence; among the most noteworthy pieces are the remains of two two-horse chariots covered in sheet bronze, with embossed decoration showing figures and animals, and iron inlay work; also an Athenian red-figure pelike depicting the slaying of the Minotaur by Theseus, covered with a bronze patera. It had been used as a cinerary urn, a most unusual occurrence.

The most celebrated finds from Vetulonia are kept here: the funerary objects from the Tomba del Duce and the Tomba del Littore, the stele of Avile Feluske, depicting a warrior armed with a round shield and a double axe, with a long inscription along the edge giving the name of the person depicted. There are also the sculptures from the Pietrera tumulus,

The Arringatore, from Lake Trasimene. Florence, Museo Archeologico

a stone funerary couch and some typical Vetulonian objects: a cylindrical sheet-bronze 'censer', with pierced sides and a removable handle, filigree gold bracelets and gold brooches.

From Roselle there is an Archaic stele of the Volterran type, depicting a warrior brandishing a sword, and other finds unearthed during the excavations undertaken between 1959 and the present day, which supply much evidence of everyday life in this city where life continued from the 7th century B.C. until the early Middle Ages.

From Talamone there is the impressive collection of decorative architectural terracottas from the Hellenistic temple and the votive offerings, which consist in the main of miniature weapons and agricultural implements.

Another magnificent collection of architectural terracottas is the one from the pediments at Luni, known as the Capitoline triad (Jupiter, Juno and Minerva) and Apollo and the children of Niobe; together with the preceding, these represent one of the most important collections for the study and appreciation of Hellenistic modelling in Italy.

The funerary objects from Marsiliana d'Albegna include some pieces of particular interest: the gold Corsini fibula (p. 131) with moulded and granulated decoration, and the ivories from the Circolo degli Avori and the Circolo della Fibula. Among other things this latter has produced a female figure with one hand on her left breast and the other holding a small ritual vessel; she is wearing a mantle of which traces survive in a thin sheet of gold from her head down her back; it did not hide her hair, which was gathered into a single tress.

From Magliano there is the famous disc (p. 129) inscribed in Etruscan on both sides; from Saturnia a series of Greek and Etruscan vases, and various typical biconical urns, whose lids show a tendency to humanize the urn that is characteristic of this part of central Etruria, as well as of the region around Chiusi.

The funerary objects from Poggio Buco and Pitigliano, the architectural terracottas and the votive offerings from Sovana demonstrate the material culture of the towns around the valley of the Fiora.

The funerary sculpture of Vulci is represented by the famous lion in *nenfro*, dating from the 5th century B.C., and the moulded decoration of a pediment with the antefixes and the slab in relief which covered the head of the *columen* (ridge-beam), dated to the 3rd century B.C. From Tuscania there are several typical terracotta and *nenfro* sarcophagi, with the figure of the deceased lying on the lid; from Tarquinia there are the characteristic Villanovan biconical urns covered by a bronze helmet, a hut-urn, and a pediment painted with a representation of a couple feasting.

The material culture of Cerveteri is represented by several urns and Archaic bronzes, that of Veii by a series of four-handled amphorae and thin-walled buccheri; from the Faliscan territory are personal ornaments, impasto mortars on tall pierced clay stands, and red-figured Athenian and locally made pottery.

The first floor of the museum houses a rich collection of small Hellenistic urns, coming mainly from Chiusi and Volterra, and sarcophagi; among these is a remarkable piece decorated with scenes of battle between Greeks and Amazons, elegantly and masterfully painted on the smooth sides of the chest. Among the numerous Greek and Roman bronzes the Idolino stands out: this is a nude youth in the act of pouring a libation before an altar, dated by some to the 5th, by others to the 1st century B.C. The Etruscan bronzes include several quite exceptional pieces, such as the Chimera (p. 43) and the Athena di Arezzo (p. 23), and an orator in a toga with his right hand stretched out towards his audience, known as the Arringatore del Trasimeno; this piece has an inscription carved along the hem of the toga with the name Aule Meteli, son of Vel and Vesi. Apart from these, there is a striking series of small votive bronzes, facing plaques with embossed decorations, and mirrors decorated with mythological scenes engraved with every type of tool.

The top floor of the building houses the prehistoric collection, illustrative of the pre- and protohistoric cultures of Tuscany, and a very fine collection of pottery. This includes Athenian black- and red-figure vases, with some exceptional pieces such as the François

Above: terracotta sarcophagus, from Tuscania

Left: lid-handle of a bronze casket. Florence, Museo Archeologico

Opposite:
1. Detail of the Sarcofago delle Amazzoni, from Tarquinia
2. Mirror depicting Hercules being suckled by Juno, from Volterra
3. Small ivory tablet with archaic alphabet, from Marsiliana d'Albegna.
Florence, Museo Archeologico

Vase from Chiusi. This is signed by Kleitias and Ergotimos and decorated with mythological scenes and various designs in six horizontal bands. In addition there are pieces of thin-walled and heavy bucchero ware, with engraved or relief decoration; Italiote red-figure vases; black- and red-figure Etruscan pottery; vases of the type known as Volsinian, decorated in relief with mythological figures or scenes, and covered with fine silver plating in imitation of the precious-metal ware with embossed decoration: black-gloss vases in various shapes and sizes, sometimes likewise decorated in relief in imitation of metal ware; Arretine vases; and 'thin-walled' pottery from the Roman period.

It is also possible to admire the paintings of the Tombe Golini, which were detached from two tombs at Orvieto in the interests of preserving them, and re-assembled here on supports that reproduce the exact structures of the tombs; they both date from the 4th century B.C. and depict banqueting scenes.

Finally, a noteworthy section of the Florentine museum is the Egyptian collection, which consists largely of the objects excavated by a Tuscan expedition headed by Ippolito Rosellini in Egypt in 1828–29, and the collection of Grand Duke Leopold II. It includes sculptures and bas-reliefs from various dynasties; a mummy from the 4th century B.C.; a portrait in tempera on wood, depicting a young woman, of the type which was placed above the face of the mummified deceased and wrapped up in the bandages. Then there are the alabaster Canopic vases, used to contain the internal organs of the dead which were removed before commencing the mummification process; fragments of papyri from various periods; bronze statuettes of deities; amulets and scarabs. One particular exhibit is the war chariot, dated to c. 1500 B.C., made of various kinds of wood, including acacia, willow, elm and oak, and originally covered with birch bark. Drawn by two horses, the chariot carried two people, the charioteer and the warrior, and was introduced into Egypt by invading peoples.

Polychrome terracotta urn, from the Chiusi area.
Florence, Museo Archeologico

Southern Etpuria

The name Cerveteri comes from *Caere Vetus* ('ancient Caere'). Called, probably, Chaire or Cheri in Etruscan, Caere in Latin and Agylla in Greek, the town is situated about 45 kilometres from Rome and about six kilometres from the sea. It stands on a tufa plateau, a southern spur of the volcanic Monti della Tolfa, which is bounded by the narrow Manganello valley to the northwest and the broader Mola valley to the southeast. These two watercourses meet south of the city to form the Vaccina (the *Caeritis amnis* mentioned by Virgil) which crosses the coastal plain and flows into the sea north of Ladispoli. On three sides Cerveteri had natural defences in the deep tufa ravines resulting from erosion by streams. At its northeastern tip, however, the plateau was linked to the surrounding hills by a tongue of land; this was cut, for strategic purposes, by a large trench. Where the natural defences were weakest, stretches of wall were built of large regular stone blocks to render access impossible.

The exact extent of the territory of Cerveteri is not known; its boundaries varied over a period of time. However, it certainly bordered on Tarquinia to the north and Veii to the south; it must have extended inland to the western shores of Lake Bracciano. Sea trade was carried on through the ports of Pyrgi (modern Santa Severa), Alsium (Palo, near Ladispoli) and Punicum (Santa Marinella).

From the Etruscan period, a complex road system provided communications with neighbouring towns. The roads were unpaved and often had picturesque rock-cut stretches running between high tufa walls. A monumental way led from Cerveteri to the port of Pyrgi. In Roman times these routes generally remained in use and were paved over; in

Left: Cerveteri. Aerial photograph of the Banditaccia cemetery

Below: plan of the archaeological zone

Right: plan of the Banditaccia cemetery

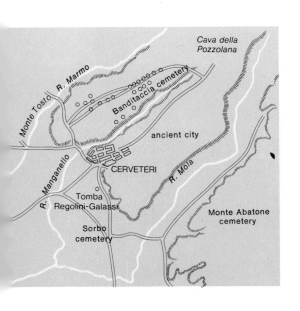

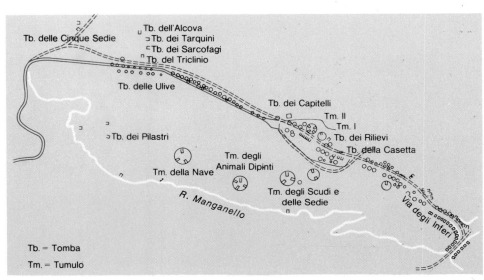

addition, the Via Clodia, inland, and the Via Aurelia, along the coast, crossed the territory of Cerveteri.

The earliest signs of urban settlement at Cerveteri date from the Villanovan period (Iron Age; 9th–8th centuries B.C.). The chief cemeteries from that time are situated to the north and south, some distance away from the inhabited area. The southern and oldest burial-ground, called Il Sorbo, extends over a rolling plateau which slopes down towards the sea. The northern burial-ground is at Cava della Pozzolana, beyond the trench which marked the city's northern boundary; it formed the nucleus of the Banditaccia cemetery, which developed during the classical age. The Villanovan tombs, cut into the soft tufa and not monumental in character, consist of both pit-tombs (for cremations) and trench-tombs (for inhumations).

The pit-tombs are of two types:
(a) simple: these consist of an almost cylindrical pit dug into the ground containing a tufa holder with lid, which in turn contains the urn with the ashes of the deceased and the burial goods;
(b) double: here a wide upper pit is filled with pebbles and stone chips, while a narrower lower pit, its opening covered with a slab, contains the cinerary urn.

For inhumation a more or less rectangular trench was dug and the body laid in it, on its back, with its ornaments and other objects. Round the body, along the sides of the trench, a narrow ledge was cut, or built up with stones, and wooden boards or tufa slabs were laid on it. These covered the body and prevented it being crushed by the stones and rubble which were used to fill the upper part of the trench.

A characteristic feature of the Sorbo cemetery was the use of a thick layer of quicklime to cover the body, probably as a hygienic measure.

The tomb furnishings of the Villanovan burial-grounds at Cerveteri are fairly poor, especially when compared with the riches of neighbouring Tarquinia. There are a few

terracotta vases and a number of objects proper to each sex: for men, razors and weapons; for women, jewels, spindle whorls (these must have been attached to wooden spindles which have not survived) and spools, used in the women's tasks of spinning and weaving.

After the Villanovan period, from the 7th century B.C., the cemeteries were transferred to the two plateaux lying parallel to the town: Banditaccia to the northwest, between the Manganello and the Marmo, and Monte Abatone to the southeast, on the left bank of the Mola. The older cemeteries were not of course suddenly abandoned: the Sorbo cemetery does in fact also contain tombs of the Orientalizing period. But the Iron Age trench- and pit-tombs give place to the first chamber-tombs, covered by a small protective earth mound and surrounded by a circle of tufa slabs. The oldest tombs of this type are rectangular; the walls are built of rows of large stone slabs which gradually close in towards the top to form an ogival false vault. In other instances (for example the Tomba Regolini-

Galassi), the chambers are semi-subterranean, that is to say partly cut into the tufa, partly built up like the type described above.

Much of the interest which the Cerveteri cemeteries have for both archaeologists and tourists lies in the fact that as the chamber-tombs gradually developed over the centuries they reflected to a large extent changes in houses over the same period. The first small, simple chambers with their ogival false vaults resemble the huts of Villanovan villages, roofed with branches and straw, while the richer tombs with two rooms on the same alignment (for example the Tomba Regolini-Galassi or the Tomba della Capanna) probably reflect extended versions of the primitive dwellings.

In the Orientalizing period (7th century) Cerveteri reached a high economic and cultural level, perhaps because of possessing the mines of the Monti della Tolfa. At this time its sea trade and naval power were at their height, and this is apparent in the sudden improvement in the quality of burial goods, from the rustic objects of the preceding Villanovan phase to the valuable objects, skilfully worked in precious metals, found in the 7th-century tombs. The city exported raw materials and imported sophisticated manufactured goods which adorned first the houses of local nobles, then their tombs.

The sumptuous furnishings of the Tomba Regolini-Galassi, now in the Museo Gregoriano, are a supreme example of the Caeretan aristocracy's high standard of living at the time; in addition to the quantities of precious gold, ivory and silver objects imported from the East, there were many imitations made locally in the workshops of Etruscan or immigrant craftsmen who gave the original models characteristic local features.

The prosperity of Cerveteri at this period attracted many foreign artists; these included the Greek vase-maker Aristonothos, who moulded, painted and signed a very fine krater, decorated on one side with the blinding of the giant Polyphemus, and on the other with a battle between Greek and Etruscan ships.

The city's power, so flourishing during the Orientalizing period, continued into the 6th and 5th centuries. Its leading position in the Etruscan confederation during this period is confirmed by historical accounts (Herodotus) and also by valuable archaeological finds, such as the inscribed gold plaques found at Pyrgi. Cerveteri was the only Etruscan city to build its own treasury (a small building to house its offerings to the god) in the sanctuary of Apollo at Delphi. The city's thriving economy also allowed it to send its own fleet to defend Etruscan domination of the Tyrrhenian Sea; about 540 B.C. it joined forces with the Carthaginians against the Greeks from Phocaea in Ionia, forcing them to abandon Corsica. Historians also relate that the Caeretans had to atone for their indiscriminate killing of Greek prisoners after this naval battle: in obedience to the Delphic

Cerveteri. Tumulus in the Banditaccia cemetery

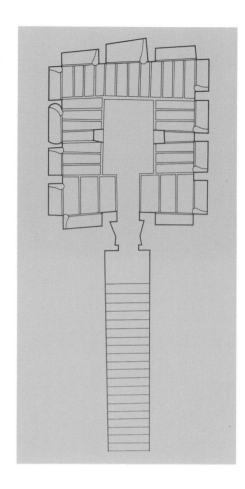

Above: plan of the Tomba dei Rilievi

Below: section and plan of the vast Tumulus II, with the Tomba della Capanna (1) and the Tomba dei Vasi Greci (2)

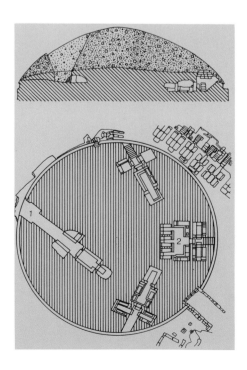

oracle, they consecrated a sanctuary to the shades of their slain enemies. It has been suggested that the site of this sanctuary may have been a sacred area discovered at Montetosto, beside the road from Cerveteri to Pyrgi.

Although Cerveteri fought to defend its economic interests against the Greeks, it was precisely in the second half of the 6th century that its cultural links with the Hellenic world were strongest, and Ionian influence was clearly apparent in figurative art. One has only to think of the painted terracotta plaques in the British Museum, the Louvre and the local museum at Cerveteri, the architectural terracottas, and the terracotta sarcophagi, including particularly the famous Sarcofago degli Sposi and the Sarcofago dei Leoni, now in the Museo di Villa Giulia. These works all exemplify the taste for soft, rounded figures and flowing lines which was prevalent in contemporary Greek art. The close links between the Hellenic world and Cerveteri are shown not only by the large amount of imported pottery, but also by a series of vases, known as the Caeretan hydriae (water pitchers), which were probably made in a workshop founded by an artist who came to Cerveteri from Ionia.

The Banditaccia and Monte Abatone cemeteries faithfully reflect the city's high level of prosperity and well-being in the 6th and 5th centuries, as described by ancient historians. During that period the tumuli, which had been of modest dimensions during the Orientalizing period, became impressive in size, with an outer ring of rock in a variety of forms. The tumuli contain groups of chamber-tombs dug deep into the tufa and becoming increasingly complicated in design, in imitation of contemporary domestic buildings.

The most usual layout consisted of an entrance vestibule with two little rooms leading off it to the sides and the main tomb at the end: this was a single rectangular room with a roof imitating a coffered ceiling or one with sloping beams; farther in, three cellae contained carved copies of household furniture (as for example in the Tomba dei Vasi Greci or the Tomba degli Scudi e delle Sedie). Dwellings built on a similar plan have been discovered at Acquarossa, an Etruscan site in the Viterbo area, confirming that tombs of this type were built in imitation of ordinary houses.

From the mid-6th century the so-called cube-tombs begin to appear alongside the round tumuli. These had rectangular constructions imitating house exteriors; below them were the chamber-tombs, with a vestibule which was sometimes reached through an opening in the ceiling, closed with a slab (the so-called trap-door tombs). It is significant that with the appearance of cube-tombs attempts were made to impose some kind of planned layout on the cemeteries. Previously the tumuli had been scattered at random over the plateau, but from the 6th century onwards the tombs were arranged according to a kind of 'town plan', with varying degrees of success. Funerary ways were laid out, crossing each other at right angles and sometimes opening out into squares cut into the tufa; cube-tombs fitted well into these rectilinear schemes.

Characteristic of Cerveteri, throughout this long and complex evolution of its chamber-tombs, was the custom of laying the dead on couches cut into the rock and shaped according to sex: the couches for men had legs worked in relief, while for women they were in the form of a chest or sarcophagus with a gabled head. All have a kind of pillow or sloping support, with a semicircular section cut out for the head.

The chamber-tombs so far described must have belonged to the aristocratic families of Cerveteri, but from the Archaic period a poorer type of tomb is also found. Scattered around the tumuli there were often sarcophagi consisting either of a stone chest with a cover, or of large slabs placed one on top of the other, with the bottom one hollowed out. Stone cippi shaped like small columns (for men) or little houses (for women) were placed on the cover of these sarcophagi or fixed with lime mortar in niches made for the purpose in tufa slabs lining the funerary way, near the tomb entrances.

Despite our detailed knowledge of the cemeteries, little is known about the area of the city itself, now partly built over by the modern town. However, archaeologists have identified no less than seven sacred areas, and partially excavated two of them, showing that the city of the living was just as rich and splendid as the city of the dead. The many fragments of Archaic and classical architectural terracottas which formed a protective facing for the wooden structures of sacred buildings further confirm the size and importance of the temples of Cerveteri.

Cerveteri was involved in the political and economic crisis which affected the whole of coastal Etruria during the 5th and 4th centuries B.C. The rapid decline of its naval power made it possible for Dionysios of Syracuse to sack the sanctuary at Pyrgi in 384 B.C. Relations with Rome, however, remained friendly on the whole, although in 353 B.C. the Caeretans endangered the alliance by aiding neighbouring Tarquinia in its struggle against the Romans. But finally a rebellion in 273 B.C. resulted in the Etruscan city's acquiring Roman citizenship without the right to vote and in the confiscation of its coastal strip, where the *coloniae* of Castrum Novum, Pyrgi, Alsium and Fregenae were subsequently founded.

Later in the 3rd century the economy of Cerveteri, and all Etruscan cities, received a blow during the Punic Wars on account of the contributions of both men and supplies that had to be made to Rome.

The changes in the city's condition are reflected in the cemeteries. From the late 5th–4th centuries B.C. the imposing tumuli of earlier days disappear. Instead there are simple rock-cut tombs, generally consisting of a single large room, its roof supported by pillars; one or two benches run right round the walls, designed to take a large number of burials. The tombs now served not a single family but a whole clan, and remained in use for a long time (Tomba dei Rilievi, Tomba dell'Alcova, and so on). The dead were not accompanied by rich burial objects as before, but by poor, roughly-made local pottery and a few valuable imported objects.

Alongside these, the poorer tombs still continued to be dug. In the Hellenistic period these consisted of the so-called *cappuccina*-tombs, with tiles arranged to form a small roof protecting the body in its trench, and of rectangular niches (*loculi*) cut into the rock faces along the funerary ways.

Although life at Cerveteri gradually declined, it never came to an abrupt stop, which would have been indicated by an absence of tombs from certain periods. As it is, the unbroken chronological succession of the tombs reflects the continuity of the town's normal life.

Excavations in the mid-19th century revealed the theatre of Roman Cerveteri; although there is practically nothing of it left, many noteworthy marble statues from the Imperial age were found there and are now in the Lateran museum.

The depopulation of the city which began in the Hellenistic period increased during the Imperial age, until finally the area was abandoned by its inhabitants, who were driven by the fear of malaria and Saracen raids to nearby Ceri.

Sorbo cemetery

Tomba Regolini-Galassi. The well-preserved state of this tomb (named after its discoverers) is explained by the fact that the original tumulus was later, at the end of the 7th century, enclosed in a larger tumulus (48 metres in diameter) to make it possible to dig new burial chambers. The older tomb thus escaped the depredations of tomb robbers and survived intact. The semi-subterranean tomb, reached through a small entrance with steps, consists of two long rooms on the same alignment. Almost at the end of the first, two small circular rooms open off, completely rock-cut. The tomb contained three burials: a cremation in the right-hand circular room and an inhumation in each of the main chambers. The tomb's burial goods, some of the richest ever found from the Orientalizing period, are now in the Museo Gregoriano.

In an area which the Comune intended to use for school buildings, a burial-ground has been uncovered. It consists of cube-tombs lining a funerary way and a most impressive elliptical tumulus which has been partially destroyed by the building of modern villas.

Cerveteri. Interior of the Tomba Regolini-Galassi

Below: plan of the Tomba Regolini-Galassi

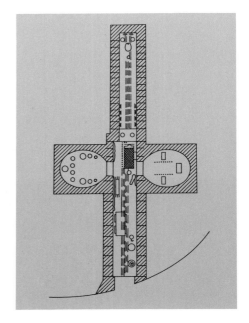

The monument has an outer ring built of squared tufa blocks, with mouldings; a section of this about 79 metres long has been discovered. The tumulus contained two tombs, one dating from the 6th and one from the 7th century; the latter may originally have had its own tumulus which was subsequently swallowed up, like the Tomba Regolini-Galassi, by the larger one which now survives.

1. Cerveteri, Tomba Regolini-Galassi: bucchero calyx. Rome, Musei Vaticani
2. Ampulla with figure, from the Sorbo cemetery
3. Tomba dell'Alcova, Banditaccia cemetery
4. Section of simple pit-tomb
5. Section of double pit-tomb

Banditaccia cemetery
On the way to the Banditaccia cemetery, following the motor road which starts below Cerveteri, the first tombs are outside the enclosed zone. Obviously only a very few of the cemetery's hundreds of tombs can be described here.

Tomba dell'Alcova ('Tomb of the Alcove'). This is an example of the funerary architecture of the 4th century B.C., like the Tomba dei Pilastri, the Tomba dei Tarquini or delle Iscrizioni and the Tomba dei Rilievi. The lower part of the façade is cut into the tufa, the upper part built of blocks. The interior consists of a single enormous room divided into three aisles by two large rectangular fluted pillars. The ceiling, flat in the side aisles and gabled in the central section, has three large main beams in relief running lengthwise and small transverse beams. A rectangular space extends beyond the end wall, reached by a short flight of steps; it contains a monumental double couch with a footstool, obviously intended for the couple for whom the tomb was made. Against the side walls are wide benches, each with many niches for other members of the family.

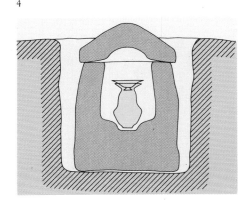

Tumulo della Nave. This tumulus is cut into by corridors which lead to five groups of burial chambers. The main group consists of three tombs, two leading off the sides and

3

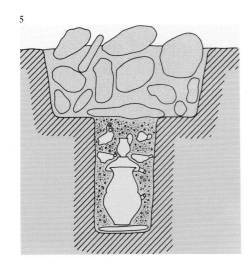

5

one at the end of the corridor. The right-hand tomb gives the tumulus its name ('Tumulus of the Ship'), since the end wall of the second of its two rooms bears traces of a roughly-painted sailing ship, its mast tilted.

The tomb to the left of the corridor is reached through a fine arched doorway decorated with cordons in relief. It consists of a single chamber with a funeral couch against the end wall and two steps along each side wall; the roof forms a tent-like canopy with prominent joists. A man's body was found on the couch, and the remains of his wife were in a wooden sarcophagus on the floor. The main tomb, which opens out at the end of the corridor, has a doorway decorated with cordons in relief and consists of an elliptical vestibule and a large chamber divided into three parts by two pairs of square pillars.

Tumulo degli Animali Dipinti. This contains four groups of chambers. The tomb which gives the tumulus its name ('Tumulus of the Painted Animals') consists of an elliptical vestibule with traces of paintings of animals, and two rooms, one leading into the other. The first contains two couches for a married couple. The woman's couch, in the form of a sarcophagus, has a lion in Orientalizing style painted on the head.

Tumulo degli Scude e delle Sedie. Around the outside of this tumulus is a plinth of smooth tufa with a triple moulding at the top; on one side there is a rectangular altar, linked to the plinth by a little bridge. The tumulus contains two famous chamber-tombs.

(1) Tomba dei Leoni Dipinti. This tomb is reached by a corridor with steps leading down; four chambers open off it (two at the sides and two on the axis of the corridor), connected to each other by passages set at an angle.

The side rooms contain a bench set against the end wall, and two couches along the side walls. The right-hand chamber has two large fluted cylinders cut in tufa, perhaps in imitation of baskets, resting on the bench at the back. Two lions in Orientalizing style (hence the name 'Tomb of the Painted Lions'), which have now almost totally disappeared, are painted on the right-hand wall; on the end wall is a painted group of two lions facing each other, with a warrior in the middle. In the left-hand chamber are traces of similar paintings. The central section of the tomb, aligned with the corridor, consists of two rooms. The first is divided into two by a pair of pillars and has a bench with a gap in the middle of the side walls, leaving a space for two couches. The second of these chambers follows on from the other; it has a gabled roof, a bench running along the end wall and two couches along the sides. The tomb dates from about 620 B.C.

(2) **Tomba degli Scudi e delle Sedie** ('Tomb of the Shields and Seats'). This is a clear and significant example of an imitation of an Etruscan house of the 6th or 5th century B.C. A corridor leads to the main part of the tomb: a large rectangular room which has a flat roof decorated with nine wide beams and three doorways opening in the back wall. There are carved funeral couches all round the chamber and large round shields sculpted on the walls. Between the doorways in the back wall are two seats with wide curved backs and small foot-rests. The doorways lead into three rooms with gabled roofs, couches for men and women against the side walls and a bench along the end wall. The rooms on the right and left are lit by two little windows as well as by the doorways. In addition to the main chamber, there is a small chamber on either side of the corridor, again with a gabled roof, couches and benches against the walls and small windows which connect with the main chamber. The chamber on the left contains six large shields in relief.

Opposite: Cerveteri. Tumulo della Nave, Banditaccia cemetery

Below: Tumulo degli Scudi e delle Sedie, Banditaccia cemetery

Following pages: interior of the Tomba dei Capitelli, Banditaccia cemetery

The monumental area of the cemetery is in an enclosure. Inside, one of the first tombs of interest is the

Tomba dei Capitelli ('Tomb of the Capitals'). This is covered by a small tumulus. There are three doorways at the end of a short corridor; the side doorways lead to two little chambers with a simple bench, the central one to the tomb itself. This is a room at right angles to the corridor, with a coffered ceiling supported on two octagonal pillars with voluted capitals of the Aeolic type; there are three small chambers at the back, lit by little windows. The atrium and the three small chambers contain funeral couches. The tomb dates from the beginning of the 6th century B.C.

Next come two large tumuli numbered I and II, with a circle of worked tufa and a large rectangular altar. Tumulus II contains two very interesting tombs.

(1) Tomba della Capanna. Dating from the first half of the 7th century B.C., this (the 'Tomb of the Hut') is an imitation of a primitive dwelling, the type of straw-roofed hut which preceded houses with tiled roofs. The tomb, which is reached by a long, wide corridor with two large irregular niches cut in its walls, consists of a chamber with a bench running round it and a smaller, lower second room, on the same axis as the first. The roofs of both chambers are steeply pitched and concave, supported by a slender cylindrical central beam.

(2) Tomba dei Vasi Greci ('Tomb of the Greek Vases'). This is similar in layout to the Tomba degli Scudi e delle Sedie and dates from the middle of the 6th century B.C. It is reached along a corridor with a short flight of steps; at the end is the doorway leading to the main part of the tomb, a large rectangular chamber with three smaller rooms at the back. All the chambers have gabled ceilings sloping down from a central beam, which runs lengthwise in the main chamber. Opening off the sides of the corridor are two more small chambers. All the rooms contain funeral couches.

Tomba dei Rilievi. This (the 'Tomb of the Reliefs') is typical of the later style of funerary architecture at Cerveteri, from the 4th century B.C. A long flight of steps leads down to the tomb, which is a single rectangular chamber with a gabled roof sloping down from an enormous central beam and supported by two pillars. Along all the walls are burial niches, and a wide bench runs the whole way round, divided by cordons in relief into thirty-two compartments, each of which contained a burial. Walls and pillars are decorated with painted stucco reliefs depicting household objects and furniture, weapons, and objects used for hunting and for games; this realistic portrayal of objects cherished by the deceased tells us a great deal about Etruscan private life. The main niche, in the middle of the end wall, has two places, for the *pater* and *mater familias*, whose likenesses were modelled on the pillars at the sides. The couch is reproduced in exact detail, with legs, pillows, stool and slippers. On the front of it are Typhon and Cerberus, to recall the underworld. The objects depicted on the two large pillars which support the roof throw an interesting light on Etruscan customs. The many painted inscriptions inside the tomb show that it belonged to the Matuna family.

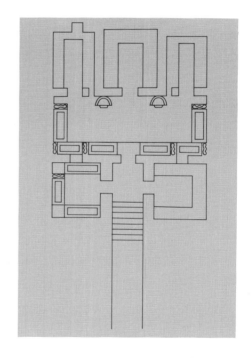

Cerveteri. Plan of the Tomba degli Scudi e delle Sedie, Banditaccia cemetery

Farther on, still inside the enclosure, is the area of the cemetery where the rows of cube-tombs are to be found. It is at present closed to tourists.

Outside the enclosure, to the right before reaching the Via degli Inferi, a burial area on a low tufa hill on the edge of the plateau has recently been excavated by the Fondazione Lerici. The many tombs cut into the tufa make this a picturesque spot. Trenches are visible on the surface, while steep little stairways lead down to rectangular chambers of the usual Caeretan type, with couches for men and women. On the edge of the plateau,

Cerveteri. Detail of the Tomba dei Rilievi

above the green Manganello valley, one can easily identify several tumuli with well-preserved outer rings, cut into the tufa or built of blocks. Beyond the valley the plateau on which the ancient city stood can be clearly seen.

Via degli Inferi. This is the name given to the last stretch of the long funerary way which runs along the Banditaccia hill and then, turning right, descends towards the Manganello valley. The roadway is cut into the tufa, with high walls on each side in which are many entrances to chamber-tombs, consisting of one or two rooms with benches, usually comparatively late in date.

Monte Abatone cemetery

Tomba Campana. This consists of a chamber divided into two by fluted pilasters: in the first part the ceiling has small beams radiating from a disc. To the left of the entrance there is a low fluted column, and to the right a relief imitating a kind of wooden throne with two seats; the rectangular back-rest is decorated in the upper corners with two horn-shaped appendages, and two stars are carved in the flat panel of the seat. In the second part of the tomb there are some remains of the funeral couches. The tomb dates from the 7th century B.C.

Tomba Torlonia. This tomb (4th century B.C.) is complex in layout, being built on two levels. The upper level finishes in a rock-cut façade, while the lower part, reached by a steeply sloping passage, has a little room for a married couple cut into the end wall and three cellae along each side.

Museum. Inside the Castello belonging to the Ruspoli family, in the centre of the modern town, a small museum has recently been opened; it consists of two long rooms on two floors.

On the lower floor, visitors should go round anticlockwise. Funerary deposits discovered in the many cemeteries of Cerveteri from the Iron Age to the 6th century B.C. are on show, arranged in chronological order. From tombs of the Villanovan period come two tufa holders, in the centre of the room, one open to show the burial goods, which are arranged as when they were first found.

On the upper floor, in the show cases along the right-hand wall, burial goods from the 6th to the 3rd and 2nd centuries B.C. are displayed, showing how over the years the vases gradually became rougher and less artistically accomplished. There is an interesting terracotta cover, perhaps for a sarcophagus, depicting a reclining boy and dating from the early 5th century B.C. Against the wall at the end there are small funerary cippi for men and women. In the showcases along the left-hand wall are a small selection of terracotta votive objects (heads, feet and so on) which were dedicated to deities in the sacred buildings, and also many fragments of the architectural terracottas which must have covered the wooden structures of the temples; particularly striking is the series of fragments of acroteria depicting mounted Amazons, and some fine antefixes in the form of male and female heads, all dating from the 6th century B.C. Next come some rectangular slabs of painted terracotta whose function is still not clear; a slab depicting an armed warrior is particularly well preserved. The last cases display a range of Athenian black- and red-figure vases from various sources.

In the middle of the room are three sarcophagi of alabastrine limestone from the Tomba dei Sarcofagi.

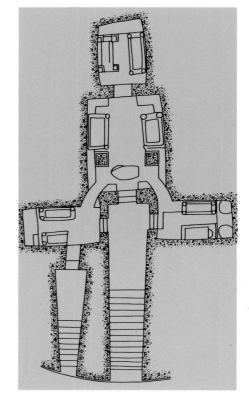

Above: Cerveteri. Plan of the Tomba dei Leoni Dipinti

Below: plan of the Tumulo della Nave

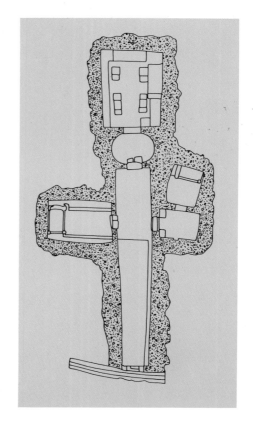

Pyrgi

The most famous of the three ports of ancient Caere, Pyrgi, was situated near the present Castello di Santa Severa, which once belonged to the Anguillara and Orsini families. The port's Etruscan name is not known, since historians have recorded only its Greek name, Pyrgoi ('the towers'). It was linked to Cerveteri by a wide road about 13 kilometres long, flanked by large tumuli of the Orientalizing period. The houses of unfired brick which made up the Etruscan settlement stood beside a small bay sheltered to the northwest by the promontory on which the Castello now stands. Part of the inhabited area has certainly been washed away by the sea; there are many tufa blocks lying on the seabed.

The history of the port naturally reflects that of nearby Cerveteri. Pyrgi flourished, in particular, from the 7th to the 5th century B.C., when Cerveteri was a dominant commercial and military power at sea. We know this not only from the rich archaeological discoveries but also from references in ancient historians to a sanctuary at Pyrgi, dedicated to a goddess whom the Greeks called Leucothea or Eileithyia, and famous all over the Mediterranean; this sanctuary has been identified with a sacred area containing two temples about 400 metres south of the Castello. Following the political and economic decline of Cerveteri, Pyrgi suffered a raid in 384 B.C. by the fleet of Dionysios I of Syracuse, who carried off the enormous sum of 1,000 talents from the goddess's treasury. After Rome annexed the coastal territory of Cerveteri in the early 3rd century B.C., a coastal *colonia* was founded on the site of the port, though it covered only part of the earlier Etruscan settlement. This was finally supplanted in the 2nd century A.D. by the nearby port of Centumcellae (modern Civitavecchia).

Pyrgi. Aerial view, showing, below, the temples and, at the top, the Roman city and mediaeval Castello

The sanctuary at Pyrgi, identified as the one described by the ancient historians, has been systematically excavated from 1957 onwards. It consists of an open space containing two temples (A and B), built parallel to one another, facing the sea, with a small sacred area (C) between them. The boundaries of the open space have not yet been excavated, except in the area behind temple A; here a section of the enclosure wall has been discovered, with an entrance gate which marked the end of the monumental way linking Cerveteri to the port. The outside walls of the two temples must have been built of tufa blocks, and the internal dividing walls of unfired clay brick, but the imposing foundations of huge squared blocks are all that remain.

Temple A (about 460 B.C.) followed the plan typical of Etruscan sacred buildings, with three parallel cellae at the back and a portico in front, enclosed between the extensions of the side walls. Temple B, however, which is older than temple A, dating from the end of the 6th century B.C., follows the Greek pattern, having a single long cella with columns all round it. Between the two temples is a small rectangular sacred area (C), paved in part with tufa blocks and containing a cylindrical altar and a sacrificial well in which the remains of an ox, a piglet, a badger and a cock were found. Although little remains of the temple buildings, many fragments of architectural terracottas have come to light; these adorned the wooden roof-beams of the two buildings. Among these is the famous mythological relief which, together with the gold plaques, is the most important discovery to date at Pyrgi and is now in the Museo di Villa Giulia. The relief must have covered the end of the main roof-beam of temple A, in line with the rear façade. It consists of two slabs with

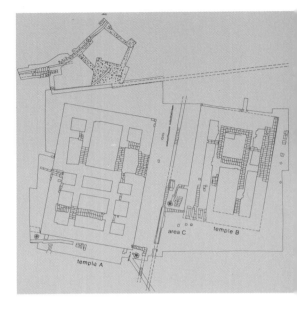

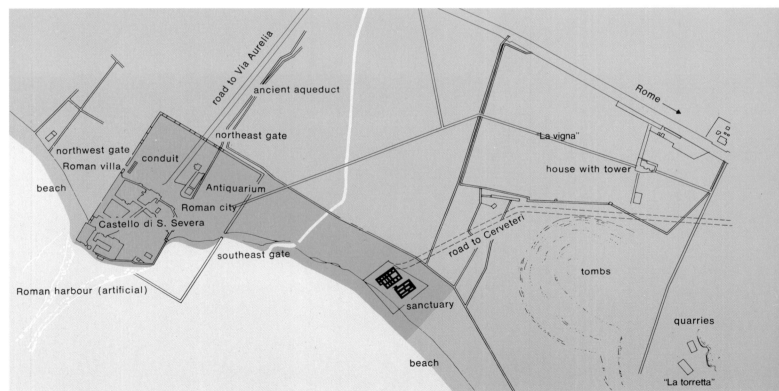

Top: Pyrgi. Plan of the sanctuary

Above: plan of the archaeological zone

a protruding cornice at the bottom to support the figures; these slabs were fixed to the wood with bronze nails. The figures which fill the scene are three-quarters life-size and modelled by hand without the use of moulds or dies (in some places fingermarks are visible). The colours are well preserved.

The episode depicted is taken from a well-known Greek legend. Eteocles and Polynices, the sons of Oedipus, quarrelled over the throne of Thebes after their father's death. Polynices fled and an expedition was organized on his behalf, known as the Seven Against Thebes; its members were Adrastus, Amphiaraüs, Capaneus, Hippomedon, Parthenopaeus, Tydeus and Polynices himself. The attempt ended disastrously with the death of all but Adrastus. The relief shows a point in the battle. At the bottom Tydeus is biting the Theban Melanippus at the back of the neck; this provokes the wrath of Athene (standing on the left), who was about to make him immortal with a miraculous potion contained in the small vessel which she bears in her hand. Beside Athene is Zeus, who is striking Capaneus with lightning; the latter's face is convulsed with pain and rage. The armed warrior between the two combatants is perhaps a Theban. Although subject and style are clearly Greek in inspiration, the artist, who must have been of local origin, indubitably gave the work a personal quality which makes it one of the most important Etruscan sculptures from the first half of the 5th century B.C.

The most sensational discovery, however, which has made Pyrgi famous even beyond the world of archaeology, was the three inscribed gold plaques. These were found between the two temples in a small rectangular enclosure made expressly to guard and preserve these

Pyrgi. Relief depicting Zeus, Athene and figures from the Theban legend

valuable and sacred objects when temple B was dismantled. The plaques are three thin
rectangular sheets of gold, found carefully rolled up, with inscriptions, two Etruscan and
one Phoenician, incised on them. The holes around the edges and the small bronze nails
with gold heads found in the same spot show that they were fixed originally to a wall or a
wooden temple door. What makes them so important is that they are the first contemporary
written Etruscan historical document to be found. The plaques confirm the international
reputation of the sanctuary at Pyrgi and provide additional proof that the buildings
excavated are those mentioned by historians. The two Etruscan inscriptions are sixteen
and nine lines long, the Phoenician one eleven lines. They state that Thefarie Velianas,
described as king (or tyrant) of Cerveteri, dedicates a sacred place to the Phoenician goddess
Astarte (identified with the Etruscan Uni); this may have been temple B, according to
some scholars, or a shrine nearby, according to others. The long Etruscan inscription and
the Phoenician one have the same general meaning, although one is not a literal translation
of the other.

The plaques, dating from the end of the 6th or beginning of the 5th century B.C., raise
a whole range of problems. First, there is the description of the dedicator, who in Phoenician
is designated king of Cerveteri, but in Etruscan is given a title commonly used by republican
magistrates.

The texts indicate clearly that there were friendly relations between Carthaginians and
Etruscans, since the highest authority at Cerveteri felt it necessary to dedicate an important shrine to the foreign goddess. Moreover, the name of the nearby city of Punicum
(modern Santa Marinella) suggests that there was a Phoenician trading colony very near
to Pyrgi itself. According to historians, relations between Cerveteri and Carthage dated
back at least to the mid-6th century B.C., when the two cities combined to fight a naval
battle in the Sardinian sea against the Greeks from Phocaea.

It is possible that Thefarie Velianas was making a gesture of friendship towards his
allies to win their favour at a time when Etruscan sea power was threatened by the Greeks.
The Pyrgi plaques are evidence of this anti-Hellenic alliance and bear out the information
contained in ancient sources.

The Roman *colonia* founded at Pyrgi in the 3rd century B.C. was situated on the promontory, more or less where the Castello now stands. The surviving sections of its sur-

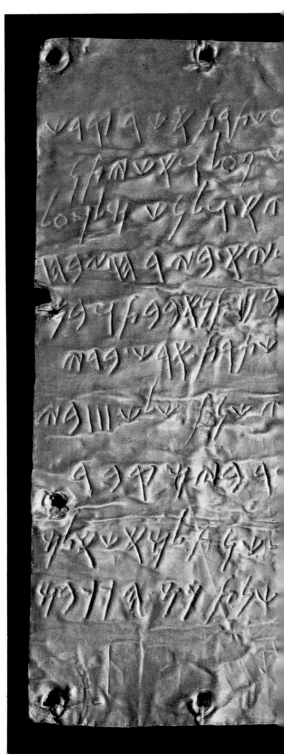

rounding walls have been excavated. These were built of large polygonal stone blocks and enclosed a rectangle measuring about 220 by 250 metres; the northeast, southeast and northwest gates have also been identified. Along the southeastern stretch of the walls have been found Roman *cappuccina*-tombs (trenches covered with tiles to form a small roof), sometimes containing amphorae with the ashes of the dead.

The excavation headquarters, near the Castello, houses an Antiquarium for the finds not on show in the Pyrgi room of the Museo di Villa Giulia. It consists of one large room with showcases containing votive objects, architectural decorations and pottery, as well as an electrotype copy of the gold plaques. A reconstruction of part of the rear pediment of temple A is mounted on the short wall to the right as you go in (some elements are original, others are casts; instead of the mythological relief, it shows a battle of gods and giants). Part of the pediment of temple B is mounted on the left-hand wall.

Below, left: Pyrgi. Polychrome antefix in the form of a head of Silenus

Below: the gold plaques from Pyrgi with, from left to right, the Phoenician inscription and the long and short Etruscan inscriptions. Rome, Museo di Villa Giulia

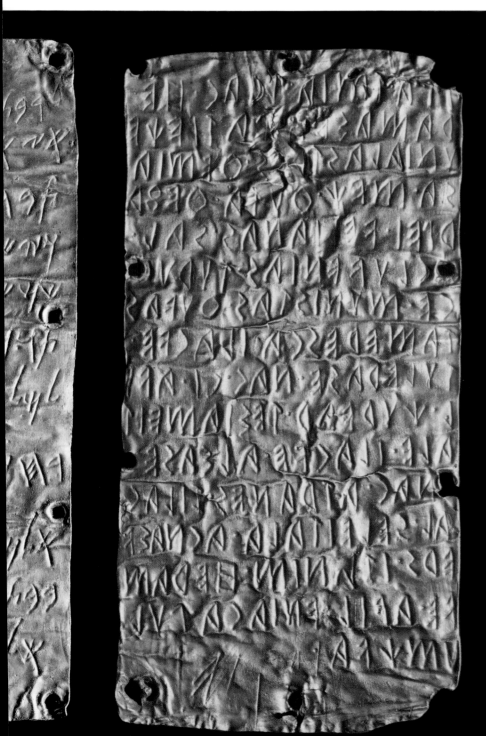

Tarquinia

Opposite: Tarquinia. Detail of the Tomba della
Caccia e Pesca

Below: archaeological plan. The numbered tombs
are: (1) Tomba della Caccia e Pesca; (2) Tomba
delle Leonesse; (3) Tomba del Tifone; (4) Tomba
del Barone; (5) Tomba dei Tori; (6) Tomba degli
Auguri

Ninety kilometres from Rome along the Via Aurelia (S.S.No.1), a road branches off to the right, leading the short distance to the modern town of Tarquinia. It stands on the northwestern tip of a hill of no great height which runs parallel to the Tyrrhenian coast, roughly six kilometres long and never more than 1,500 metres wide. In mediaeval times the town of Corneto stood on the same spot; this was still an important centre in the Renaissance, when the 15th-century Palazzo Vitelleschi was built, now the home of the Museo Archeologico Nazionale.

The outward appearance of the old town, with its characteristic walls and towers and the gable-belfries of its many Romanesque churches, has, alas, been utterly ruined by intensive and often uncoordinated building activity in the surrounding area during recent years. This expansion is not even confined to the immediate outskirts of the town: ill-conceived development plans are allowing it to spread towards the rest of the hill, south-east of the old town centre, where the vast cemetery of the Etruscan city (ancient Tarquinii) lies. The hill is known by the popular name Monterozzi because many tombs were once visible on the surface as hillocks of earth; they are now much reduced in size and scarcely discernible. These are only some of the thousands of tombs which have been discovered on the plateau since the beginning of the 19th century; an additional 6,000 or so have been identified during the last fifteen years by the geophysical surveys conducted by the Fondazione Lerici.

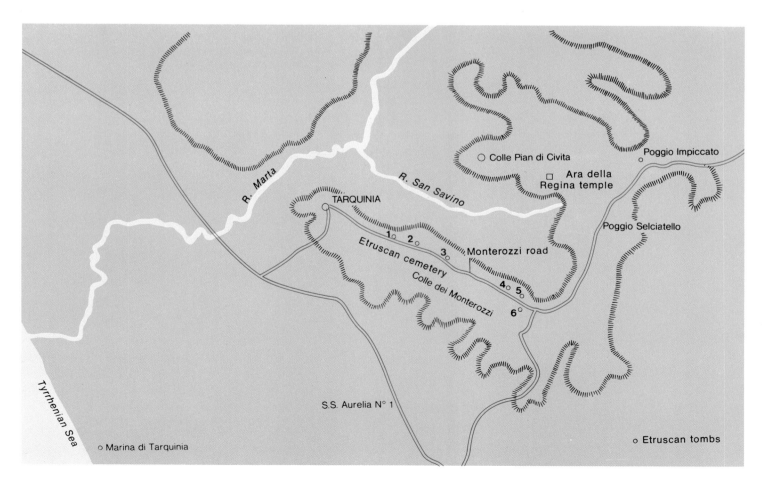

The Etruscan city and the Roman *municipium* were situated on a second hill, called Pian di Civita, which lies more or less parallel to Monterozzi, but farther inland. The two plateaux are linked on the southeast by a series of hillocks which lead gradually inland to the foothills of the Apennines of Latium. At their other (northwestern) ends they extend towards the valley of the river Marta, flowing from Lake Bolsena. At this point, as it nears the sea, the river is joined by the San Savino stream, which flows along a green valley between the two hills.

This brief account of the topography of the area shows that the Etruscan city occupied an extremely favourable geographical position: near the sea, lying between the principal

towns of coastal southern Etruria—Vulci and Cerveteri—and well placed for communication by way of the Marta with a large inland area including Tuscania and Bisenzio. All these factors contributed to Tarquinia's political and cultural importance, for which there is evidence from the earliest stages of Etruscan civilization (9th–7th centuries B.C.).

Tarquinia continued to be one of the leading cities of Etruria; from it comes some of the most valuable archaeological evidence to be found, not just in Italy, but in the whole Mediterranean area. The painted tombs on the Colle dei Monterozzi, the architectural remains of the city walls and of the Ara della Regina temple on Pian di Civita, the quantities of sculpture, terracottas, imported Greek and local pottery, and Etruscan and Latin inscriptions all provide a precious archaeological legacy which will be increased further when the area of the city on Pian di Civita, as yet scarcely studied at all, is systematically excavated.

Reconstructing the political and military history of Tarquinia, as with that of other Etruscan cities, presents problems, since written evidence is scanty and fragmentary. A few Latin inscriptions, found at Tarquinia itself, give first-hand information on individual episodes of Etruscan internal history; but other information, handed down by classical Latin and Greek authors, is second-hand and often very vague. The rich archaeological evidence which exists thus becomes of prime importance, making it possible to follow the development of the cultural phases which succeeded each other at Tarquinia, alongside parallel developments in the other important Etruscan cities.

The historical city of Tarquinia developed around the first settlement, which dates from the beginning of the Iron Age, according to the evidence provided by the Archaic cemeteries. These first appeared on the hills east of Pian di Civita—Selciatello, Impiccato and Sopra Selciatello—where the oldest tombs, typical of the earliest Villanovan phase (9th century B.C.), have been discovered: pit-tombs, usually cylindrical, dug into the ground and covered by a stone slab. These contained the biconical urn of dark impasto, decorated with an impressed or incised geometric pattern and covered with the usual bowl or helmet, according to the sex of the deceased. In richer graves the biconical urn is

Below: Tarquinia. Cemetery on the Scataglini estate: street of tombs

Right: podium of the Ara della Regina temple on the Pian di Civita

Cinerary hut-urn, from the Monterozzi cemetery.
Tarquinia, Museo Nazionale

replaced by a hut-urn, made of the same dark-coloured impasto. The grave goods consist of various types of vases, also in impasto, and the usual objects, some (fibulae, razors) being of bronze.

During the 8th century the Archaic cemeteries continued to develop, as before, on the hills to the east of Pian di Civita. From about 750 B.C., however, date the first burials on the Colle dei Monterozzi, at Le Arcatelle, by one of the three deep natural gaps in the hillside facing Pian di Civita. The increasing cultural enrichment of these cemeteries, right from the beginning, is closely connected with Tarquinia's new commercial role during the second Villanovan phase, which developed as a result of the exploitation, then just starting, of Etruria's vast mineral riches. In the early stages it was the cities of coastal Etruria, including Tarquinia, that found themselves in direct contact with the great Mediterranean trade-routes, and were thus able to benefit immediately from the exploitation of this wealth. It was with these cities, in particular, that the earliest Greek colonies in Italy (Ischia and Cumae) established the first important trade links.

Besides the pit-tombs for cremated remains, as the practice of inhumation spread, new types of tombs appeared: rectangular trench-tombs dug into the ground and covered with a tufa slab or gabled lid, or corridor-tombs, again cut into the ground, consisting of small rectangular chambers with a vestibule, a narrow bench on one side for the body and a rudimentary vaulted ceiling. In an older version of the second type, the walls curve slightly inwards at the top, leaving a narrow opening covered with tufa slabs.

The grave goods for these tombs included for the first time many bronze objects. Most of the vases and many of the personal items of the deceased are made of sheet bronze decorated with a distinctive pattern of raised ridges and bosses.

Faience situla with hieroglyphic inscription giving the name of the Twenty-Fourth Dynasty pharaoh Bocchoris, from the Tomba di Bokkoris. Tarquinia, Museo Nazionale

The furnishings (now in the Staatliche Museen zu Berlin) found in one trench-tomb of the period, known as the Tomba del Guerriero ('Tomb of the Warrior'), are of particular interest, since they provide complete evidence of an outfit of bronze armour, skilfully embossed, which must have been used by a Tarquinian warrior of the Archaic period. This consisted of a cloth jacket fastened with bronze conical buttons and little hooks, and with bronze shoulder-pieces; a breastplate, roughly rectangular in shape; a shield decorated with concentric circles, with an armlet inside by which to grasp it; a lance and the chape (tip) of a scabbard.

As well as bronze-work, Tarquinia began to produce at this period a type of fine pottery decorated with thin parallel lines and other motifs, such as rows of stylized birds, painted in a reddish gloss on the smooth, light-coloured surface of the vase. The similarities between this pottery and contemporary pottery discovered at the Greek colony of Cumae are clear proof of the cultural and commercial links between the two areas.

Archaeological finds from the Archaic period thus show beyond a shadow of doubt that Tarquinia was a city of very ancient origins which developed rapidly and at an early stage became a leading cultural and perhaps political power among the other Etruscan cities. Although the remains of the Archaic settlement have not yet been discovered—work so far has been confined to a few preliminary investigations—it is assumed that it stood on the Pian di Civita, since the contemporary Villanovan cemeteries are situated on the hills nearest this one.

Classical authors also mention the city's ancient origins. Tarchon, brother of the Tyrrhenos who led the Etruscan migration from Lydia in Asia Minor, was said to have founded the city, which was called after him; Virgil refers to him in the *Aeneid* as an Etruscan king who was Aeneas's ally in the war against the Latins. Cicero (thereby attributing a leading religious role to the city) claimed that Tarquinia was the site of the legend of Tages, the child who sprang from the earth to teach the Etruscans the art of foretelling the future by the interpretation of the flight of birds and the entrails of animals.

Between the early 7th and early 6th centuries B.C. Tarquinia's cultural development was an integral part of the Orientalizing culture of contemporary Etruria. During this period of vigorous commercial activity all around the Mediterranean it remained an important market for unworked metals, a function it had first acquired in the previous century, before the other Etruscan cities. Its commercial role is shown by increasingly frequent finds among the grave goods of precious Eastern, Phoenician and Greek objects, acquired in return for its exports of metal. It would appear, however, that during this period Tarquinia did not maintain the cultural and perhaps political leadership of southern Etruria for which there is evidence in the earlier period: contemporary archaeological finds in the tombs of Cerveteri and to a lesser extent Vulci are far richer in gold, ivory and other precious objects.

The grave goods from the Tomba di Bokkoris are typical of the early Orientalizing phase in Tarquinia. The name comes from the most important discovery in the tomb: a Phoenician vase of faience (glazed terracotta) bearing the name of the pharaoh Bocchoris in Egyptian hieroglyphs and depicting his military campaigns in Ethiopia. The vase is not just an important indication of commercial links between Tarquinia and the Near East; it also supplies a precise chronological reference-point for Archaic Etruria in the years of the pharaoh's reign, which Greek and Egyptian sources give as 715–709 B.C. The tomb also contained other imported Eastern objects, in particular the personal ornaments of the deceased, including the faience beads of a necklace in the shape of figurines of Egyptian deities, and embossed gold plaques. The other vases found are local products, among them a number of distinctive items: two large globular kraters on tall open-work stands, made of red impasto but of a design obviously derived from metal-work; a small rounded amphora made of dark impasto and decorated with incised spirals; two pitchers of fine clay painted in red with a decoration of geometric motifs and rows of schematized animals.

In the second half of the 7th and the beginning of the 6th century B.C. the Orientalizing culture of Etruria was greatly affected by Greek artistic trends, particularly the influence of Corinth. In Tarquinia this new dimension expressed itself in a number of ways. Magnificent tumulus-tombs (which have now largely disappeared, though there is still one which can be visited near Doganaccia) appeared on Monterozzi. They consisted of an artificial mound of earth bounded by a circular base with a gap or gaps for one or more corridors leading to the underground chambers. Inside, these rooms, entirely rock-cut, followed closely the by now standard pattern for chamber-tombs of the time, with gabled ceiling and a bench along the walls for the remains of the dead and the tomb furnishings.

Pottery is now dominated by Corinthian imports, with their characteristic decoration of incised and painted figures and motifs drawn from the traditional Eastern repertoire of fantastic animals (sphinxes, chimaeras, centaurs and winged beasts). This style of pottery was widely imitated by local craftsmen, who also at this time produced the first bucchero ware, influenced in its decoration by current Orientalizing trends.

In the field of sculpture, too, the fantastic animals typical of contemporary Greek and Etruscan decoration appear on the richly carved bas-reliefs of the large limestone or *nenfro* slabs which were used as tomb doors. Large numbers of these have been found in the cemetery of Tarquinia (though nowhere else), and they can now be seen in the court-yard of the museum.

Another indication of Tarquinia's links with Corinth appears in a legend preserved by classical authors. Demaratos, an eminent Corinthian who had grown rich on the trade between Greece and Etruria, was forced to leave his homeland for political reasons

Nenfro funerary slab. Tarquinia, Museo Nazionale

Tarquinia. Aerial view of the Etruscan city

and fled to Tarquinia, taking with him a group of Greek artists. The legend claims that he was the father of Tarquinius Priscus who, tradition has it, was fifth king of Rome and founder of the Etruscan dynasty of the Tarquins who ruled that city from the end of the 7th to the end of the 6th century B.C.

The ancient sources thus refer explicitly to an Etruscan phase in the history of Archaic Rome. Archaeological discoveries confirm this, showing clear signs of Etruscan influence in Rome and Latium at precisely the period referred to by the ancient authors. It seems likely, as has been inferred from the legend, that Tarquinia, one of Etruria's leading cities, did play a decisive part in the spread of Etruscan civilization to Rome and Latium. However, as yet no written evidence or historical reference has been discovered to support the legend's account of Tarquinia as the origin of the Tarquin dynasty.

About the middle of the 6th century B.C. the first signs of tomb painting appear at Tarquinia. From then on, the use of figurative paintings to decorate tomb walls and ceilings becomes a permanent feature of the cemetery, continuing without a break until the end of the 2nd century B.C. However, the painted tombs are relatively few compared with the enormous total number of tombs excavated on Monterozzi, and this indicates that they belonged to a select group of high-ranking families who could afford to build and decorate such magnificent tombs.

The paintings at Tarquinia are the most important group to survive from the classical world before the Roman Imperial age. They are thus vital to an understanding of the development of ancient painting, in particular Greek painting, which so much influenced them. They also provide valuable documentary evidence of Etruscan social life, customs and beliefs.

There are about 150 painted tombs known today. A number of these have been discovered in recent years by means of new investigatory techniques. Two processes are involved. First, electrical and magnetic instruments transmit a current to test the resistivity of the ground, which offers different resistance at points where there are tombs.

188

When a tomb has been located, a photographic probe is lowered through a narrow hole drilled in the ground into the unexcavated chamber, and its paintings are photographed.

With only a few exceptions, all the paintings were executed by the fresco technique, on a thin coat of plaster applied directly to the tufa walls of the chamber, this layer of plaster being thicker in later tombs. The colours, made from mineral and vegetable bases and dissolved in water, were fixed permanently by the chemical reaction (calcium carbonate) produced when they came into contact with the lime contained in the still damp plaster. Usually a preliminary design, giving the outline and a few details of the figures, was sketched in with a metal point or stick before the colours were applied.

The largest group of painted tombs dates from the period between the mid-6th and mid-5th centuries B.C. The internal structure of the chamber-tombs did not change appreciably at this time, despite the important innovation which the introduction of paintings represented.

The typical tomb still consists of a rectangular rock-cut room, between two and five metres long, reached by a stepped corridor or opening directly off the steep slope of the hillside. The ceiling slopes from a central beam, either painted or carved in relief. The bench along the walls for the deposition is often replaced by wooden funeral couches with applied bronze decoration.

There are only a few examples of more complex tombs with several rooms. The Tomba dei Tori, for example, has a rectangular entrance chamber with two adjoining chambers leading off it at the far end. The Tomba Bartoccini has a cruciform plan, with a central room and three rooms opening off three sides of it: These types of tombs, which appear more frequently during the next period (4th–3rd centuries B.C.), follow the layout of rooms in Etruscan dwellings; recent excavations at Marzabotto have brought very similar structures to light.

There were two distinct aspects of tomb painting during this period: the structural and architectural element, decorating the ceiling and pediment spaces of the walls; and the purely figurative paintings on the walls themselves. The central ceiling beam was decorated with a simple red-painted band, emphasizing the structure, or, more often, with a series of concentric circles, sometimes alternating with ivy leaves (Tomba delle Bighe), or with a frieze of branches and ivy leaves (Tomba del Letto Funebre). On the

I

ceiling itself there might be a regular pattern of rosettes made of red spots on a white ground (Tomba degli Auguri, Tomba della Caccia e Pesca), or a chequerboard pattern in two or three colours (Tomba delle Bighe, Tomba dei Leopardi, Tomba del Triclinio). The decoration of the pediment spaces generally followed a set scheme based on an architectural feature of a house interior, namely some form of short central pillar, with an animal on either side of it, facing each other. These may be felines (Tomba delle Leonesse, Tomba dei Leopardi), monsters and sea horses (Tomba dei Tori, Tomba del Barone), groups of hunting lions with birds, deer, rams and gazelles (Tomba degli Auguri, Tomba del Letto Funebre).

Tarquinia
1. Detail from the end wall of the Tomba degli Auguri
2. Detail from the pediment of cella II of the Tomba della Caccia e Pesca
3. Diver, detail from the left-hand wall of cella II of the Tomba della Caccia e Pesca
4. Dancer and lyre-player, from the Tomba del Triclinio
5. Banquet, from the end wall of the Tomba dei Leopardi

Below: Tarquinia. Detail of painting in the Tomba delle Leonesse

Right: end wall of the Tomba del Barone

But the most important part of the painted decoration of these tombs is the frieze of figures which runs right round the walls, usually occupying about half the height. Only once, in the Tomba dei Tori, is the composition confined to the central section of the back wall, so that it is more like a proper picture. Finally, in some 5th-century tombs it is not unusual to find a double frieze (Tomba delle Bighe).

Scenes from real life are the most frequent subjects of such friezes. Banquet scenes are common, with one couple or more, sometimes of the same sex, reclining on couches while they talk and eat. Often the atmosphere is enlivened by the presence of musicians and dancers, while numerous attendants, depicted nude and smaller than the other figures, carry out their tasks in the background.

Representations of games and sporting contests are equally common. These show, as well as the athletes, trainers at work with their assistants, and in one case (Tomba delle Bighe) the great sporting public ranged on wooden tiers. The lively and varied themes are drawn from a number of sports of the time: wrestling, boxing, pole-vaulting, discus-throwing and a strange type of fighting involving masked men and a dog (Tomba degli Auguri, Tomba dei Giocolieri, Tomba delle Olimpiadi).

Less frequently, there are hunting and fishing scenes, wonderfully conveyed on the walls of the Tomba della Caccia e Pesca, with their naturalistic portrayal of the sea full of fish and the sky criss-crossed by flying birds.

Tarquinia. Tomba dei Giocolieri: below, detail of right-hand wall; opposite, end wall

The only example of a mythological subject is the scene from Greek mythology in the Tomba dei Tori. This shows Achilles lying in wait for Troilus, one of Priam's sons, during the siege of Troy.

The belief that the afterlife would take the form of everyday existence explains the wish to create realistic and convincing scenes of earthly life around the deceased, who, as we know, must have belonged to the local aristocracy. This is clearly apparent in all the figurative wall paintings in the tombs, apart from the mythological scene of the Tomba dei Tori.

However, although these themes are drawn from scenes of local life, they must not be thought of as exclusive to Etruscan art, since they appear on many painted vases and other artistic products of Archaic Greece. Moreover, paintings showing banquets and sea-diving discovered recently in a tomb at Paestum dated to 480 B.C. show that a style of Greek funerary art akin to the tomb paintings of Tarquinia was to be found at this time farther down the Tyrrhenian coast.

However, the influence of Greek models does not mean that certain subjects were not given an original treatment. One example is the masked dog-fighting depicted in the Tomba degli Auguri and the Tomba delle Olimpiadi, or the funeral ceremony of the Tomba del Letto Funebre.

In any case, the originality of the compositions lies not so much in their subject-matter as in their strong local flavour, with their exact portrayal of episodes of daily life, and the outstanding skill of the craftsmen in conveying these realistic details in an expressive and lively fashion.

Greek influence is apparent in the pictorial style of the friezes, as well as in their subject-matter. The oldest series of paintings, from the last decades of the 6th century B.C. (Tomba degli Auguri, Tomba della Caccia e Pesca, Tomba del Barone, Tomba delle Leonesse, Tomba delle Olimpiadi, etc.), clearly shows the influence of the Ionian style which spread to Etruria from the Greek cities of the western coast of Asia Minor and was undisputedly the dominant factor in Etruscan representational art in the second half of the century.

On the other hand, the paintings from the first half of the 5th century (Tomba delle Bighe, Tomba del Triclinio, Tomba dei Leopardi, Tomba del Letto Funebre) reflect new trends originating in mainland Greece, particularly Athens.

However, the Etruscan painters were not passive receptacles for foreign influence. In fact the different levels of artistic accomplishment and the range of styles, including a number of personal touches, found in these paintings suggest that here were gifted local artists engaged in creative and innovatory work, but familiar both with the legacy of the ancient Etruscan representational traditions and with the teachings, perhaps at first hand, of skilled foreign craftsmen.

The decoration of the tombs was probably entrusted to the best-known and most highly esteemed painters, either because the Etruscan magical and religious mentality considered these paintings of great significance, or because of the financial means and social pretensions of those who commissioned them, who as members of upper-class families could afford the expense of such fine private monuments.

Pictorially, the outstanding feature is the outline drawn more or less continuously round subjects and used to divide areas of colour inside single subjects. The colours are applied evenly and are particularly vivid in the oldest paintings, with strong and totally improbable contrasts. In the portrayal of certain details in some more sophisticated monuments there is occasionally an attempt at shading, though this never really succeeds in giving an effect of genuine chiaroscuro (Tomba del Triclinio). In paintings influenced by Ionian art the soft plump figures, drawn with characteristic curving outlines, are usually portrayed in attitudes of movement, but these are not naturalistic and sometimes tend to be exaggeratedly stylized (Tomba del Barone). However, the influence of Athenian art brought a less abstract concept of the human figure, an interest in anatomical study of the male nude and a taste for subtle movement, sometimes coupled with timid attempts at perspective. Finally, a characteristic common to all the paintings is the slight hint of a background given by lines indicating the earth, often decorated with plants and flowers, or rows of little trees placed in between the figures.

This intensive production of paintings in the 6th and first half of the 5th centuries slowly tailed off between the mid-5th and the early 4th century B.C. This sudden break in cultural activity, which also affected the other cities of coastal Etruria, resulted from the cities' loss of naval supremacy in the Tyrrhenian Sea. Etruscan domination of the sea, which had several times been threatened during the 6th century by the gradual consolidation of the political and commercial power of the Greek colonies in Italy, declined totally after the victory of the Syracusan fleet off Cumae in 474 B.C.

The cities of coastal Etruria thus became modest little land-based states, cut off from the main cultural currents of the Mediterranean. Only isolated motifs and conventions of contemporary Greek art of the classical period reached them, and these were reworked without any full understanding of the underlying reasons for such modes of expression. The rare tombs of this period at Tarquinia (Tomba della Nave, Tomba della Scrofa Nera) repeat in a remarkably uninspired way the same old figure designs, with only an occasional timid attempt at innovation in the field of perspective or chiaroscuro technique.

At the beginning of the 4th century B.C. Tarquinia once again became a powerful city and a member of the league of twelve major Etruscan cities which was the basis of the political and religious organization of Etruria at the time of its struggles against Rome.

End wall of the Tomba della Nave. Tarquinia, Museo Nazionale

The first armed conflict between Rome and Tarquinia erupted about the middle of the 4th century, following the insidious increase of Roman incursions along the southern reaches of the territory of Tarquinia. The indecisive outcome of the war, which was followed by a forty-year truce, made a further flare-up of hostilities at the end of the century inevitable. The second conflict ended with the signing of an alliance which in fact brought Tarquinia within Rome's political orbit. It established that foreign affairs came under Roman control, while the government of the city was responsible for internal administration only. The agreement remained unchanged for about two hundred years, until the Lex Julia of 90 B.C. granted Roman citizenship to the entire Etruscan territory.

Above: Tarquinia. Tomba Giglioli

Left: Tomba dell'Orco II: Geryon, Hades and Persephone

Opposite: Tomba dell'Orco I: profile of Velia

Following pages: Tarquinia. Tomba del Tifone: general view, and detail of the painted pillar showing a figure of Typhon

Archaeological data from the cemetery provide a clear picture of the city's organization at this time. Inscriptions found in the large, rich tombs designed to house many burials show that each of these belonged to an entire clan and also prove the existence of an organized social class of nobles. The inscriptions also record the titles of political and religious offices, held by members of these same families for a limited time, probably with colleagues; this suggests an oligarchical structure of government with temporary, collegiate offices, similar to the system found at this time in Rome (where, for instance, pairs of consuls were appointed annually) and other city-states of the ancient world. The number of these rich tombs is not great and becomes smaller as time goes on, showing that the main groups of nobles which formed Tarquinia's ruling class gradually dwindled until the last survivors were absorbed into the Roman ruling class; only three large noble chamber-tombs from the 2nd century are known, compared with a dozen from the period between the mid-4th and the mid-3rd century B.C.

A number of distinctive elements give a new look to the tombs of this period: the remarkable size of the chambers, which vary considerably in form; the style and content of the wall paintings, which are dominated by scenes of the afterlife, depicted according to conventions and motifs borrowed from contemporary Greek models, but not further elaborated in any way as in the Archaic period; the use of stone sarcophagi for inhumation; and finally, as already mentioned, the large numbers of inscriptions painted on the walls.

Most tombs follow the earlier custom and consist of a single enormous chamber with a very slightly gabled ceiling and a central beam in relief (Tomba dell'Orco I, Tomba Giglioli). However, as in earlier times, there are a few rare examples of more complex

L·F·LOVD·TARDIVINVS·TARDI·ARNTH·CLAN·PANOMAS·CVCLNIAL·FIL·I·CELANEDI·TENOAS·ATI·
A·FLORS·φ·H·HI

cruciform structures (Tomba degli Scudi) or of tombs with an entrance chamber leading to two small cellae. Another typical form, from the first decades of the 3rd century B.C. onwards, is the tomb consisting of a single large chamber with a flat roof supported by one or more pillars. Along the walls runs a bench with two or three tiers on which the sarcophagi were placed; or else, more economically, the niche for the dead body was simply cut into the wall itself (Tomba del Tifone).

In the wall paintings of figures the theme of the banquet again appears, but in accordance with new religious ideas the banquet now takes place in the underworld in the presence of Greek and Etruscan infernal deities and demons. Charun, the monstrous underworld creature, is portrayed, armed with a heavy hammer, as a semi-bestial figure with greenish skin, a huge hooked nose and enormous pointed ears (Tomba dell'Orco, Tomba degli Scudi).

Many scenes show the dead man's journey to the underworld. The aim of these paintings was clearly to honour important individuals who had in life held political or religious office; the deceased is accompanied by a long procession including, as well as members of his household, figures bearing symbols and insignia indicating his social rank (Tomba del Tifone).

Stylistically, despite some naïve attempts at simplification, these paintings have obviously been greatly influenced by the important discoveries made by the great Greek painters of the 5th century concerning perspective and light-and-shade effects arrived at by means of colour contrast (Tomba dell'Orco, Tomba Giglioli, Tomba del Tifone).

Another distinctive feature of the tombs of this period, as has been mentioned, is the use of sarcophagi for burying the dead. A considerable number of these have been found, suggesting that Tarquinia was one of the chief centres of their manufacture.

The rectangular chest, made of *nenfro*, or less often of marble or alabaster, is decorated with reliefs illustrating incidents from Greek mythology (for example, the battle with the Amazons), depicting the journey of the deceased to the underworld (similar to the scenes depicted in wall paintings), or simply ornamental (for example, felines attacking a domestic animal). In the richest examples the lid depicts the deceased half-reclining, portrayed, typically, as solid in build, often exaggeratedly and unnaturally obese; certain salient facial features are picked out to convey expression. However, usually these sculptures are not actual portraits of individuals. The frequent repetition of similar forms indicates, instead, that they were meant to show merely that the deceased belonged to a particular category: an old man, a young man, a matron.

One of the most interesting of the sculptures, now housed on the ground floor of the museum, is the sarcophagus of Velthur Partunu who, according to the inscription carved on the chest, died at the age of 82 after holding important magisterial offices. Another noteworthy sarcophagus belonged to a member of another noble clan, the Pulena, who is shown unrolling a scroll listing his ancestors and, again, the offices they held (p. 28).

Finally, something must be said about the archaeological remains, dating solely from this period of its history, of the city of Tarquinia itself on the Pian di Civita. Since excavations in the city area have to date been far less intensive than in the cemetery zone, the monumental remains are scanty. However, it is possible to identify most of the eight-kilometre perimeter of the city walls, built in the early 4th century when the city was threatened by the growth of Roman power in central Italy. Built of huge limestone blocks and 1.80 metres thick, the imposing wall followed the irregular contours of the hill-top.

Inside the wall there are visible signs of a regular town plan with straight streets crossing at right angles. The most important construction so far discovered is the podium of a large temple called the Ara della Regina, which was also built in the first half of the 4th century B.C. It follows a plan common in Etruria: a rectangular cella is flanked by two corridors (alae) and preceded by an area of the same width with four columns arranged in two rows in front.

From the Tomba dei Partunu, Tarquinia

Above: the Sarcofago del Magnate, with figure of the deceased and polychrome scenes

Below: sarcophagus with figure of the deceased. Tarquinia, Museo Nazionale

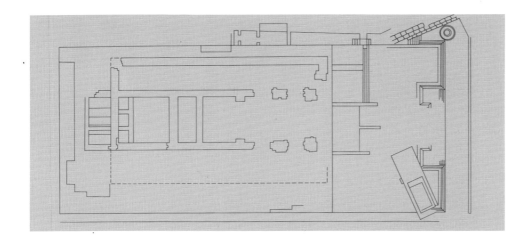

Left: Tarquinia. Plan of the Ara della Regina temple

Below: winged horses, from a pediment of the Ara della Regina temple. Tarquinia, Museo Nazionale

General view of the Tomba del Cacciatore, Tarquinia

The beautiful terracotta slab with the relief of two winged horses, now displayed in a little room on the first floor of the museum, was part of the pediment decoration of the temple. It covered part of the end of the central roof-beam and would have been completed by a second slab on the right; all that remains of this is the bottom section, showing a female figure, perhaps standing, in a chariot which must have been drawn by the two horses. This female figure, whose name is at present unknown, may have been the deity worshipped in the temple.

Monterozzi cemetery. The painted tombs of the Colle dei Monterozzi cannot be visited without a guide from the museum, who conducts a tour, generally in topographical order.

At the head of the road which runs the entire length of the hill, a considerable number of painted chamber-tombs lie to the left, not far from the outskirts of the modern town, at Calvario.

These include the Tomba della Caccia e Pesca ('Tomb of Hunting and Fishing'), which dates from about 530–520 B.C. and belongs to the oldest group of painted tombs, those influenced by the East Greek style. It is made up of two rooms on the same alignment. In the first, the frieze running round the walls depicts a feast: musicians and dancers alternate with trees decorated with ribbons and little garlands. The pediment shows a return from the hunt, in place of the usual Greek-inspired design of animals facing each other on either side of a central pillar.

On the walls of the second room is a marvellous seascape, showing details of life by the sea, while the pediment is decorated with a banquet scene.

The sea scene is one of the most original works of ancient painting, depicting with lively and exuberant realism the different aspects of nature. Flocks of gaily-coloured birds fly across the sky; dolphins frisk among the waves; small rocks break through the surface of the water; a naked boy is diving from one of them, while on another a man is aiming his sling at the birds. In a boat with an eye painted on the prow for luck other boys are fishing with nets, while one boy steers.

Nearby is the single-chamber Tomba del Cacciatore ('Tomb of the Hunter'), which is in the same general artistic style as the Tomba della Caccia e Pesca, though possibly a little later (530–510 B.C.).

The extremely unusual painted decoration represents a hunting pavilion. The wooden framework, painted a reddish-brown colour, is roofed over with a heavy, brightly-checked material with a narrow border decorated with a continuous row of animals, hunters and horsemen. On the walls hangs a curtain, embroidered with tiny regular ornamental motifs; through its thin material the surrounding countryside can be seen. A roebuck is shown grazing on the gently undulating lines of the ground. Another has been slain and now

Tarquinia. The Palazzo Vitelleschi, home of the Museo Nazionale: interior courtyard, with Renaissance well in the centre
Below: detail, showing sarcophagi found in noble tombs of the 4th–2nd centuries B.C.

Bronze shield boss with animal head. Tarquinia, Museo Nazionale

hangs from one of the poles inside the tent, where other items of hunting equipment are also depicted.

East Greek influence is particularly strong in the paintings of the Tomba delle Leonesse ('Tomb of the Lionesses'; 540–530 B.C.), wrongly so called after the two panthers painted on the pediment of the end wall.

On this wall, beside an enormous krater which was assumed to contain the ashes of the deceased, are two musicians, one playing a lyre, the other a double flute. To the right of this group a man and a woman are dancing with total abandon. The woman, dressed in a light transparent tunic, is playing the castanets with her right hand, and making with her left the gesture of the horns, which no doubt has a ritual significance; the man has long fair hair and skin painted the brick-red colour conventionally used for male figures. On the other side of the krater is a single female dancer, richly dressed in a transparent tunic and full cloak. Her hair is covered by an elongated hat in the Ionian fashion.

On the side walls, under a portico indicated by three columns on each side, four male figures are banqueting. They are depicted as much bigger than the figures on the end wall, an artistic convention common in antiquity to show that they were of high social rank, belonging to the family of the deceased.

The Tomba del Tifone is situated near Casale di Ripagretta, not far from Primi Archi, the first natural break in the hill. It is the latest in date (about 150 B.C.) of the cemetery's noble painted tombs, and also one of the largest (nine by twelve metres). It consists of a single chamber with a flat roof supported by a central pillar. Like most chamber-tombs of the late period (3rd–2nd centuries B.C.), it contains a three-tiered bench round the walls on which the sarcophagi were placed.

Figure-painting is found only on the faces of the pillar and on a short stretch of the right-hand wall; simple decorative motifs (rosettes, dolphins leaping over the waves) extend along all the walls.

Two winged giants (Typhons) with serpents in place of feet are depicted on two faces of the pillar, holding up the ceiling with all their might. These are not figures drawn from local tradition like most of the demons and monsters of late Etruscan funerary art, but derive from a Greek model which can be seen in the reliefs of the great altar of Pergamum in Asia Minor.

However, the scene on the tomb's right-hand wall does belong to native tradition. It shows the last journey to the underworld of a member of the noble Pumpu family to whom the tomb belonged. A long procession accompanies him, as befits an eminent figure who, the inscription tells us, held the highest political and priestly offices in the city.

On the right-hand side of the road which runs along the north side of the modern cemetery is the Tomba dell'Orco, consisting of two separate tombs built at different times and connected at a later date by a small third room. The older chamber is the first of the cemetery's great noble chamber-tombs from about the mid-4th century B.C., as is shown by the remarkable size of the tomb, the content and style of its paintings and the painted wall inscriptions which give the names of some members of the noble Spurinna family which owned the tomb.

The wall paintings, surviving only in fragments, show scenes of a banquet being held in the underworld in the presence of monstrous demons, according to the new pessimistic religious concepts of the time. On the end wall one of these monsters appears, characteristically shown as half man, half beast, greenish in colour, with a huge hammer grasped in his left hand. Nearby, in the right-hand corner, the beautiful profile survives of a woman reclining beside her husband on the banqueting couch. The inscription gives her name as Velia. Her hair is gathered at the nape of her neck and held by a band, and she wears a diadem, cluster earrings and two necklaces. The pure outline of her profile and the delicate shades of colour bringing out the facial features make this painting a highly accomplished work.

The walls of the second tomb show the underworld, peopled, as in Greek mythology, by infernal deities, the spirits of ancient heroes and the shades of the dead. The names of the legendary figures are given in the painted Etruscan inscriptions.

On the end wall Hades (Pluto) and Persephone (Proserpina), the king and queen of the underworld, are seated on their thrones. He wears a wolf skin on his head and grasps a snake in his left hand. Her hair is interwoven with snakes and she wears a sumptuous dress. In front of them stands Geryon, the three-headed warrior, fully armed. On the left-hand wall are the Homeric heroes, including Agamemnon in a solemn attitude and the seer Tiresias; beside the latter are the shades of the dead he has called up, represented as small stylized black figures leaping among the branches of a small tree. On the right-hand wall Theseus is seated by a table behind which is a terrifying demon with the face of a vulture and the ears of an ass, armed with snakes.

The decoration of the whole tomb complex is completed by a large painting of the killing of Polyphemus on the end wall of the third room.

To the left of the road which cuts along the last section of the Colle dei Monterozzi is the Tomba del Barone. The figured frieze running round the walls is striking for its elegant and rhythmic composition and for the symmetrical use of colour contrasts to distinguish the different scenes. On the end wall a bearded figure embraces a young man playing a double flute, while at the same time offering a cup to a richly dressed noblewoman, perhaps his wife; she is raising her arms in response to this courteous gesture. On either side of the group, separated from them by green shrubs, are two young men on horseback. A second family scene on the left-hand wall shows the same woman talking to the two young men, who have now dismounted. The tomb was built and painted for this woman, who perhaps predeceased the other members of the family.

Bronze shield boss with head of Acheloüs.
Tarquinia, Museo Nazionale

The techniques of these paintings differs from that of the other tombs. The silhouette of the individual figures is first filled in with a greyish wash of colour spread directly on to the rock surface. The outlines are then drawn in, but are toned down when the unusually strong, bright colours are applied over them. The slender, elongated figures bear the mark of the elegant Ionian style towards the end of the 6th century (520–510 B.C.) in contrast to the vigorous, solid representational style of the period immediately preceding (Tomba delle Leonesse, Tomba degli Auguri).

Not far from the Tomba del Barone is the Tomba dei Tori ('Tomb of the Bulls'), the oldest painted tomb at Tarquinia (550 B.C.), which contains the only mythological scene depicted on the walls of the 6th- and 5th-century chamber-tombs. Its layout is also an unusual one for this cemetery: it consists of a rectangular entrance chamber with two small adjoining rooms opening out of the back wall. Another exceptional feature, considering the tomb's early date, is the inscription painted on the back wall of the entrance chamber, giving the name of the noble family which owned the tomb.

Painted in the space between the two doors leading to the small rooms is a scene drawn from Greek mythology which occurs a number of times in Greek sculpture and pottery of this period: the Greek hero Achilles lying in wait for Troilus, one of Priam's sons. The young Trojan, mounted on horseback, approaches a fountain behind which Achilles is waiting, armed with helmet, greaves and dagger, ready to leap out from his hiding-place and strike the fatal blow. The scene takes place in the midst of shrubs and bushes, which are painted in every empty space around the two heroes. The painter is not a great artist, and his changes of mind can often be seen, both in the preliminary design and in the actual painting. However, his skill as a decorator is apparent in the rendering of plant

Above: vase in the shape of a female head, by the potter Charinos. Tarquinia, Museo Nazionale

Right: large cup in the miniaturistic style, depicting Heracles wrestling with Triton and, round the edge, girls dancing. Tarquinia, Museo Nazionale

and ornamental motifs in the tomb, and this suggests that he spent some time as a vase-painter.

Finally, the little frieze which runs along the back wall above the mythological scene is unusual in its subject-matter: two erotic groups with a bull beside each one. The bull on the left is more or less indifferent to what is going on, but the one on the right, depicted with a human head, has his horns lowered ready to charge the second group.

In this same northern area of the hill, to the right of the road, is the Tomba degli Auguri. It consists of a single rectangular chamber with a gabled ceiling and wide painted central beam. All four walls and the ceiling are painted, as was usual in the chamber-tombs of the 6th and 5th centuries B.C.

On the end wall there is an imitation door, representing the entrance to the place where the deceased was imagined to be. On either side are figures making a gesture of lamentation, each touching his forehead with one hand and stretching out the other arm.

The side walls show vividly realistic scenes from the athletic games held in honour of the deceased. In the centre of the right-hand wall there are two wrestlers; the younger, still beardless, has seized his opponent firmly by the wrists. To the left of them two judges watch the contest, holding in their right hands a curved stick as their badge of office; they are accompanied by two servants, one of whom carries a folding stool on his shoulder.

The winner will receive as his prize the three metal basins depicted, one on top of the other, between the two athletes. Another scene of contest between two people is also painted on the right-hand wall. The first figure is described in the inscription by the name *phersu* (corresponding to the Latin *persona*, 'masked man'); he is wearing a short red garment, a pointed cap on his head and a mask with an extremely long beard covering his face. He is inciting a dog, which he is holding on a very long lead, to attack the second figure. The latter is naked and his head is completely covered by a white cloth; with a club he is trying to fend off the dog, which is about to sink its teeth into his left leg.

A later stage of the same contest is shown on the tomb's left-hand wall. The masked man, who has obviously had the worst of it, has taken to his heels, having lost all vestiges of clothing, and casts a terrified look back at his pursuing opponent.

This sport, which appears only at Tarquinia, in this and some other painted tombs, is a theme typical of the use of local subject-matter in tomb-decoration. However, these native realistic paintings also reflect the influence of the Ionian style which was dominant in Tarquinia in the last years of the 6th century and is apparent in the figures of the two wrestlers with their solid bodies, round heads, receding foreheads, large noses and fleshy lips.

After the visit to the tombs on Monterozzi, the tomb paintings housed on the top floor of the Museo Nazionale deserve special attention. These were removed from their original settings by the Istituto Centrale del Restauro to prevent further deterioration.

The walls of the Tomba delle Olimpiadi ('Tomb of the Olympic Games') show a series of athletic competitions. On the right is the cruel contest, already encountered in the Tomba degli Auguri, between a masked man and a strange figure, his head wrapped in a cloth, who is frantically using a club to ward off an angry dog set on him by his opponent. Then come a discus-thrower in action and an athlete about to make a jump. Finally there is a race which is going to be won by the oldest of the three runners, humorously characterized by a long pointed beard.

The left-hand wall shows a boxing match and a race of two-horse chariots, with four contestants. In this last scene the artist's personality emerges: he does not just depict the incident, but shows all the lively and picturesque details. The first charioteer turns a worried look towards his pursuers; the third leans forward to shout encouragement to his horses as they overtake the chariot in front of them; lastly, the fourth charioteer comes to grief and is thrown into the air, while one of his horses has fallen to the ground with its legs in the air. The tomb obviously dates from the last decades of the 6th century, since the style reflects the Ionian influence usual in that period.

In the Tomba delle Bighe ('Tomb of the Chariots'), athletic games again form part of the subject-matter of the wall paintings. The narrow frieze along the top of the walls shows several contests (two-horse chariot-racing, boxing, discus-throwing and so on) taking place in a stadium surrounded by wooden stands, on which the spectators are seated. In style these paintings, dating from about 500 B.C., are very interesting because they show the first attempts at naturalistic representation of the human figure, following the new trends in Athenian art in the early 5th century B.C. In the athletes' movements and gestures there is also a timid attempt at perspective, in place of the conventional abstract schemes of earlier paintings.

The tomb walls are also decorated with a second frieze which deals for the first time with themes which reappear in other tombs of the first half of the 5th century B.C. The end wall shows a banquet scene with two male figures, while on the side walls there are musicians and dancers.

The theme of the banquet, taking place in a joyous atmosphere among the flowering shrubs of a garden, with musicians and dancers, recurs in the paintings of the Tomba del Triclinio ('Tomb of the Dining Room'). The participants, painted on the end wall, are two couples half-reclining on couches. Their poses, their slightly inclined heads and the

Biconical Villanovan urns with, respectively, a bowl and a helmet as lids, from the Monterozzi cemetery

Right: Etruscan black-figure amphora, depicting a troop of marching warriors. Tarquinia, Museo Nazionale

solemn, languid gestures of their arms make a harmonious and graceful composition, obviously inspired by the models of Athenian art of the early 5th century B.C. The delicate curving contours of the individual figures, with their fluid, sinuous outlines, are painted in mellow colours, sometimes lightly shaded. These highly accomplished works are among the most important examples of ancient painting.

Similar in style to the paintings of the Tomba del Triclinio are those of the slightly later Tomba del Letto Funebre ('Tomb of the Funeral Couch'; 470 B.C.), but their subject-matter, on the entire end wall and part of the side walls, is original. An enormous couch, decorated with heavy multicoloured covers, dominates the centre of the scene, which is set in a large pavilion roofed over with an awning supported by columns decorated with leaves. On the bed are spread two white mantles, while two strange conical objects, with a garland of leaves round the bottom, are resting on two cushions. On either side of the bed a banquet scene is depicted on one plane; in the background, young men are standing facing the bed, their arms raised in salute and homage. The composition provides the first example of a single coherent funeral scene, probably representing a specific moment in the ceremony in honour of the dead owners of the tomb. The decoration is completed by the usual figures of musicians and dancers.

The Museo Nazionale also contains one of Italy's most important collections of Etruscan antiquities and Greek pottery. The most interesting exhibits on the ground floor are the series of outstanding sarcophagi from the great noble tombs of the 4th–2nd centuries B.C. and the many Archaic burial reliefs decorated with animals in the Orientalizing style.

On the first floor can be seen the slab of pedimental decoration from the Ara della Regina temple, with the relief of the two winged horses. Also on show, arranged in chronological order, are pottery and other finds from the cemetery: sheet bronzes from the Villanovan period; the Orientalizing grave goods of the Tomba di Bokkoris; a series of Corinthian vases and locally-made imitations; Athenian black- and red-figure pottery, including the remarkable cup signed by the painter Oltos, and a vase modelled in the form of a woman's head, signed by Charinos.

On the same floor are some fine heads and other votive objects (models of swaddled babies and parts of the body) from the deposit found near the great temple of Pian di Civita.

Sanctuary at Punta della Vipera

North of S. Marinella, at the mouth of the Marangone stream, the remains of a little sanctuary dedicated to the goddess Minerva have recently been excavated at Punta della Vipera. This sanctuary lay in the open country, away from any towns, and served the religious needs of the scattered rural population.

The excavations revealed the history of this temple. It was built during the second half of the 6th century B.C.; after a period of prosperity, it was destroyed in consequence of hostilities (about which nothing is known) towards the beginning of the 4th century B.C. The area was subsequently levelled by means of a terrace of earth mixed with rubble from the original building and its votive deposits, and about 350 B.C. a new temple was built on the site, probably on the same plan, but decorated with a new series of terracotta facing plaques. After 273 B.C. the coastal strip of land belonging to the territory of Cerveteri was requisitioned by the victorious Romans, who founded several *coloniae* there, including Castrum Novum (probably in 264), about 700 metres from the sanctuary at Punta della Vipera. This led to a further renewal of its terracotta decorations; it is known that in fact these slabs needed replacing with new pieces quite frequently, since they quickly deteriorated as a result of exposure to the atmosphere.

The sanctuary went through a period of decline from the 3rd century B.C. until the time of Augustus, when its ruins were used as a quarry for building materials for a villa, part of which was constructed over the eastern side of the former sanctuary.

The sanctuary appears to have consisted of an enclosure, with the temple in its north-western part; the temple probably had a single, almost square cella and a colonnade in front.

Behind this, in the direction of the Via Aurelia, which runs about 50 to 70 metres inland of this site, were rooms added no earlier than the 4th century B.C., possibly a service area. In front of the temple are the remains of an altar, also dating from the 4th century, i.e. from the second building phase of the sanctuary; it was almost square and had a base and central part of rock chips, with facing in *nenfro*.

To the east of the temple, two wells have been found near the altar; the second was filled up with animal bones, vases, fragments of architectural terracottas, and a sheet of lead with an inscription, about 70 words long, containing formulae of a ritual nature.

A votive deposit was found lying against the boundary wall; this consisted of models of parts of the body, coins, vases with inscriptions, and objects of everyday use, such as fish-hooks and weights for fishing-nets.

Porto Clementino

The archaeological importance of Porto Clementino was unknown until a few years ago. All that was known was that the *colonia* of Gravisca had been founded in Roman times at this site on the Tyrrhenian coast, near the modern lido of Tarquinia. Nothing was visible on the surface, but aerial photography revealed the ground-plan of the *colonia*, consisting of a series of straight roads that intersected at right angles, forming a regular grid system.

In 1969 the land was divided into building lots and the archaeological status of the area was threatened; so the Soprintendenza alle Antichità dell'Etruria Meridionale began the systematic excavation of the whole area. This led to a series of surprises: not only were the remains of the Roman *colonia* uncovered and the successive phases identified of its continuous occupation from its foundation in 181 B.C. to the late Imperial age, but the earlier Etruscan settlement, dating back to the early 6th century B.C., was also found on the same site, covered in part by the Roman ruins. This was the ancient port of Tarquinia. Its name is still unknown, but it was certainly large, covering a vast, roughly rectangular area: its longer side ran for 800 metres along the coast, and its shorter side followed the road leading to Tarquinia for 300 metres.

Only small trial excavations were made to the oldest levels (6th and 5th centuries B.C.) and it was not possible to gain a clear and coherent picture of the plan of the Archaic town; the structures brought to light are of interest, nevertheless. They consisted of short stretches of streets and remains of private houses: the lower parts of the walls of

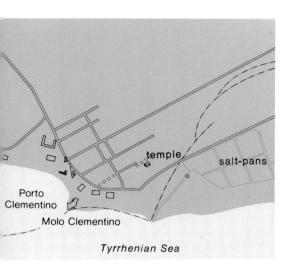

Gravisca. Archaeological plan

Excavated area of Gravisca, with remains
uncovered since excavations began in 1969

these houses were exceptionally well preserved, consisting of large limestone blocks that must have supported the unfired brick of the upper part.

One really remarkable fact of historical importance has, however, emerged from the excavations in this area: they provide for the first time evidence of Greek settlement on Etruscan soil in the 6th century and the first decades of the 5th century B.C. This evidence came with the discovery, on the extreme southern edge of the Etruscan settlement, of a sacred area where the rites of an exclusively Greek cult were performed in the Archaic period, as is indicated by the inscriptions and pottery found there. The deities worshipped were Hera and Aphrodite, as we know from numerous inscriptions incised on vases offered to them. Furthermore, since the alphabet and dialect of these inscriptions are Ionian, that is, those used by the Greeks living on the coast of Asia Minor, it can be assumed that it was the Ionians who established their cult in this sanctuary in Archaic times. This is confirmed by the discovery of a high proportion of Ionian pottery and, significantly, of a large number (about 2,000) of terracotta oil-lamps, a form of votive offering frequently found in East Greek sanctuaries (Samos, Rhodes).

Another important object (p. 24) discovered in this sacred area was a roughly pyramidal cippus 1.30 metres high, with a Greek inscription on one face, dating from the end of the 6th century B.C., that reads: 'I belong to Apollo of Aegina. Sostratos had me made'. This was obviously a sacred image of Apollo (other representations of the god in this form are known) and was set up in the sanctuary as an offering by the person named on it. He was a citizen of Aegina (a city of Greece proper); Herodotus mentions him as one of the most successful Greek traders of all time.

The Etruscan port of Tarquinia was therefore an important port of call for Greek traders in the 6th century and the first decades of the 5th century B.C.; this fact adds greatly to our knowledge of the links between the Greek world and Etruria, which were particularly strong during this period.

The remains of buildings discovered in the sanctuary area are also worth mentioning. Excavations still in progress have uncovered remains of buildings, all constructed after the period of Greek occupation (6th–beginning of the 5th century B.C.), except perhaps for some short stretches of a dry wall. In fact, the area was occupied, from the beginning of the 4th to the end of the 3rd century B.C., by a second sanctuary, this time dedicated to a native cult. Inscriptions found at levels of later occupation show that the Etruscan goddesses Turan (Aphrodite) and Uni (Hera) were venerated there. The construction of this new sanctuary must have resulted in the almost total destruction of earlier buildings on the site, although it has been possible to reconstruct them from the discovery of their foundation trenches cut into the ground.

Three buildings belonging to the Etruscan sanctuary have been discovered: they have dry walls made of large stones and pebbles from the river bed, though only the foundations below ground level have been found. These buildings open on to a street running north-west in the direction of the ancient port. The largest consists of a rectangular courtyard, where two altars and a well can be seen, with two adjacent rectangular rooms opening off it; to the west of one of these is a second irregular four-sided courtyard. Of the other buildings, one is situated to the east of the street, and consists of a single room containing several bases for votive offerings; the other building, farther to the south, consists of a rectangular room with a vestibule in front, and a central well.

Vulci was one of the major cities of southern Etruria, situated on the right bank of the river Fiora, some 12 kilometres as the crow flies from the Tyrrhenian coast and 110 kilometres north of Rome. The ruins of the city, together with the remains of its desolate burial-grounds, today stretch over a wide uninhabited region lying between the two small towns of Montalto di Castro and Canino; this is one of the most picturesque areas of the Maremma.

Geographically speaking, the region is characterized by the presence of hills of volcanic origin, with frequent plateaux which have been much eroded by the small watercourses of the Fiora basin.

The ancient settlement arose on one of these tufa plateaux, fairly low in height and roughly oblong in shape. From its northeastern corner there extends a long narrow tongue of land, falling sharply away on three of its sides, orientated east–west; this is the presumed site of the ancient acropolis. The remains of the city, as brought to light to date, do not date back beyond the 4th century B.C., and supply evidence only of the last period of development of the Etruscan city, which came under the political authority of Rome in the year 280 B.C., was transformed into a Roman *municipium* after the Social War (90 B.C.) and progressively declined in the Imperial period.

Basically, the cemeteries occupied two areas, both very extensive and both crowded with tombs: one is situated to the east of the Fiora and comprises three main nuclei, known respectively—from north to south—as Cavalupo, Ponte Rotto and Polledrara; the other is to the north of the city on the right bank of the Fiora, near the modern village of Osteria. The period during which these two cemeteries developed was long; as attested by the archaeological data they furnished, it lasted from the early 8th century B.C. down to the 1st century A.D. The extraordinarily large number of tombs and the richness of

Vulci. Aerial view of the ancient settlement

funerary objects from between the end of the 7th and the mid-5th century B.C. conclusively illustrate the importance of this Etruscan city during those centuries. During this period Vulci seems to have exercised its cultural influence and possibly its political authority over the surrounding area, and in particular over the minor centres situated farther up the Fiora valley (Sovana, Statonia and Poggio Buco) and the hills to the west of Lake Bolsena. Proof of this is provided once more by the cemeteries in the neighbouring centres of Ischia di Castro, Pescia Romana and Sovana which, among other things, have yielded objects very similar to those from contemporary Vulcian tombs.

Furthermore, it is only on the basis of archaeological data that we can piece together the history of Vulci. In fact, nothing has been recorded by the ancient historians, and inscriptions referring to the place are few and far between. Its actual Etruscan name is uncertain (Velh- ?), and the only reliable historical mention refers to Vulci's ill-fated

Vulci. The Ponte della Badia across the river Fiora

Following pages: Vulci. Ruins of a house of the late Republican period with a fine mosaic floor of black and white geometric designs

conflict with Rome (280 B.C.), as a result of which it was deprived of part of its territory and also of its access to the sea, where the Roman *colonia* of Cosa was founded in 273 B.C.

The early Iron Age saw the start of the development of the Vulcian cemeteries. The oldest Villanovan tombs (9th century B.C.) have been found both in the three clearly defined cemeteries in the eastern area and in the northern, Osteria area. These are pit-type tombs for cremated dead, dug into the soft local limestone (*murcio*), containing the usual biconical urns of dark impasto, placed in tufa or *nenfro* holders, or else in holes dug inside larger pits.

Later, around the original nuclei represented by these pit-tombs, the 8th and 7th centuries saw the appearance of countless trench-tombs, which were linked with the establishment of the inhumation rite.

The cultural level of this original Villanovan concentration was notably high, particularly as regards the funerary objects from the Osteria cemetery. One of these funerary deposits, still in the Archaic period (early 8th century), includes a bronze statuette of a warrior which is a typical product of the culture of the first inhabitants of Sardinia. Together with the various other Sardinian pieces found at Populonia and Vetulonia, this provides evidence of the existence—in those remote days—of trading relations between the two areas, both of which are known to have been major producers of metals.

In another tomb, from the mid-8th century, was found a hut-type cinerary urn, exceptional in being made of sheet bronze instead of the usual dark impasto. It is finely decorated with rows of small dots and studs; furthermore, the precision with which certain architectural elements are rendered (the pronounced overhang of the roof, the outer framework of the ceiling) makes it a real model of an oval-plan hut with a low conical roof, such as must have been familiar in contemporary Etruscan domestic architecture.

In the first half of the 7th century B.C. the Vulcian cemeteries went through a period of stagnation: the sudden rapid cultural advance that accompanied the establishment of the Orientalizing culture in the major cities of Etruria does not appear to have affected Vulci. The riches of the tombs of Cerveteri or Vetulonia are unknown, as are the early precious objects imported from abroad; pottery techniques show no startling development, and there are few examples of the finer and thinner bucchero-ware.

In the last decades of the century, nevertheless, the cemeteries underwent a slow but steady revival, which became gradually more noticeable. From this moment onwards Vulci may be considered one of the cities of Etruria with the liveliest cultural progress. The Tomba di Iside, in the Polledrara cemetery, with its rich funerary objects dating from about the first decades of the 6th century, attests the now fully-fledged renaissance. Among the many imported objects found in this tomb is a small statue in alabaster, 88 cm high, of a woman richly clothed in a long robe covered by a mantle; her arms are held forwards at right angles from the elbows and in her left hand she holds a strange long-horned animal (possibly not part of the original sculpture). This is a fairly important example of Archaic Greek sculpture (580/570 B.C.); its stylistic characteristics are displayed above all in the stiff appearance of the figure and the features of the rather square face, which seems engraved rather than sculpted in the stone. Other objects of foreign origin found in the tomb are Egyptian scarabs, painted vases and five decorated ostrich eggs.

In this period of the greatest development of the cemeteries, which continued until well into the 5th century, the characteristic type of tomb is the so-called *cassone* or chest; this consists of a small chamber, usually containing one body, with benches along the walls and a barrel-vaulted ceiling. One exception is the monumental Tomba del Sole e della Luna, discovered in the Osteria cemetery. This consists of eight chambers, the ceilings of which are carved in rock to imitate wooden structures; they have a central beam and at right angles to this a row of smaller joists in relief or, in one case, a series of small beams arranged in a fan shape.

Tumulus-tombs, which are typical of the cemeteries of this date at Tarquinia and Cerveteri, are rare. However, Vulci does boast one unusual and remarkably monumental

example of this type, known as the Cuccumella. It has been excavated on several different occasions from the 19th century onwards, but has still not been explored completely in every part. The tumulus is about 18 metres high, has a diameter of some 65 metres and is bordered by a circular enclosure made of *nenfro* slabs fixed into the rock, which is cut all around the circumference to a depth of about 5 metres. At the centre of the enclosure, at the end of a long corridor, was an apparently unroofed area; it was cut into the rock and its upper part completed with blocks of stone; at the sides are two small rooms covered by a false vault, and beyond these there are two further chambers furnished with benches. A steep ramp from the last room led to the centre of the tumulus, where complicated underground tunnels have been excavated.

A characteristic feature of the tombs of this period (7th–5th centuries) is the presence of stone sculptures at the entrance of the corridor giving access to the tomb, or at the sides of the main door of the burial chamber. These sculptures generally depict animals or monsters, such as panthers, lions, centaurs or sphinxes, taken from the traditional repertoire of the Orientalizing culture and repeated, almost ritually, in later periods too. Two of the most interesting examples of these which, among other things, reflect two different phases in the development of Etruscan art, are in the Museo di Villa Giulia: a centaur, and a sea-horse with a human rider. The former, it is true, displays typically Etruscan emphases in the rendering of certain of the facial features, the large deep-set eyes, large flattened nose, curved full-lipped mouth, but it is inspired by a Greek model, and its heavy, compact structure shows the influence of Greek, in particular Corinthian, artistic trends. The latter, on the other hand, which is some fifty years later (dating from *c.* 540/530 B.C.), although unique in Archaic Mediterranean statuary, reveals the influence of Ionian Greek art in the rhythm and movement of the sculpture as a whole.

Among the funerary objects from these same tombs the quantity and quality of the

Vulci. Detail of the *viridarium* (garden) of the same house

vases discovered are such that Vulci, of all the centres in the ancient world, may be considered to provide the greatest wealth of evidence for the study of Greek vases. The most important groups of Greek-made vases are first the Corinthian (end of the 7th–mid-6th centuries B.C.), followed by the Ionian and by the Athenian black-figure and red-figure pottery (6th–mid-5th centuries). There are also countless imitations of these products. Fairly notable examples of these are provided by the Etrusco-Corinthian vases, with distinctive animal friezes in rows one above the other, like the imported originals, though executed with less accurate draughtsmanship, and the Pontic vases, whose decorative repertoire (large palmettes and lotus flowers, mythological figures, and so on) is inspired by the designs and conventions of Ionian vase-painting.

Besides pottery, there was a particularly flourishing industry producing bronze objects which were exported throughout Italy from about the mid-6th century B.C. onwards. These included candelabra, censers, statuettes, vases with figured handles, and tripods standing on tall slender rod-legs with applied figures: all of these show considerable technical refinement and rich decoration.

Shortly after 450 B.C. Vulci was in the grip of that general economic and artistic crisis which affected more or less all the cities of Etruria, and lasted until the mid-4th century B.C. Its recovery was nevertheless dazzling. In the larger noble tombs, in some cases decorated with paintings, the signs of a new affluence are to be seen. These tombs are in a variety of shapes and sizes; from the 4th century until Roman times they were built here, there and everywhere at various heights on the rocky slopes which overlook the left bank of the river Fiora (Cavalupo) and, to a lesser extent, in the Osteria cemetery as well. The oldest type (4th–3rd centuries B.C.) consists of a long corridor which ends in a large covered vestibule, which in turn extends into a rectangular chamber off which there are several other rooms: the whole complex is a copy of the typical Etruscan house, with

Below: cast bronze tripod, from Vulci. Rome, Musei Vaticani

Right: oval casket in bronze with embossed decoration. Rome, Musei Vaticani

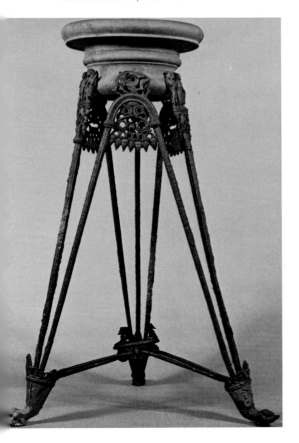

the *atrium* (the vestibule), *tablinum* (the rectangular chamber) and secondary rooms. Other elements of obviously architectural derivation to be found in this type of tomb are the fine gabled roofs with beams in relief and the carved imitation doors (Tomba François, Tomba dei Tori).

A later type of tomb (3rd–2nd centuries B.C.) is the so-called corridor type. This consists of a large number of small cell-like rooms, symmetrically arranged along the sides of an extremely long corridor which leads to a large chamber, off which there are still more rooms. A less common type, similar to some of the tombs at Cerveteri, consists of a single large chamber with one or more piers supporting the ceiling, and burial niches cut into the walls. The Tomba Campanari (end of the 4th century B.C.), discovered in the Osteria cemetery, is an example of this type; its central column has an ornate capital decorated with leaves and female heads.

In this last phase of the development of Vulci, the remains unearthed in the urban area supplement the archaeological evidence provided by the cemetery. The city appears to have been defended by a wall, parts of which are still standing, made of large blocks of tufa with considerable rustication and with strengthening in *nenfro*. There are the remains of two gates, one to the east and one to the north, with single openings probably in the form of arches.

Of the street network, the steep *decumanus* has been found, with some of the buildings facing it; in the eastern stretch of this a small building is visible, of religious character, dedicated to Hercules, with two distinct phases of existence, one dating from the 3rd century B.C., the other from the height of the Roman Empire.

Along the central section of the *decumanus* a nymphaeum and a portico have been discovered on the southern side, at the intersection with a road which seems to climb up towards the acropolis; on the other side are the foundations of a large building, possibly a temple, situated at the centre of an enclosure. Beside this a fine house of the late Republican period (1st century B.C.) has been discovered, with its own baths. The rooms are arranged axially and have beautiful mosaic floors with black and white geometric designs; it is possible to identify the *atrium*, the *tablinum*, a large peristyle (inner courtyard) and a small nymphaeum. The numerous subterranean vaulted tanks were supplied by an aqueduct connected with the river Fiora.

Among the buildings erected in Roman times, particular mention should be made of the two bridges over the Fiora, which must be associated with the ancient road network of the Vulci region (still obscure). The Ponte della Badia, situated to the north near the Castello, is an impressive structure dating from the first half of the 1st century B.C.; it has three arches, the easternmost one being a blind arch, while the central one measures 20 metres across; it is built of *nenfro* and travertine with tufa pillars as buttresses. The second bridge, no longer standing (Ponte Rotto), was farther to the south; it had five arches, each 12 metres across, supported by 'flat-iron' piers.

A visit to the remains of the city of Vulci, which we have now briefly described, may be extended to include some of the larger noble tombs discovered in the cemeteries to the east of the Fiora (visitors should apply to the Castello).

One of these, situated near the Ponte Rotto, is the Tomba François; it stands out from the other tombs by the greater complexity of its architecture and above all by the paintings that once decorated its walls. A very deep corridor some 27 metres long leads via a door with a hawksbeak architrave into a rectangular antechamber, end-on to the corridor; on the side opposite the entrance door there is an almost square room which would correspond to the *tablinum* in the plan of an Etruscan house. The ceiling of the antechamber imitates the wooden framework of a gabled roof, while the *tablinum* has a ceiling with imitation beams and at the centre a slab with a low relief depicting the face of Charun, the monstrous demon of hell. Three rooms open off the antechamber on the left, and three on the right; at the end of the *tablinum* is the main room, with its gabled roof and walls decorated with an imitation marble facing. The tomb, which was discovered apparently intact, has yielded

Above: Vulci. Alabaster statue, from the Tomba di Iside. London, British Museum

Below: general plan of Vulci

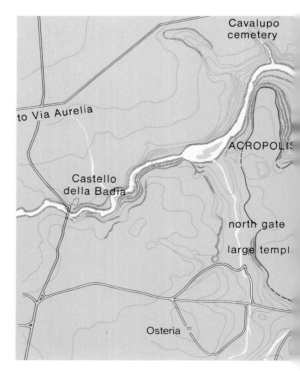

Above: portrait of Vel Saties

Right: sacrifice of the Trojan prisoners. Paintings from the Tomba François. Rome, Villa Albani

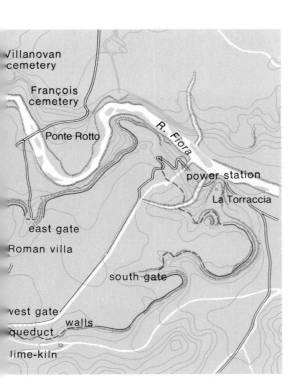

a very large number of vases and items of gold-work; it was used for about 250 years, from the beginning of the 4th century to the mid-2nd century B.C.

The famous paintings (now kept in the Villa Albani at Rome, belonging to the Torlonia family) were on the walls of the antechamber and the *tablinum*. In the first room they were painted at the sides of each door leading to the six side rooms; they depict six pairs of people, among whom are the two owners of the tomb, members of the aristocratic family of the Saties; a figure from Etruscan history killing a Roman, named by the inscription as Cneus Tarquinius Romanus; and Greek heroes (Sisyphus and Amphiaraüs, Eteocles and Polynices).

The long side-walls of the *tablinum*, on the other hand, showed more complicated mythological and historical scenes. On the left was the scene of the sacrifice of the Trojan prisoners in the presence of the shade of Patroclus and two Etruscan demons, Charun and Vanth; on the right, however, was depicted an incident in Etruscan history with a battle between heroes, perhaps from Vulci, and people whom we know from the accompanying inscription to be from other Etruscan cities (Sovana and Volsinii). Each of these is depicted in the act of submission to the foe. The composition also includes the figure of Macstrna, identified in Roman tradition with the Roman king Servius Tullius, depicted releasing an Etruscan hero from the bonds holding him captive.

A few feet away from the Tomba François is the Tomba dei Tutes, dating from the 3rd century B.C., which is very similar to the above in both plan and architecture, although it has no paintings.

The nearby Tomba dei Due Ingressi has an unusual plan: here a single corridor leads into two separate tombs consisting of a narrow vestibule, an antechamber and a room containing two sarcophagi. An interesting detail is the presence on the walls of one of the antechambers of nails for hanging the funerary objects.

Lastly, the Tomba delle Iscrizioni (dating from the end of the 4th century B.C.), not far from the above-mentioned tombs, has a very irregular plan: it has a very long corridor and a large chamber off which there are six small irregular rooms; above the doors to these rooms there are long funerary inscriptions, either painted or inscribed.

A tour of the ruins of Vulci may be completed by a short visit to the Castello della Badia, where there is a small Antiquarium which is in course of arrangement.

Ischia di Castro

Around the city of Vulci there were numerous settlements, smaller in size, but still important. In an area approximately bounded by Monte Argentario to the north, the river Arrone to the south, and the heights around Lake Bolsena to the west, were the centres of Forum Aurelium, Cosa and Ischia di Castro and the small villages of Pescia Romana, Cellere, Canino and perhaps Poggio Buco. Over this wide area, which was crossed by two major highways, the Via Aurelia along the coast and a second main road inland, Vulci must have exercised its artistic influence and perhaps its political authority, at least in the period of its heyday (end of the 7th–mid-5th centuries B.C.). This is attested by the evidence of the Vulcian cemeteries and, among others, those at Pescia Romana and Ischia di Castro, which show designs and conventions that are quite similar as regards the style of the tombs and the funerary objects.

For instance, numerous chamber- and chest-tombs, typical of Vulci in the 6th and first half of the 5th century B.C., have been discovered in the vast Castro cemetery, which has been excavated in recent years near the hill where the ruins of the old mediaeval town stand in their rather picturesque position. The town was destroyed in 1649 by Pope Innocent X after a bitter struggle between the Church and the Farnese lords of the stronghold; it is situated 20 kilometres north of Vulci on the right bank of the Olpeta, a tributary of the Fiora. In particular, in one tomb from this cemetery an exceptional discovery was made, a few years ago, of a two-horse chariot of wood and iron covered with sheet bronze, buried in the corridor giving access to the tomb; the horses were still harnessed, having probably been sacrificed to the shades of the deceased. Thanks to the extremely careful and prompt intervention of the Istituto Centrale del Ristauro, it was possible to recover this valuable object, which would have been lost for ever if provision had not been made to extract it with special apparatus from the mud in which it was sunk. It was in fact necessary to construct a temporary framework by the use of a plaster jacket to hold the fragile parts of the chariot together at the moment of removal. The painstaking work of reinforcing and reconstructing the piece is not yet completed: we know, however, that this was a ceremonial chariot with a curved frame, a high curved front and wide hand-bars, similar to other examples discovered in Umbria at Monteleone di Spoleto (now in the Metropolitan Museum of Art, New York) and at Castel S. Mariano near Perugia. Particularly elegant embossed decoration embellishes the bronze plating along the sides of the front panel: following the typical design of an Archaic Greek statue, it depicts two nude young men, facing towards the front of the chariot, with one leg thrust forward, arms extended down their sides, heads up and eyes looking straight ahead. From the style of these two small reliefs, which are influenced by the Ionian artistic tradition, the chariot may be dated to the end of the 6th century B.C.

Veii, the southernmost Etruscan city, and thus the closest to Rome, stood on a tufaceous plateau bordered by the Valchetta (the ancient Cremera) and one of its tributaries, the Piordo, giving an overall area of about 350 hectares. To the north its territory adjoined the Faliscan territory, to the west that of Cerveteri, and to the south it reached the sea; to the east the river Tiber separated it from Rome; Veii held the right bank of the Tiber at least from Fidenae to the estuary, including the districts of present-day Rome that lie on that side of the river.

This important Etruscan city was served by a highly-developed road system which linked it with the neighbouring areas. Along the city wall no less than seven main gates have been clearly identified; from each of these gates a road left the city, some dating from the Villanovan period (as is confirmed by the siting of the Iron Age cemeteries along them),

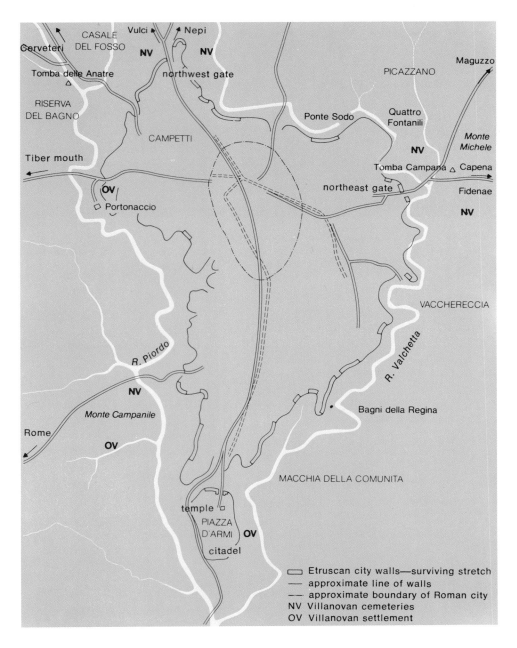

Veii. Plan of the archaeological zone

others from a later stage in the city's development. A certain number of routes remained in use after the fall of Veii until the construction of the Via Clodia and the Via Cassia in Roman times.

Although there are very occasional finds of objects dating back to the Bronze Age, the area was permanently settled only during the Villanovan period. According to some scholars, Villanovan Veii was not a single centre of habitation, but rather a group of separate villages, each occupying a corner of the plateau, with its own burial-ground on the road which linked it to other nearby settlements. Other archaeologists, on the other hand, maintain that there was a single inhabited area.

The most substantial discoveries from the Iron Age settlement, revealing traces of the wooden huts that must have formed it, have been made near the northwest gate, at Piazza d'Armi and at Portonaccio.

Archaic architectural slab from Piazza d'Armi (Veii). Rome, Museo di Villa Giulia

Villanovan cemeteries have been discovered at Grotta Gramiccia, Valle La Fata, Vaccereccia and Quattro Fontanili. The oldest tombs are of the simple pit type (with a diameter hardly greater than that of the cinerary urn they contained); later the pits became more complex (with burial niches in the sides or with a second smaller pit and the urn placed in a tufa holder or a terracotta jar). Large roof-like tufa discs were possibly used to mark the burial-place. Alongside the more developed pits there are trench-tombs for inhumation, often with a niche in which the funerary objects were placed, cut into one of the longer sides.

Villanovan Veii does not appear to have been as rich as the coastal cities; the funerary objects are relatively poor, but show an interesting affinity with the neighbouring contemporary Iron Age cultures of Latium and the Faliscan territory, with which they clearly maintained commercial relations. The discovery of cups imported from Cumae shows that, from as early as this period, such relations extended as far as the Greek colonies in Campania; it seems likely that the southernmost Etruscan city acted as intermediary in trading iron and other raw materials between the rich mining cities of northern Etruria and the oldest Greek settlements in Italy.

Given the lack of systematic archaeological excavation, it is not possible to say much about the Etruscan city and its internal topography. The city centre was most probably situated at the highest point of the plateau, where the various roads met and where the Roman *municipium* was later built. The acropolis, on the other hand, has been identified at Piazza d'Armi towards the southeastern tip of the plateau where the hillsides become overhanging: this is separated from the rest of the city by a deep, in part man-made ditch.

It was not until late in the 5th century that the inhabitants of Veii felt the need to erect a city wall (except perhaps around the citadel itself), and it was only following the threat of an invasion by Rome that the plateau was surrounded by a high earth rampart which also incorporated a wall made of tufa blocks. From finds made near the northeast and northwest gates and on the acropolis, we know that the houses of Veii had foundations of roughly-squared tufa blocks and walls built of mud-bricks or wattle.

Recent excavations at Piazza d'Armi have brought to light a series of streets intersecting at right angles, following a proper town-plan of the Greek type. There must have been many sacred buildings in the city; at the present time, thanks to the discovery of the monument itself or of votive deposits, at least five such buildings have been identified: on the acropolis, at the foot of the citadel, at Campetti, near the Porta di Cere and finally at Portonaccio, outside the walls.

The cemeteries belonging to the Etruscan city (Macchia della Comunità, Vacchereccia, Monte Michele, Picazzano, Casale del Fosso, Grotta Gramiccia, Riserva del Bagno, Pozzuolo, Oliveto Grande and Monte Campanile) extend over the hills all around the city wall, which was thus completely surrounded by burial-grounds. Some of these developed without interruption out of the previous Villanovan cemeteries, while others were new. The special feature of the cemeteries of Veii is their chronological succession from the top to the foot of the hills on which they are sited: the Iron Age tombs are the oldest and are to be found at the top of the hills; lower down are the chamber-tombs opening on to the hillside, and the *area scoperta* tombs, characteristic of Veii, which consist of a trench which is almost a room without a ceiling, reached by means of steps, with niches cut into the sides. The chamber-tombs are usually very simple, oblong in shape, with one or more funerary couches.

The cemeteries of Veii have not been much studied. From the information available, it would appear that at the beginning of the historical period (7th century B.C.) the city never achieved the splendour of neighbouring Cerveteri and Tarquinia. Outside the burial-grounds, along the routes of the ancient roads, there are, it is true, many large isolated tumuli with tombs of this period, but the funerary objects of the deceased are on a modest level: there is hardly any gold-work at all, and the bronzes are rather poor. But, to be fair, it should be mentioned that in the tumulus sited on the top of Monte Aguzzo, in the direction of present-day Formello, there was found one of the most beautiful Greek vases of the Orientalizing period, now in the Museo di Villa Giulia: the Chigi olpe.

The only paintings to be found so far at Veii, which decorate the walls of the Tomba delle Anatre in the Riserva del Bagno cemetery and the Tomba Campana in the Monte Michele cemetery, must also be attributed to the 7th century. These are among the oldest examples of frescoed tombs discovered to date in Etruria, following a tradition later characteristic of the coastal city of Tarquinia, rather than of Veii.

In the course of the 6th and 5th centuries Veii was at its most splendid; it became one of the most important artistic centres in Etruria, especially in the field of terracottas, thanks to its famous workshops of modellers. The clay decorations that covered the wooden structures of the temple discovered on the acropolis are among the oldest of their kind and are made after Archaic Greek designs.

But in the second half of the 6th century the fame of the artists of Veii crossed the frontiers of Etruria itself. Ancient authors mention a great modeller from Veii by the

name of Vulca, whose skill was so renowned that he was summoned to Rome by the Tarquins with the task of making the statue of Jupiter for the temple on the Capitol. The quadriga (four-horse chariot) on the top of the roof was likewise attributed to Veian workmanship.

Vulca is the only Etruscan artist whose name has been recorded. References in the various sources have become of considerable interest since the discovery in the area of the Portonaccio sanctuary of a group of terracotta statues which must have been placed on the great central beam at the top of the temple roof. These figures are larger than life-size; of notable beauty are the famous Apollo, Heracles with the hind, Hermes and a goddess and child, now in the Museo di Villa Giulia. The group, which shows the influence of East Greek art dominant throughout Etruria in the second half of the 6th century, as well as Athenian influences, can be dated to between 520 and 500 B.C. Who could have been the author of works of such a high artistic level if not the Vulca mentioned by ancient writers? Archaeologists have in fact attributed the statues to the great artist, or at least to his school. The workshops of the modellers of Veii also flourished during the 5th century, to judge from the discovery of pieces of considerable artistic interest inspired by contemporary Greek art.

There is, however, one somewhat obscure circumstance that contrasts with the prosperity that Veii must have enjoyed at this period, namely the scarcity of high-quality imported objects during the whole 5th century; this phenomenon might be explained in part by our still slight knowledge of the cemeteries, and future excavations may well shed further light on it.

The position of Veii, whose territory bordered on Rome's, was a constant source of conflict between the two neighbouring cities. Growing Roman territorial ambitions and competition for the trade along the Tiber made a clash inevitable. In the course of the

Above: detail of the Chigi olpe. Rome, Museo di Villa Giulia

Below, left: terracotta antefix with female head, from Portonaccio (Veii). Rome, Museo di Villa Giulia

Below: terracotta female figure, with baby, from Portonaccio. Rome, Museo di Villa Giulia

Above: antefix with gorgon mask, from
Portonaccio. Rome, Museo di Villa Giulia

Right: head of Hermes, from Portonaccio. Rome,
Museo di Villa Giulia

Below: terracotta statue of Apollo, from
Portonaccio. Rome, Museo di Villa Giulia

5th century there was the famous incident of the private war waged by the clan of the
Fabii against the Etruscan city, ending in their being slaughtered, almost to a man, in the
Cremera valley.

In 442 B.C. Veii came to the aid of the small settlement of Fidenae which had rebelled
against Rome, but suffered defeat and was forced to ask for a truce; as a result, Veian
navigation on the Tiber was controlled by the enemy. Abandoned, moreover, by the
confederation of the other Etruscan cities, Veii was unable to halt the Roman plans of
conquest, and after a war ten years long it was subdued in 396 B.C. by the legendary Camillus.
Having surrendered, Veii never regained its independence, but its territory, which became
an area of agricultural settlement, lost none of its importance. For at least two more
centuries, until the construction of the Via Clodia and the Via Cassia, the main roads
from Rome to Nepi, Sutri, the Faliscan territory and the inland cities of Etruria passed
through the site of Veii. There is also evidence of the continuance of worship in the
sanctuaries at Campetti and Portonaccio, and in those at the foot of the acropolis and
near the Porta di Cere.

On the site of ancient Veii, Augustus founded the *municipium Augustum Veiens*; this
occupied only a small part of the area of the Etruscan city: about 20 hectares in the central
part of the plateau, at the centre of the road system. The place was ransacked in the 19th
century by numerous excavations aimed at collecting valuable objects; no ground-plan
of the area was drawn up, since the remains of the ancient buildings were regarded only
as sources of marble, and virtually no trace of them now remains. A considerable number
of statues of emperors of the Julio-Claudian family passed to the Vatican and Lateran
museums.

Among the remains from Roman times should be mentioned the so-called Bagni della
Regina ('Queen's Baths') in the little river Valchetta north of the city, belonging to a

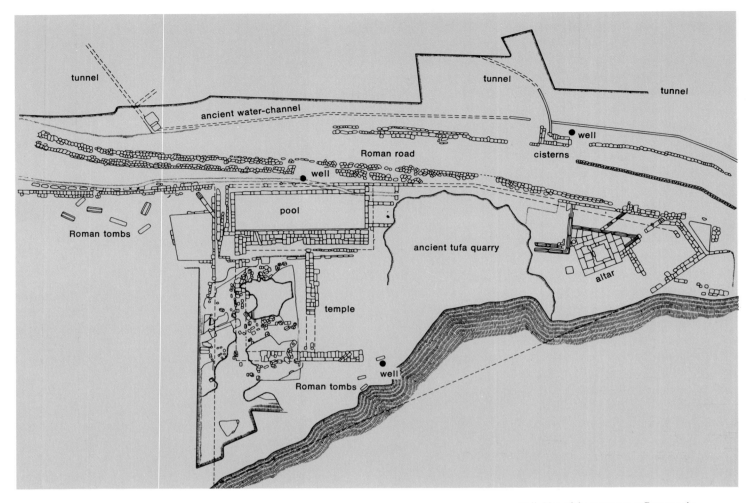

bath-building of the Augustan period, and traces of the cemeteries outside the northeast gate (niches for cremated remains) and in the Vignacce region (chamber-tombs).

After a period of moderate prosperity under Augustus and his immediate successors, the life of the *municipium* underwent a rapid decline in the late Imperial period. The importance of Roman Veii lay not so much in the actual city as in the numerous country villas (of which considerable remains have come to light both on the plateau and in the surrounding countryside) which were scattered throughout the region. It would seem that many of these villas survived until the Middle Ages.

The founding of the *Domusculta Capracorum*, an agricultural colony which emerged in the 8th century at the wish of Pope Adrian I at S. Cornelia (two kilometres north of Veii) and the construction of the fortress of Isola Farnese about A.D. 1004 marked the final and total abandonment of the site of the ancient city.

Portonaccio. This is a sanctuary comprising a temple and other noteworthy religious buildings, situated outside the walls of Veii, on a plateau midway in height between the one on which the city stood and the deep valley of the Piordo. The whole sacred area was surrounded by a wall, stretches of which survive on the west and north, while the southern side, which must have followed the edge of the cliff, has been destroyed by landslides.

The western section of the sanctuary was occupied by the temple and a large rectangular pool beside it. Only a few courses of tufa blocks from the temple building have been found, because of the collapse of the roof of a gallery in a quarry beneath it, possibly

Veii. Remains of the temple at Portonaccio

dating back to Roman times; the only original parts are the north wall, the northwest corner, part of the south wall and the front wall of the cella: the re-establishment of the plan is the result of restoration. The temple, facing southeast, probably had a triple cella at the back and an area in front enclosed between the extensions of the side walls, in accordance with the plan Vitruvius has recorded as being typical of Etruscan temples. Though commonly and mistakenly known as the temple of Apollo, because of the famous statue found in it, it was in fact dedicated to Minerva, who is mentioned in some of the inscriptions cut on votive offerings. A great many fragments have been recovered of the terracotta decoration that adorned and also protected the wooden structure of the temple; these fragments date from the end of the 6th and the whole of the 5th century B.C. In particular, the discovery of the group of statues already discussed is remarkable; these are larger than life-size and their bases were placed on the great longitudinal beam of the roof in such a way that pilgrims approaching the temple would see them in profile. Contemporary with the construction of this sacred building was that of the large pool along its north side; this was built with walls made of tufa blocks, carefully worked and fitting together exactly, and covered with a thick layer of clay which stopped the seepage of water. It is almost perfectly preserved to this day.

About 30 metres to the east of the temple there is a paved area; in the centre of this are the remains of an altar with trenches for sacrifices. The building, in large tufa blocks, is rectangular; to the west stands the altar, with two steps in front of it, and to the east the trench, which, at the time of discovery, showed a large, dark red patch of greasy ash with carbonized remains. Around the altar are rain-water gutters.

The eastern end of the sanctuary was occupied by a rectangular enclosure, of which the foundations on the south side remain, and in which a large number of vases and a group of inscriptions were found.

To the north the sanctuary is flanked by a paved Roman road, probably constructed on the line of an earlier Etruscan one. Three tunnels emerge beyond the road, dug to carry water running off the mountainside: tunnel A (contemporary with the temple) carried water to the pool along a channel; tunnel B (built after the temple was destroyed) filled a cistern covered by a large slab with a hole in the middle; no trace remains today of tunnel C. Water obviously played an important part in the rites of divine worship.

Campetti. Here are the ruins of a Roman villa of the Imperial period with a small nymphaeum consisting of three small fountains with apses into which the water spouted. Farther north, towards the cliff edge, were the remains of five large cisterns, three of which had almost completely collapsed into the void below. In the surviving two, the barrel-vaulting can be seen, also the open arches in the longer walls which allowed intercommunication between the cisterns.

Piazza d'Armi. This was the fortified citadel, already occupied in the Iron Age: beneath the remains of the Etruscan period many traces of Villanovan huts have in fact been found.

Remains of the gate which permitted communication between the acropolis and the city have been preserved, and there is a notable stretch of city wall on the northern and western sides of the hill.

The plateau itself, which has been to some extent the object of systematic excavation, seems to have been largely occupied by buildings arranged according to a proper grid plan along streets intersecting at right angles. Of especial interest are the partially-uncovered remains of a wide road that crosses the citadel lengthwise and, almost on the top of the hill, runs alongside a large square; in the centre of this there is an elliptical cistern dug in the ground and lined with tufa blocks; the bottom of the cistern was reached by means of a small stairway.

To the north of the cistern, in the direction of the gate giving access to the citadel, are the remains of a temple orientated northeast–southwest; the building consists of a simple rectangular cella and was decorated with a series of terracottas, some good fragments of which have been discovered, dating from the first half of the 6th century B.C.

Northeast gate. At this gate, from which the road led to Capena, there remains a section of the actual roadway, enclosed between tufa walls. The well-preserved paving, pavement, surface-water drains and clearly visible ruts of cart wheels all date from Roman times.

Just outside the gate is one of the cemeteries belonging to Roman Veii. Small niches of varying shapes and sizes (rectangular, with tops either rounded off or triangular) were cut in the rock alongside the road, and here the ashes of the dead were placed in urns. The niches were faced with coloured plaster, which can still be seen in some places. On the left, as you leave the gate, is a small chamber-tomb with a single funerary couch.

Ponte Sodo. Here there is a tunnel some 70 metres long that channels the Valchetta through a rocky outcrop running north from the plateau where the city stood, between the Porta di Capena and the Porta di Formello.

Its purpose was possibly to cut across an inconvenient loop in the river at a place where floods were frequent; at the same time it was a kind of natural bridge between the city and the countryside lying beyond the stream. In the ceiling one can see air-vents for the benefit of those working the tunnel. Chronologically, the tunnel perhaps precedes the 5th-century city wall, which was weakened by this water passage. The Ponte Sodo is only

Top: Veii. The Macchia Grande *columbarium*

Above: Tomba delle Anatre, Riserva del Bagno cemetery

Top right: Ponte Sodo

one example (although the most spectacular) of the projects of highly advanced water-engineering carried out by the Etruscans, numbers of which have been found in and around Veii.

Tomba Campana. When discovered by the Marchese Campana, this tomb had already been desecrated by unofficial excavators, who fortunately only made off with the objects in precious metal. The two burial chambers of which the tomb consists are reached by a long corridor in the walls of which there are two small secondary rooms.

The first chamber, with a gabled roof, had two large benches upon which were found the bodies of a woman and a man; the man's bronze helmet had been pierced by a blow from a spear. The back wall, in the centre of which is the door giving access to the second chamber, was painted with bright colours applied directly to the rock face. The actual paintings are now unfortunately almost completely lost. At the sides of the door, which is framed by a geometric design of triangles, the walls are divided into three bands: the top bands are painted with lotus flowers, the bottom ones with animals, both real and fantastic, and the central bands show figures on horseback preceded and followed by people and animals.

The second chamber, with a low bench on which were found three small terracotta urns with heads on their lids, containing the ashes of the dead, also has a painted back wall, this time with a stylized design of shields. The paintings are clearly inspired by Eastern designs, and the tomb dates from the last decades of the 7th century B.C.

Tomba delle Anatre. This is the oldest painted tomb so far discovered in Etruria, dating from the first half of the 7th century B.C. The rectangular chamber has a funeral couch against the left-hand wall; the rock above the couch shows deep holes which were probably used to support a kind of canopy. The ceiling is painted in sections, alternately red and yellow. The walls are in two coloured bands (the lower being red, the upper yellow), separated by a series of parallel stripes; the end wall shows a line of ducks facing left (hence the name 'Tomb of the Ducks'). The colours used for the stripes and the ducks are black, red and yellow.

Monti della Tolfa

The Monti della Tolfa are of volcanic origin and in ancient times were known as the Caeretan hills, since they were in territory belonging to the city of Cerveteri in classical times; they are an area of great interest for their landscape and for their archaeological remains. They are bounded from northwest to northeast by a bend in the river Mignone. The hills are covered in part by thick woods of chestnut, beech and ilex, in part by the typical Mediterranean *maquis* of arbutus, mastic and broom, and are honeycombed with quarries and mines, both ancient and modern, testifying to the riches lying underground. It was on account of the rich deposits of alunite, limonite and pyrite that these volcanic heights were quite densely inhabited from ancient times onwards.

Scattered discoveries of stone implements prove that the area was occupied as early as the Neolithic and Chalcolithic ages. Late Apennine (late Bronze Age) culture is represented by a wealth of material found at Monte Rovello.

However, the first really consistent evidence for human settlement dates from the final period of the Bronze Age, belonging to the culture of the early 1st millennium B.C. that is known as the proto-Villanovan. At least nine tombs from this period have been found, also two hoards and a village. Excavations carried out at the village, at Monte Rovello, have revealed rudimentary defensive walls built approximately half-way up the hill, and foundations of huts. There were very many objects of domestic use: terracotta stoves in various shapes, crude millstones for grinding wheat, consisting simply of a slab of trachyte and a stone crusher, and so on. The pottery is decorated with simple geometric motifs made by rollers, prickers or punches.

The principal proto-Villanovan cemetery is at Poggio La Pozza near Allumiere, not far from the village of Monte Rovello. The ashes of the dead were placed in typical biconical pottery urns with modest geometric decorations incised on the neck and body. The urn, enclosed in a rounded tufa holder or in a coffer made of stone slabs, was then buried in a pit-tomb. The tomb furnishings usually consist of simple small pots (cups, jugs, and small jars), and personal items such as fibulae, rings and necklaces. In the cemetery of Poggio La Pozza it was customary, in addition, to pile up stones over the tombs as markers.

The bronzes are best represented by the two hoards (Monte Rovello and Coste del Marano); they comprise cups of embossed sheet bronze, giant fibulae, bell pendants, axes, hatchets and foundry waste.

The proto-Villanovan culture of the Monti della Tolfa is similar to contemporary cultures already known in many other areas, including nearby S. Giovenale and Luni sul Mignone.

So far nothing has been found that clearly belongs to the Villanovan culture typical of the Iron Age; it is rather an instance of a late survival of the proto-Villanovan culture.

However, there are many finds belonging to the Archaic Etruscan period (7th–6th centuries B.C.), showing that the population was increasing as a result of intensive cultivation of the area. Small villages have been identified on high ground at Pantanelle, Ferrone, Monte S. Angelo, Casalone and Tor S. Cimino. There was probably also a settlement on the site of modern Tolfa. The village of Monte Rovello likewise shows signs of continuous occupation from prehistoric or early historical times to the 4th–3rd centuries B.C.

We know of a considerable number of cemeteries with tombs dating from the 7th and 6th centuries that are obvious imitations of tombs at Cerveteri. In the cemetery of Colle di Mezzo the chambers are built of great trachyte slabs and covered with stone tumuli. In the small cemeteries that extend in an arc round Tolfa (Castellina di Ferrone, Pian Cisterna, Pian Li Santi, Pian Conserva, S. Pietro, Brandita), however, the tombs are cut into the tufa.

Above: Tolfa. Rocca dei Frangipane

Right: remains of the Etruscan sanctuary at Grasceta dei Cavalieri

Since the furnishings appear to indicate that these tombs were abandoned during the course of the 5th century, it would seem that many small settlements in this area disappeared at this time, perhaps in consequence of the social crisis that affected the city of Cerveteri, upon which the whole territory was dependent.

Among the archaeological remains of the Hellenistic period is an interesting little rural sanctuary at Grasceta dei Cavalieri, on the pass over the Monti della Tolfa leading to Tarquinian territory. Only the foundations remain. The sanctuary consisted of a shrine in the middle of an enclosed area with a wooden portico; a second shrine, with two benches running along the side walls, contained the base of a statue; and a third building, in the shape of a U, completed the sanctuary. Several terracotta votive objects have been found at the site.

In Republican and Imperial times the territory was dotted with country villas.

A little Antiquarium has been opened in the Palazzo Camerale at Allumiere, and contains items found in the cemetery of Colle di Mezzo and the settlement of Monte Rovello, and also proto-Villanovan tomb furnishings excavated in cemeteries in the area since 1945.

The Museo Civico di Tolfa, in the Palazzo Comunale, contains tomb furnishings recently discovered in the cemeteries of the area, and material from the rural sanctuary at Grasceta dei Cavalieri and the Roman villas.

Civitavecchia

Trajan (emperor A.D. 98–117) had the ancient port of Centumcellae built, on the site of present-day Civitavecchia. It lay between the ports of Cosa (by Monte Argentario) and Ostia (at the mouth of the Tiber) and was an impressive complex built on the same model as the port of Ostia, with an outer basin protected by a series of moles and an artificial island, and an inner basin linked to the outer one by a wide channel.

At the same time as the harbour, Trajan began the building of a sumptuous villa on top of the Colle Belvedere, about four kilometres northeast of Civitavecchia, with huge bath-buildings attached. There were already public baths in the area, dating from the Republican age and using a hot spring known since earliest times. According to a legend preserved by the Roman poet Rutilius Namatianus, a god, taking the form of a bull, caused this spring to flow; from this event derived the name Thermae Taurinae given to this place.

The modern road that leads from the centre of Civitavecchia to the autostrada to Livorno (the N. 16) divides the impressive ruins of this Imperial building into two parts. Excavations carried out to the right of the road have only been partial, but they have revealed several rooms that made up the living area of the villa, among which are a library and a series of rooms built around a huge central *atrium*. To the left of the road are the remains of the baths, including Trajan's buildings (subsequently remodelled) and the older baths that were incorporated in them.

Civitavecchia. Baths of Trajan

The baths consisted of a two-storey building. On the lower floor can be seen, running along a single axis, the rooms typical of all Roman baths: from south to north, they are the *frigidarium*, the *tepidarium* and the huge *caldarium*, and beside them the indispensable service rooms, such as dressing-rooms, little rooms for applying and removing oil after the bath, and rooms for the heating plant. The *frigidarium* was open to the sky and had a rectangular pool with three steps running round the sides. The other rooms had cross vaults with plaster decorations, and fine pavements with polychrome marble intarsia; along the walls, frequently faced with coloured plaster, were several niches for statues. Inside the *caldarium* was a large swimming-pool (20 by 10 metres), fed by water from the hot spring that reached a temperature of 47°C; a bench 40 cm high ran along three sides of the pool and was lined with thick slabs of white marble where the bathers sat.

The oldest part of the baths lies to the west of this room. A second *caldarium* and a circular *sudatorium* can be seen.

Little remains of the upper floor except a few fragments of wall surviving to a low height; there was a large square room surrounded by broad terraces which had a magnificent view of the wooded Monti della Tolfa to the east and of a wide expanse of blue sea to the west.

The most important archaeological discoveries from the Civitavecchia area are now in the Museo Archeologico Nazionale, recently set up in the former Palazzo Genio in Civitavecchia. The objects are displayed in a simple linear order, and there are numerous explanatory labels and maps which give a complete picture of the history of the whole area. On the ground floor numerous Roman sculptures, from the port of Centumcellae and neighbouring villas, are most effectively displayed. A statue of Apollo from the time of Hadrian and several gladiatorial reliefs belonging to a funerary monument from the Roman *colonia* of Castrum Novum are of exceptional interest. On the first floor are objects from the small settlements in the area, laid out in topographical order; of these, the items from Allumiere, Aquae Tauri and Castellina are outstanding for the richness of their culture.

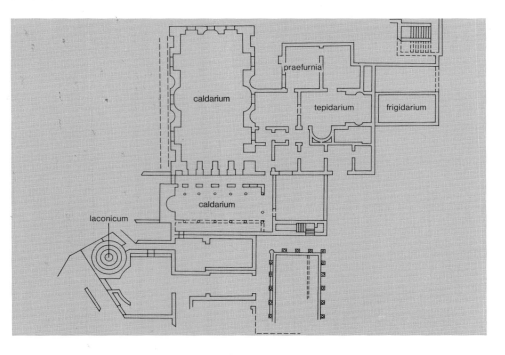

Civitavecchia. Plan of the baths of Trajan (top of plan = east)

Region of the Cliff Cemeteries

The part of inner Etruria lying roughly between the river Marta, the Monti Cimini, Lake Vico and the upper course of the Mignone can rightly be called the region of the cliff cemeteries, because of its distinctive tombs with façades cut in the high rocky walls of the valleys eroded by its rivers.

Within this area lies some of the most picturesque scenery in southern Etruria, which has remained almost completely unaltered because upper Latium still has a primarily agricultural and pastoral economy, with very little industry. The countryside is quite unspoiled and must have changed little since ancient times: the area is geologically homogeneous, consisting of a series of tufa plateaux (where most of the settlements were situated), separated by the deep green valleys of the left-hand tributaries of the Marta; the tomb façades are cut into the sides of these valleys.

The area was inhabited in prehistoric times, but whereas Bronze Age settlements occupied naturally strong positions on top of the rocky outcrops at the convergence of the river valleys, at the beginning of the Iron Age the Villanovan communities abandoned the sites of the early settlements; economic and social changes had clearly brought about a period of peace which enabled them to move to more accessible places better suited for agriculture. During the final period of the Iron Age these communities were forced by renewed hostilities to move again, returning to the primitive fortified positions where they remained until the Middle Ages.

In the historical period the area was dotted with many small settlements; these owed their prosperity chiefly to their position along the trade routes that ran parallel to the coast from Vulci and Tarquinia to Veii and Latium, and others that ran from Tarquinia and Cerveteri inland towards Orvieto and the valley of the Tiber.

The oldest routes must have been those along the river valleys, where natural pathways made the going easier, and indeed the most important settlements lay along the course of the rivers: S. Giuliano, Blera and Norchia on the Biedano, Castel d'Asso on the Leia, Tuscania on the Marta.

In the Archaic period, when Cerveteri was at the zenith of its prosperity (7th–5th centuries B.C.), that coastal city had a strong cultural and artistic influence over the whole area, which encouraged the growth of settlements affected by the extensive trade coming from and through Cerveteri. This influence is particularly clear in the field of funerary architecture; the cliff cemeteries with their tombs with façades, so typical of the area, are in fact inspired by the cube-tombs of Cerveteri: they have the same mouldings on top, carved door frames and internal decorative elements (funerary couches for men and women, coffered ceilings, etc). Both these cliff tombs and the cube-tombs of Cerveteri provide valuable evidence of the external appearance of Etruscan houses, and the impressive cities of the dead carved in the tufa cliffs give us an idea of what the cities of the living must have been, now sadly vanished without trace.

From the 4th century, with the economic decline of Cerveteri and the simultaneous expansion of Tarquinia, the latter city developed commercial links with inner Etruria, which fell permanently under its economic and cultural domination. This is a period of particular prosperity for the settlements between Tuscania, Norchia and Castel d'Asso, along the route from Tarquinia to the Tiber.

In Roman times the Via Cassia skirted the area, and it was crossed by the Via Clodia (built perhaps as early as the end of the 3rd century B.C.) which followed ancient Etruscan

Opposite: gorge of the Biedano

Isometric diagram of a semi-cube cliff tomb

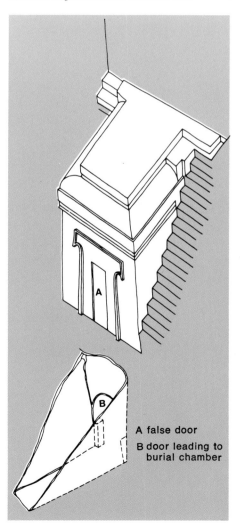

A false door
B door leading to burial chamber

routes over the hills to the west of S. Giuliano (where a road led to S. Giovenale and Luni), passing Blera and Norchia in the valley of the Biedano and Tuscania on the Marta, and then going on in the direction of Statonia. The Via Cassia and the Via Clodia were linked by cross roads, one of which followed the river Leia, passing through Castel d'Asso.

Types of cliff tombs. These tombs, cut into the rocky sides of the river valleys, vary in form, not only because of normal chronological development, but also as a result of adaptation to their natural setting (depending, for instance, on whether they are cut in a rocky outcrop or a smooth cliff face).

Cube-tombs: these rectangular tombs stand completely free of the cliff face from which they are cut; they have mouldings at the top and an upper terrace, reached by an outer staircase, on which stand cippi of various shapes set in the tufa.

Semi- and pseudo-cube tombs: these are similar but have only one or three sides isolated, the other(s) being part of the cliff face.

Sometimes the cube- or pseudo-cube tombs have a gabled roof instead of the upper terrace (shrine-tombs).

In the oldest cemeteries the burial chamber is generally situated within the cube of the tomb; later it is cut below the monumental part, but a false door is still carved on the façade for symbolic reasons.

A final development is the double-façade tomb, with a front part added at the base of the cube, containing a room with benches along the walls, a false door in the end wall and a little roof with realistic imitation tiles. The tomb thus had an upper and a lower façade, both with a false door, and a burial chamber cut on a lower level and reached by a corridor opening into the area in front of the lower façade. The room behind this façade was probably used for religious ceremonies; especially in the cemetery of Norchia, it is sometimes in the form of a real portico supported by columns.

The tombs so far described resemble private dwellings, but there were also tombs built to look like sacred buildings, with proper colonnades or carved pedimental decorations.

Chronology of the cliff tombs. The oldest cube-tombs belong to the early 6th century; the most elaborate, the double-façade tombs, are unlikely to be earlier than the 4th century. Temple-tombs generally date from the Hellenistic period (3rd–1st centuries B.C.). S. Giuliano and Blera have older cemeteries than Norchia and Castel d'Asso.

S. Giuliano

The Colle di S. Giuliano, the site of an Etruscan settlement, lies about two kilometres northeast of Barbarano Romano. The plateau runs east–west and has a distinctive shape, like the sole of a shoe; it is bounded on the north and south by two deep gorges cut in the rock by the Chiusa Cima and the S. Giuliano respectively; these two watercourses converge to the west of the hill to form the Biedano. The cemeteries are cut into the steep cliffs of the hills of Serignano, Chiusa Cima, S. Simone, Tesoro, Caiolo, Cenale and Greppo Castello, which radiate in all directions from the settlement on the plateau of S. Giuliano.

S. Giuliano is presumed to be the Manturanum or Marturanum recorded by mediaeval geographers; after the fall of the Western Roman Empire, this town was moved to a nearby site, for unknown reasons, and changed its name to that of Barbarano, which it retains to this day. The importance of Manturanum can be seen from the fact that it was the seat of a bishop until the 10th century A.D.

The Colle di S. Giuliano still has remains of Etrusco-Roman defensive walls and is accessible only from the south, where its rocky cliff is less precipitous than on the other sides. The highest point of the plateau (about 350 metres above sea level), is still called

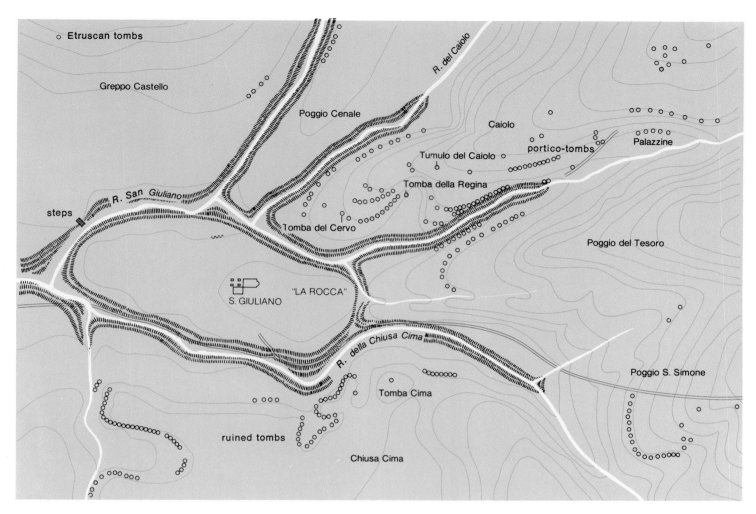

Above: S. Giuliano. Plan of the cemetery

Right: cliff tomb

'La Rocca' and was probably the site of the fortified citadel. The settlement was linked to the Via Clodia (which runs about two kilometres to the west of Barbarano) by two roads, one running north to link the northern settlements and joining the Via Clodia near Blera, the other running south. The impressive Greppo Castello steps may be associated with the former road: carved out of the tufa, they go up about 40 metres and are a remarkable sight even now. The southern road, on the other hand, runs through the deep cutting in the Colle di Serignano, which can stand comparison with the Cava Buia at Norchia. Nothing remains of the Etruscan settlement, which was built of highly perishable materials (wood, or unfired clay bricks). As in practically all the towns of the region of the cliff cemeteries, the only remains of the town are the water-engineering works (in which the Etruscans excelled) built to control rain-water. Channels cut below ground level collected the water and conveyed it to the brow of the hill, where it was discharged into the valleys below; this was an attempt to avert the risk of malaria by preventing the collection of stagnant surface water. The outlets of three of these drains (two on the south slope and one on the north) are still visible today.

A tank survives about 200 metres southwest of the little Romanesque church of S. Giuliano; it collected water in a huge underground chamber, and at a later period (perhaps in Roman times) was converted into baths.

The Etruscan cemetery occupies the ridges and plateaux of the hills that radiate from S. Giuliano; the most important tombs are cut on the heights of Chiusa Cima (which is the oldest part of the cemetery) and Caiolo (see below, pp. 255–256). The later tombs are mostly situated on Poggio S. Simone and Poggio del Tesoro, to the east of the city.

There are four types of tombs at S. Giuliano: tumuli, chamber-tombs (entirely rock-

Above: S. Giuliano. Cliff tombs

Below: side elevation of a cube-tomb

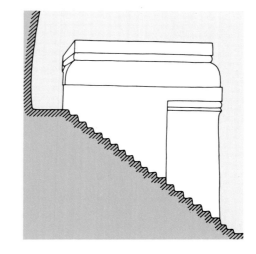

cut, with no façade), cube-tombs (true, semi-cube and pseudo-cube tombs), sometimes with gabled roofs, and portico-tombs.

Generally the cube-tombs are of the oldest type, with the burial chamber cut into the monument itself.

Blera

The modern village was known as Bieda until 1952, when it reverted to its ancient name of Blera; it covers only a small part of the site of the Etruscan settlement, on a long, narrow tufa plateau between the Biedano and the Ricanale. Blera is mentioned by Pliny, Strabo and Ptolemy; it occupies a strategic and naturally fortified position which made it an important post on the busy Etruscan commercial route which the Via Clodia followed in Roman times.

Archaeological finds indicate that Blera was continuously inhabited from the Etruscan period to mediaeval times, when the little town became the seat of a bishop with a vast diocese stretching from the Mignone in the south to the Via Cassia in the north. It reached the zenith of its prosperity in the Archaic period (7th–5th centuries B.C.) when the whole area inland of Cerveteri was also at its most prosperous through lucrative trade links with the powerful coastal city. This is obvious from a study of the extensive cemetery, which revealed a great number of rich tombs built during this period. From the 5th century, however, it appears that although new tombs were still being constructed at Blera, the inhabitants were more inclined to re-use existing tombs, as a result of a change in their economic situation and a lower standard of living. Of the city itself, there survive only short stretches of the walls (generally dating from the late Roman period) and the usual tunnels and shafts that were part of the system for draining off rain-water.

Although there is so little to see of the settlement, impressive remains of the Via Clodia are still visible. Coming from Lake Bracciano, this road, before it reached Blera, crossed the Biedano by a three-arched Roman bridge, called the Ponte del Diavolo (A on plan), which remains an imposing monument to this day. After Blera it went in the direction of Tuscania, running for a while almost parallel with the Biedano until it crossed a tributary coming in from the right, the Ricanale, just before the two streams converged. Here

stands a second bridge, called the Ponte della Rocca (B), which is older than the Ponte del Diavolo and has a single arch rising about 7.50 metres above water level; it is built of large squared blocks of tufa. Much of the bridge visible today is the result of modern restoration.

The cemeteries are situated on the slopes surrounding the city and in an extension of the valley of the Biedano to the north of the settlement.

In 1914 and 1915 a team of German archaeologists made a thorough study of the area and estimated that it contained two to three thousand tombs, of which a thousand were visible.

The cemeteries of Blera and S. Giuliano contain the oldest cliff tombs known to date. The most common types at Blera are tumulus- and cube-tombs. However, there are also

Above: Blera. Plan of the archaeological zone

Blera. Cliff tombs

Blera. Roman bridge

Blera. Roman bridge

niche-tombs, often with an arched upper part (the so-called *arcosolium*-tombs); these are later, as a rule, and are forerunners of the Roman *columbaria*.

The tumuli have an external ring cut into the tufa or built of tufa blocks. Sometimes they contain corridors and burial chambers with a gap at the top, showing the influence of Tarquinia, or else they have one or more rectangular rooms with funerary couches for men and women of the type well known at Cerveteri. Their furnishings date the tombs to the 7th–5th centuries B.C.

During the 6th century cube-tombs (pseudo- or true) appeared; these were generally of the most archaic type, with a burial chamber cut into the cube itself and reached by a real door. However, there are also cube-tombs with false doors and three examples of tombs imitating houses with gabled roofs. There is only one cube-tomb at Blera with a lower façade and a room in it, but even this has archaic features, in the shape of real doors.

The best-preserved part of the cemetery is in the region of Pian del Vescovo, which extends for about a kilometre northwest of the city, beyond the Ponte della Rocca, along the side of a hill whose slopes descend fairly steeply towards the Biedano. The Via Clodia runs along the bottom of the valley, between the tufa cliffs and the stream. The numerous tombs cut at several levels up the slope resemble an enormous staircase.

The Tomba della Sfinge (1 on plan) is a good example of a Bleran tumulus-tomb. Its name is derived from the fragments of a stone sphinx, found inside the tomb but probably originally placed outside it as a symbolic guardian; this sculpture is now in the Museo di Viterbo. The tumulus has two burial chambers of the Caeretan type, containing funerary couches with cylindrical legs ending in knobs. In the first room, besides the funerary couches for husband and wife, there are also two other small couches for children.

Also in the area of Pian del Vescovo are two of the three cube-tombs at Blera with gabled roofs; the first (2) has a moulding below the eaves and two real doors with no frame; the second (3) has a false door and a little platform in front of the façade.

There are examples of funerary architecture of the Roman period in three *columbaria* (4, 5 and 6) cut in the rock and an impressive circular mausoleum (7) on Pian Gagliardo, northeast of Blera.

The visitor is recommended to take the picturesque walk from Blera along the gorge of the Biedano to Barbarano Romano. Both the reddish tufa cliffs, 50 to 60 metres high, and the valley bottom are covered in luxuriant vegetation.

Norchia

There was an Etruscan settlement in the valley of the Biedano, on the Via Clodia between Blera and Tuscania, where the remains of the mediaeval castle of Norchia now stand; its Etruscan name is unknown, but in Roman and mediaeval times it was called Orclae. It was continuously inhabited from the Etruscan period until 1435, when malaria drove the inhabitants to Vitorchiano, to the east of Ferento. The town occupied a long, narrow tufa plateau bounded on the west by the Biedano and on the east by the Pile; to the north of the town, these two streams converge and join the Acqua Alta.

Because of its position, the town needed artificial defences only on the south, where a deep ditch (I on plan) was dug for that purpose. In mediaeval times the population declined and the town gradually retreated to the highest part of the plateau; as a result, at least four more defensive ditches (II–V) were dug farther north.

Nothing remains from the Etruscan and Roman period except a few stretches of walls, streets dug into the tufa and the drainage system (underground channels with shafts and cisterns to the north of the castle). The ruins of a crenellated castle and the small Romanesque church of S. Pietro are all that remains from the mediaeval period.

The Via Clodia crossed the southern ditch and continued lengthwise through the town, coming out at the northern end (where the mediaeval gate survives, on the site of the Etruscan one), turned left down to the Biedano, crossing it by a bridge to go on in the direction of Tarquinia through a most impressive deep cutting about 400 metres long, generally known as the Cava Buia. This part of the road is two to three metres wide and runs between rock walls more than ten metres high; it was constructed to avoid the steep gradient of a little hill just outside the town and is one of the most important examples of Etruscan road-building known. In the centre of the roadway the deep drainage channel is still visible; about half-way along, high up on the rock face, is a Latin inscription by C. Clodius Thalpius (who may have been the official in charge of the work that transformed the ancient Etruscan track into a Roman road), giving the distance from Rome as 40 Roman miles. At the entrance to the Cava Buia the tufa cliff contains a complicated system of little intercommunicating tanks, cut to collect and convey any water seeping through the rocky cliff.

The cemeteries are situated all round the settlement, along the faces of the cliffs that overhang the Biedano, Pile and Acqua Alta. These hundreds of tombs cut at two or even three levels in the rocky walls, their façades decorated with architectural features, make an impressive sight, especially at sunset when the tufa glows with a rosy light. The cemetery of Norchia, like that of Castel d'Asso, developed at a late period (no earlier than the 4th century B.C.).

Its most important tombs will now be described.

Tomba Lattanzi (on the Biedano). The tomb consisted of three parts, one above the other: a high podium with a flight of steps, a central colonnade, and an upper storey set slightly back, made up of three rock-cut rooms. The burial chamber was situated seven metres below the level of the central portico. Little steps cut at the side of the façade led from one floor to another. The three rooms of the upper storey were plastered and painted, and separated by walls ending in front in fluted pilasters. The pillars of the central portico supported an architrave decorated with a frieze of griffins. On the left-hand side the portico was separated from the flight of steps at the side by a fluted pillar that stood on an enormous stone animal crouching on its front paws; there is no trace of its head.

Doric or temple-tombs (on the Acqua Alta). These two tombs, standing side by side, imitate sacred buildings with pediments decorated in relief. The eastern tomb is complete, whereas the other is half destroyed by landslides; the missing half of its pediment is in the Museo Archeologico in Florence. The tombs consist of a lower part imitating the

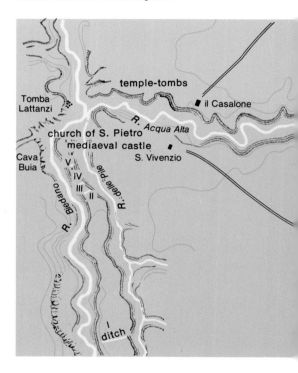

Norchia. Plan of the archaeological zone

podium of a temple, a central part imitating its vestibule and portico, and a roof with an architrave surmounted by a pediment. Both the triangular pediments are surrounded by a fascia with dentils in relief and have at their corners the typical monstrous gorgon heads (*gorgoneia*) with terrifying expressions. The decoration of the eastern pediment is complete but in a bad state of preservation; the whole left-hand part has been worn away. In the right-hand corner is a recumbent figure. In the centre three figures can be seen kneeling in a dramatic pose: the two at the sides are female, while the central figure is male and winged. Scholars believe the scene illustrates the legend of Niobe: Niobe, the daughter of Tantalus and wife of Amphion, was proud of her fourteen children and dared to mock Latona, the mother of Apollo and Diana. The angry goddess had Niobe's children slain. The central winged figure is Apollo, shown in the act of striking his victims with arrows.

The western pediment (part being in Florence, the rest still in its original position)

Norchia. The Doric or temple-tombs

has carvings of nude and armed warriors fighting. The meaning of this scene is unclear, although it may perhaps also illustrate some mythological episode.

The western tomb has a low relief (of which only half survives, now barely visible) carved on the wall of the vestibule, behind the portico: a procession of figures moves from right to left in front of a wall hung with trophies (a shield, a knife, helmets, etc.). The procession consists of a winged figure, seen in full face, followed by male figures: the subject is the descent to the underworld of the dead (depicted on the part that is now missing), accompanied by Charun, the Etruscan demon of the underworld, and people bearing offerings. Traces of coloured plaster are still visible.

Tombs on the Pile. In this area the tombs are particularly close together, cut in the rock at two or three levels. There are some splendid examples of double-façade tombs, and especially many in which the room in the lower façade takes the form of a real portico, with a roof supported by columns. In many cases the flat tops still have the original cippi of various shapes fixed in their cavities. Many bear inscriptions with the name of the deceased incised in large characters on the façade. In the rooms of the lower façade, traces often remain of the coloured plaster that originally covered the walls and false doors.

Castel d'Asso

The mediaeval castle of Castel d'Asso was built on the site of an ancient settlement; its Etruscan name has been lost, but not its Roman name: Cicero mentions an Axia in the territory of Tarquinia, about 50 miles from Rome. In the Middle Ages a castle was built there to defend the surrounding territory, which is still dotted with numerous caves belonging to that period, used either as stables or as dwellings; in many cases remains of hearths and chimneys have been found.

Like nearly all the settlements of this inland area of Etruria, Axia was built on an outcrop of tufa bounded by the two steep valleys of the Riosecco and the Freddano. From Etruscan times it was at the centre of a dense network of roads linking it to neighbouring towns; in Roman times various tracks connected it with the two main roads of the region, the Via Clodia and the Via Cassia.

The very steep slopes that protected the city to the north and south were reinforced where necessary with walls of squared tufa blocks. Thus only the eastern side of the plateau lacked any form of natural defence, and this was remedied by digging two parallel ditches bending at an obtuse angle (A and B on plan), about 450 metres apart. Thus there were two distinct areas, covering a total surface of about ten hectares: the larger lay to the east and must have contained the settlement itself, while the smaller, western one was probably a fortified citadel. The town centre became gradually smaller over the centuries until in mediaeval times it occupied only the castle area, at the extreme end of the plateau; at the same time a third defensive ditch was built farther back (C).

No trace remains of the settlement today apart from the usual drainage system for rainwater (shafts and tunnels); this was uncovered on the acropolis in the early 1960s by landslides.

However, since several Archaic architectural fragments have been found, it seems possible that a sacred building, dating from the 6th century B.C., was situated along the road which cuts lengthwise across the plateau.

There are, on the other hand, imposing mediaeval remains of the castle, consisting of an irregular-shaped court surrounded by a wall, with a keep, and with its entrance defended by a watch tower.

The cemeteries surrounding the city are cut in the walls of the river valleys, but the cliff tombs with rock-cut façades are limited to a single zone, quite small in relation to the total area of the cemetery. They are situated on the north slope of the Freddano, opposite the castle; the area also includes both banks of a side valley that comes in just at this point and in ancient times was the only possible route for roads coming from the city to climb up to the Vaccareccia plateau. The cemetery was therefore closely linked with the ancient road system. The scenery in this little valley is most picturesque, with both its high sides carved with two or even three levels of tombs.

The tombs most frequently found at Castel d'Asso are simple cube-tombs (especially semi- or pseudo-cube tombs) and those with a room in the lower façade; there is only one example of a colonnaded portico of the type found at Norchia.

The oldest tombs have small, quite accurately cut chambers with funerary couches, while the later tombs (generally with a lower façade) have large, roughly-cut chambers with long benches hollowed out to receive the bodies.

The cemetery of Castel d'Asso is fairly late: apart from a few Archaic tombs, it developed to its greatest extent between the 4th and 2nd centuries B.C. The cemetery was still in

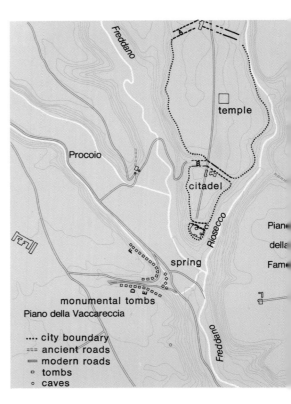

Castel d'Asso. Plan of the archaeological zone (top of plan = east)

use until the 1st century A.D., but instead of new tombs being cut, existing ones were used; the rooms in the lower façade, in particular, were disfigured with niches and *loculi* carved everywhere in the walls.

Tomba Orioli (D). This is a semi-cube tomb with a double façade, unique among the cliff tombs so far known in that it has a rectangular buttress against the right-hand edge. This forepart bounds the room in the lower façade; at the levels of the façade and the lower façade it contains two doors, in addition to the two normally found in this type of tomb. On the opposite side, to the left of the tomb, is a similar buttress, but it is lower and has no doors. The false door of the room in the lower façade is inscribed with three rows of numerals (reading from right to left) giving the number 41; this may refer to the dimensions of the area adjacent to the tomb.

The burial chamber below is enormous (about 17 metres long) and has benches hollowed out to provide at least 70 spaces (including the *loculi* cut in the walls) for burials, some intended for children.

The cemetery of Castel d'Asso is particularly interesting for the number of Etruscan inscriptions cut in large characters on the façades of the tombs, which have fascinated scholars and tourists alike since the 19th century. Three tombs in a row should be mentioned here (E), two of the semi-cube type with a lower façade, and one pseudo-cube tomb with inscriptions carved between the upper mouldings, designed naturally to be read from right to left.

The first tomb bears the name of its owner V[elus] Urinates Salvies. On the second, central, tomb are the words *eca suthi nesl* ('Here lies the deceased . . .'), followed by the family name of the deceased (Tetnie).

The third tomb, on the right, has an inscription similar to the previous one, but the name of the owner has disappeared.

The **Tomba Grande** (F) is the largest tomb at Castel d'Asso, and is a semi-cube tomb with a lower façade, flanked by two flights of steps. The room in the lower façade has a roof imitating that of a real house, with tiles carved in the tufa. Because of the width of the tomb (about ten metres) there is not just a single door into this room, as is usual in the cemetery, but three doors. Inside were benches running along the walls; these have almost all been removed in modern times.

The corridor leading to the burial chamber was also of great size and must formerly have had steps cut in it.

The dead were laid out inside the burial chamber in sarcophagi, made of either stone or terracotta, ranged on the floor along the sides of a central passage.

S. Giovenale

The tufa plateau of S. Giovenale lies within the Comune of Blera; it is crescent-shaped and bounded by two gorges made by the Vesca (a tributary of the Mignone) and two of its tributaries. The plateau is dominated by the impressive ruins of a 13th-century castle and its adjacent chapel, which gave its name to the plateau. East of the castle, separated by a steep artificial ravine, is the so-called Borgo, situated at a lower level and consisting of a little hill about 100 square metres in area.

This area has been under excavation by the Swedish Institute in Rome since 1956, and a series of dwellings dating from the Bronze Age to the Etruscan period has been revealed.

A little village of huts, dating from the late Bronze Age, has been discovered at the eastern end of the plateau, at the place where the castle was built in the Middle Ages. Fragments of vases found there are similar to the pottery of the nearby Monti della Tolfa area.

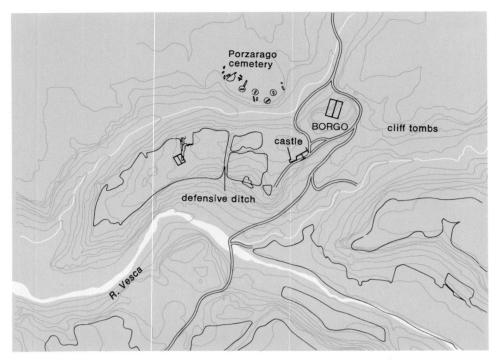

Left: S. Giovenale. Plan of the archaeological zone

Left: S. Giovenale. Plan of the archaeological zone

Below and left: S. Giovenale. Foundation walls, in tufa blocks, of Etruscan houses

A settlement belonging to the late Iron Age was built on top of this Bronze Age village, perhaps after an interval during which the site was temporarily abandoned. Its extent was much greater than that of the earlier village, and it consisted of almost identical huts. The foundations of two large oval huts were in a particularly good state of preservation; they were 11 metres long and about five metres broad, and their outline could be traced by the channels cut in the tufa for the drainage of water from the eaves. Holes dug in the rock for the wooden stakes that made up the framework of these primitive dwellings are also visible; the walls were made of reeds and branches plastered with clay. In this period too, it is clear from the pottery found that the culture here was akin to that of the region of Tolfa and Allumiere.

The Etruscan settlement was built over the Villanovan village; the acropolis must have been situated at the highest point, where the castle now is; about 100 metres west of the castle is a defensive ditch, 80 metres long and 10 metres wide. Of the houses only the tufa-block foundations remain, mostly in a poor state of preservation. In one case the rectangular plan of a two-roomed dwelling is clearly visible; one of the rooms has a low bench, made of stones from the river-bed, running along three sides of it. Another noteworthy Etruscan settlement was discovered on the north side of Borgo, dated to about 600 B.C., with foundation walls, also in great rectangular blocks of stone, preserved to a height of a metre or more. The houses are separated by alleys and consist of two rooms, like the house found on the acropolis. Storerooms have also been identified, containing large terracotta jars.

In the course of the 4th century B.C. a defensive wall was constructed in large squared blocks of stone along the eastern end of the plateau.

The Etruscan settlement appears to have declined towards the end of the 3rd century, when the plateau of S. Giovenale was abandoned; no trace of occupation in Roman times has been found.

The cemeteries were, as usual, situated along the rocky hills surrounding the settlement. At Porzarago thirteen tumuli have been excavated; they were grouped in a semi-circle, with corridors opening on to the tufa cliff-face that overlooks the stream flowing to the north of the city. The burial chambers are either of the Tarquinian type (with an opening in the roof) or of the Caeretan type (with a roof imitating beams, and funerary couches). On three sides of a little square, to the right of the lane leading to the plateau where the city stood, are cliff tombs with carved façades, some of which contain a single chamber and others two.

In the early Middle Ages the chapel of S. Giovenale was constructed on the acropolis, and in the course of the 13th century the castle was built to guard the road linking Tolfa with Viterbo at the point where it forded the Vesca.

Luni sul Mignone

The Pian di Luni lies in the Comune of Blera, about six kilometres west of S. Giovenale. It is situated between the two deep valleys of the Canino (to the north) and the Vesca (to the south), near where these streams join the Mignone. The plateau is being systematically excavated by the Swedish Institute in Rome; these excavations have revealed interesting remains of settlement from the Bronze Age to mediaeval times.

Bronze Age. Three long dwellings (the largest measures at least 42 metres by four metres) were found approximately in the centre of the plateau, in part cut into the tufa. The discovery was all the more important because Bronze Age villages hitherto discovered consisted of caves or simple huts, whereas the houses at Luni had walls made of irregular-shaped stones and roofs of straw or twigs woven together over a framework of wooden beams. The clay floors were laid over insulating layers of sand and stones. These long dwellings must certainly have housed several families and been subdivided into different areas by walls of which no trace remains because of the perishable nature of their building materials.

Finds of Mycenaean sherds dating from 1400–1100 B.C. provided not only a valuable means of dating the village, but also definitive proof that cultural and commercial links between central Italy and the Aegean world existed even at that early period.

Iron Age. Remains of the foundations of oval huts belonging to the Iron Age were found on the plateau of Luni and also in the valleys and on the surrounding hills. The most interesting element of the Villanovan settlement was a monumental building situated on the western part of the plateau. It is a rectangular construction (nine metres by 18) with foundations cut at least four to six metres into the ground. The upper part of the walls must have been built of irregular tufa blocks, while the roof was of the usual wood and straw construction. It is undoubtedly the most ancient monumental building to be found in central Italy. The care with which it was built and its impressive dimensions indicate that it was probably a public building or, perhaps, the house of the village headman. It was destroyed by fire towards the end of the 8th century B.C.

Bronze and Iron Age finds consist mainly of hand-made domestic pottery, rough in appearance and with very simple decoration, often merely with finger impressions or nail scratches; they are very similar to contemporary material from the nearby Monti della Tolfa.

Etruscan period. The plateau was fortified around the second half of the 5th century B.C., perhaps as a result of the expansionist policy of Rome. To this end, stretches of wall were built of large blocks to strengthen parts where natural defences were lacking. The eastern end of the plateau was the weakest part and there a little artificial hill was constructed, about ten metres high, and on it an almost rectangular fort. The usual defensive ditches were also cut in the plateau.

One stretch of the wall, preserved along the north side, contained a gate from which a path led out of the settlement. Immediately to the east of this gate the foundations of an Etruscan house (measuring about seven metres by 12) have been excavated, built of small blocks of tufa. The walls must have been made of logs; in the centre of the house is a large hole cut in the tufa to hold the wooden pillar that supported the roof beams. The house dates from the 5th century B.C. and is built over a 6th-century building.

In the same area as the monumental Villanovan building described above is a sacred area dating from about 500 B.C., consisting of a cave and a rectangular precinct. The floor level is about two metres higher than that of the Villanovan building. The cave is probably natural but was later enlarged and modified; it has a series of drains and a hole in the roof with a sort of basin carved in the floor underneath it. This probably served to catch the blood of victims sacrificed above the cave, while the religious ceremonies took place inside. This sacred area was in use for centuries, until it was converted into a Christian church.

The Etruscan cemeteries cover the surrounding hills (Monte Fortino to the west of the settlement, Poggio del Tempio and Vignolo to the east, and Pianarolo to the southeast) and contain more cliff tombs with carved façades.

Chiusa Cima

This hill at S. Giuliano contains the oldest cube-tombs. Along the western slopes the façades have mostly disintegrated. The burial chambers that can be seen are similar to tombs at Cerveteri, being rectangular, with funerary couches along the walls and roofs either flat or gabled with imitation beams. In a little square practically in the bottom of the valley is one of the few examples of a tomb copying a house with a gabled roof; it has a small door, framed by a square panel, leading into a small chamber that may have contained cinerary urns. On the extreme northern edge of the plateau is the Tomba Cima (end of the 7th–beginning of the 6th century B.C.), a chamber-tomb cut into a little hill 25 metres in diameter, with a complex plan and numerous rooms. In size it is comparable only to a few tombs at Cerveteri and Vulci. The walls are partly decorated with paintings. It has been recently excavated under the auspices of the Soprintendenza alle Antichità dell'Etruria Meridionale. Its rooms have a variety of roofs; one single room may have three different types of roof: gabled, flat and umbrella-shaped.

Caiolo

At the eastern end of the hillside is a row of tombs that are such a perfect imitation of a street in an Etruscan town that they are generally known as the Palazzine. They are either pseudo- or semi-cube tombs in a good state of preservation with real doors cut in the façades;

the burial chambers have ceilings with beams carved in relief and funerary couches along the walls.

In the valley bottom is a little square formed by a bend in the hill, with a semi-cube tomb (called the Tomba della Regina), projecting some way from the cliff face. It is a large tomb and is very well preserved. The façade is decorated with complicated mouldings at the top and has two real doors leading into two rectangular chambers with flat ceilings, and funerary couches and benches along the walls. On the left a staircase leads to the upper terrace.

The only true cube-tomb (that is, with all four walls free-standing) in this cemetery is the Tomba del Cervo ('Tomb of the Stag'), so called because of the animated scene of a fight between a stag and a dog carved on the wall of the left-hand flight of steps. There is a false door in the façade; the underground burial chamber is reached by way of a corridor. A series of steps carved at the sides of and behind the tomb leads to the top of the hill.

The southern brow of Caiolo has a group of tombs known as portico-tombs; these are unlike other cliff tombs and should not be confused with the portico-tombs common at Norchia, which look completely different. They are cube-tombs, generally lacking an upper cornice, with a sort of covered loggia on top, the roof of which is supported by pillars. These upper porticos are reached by flights of steps.

On the plateau of Caiolo are a great number of tumuli; the most characteristic of these is called the Tumulo del Caiolo. Its plinth is carved out of the tufa and only half of it shows; it is at least 2.50 metres high, however, and 5.50 metres across, and decorated with rich mouldings. Inside are two burial chambers, the first of which is rectangular and has a flat roof with large beams; three doors in the back wall lead into a rear burial chamber, where there are two funerary couches (7th century B.C.).

Tuscania

Tuscania stands on the right bank of the river Marta, an outlet of Lake Bolsena which passes the coastal city of Tarquinia shortly before flowing into the Tyrrhenian Sea. Etruscan Tuscania probably owed its good fortune to its well-placed geographical position, at the crossroads of the inland trade route running parallel to the coast (later covered in Roman times by the Via Clodia) and the road which ran upstream from Tarquinia to Lake Bolsena and thence to Orvieto and the Tiber valley.

Generally considered as a satellite, both economically and culturally, of nearby Tarquinia, Tuscania was treated until recently as a city which became of some importance only in the 4th century B.C. But recent discoveries and more careful evaluation of the monuments already known have led to a reassessment of the question, and today Tuscania is revealed as a major urban centre in the Archaic period (7th–5th centuries B.C.) as well, with connections not only with Tarquinia, but also with the nearby towns of the region of the cliff cemeteries, and thus with Cerveteri. This general openness to different influences is especially evident in the field of Archaic funerary architecture: alongside tombs with ogival roofs with a gap at the top (at S. Giusto, Sasso Pizzuto, Ara del Tufo etc) which indicate contact with Tarquinia, we find cliff tombs (at Pian di Mole, Peschiera etc).

From the 4th century B.C. onwards, as a result of the increase in traffic inland from Tarquinia, Tuscania enjoyed a period of particular prosperity, but also showed itself henceforward completely dependent, both economically and culturally, on its important coastal neighbour: in fact the cemeteries of this date, with their chamber-tombs con-

Tuscania. A view of the Colle di S. Pietro, with the remains of the Etruscan and Roman walls

taining one or more rooms, usually with flat roofs, have yielded funerary objects which are closely akin to those found in contemporary tombs at Tarquinia. The deceased are normally laid in sarcophagi, sometimes made of tufa but more often of terracotta painted in bright colours, which resemble the later type found at Tarquinia: on the lid, the deceased is represented half-reclining, as if at a banquet, in full relief, while the chest is decorated in relief on the front with figures (funeral processions and mythological subjects) or purely ornamental designs. These sarcophagi, in particular the clay ones which never attain a high artistic level but are all the same vividly expressive, may be attributed to local workshops inspired by contemporary work at Tarquinia.

The wealthy families belonging to the local aristocracy have left us tombs which contain a remarkable number of burials: the Tomba degli Statlane housed a good 50 sarcophagi, most of them now dispersed; the Tomba dei Vipinana had 27 sarcophagi arranged in two concentric circles, the women on the inside and the men on the outside; the tomb commonly known as the Grotta della Regina yielded 21 intact sarcophagi and 12 in fragments. Some years ago two tombs were excavated which belonged to the Curunas family, and these contained not only 34 *nenfro* sarcophagi, now considered as cornerstones of Etruscan portraiture, but their funerary objects as well, almost intact (only gold and silver was missing, obviously removed in ancient times); a large number of bronze objects (vases and decorative pieces for attaching to wooden frameworks), with ornamental designs incised and in relief, are remarkable for their beauty and craftsmanship.

Among the discoveries at Tuscania mention should also be made of the famous ivory dice, now in the Bibliothèque Nationale in Paris, inscribed with the Etruscan numbers from one to six.

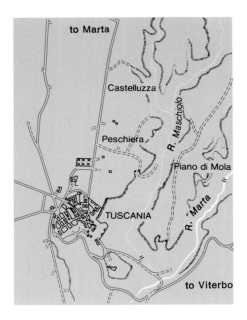

Above: Tuscania. Plan of the archaeological zone

Cinerary urn in the form of a shrine, from Chiusi. Florence, Museo Archeologico

In the Roman Imperial period the city was an important staging-post on the Via Clodia; in the early Middle Ages, when it was known as Toscanella, it was a bishopric, and its influence increased until about A.D. 1000 it embraced within its jurisdiction almost all the territory which had once belonged to Tarquinia. It is no accident that Tuscania is known not only for its archaeological remains, but also for its valuable mediaeval monuments, the most outstanding of which are the countless Romanesque churches, and in particular the church of S. Pietro, which has now been restored after the serious damage caused to it by the earthquake of 1971.

There are only very scanty remains now of the Etruscan and Roman city, which stood on the site of the modern town on a tufa spur where the Maschiolo flows into the Marta. The Colle di S. Pietro, being the highest point and steep-sided, was probably the site of the acropolis; it still has traces of Etruscan and Roman walls, incorporated into the church of S. Pietro, and terracing work on the lower hillsides. Ancient buildings have likewise come to light beneath the church of S. Maria Maggiore, and in its immediate vicinity the remains of a bath-building, dating from the 2nd century A.D.

The cemeteries were distributed all around the city. Particular interest attaches to the groups of tombs on the slopes of the Pian di Mole, along the right bank of the Marta, and on the two steep hillsides between which the Maschiolo flows. The chamber-tombs, on several levels from the top of the plateaux almost to the valley bottom, are interspersed with tombs with façades cut in the cliff.

A visit to the cube-tomb at Peschiera is not to be missed; this tomb has recently been restored and made easily accessible by the Soprintendenza alle Antichità dell'Etruria Meridionale. The tomb is rectangular in shape (5 metres by 9.40 metres), with all four sides

Detail of the Sarcofago della Suocera ('Sarcophagus of the Mother-in-Law'), from Tuscania. Rome, Museo di Villa Giulia

free-standing, situated on an artificial shelf in the rock, and intentionally made to imitate an Etruscan house with a gabled roof. Outside there is a step running around the base, then the main body of the tomb, with smooth walls ending in a moulded cornice; above this, on the longer sides, there is a second cornice imitating the overhang of a sloping roof, while on the shorter ends there are two small triangular pediments. The entrance is set in the middle of the front long wall, leading to three rooms with flat ceilings, the central one acting as a vestibule and the side rooms (the true burial chambers) furnished with funerary couches. This tomb, dating from the first half of the 6th century, puts Tuscania firmly among the cliff cemeteries.

To the east of the church of the Madonna dell'Ulivo, on the rocky hillside overlooking the right bank of the Marta, there is a whole series of chamber-tombs built at various levels. In this area is the so-called Grotta della Regina, which was already known in the 19th century and consists of a sizeable natural hollow which has been artificially worked

Left: Tuscania. The so-called Grotta della Regina

Above: rock-cut cube-tomb at Peschiera

and was used during the late Etruscan period as a tomb; from this, several underground passages lead off into the irregular rock face. Also in the same area are the two tombs of the Curunas family, already mentioned above.

Before the disastrous earthquake of 1971, Tuscania had a small Museo Comunale in the rooms adjoining the basilica of S. Pietro. The main feature of the museum was the numerous typical sarcophagi in stone and terracotta. At the present time the material is housed in the museums at Viterbo and Tarquinia.

Seven sarcophagus lids are to be found on the parapet of Piazza Basile, which is the site of the Ospedale Civile, the Palazzo Comunale and the Collegiata; from here there are fine views over the countryside below.

Acquarossa

On the Colle di Acquarossa, six kilometres north of Viterbo on the right of the main road S.S. No. 71, recent excavations, carried out by the Swedish Institute of Classical Studies (at Rome), have revealed the remains of an Etruscan settlement which flourished only in the Archaic period, during the 7th and 6th centuries B.C., and was completely destroyed about 500 B.C. After this date the hill was immediately and permanently abandoned; there was no further building there, and the Roman town of Ferento, the successor of this first Etruscan settlement, was built farther to the north, on the nearby heights of Pianicara.

The tufa plateau of Acquarossa, with its steep sides providing natural defences from all quarters, is about 1,000 metres in length and 800 metres wide, thus offering a particularly advantageous site for settlement. The oldest evidence of such a settlement dates back to the late Iron Age (end of the 8th and beginning of the 7th centuries B.C.). It consists of a small group of huts, whose ground-plan is exceptionally well preserved: they are dug into the earth and are either oval or round in shape, varying in size between nine and two metres in diameter. The upper part must have been made of branches and sticks, supported by a wooden framework, and reinforced by a layer of clay: the floors of some of these huts have yielded a large number of fragments of this clay covering, showing the imprint left by the sticks.

The main point of interest of the Acquarossa excavations, however, is the abundant archaeological evidence they supply for the study of Etruscan town-planning and architecture during the Archaic period. The absence on the hill of any building work after

Acquarossa. View of the excavated area

Below: Acquarossa, zone G: painted tile from an Archaic house

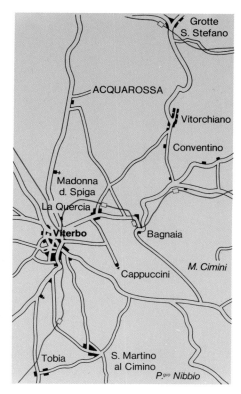

Above: map of the Viterbo region, showing the archaeological site of Acquarossa

Below: Acquarossa. Plans of Etruscan houses

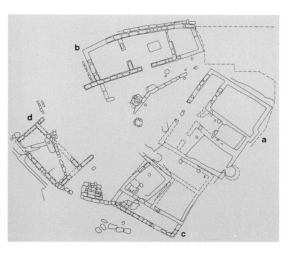

500 B.C. has in fact produced a situation hard to find in other Etruscan cities, which have been destroyed either totally or partially by later urban building, especially in the Roman period, and has preserved almost completely the ancient topography of the town and its Archaic buildings.

In the western and northern parts of the hill, the remains of numerous private houses have so far been unearthed, as well as the ruins of some monumental buildings, stretches of roads and squares, all dating from the period of the settlement's greatest expansion (late 7th–6th centuries B.C.). The buildings do not appear to be arranged according to a preordained regular plan; in other places such plans are known, typically based on a system of regions separated by streets intersecting at right angles. Instead, the buildings are seen to be grouped at random, sometimes being arranged around an open space of irregular shape.

There are some twenty dwellings whose plans are known (and also quite a few structural and decorative elements above ground level). The plans most frequently encountered are of two kinds: the simpler one generally covers a surface area of ten by five metres and consists of two or three rooms side by side, with the entrance in the long side or in one of the shorter ends; the other plan, substantially similar to the first, has an additional room situated in front of the others which opens—possibly by way of a portico—on to the area in front. It is worth noting that houses of this second type inspired the plans of many contemporary Etruscan tombs found, for example, at Cerveteri (Tomba della Cornice, Tomba degli Scudi e delle Sedie, and so on); another building which corresponds to this plan is the Regia, the house in the Forum at Rome which was the residence, according to ancient tradition, of the king, and after him of the *pontifex maximus*, the chief priest of Rome. The fact is of some significance, because it provides clear proof of the existence of conventions and designs that were common to the cultures of the Tyrrhenian region of Italy.

The foundations of these houses were cut into the calcareous tufa and built of blocks cut from the same stone and laid in two or more courses. In some cases these blocks are found in the walls as well; their upper sections were built of unfired, sun-dried brick. In addition, following a technique which we have seen was used in the construction of the primitive huts, the walls of some houses may have been made of a framework of wooden beams, covered with interwoven branches and these in turn covered with a layer of clay.

As far as the roofs were concerned, these were of the gabled type and projected some way beyond the walls, which were thus protected from the weathering caused by the elements. Large flat oblong tiles, the longer sides of which had raised edges, linked by semi-cylindrical tiles formed the heavy, solid roof covering. This was frequently enhanced by a large variety of architectural terracottas, whose function was purely ornamental. On the very top of the roof, for example, the uppermost large curved tile, ending at the gable of the house, appears in one instance to be decorated with the heads of two dragons facing each other. The curved tiles at the sides, on the other hand, were decorated along the line of the eaves with small heads in relief of griffins, or else closed off by semicircular slabs painted with rosettes. Finally, as in the architectural decoration of temples (which re-sembled this house decoration in other ways), there were cornices decorated with inter-linking geometric designs or with animals (horses, deer, birds) covering the wooden beams of the gables.

In the northwestern part of the hill, the structures brought to light belong to a complex of buildings which were monumental in character, reached by a road a good seven metres wide which came up from the valley by a steep route. The area is dominated by two buildings, both consisting of a series of rooms arranged side by side, with a portico in front; the bases of a few columns belonging to the portico remain. These were arranged in such a way that between them they formed almost a right angle, marking off a central open space.

Both buildings have produced rich architectural terracotta decoration: there are antefixes (the ends of the curved tiles along the eaves) in the shape of female heads, and facing slabs for the wooden beams of the pediments, decorated with polychrome low reliefs. Two series of slabs (there are 70 in all) depict scenes of the labours of Heracles. In one we see the hero, identified by his bow and quiver, grappling with the Cretan bull by a horn and a hoof and driving it forwards, behind a chariot, which is drawn by two winged horses and driven by a charioteer, bearing the goddess Athene, the hero's protectress; to the right, a man's figure with a tall staff—possibly king Eurystheus—greets the whole procession. The second series depicts Heracles in combat with the Nemean lion, preceded, on foot or on horseback, by a group of warriors armed with spears, shields and helmets.

1

The two types of slabs are stylistically alike: they are characterized by an emphatic simplicity in the depiction of the human figures, which tend to be partly hidden by the other elements portrayed.

The scenes depicted on two other series of slabs are less schematic and rich in representational detail; they are by a different hand and undoubtedly later (530–500 B.C.). One shows the customary banquet scene, with men and women drinking and conversing, while flute- and cithara-players enliven the feast. The other series depicts an abandoned orgy being enjoyed by various drunken people, while servants carry in full wineskins on their shoulders.

The whole group of terracottas, which is at present in the Museo Civico at Viterbo, is one of the most important discoveries made during the excavations at Acquarossa; what is more, these excavations are by no means finished, and in the years to come there is the possibility of more sensational discoveries.

For a visit to the remains of the town, it is advisable to make for the southwestern part of the plateau, taking the modern road which climbs up from the valley of the river Acquarossa. In this area can be seen traces of houses cut deep into the rock, with walls made apparently entirely of several courses of tufa blocks. Slightly farther north (zone B), the foundations can be seen of huts of the oldest inhabited part, dating back to the early Iron Age. They are round or oval in shape, varying in size between 9.50 and 2.50 metres and 1.55 by 1.10 metres. Along the lip of the western part of the hill (zone C) are the remains of a group of private houses built according to a plan which, as we have seen, was widely used in Acquarossa, having two or three rooms set side by side, with or without a portico in front; the houses are arranged around an open irregular-shaped area. In the northwestern zone of the plateau (zone D), finally, can be seen the remains of the complex of monumental buildings described above.

2

3

4

Acquarossa, zone F:
1. Terracotta architectural facing slab, depicting a banquet scene
2 and 3. Curved roof tile with an antefix in the form of a female head

Acquarossa, zone B:
4. Ridge-tile with an acroterion in the form of stylized animals

Ferento

Not far from the Colle di Acquarossa, on a very elongated tufa plateau extending in an east–west direction between two streams, stand the ruins of the Roman town of Ferento (Latin Ferentium).

We do not know much about the history of the place: in the 1st century B.C. it became a Roman *municipium*, in other words a town within the territory of Rome but autonomous as far as its internal administration was concerned. The emperor Otho was born there. It declined at the end of the Empire, when the settlement was reduced to a tiny nucleus, as is shown by the barbarian burials discovered among the ruins of the baths. Nevertheless, the town survived until 1172, when it was taken and destroyed by the people of Viterbo.

The town was protected by a wall, of which only a few blocks of the eastern section remain today; at the point where the plateau separates from the other hills, it was also defended by an *agger* (earth rampart) which is still partly visible.

Excavations inside the wall have been confined to exploration of the two important public buildings whose impressive ruins survive: the theatre and the baths. There are only scattered traces of the street plan and the other buildings in the town.

The theatre was built during the reign of Augustus, and remodelled and restored in the first half of the 3rd century A.D. There are well-preserved remains of all the structural elements which are generally characteristic of the construction of a theatre in Roman times. The *cavea* (the auditorium for the spectators), which was in the form of a sweeping semicircle, still retains all the bottom row of its outer arches, built in large blocks of *peperino*. In front of the *cavea* the *orchestra* survives, semicircular in shape with the seats around its curve, and two arched passages running along the sides, linking the *cavea* with the stage. The stage, following the typical plan of a Roman theatre, consisted of the podium, where the players performed, and the back (the *frons scaenae*), whose function was purely decorative. The podium and the lower part of the *frons scaenae* survive; the latter, adopting a form commonly found in the western Roman Empire, has a semi-circular *exedra* at the centre and two large rectangular niches at the sides. In addition, it was decorated with statues of Muses and one of Eros, now in the Museo Archeologico at Florence; its brick structure, which is now visible, was faced with marble slabs.

Next to the theatre are the baths; these were also built during the reign of Augustus, and later restored and extended more than once. The building is a grandiose construction in brick with facing in *opus reticulatum*; it is easy to recognize the remains of the typical rooms of a bath-building, such as the *frigidarium*, *tepidarium* and *caldarium*.

Ferento. Remains of the Roman theatre

Right: Lake Bolsena, and the excavated area of Volsinii

Volsinii and Lake Bolsena

In ancient times Lake Bolsena was called both *Lacus Volsiniensis* (that is, belonging to the city of Volsinii) and *Tarquiniensis*; in the historical period, at least its western shore, including Visentium, must in fact have been under the rule of Tarquinia.

Its shores were inhabited from prehistoric or early historical times. On the heights near the eastern shore, at Capriola, recent excavations have revealed the existence of the foundations of roughly oval huts dating from the Bronze Age (the Apennine culture). The evidence for life during the Iron Age is much more consistent and occurs here, there and everywhere on the shores of the lake. On the slopes of Colle Capriola, about 500 metres from the Apennine settlement, a small Villanovan cemetery has been discovered. A little farther to the south, in the actual lake itself (whose water-level was clearly much

lower in ancient times than it is today), a village of huts belonging to the early Iron Age was discovered in 1965 by underwater exploration at a depth of four to five metres at the place called Gran Carro.

But the most consistent Villanovan finds have been made on the opposite side of the lake, on the western shore to the north of modern Capodimonte, at Bisenzio, where Roman Visentium stood on the site of an earlier Etruscan town. The settlement sprang up on Monte Bisenzio and survived from the Iron Age to the Etruscan period, then into Roman times (the *municipium* of Visentium) and finally the Middle Ages (Bisenzo).

The cemeteries are scattered at the foot of the mountain, at Polledrara, S. Bernardino, Porto Madonna, Bucacce, Olmo Bello and Palazzetta. The oldest are also the farthest away from the urban centre. The Villanovan tombs are of the simple pit type, or else contain a cylindrical tufa receptacle for cremated remains; there are trench-tombs for inhumation.

Bolsena. Wheeled stand in bronze, from the Olmo Bello cemetery. Rome, Museo di Villa Giulia

The finest and richest funerary deposits, belonging to the late Villanovan period, include a large number of bronzes and pottery vessels painted in the Geometric style. Of the pottery, one of the most important pieces is a jar, now in the Museo Archeologico at Florence, from the Bucacce cemetery. The decoration is painted in red and brown on a white background; in addition to the usual abstract geometric designs, it shows a line of small schematic female figures holding hands with one another.

A typical example of the highly original bronze-work from Bisenzio is a wheeled stand found in a tomb in the Olmo Bello cemetery and now in the Museo di Villa Giulia. This consists of a small bowl, in the shape of a truncated cone, standing on four wheels and richly decorated with moulded human figures (warriors, hunting scenes, a ploughman, etc) and animals. The object, which is thought to be either an incense-burner or a container for offerings, is based on Eastern models and dates from the late 8th century.

But the Etruscan city which in historical times undoubtedly had the largest population and greatest political influence of the settlements on the shores of the lake or in its immediate vicinity (to the extent of giving its name to the lake) is Volsinii, which has received considerable mention from ancient historians.

These tell us that the city (whose Etruscan name was Velsna, Volsinii being the Latin version) was taken by the Romans in 265–264 B.C.; the inhabitants who survived the massacre were moved to a site which could be captured more easily. The victors took possession of at least 2,000 bronze statues, which they transported to Rome. Ancient sources also tell us that the principal deities worshipped in the Etruscan city were the goddess Northia and the god Vertumnus.

To the northeast of the modern town of Bolsena, excavations carried out by the École Française de Rome from 1946 onwards revealed the remains of a city which was identified beyond a shadow of doubt as Roman Volsinii. There was, however, immediate and lively debate among scholars as to the site of the Etruscan city. Where was that city before it was destroyed by its enemies? Some archaeologists identify it with the Etruscan settlement found at Orvieto; the victors would thus have deported the inhabitants of Velsna to a site a good 13 kilometres away. Other scholars maintain, on the other hand, that the move was to somewhere considerably nearer and that both cities coincide with the city excavated by the École Française; whereas Etruscan Volsinii stood on the higher, more easily defended part, after its destruction the city would have been moved to a less impregnable site lower down, closer to the lake. This second thesis is supported by information handed down by the historical sources, according to whom the Etruscan city was protected by a solid wall. Orvieto, with its naturally strong position, would not appear to have needed defence works, whereas at Bolsena traces have been found of a wall built of large squared blocks. The question, however, appears to be still open.

The city identified by the French is built on terraces at different levels: Mozzeta di Vietena, Montebello, Casetta, Le Grate and Mercatello. The first four, which are the highest, are where Velsna would have stood, according to supporters of the second theory, the lowest terrace, Mercatello, being the site of Roman Volsinii.

The city, as we have said, had a surrounding wall built of large squared blocks, with double walls in the weaker spots. Two sacred buildings have been identified inside the wall. The first, on Poggio Casetta, dates from the 3rd century B.C. and consists of a small enclosure at the back of which is a rectangular cella. It is not known what deity was worshipped here. At Pozzarello a second sacred building was identified and excavated at the beginning of the century, with a roof canopy set at one corner, a well and an altar. The excavators identified it with the temple of Northia; to bear out this hypothesis, they sought to recognize the figure of the goddess in certain bronze female statuettes found among the votive offerings. But in 1961, near the enclosure, a squared *nenfro* cippus was unearthed with an inscription in Etruscan to the god Selvans, which has definitely revealed the deity to whom the temple was dedicated.

In the lower part of the city, on Poggio Mercatello, very numerous remains of Roman Volsinii have been recognized. The city presents a regular plan, with streets intersecting at right angles. The forum, amphitheatre, baths and theatre have all been located. Up to 1962 the plans of only two private houses were known, one of them belonging to a certain Laberius Gallus. Between 1962 and 1969 the researches of the École Française were concentrated in the southwestern zone of the built-up area, at Poggio Moscini, close by the modern road from Bolsena to Orvieto. Both public and private buildings have been found, positioned on various terraces, dating from between the mid-3rd century B.C. and the 4th century A.D.

The cemeteries extend all around the inhabited centre, at Poggio Sala, Vietena, Poggio Pesce and Barano. The oldest tombs date from the 7th century B.C.

Four kilometres south of Bolsena, at La Civita, on a hill with good natural defences, there is a small Archaic Etruscan city. Remains of city walls and buildings have been found. From the material brought to light, it can be inferred that the site was inhabited from the 6th to the 4th centuries B.C.

Orvieto

The town of Orvieto stands on an oval-shaped volcanic plateau surrounded by impressive overhanging cliffs; from here it overlooks the wide valley of the Paglia, a tributary of the Tiber.

We know both its Latin name (Urbs Vetus) and its Greek one (Ourbibenton), but not its Etruscan name. Since it was immediately obvious from archaeological finds that here was an important city of considerable size, there has been lengthy dispute among scholars, from the 19th century to the present day, in an attempt to give a name to the Etruscan city. For a long time Orvieto was identified with the older city of Volsinii, conquered in 265–264 B.C. by the Romans, who destroyed it and settled the inhabitants elsewhere; some archaeologists, however, are now inclined to situate both cities of Volsinii, the old and the new, near present-day Bolsena. Others have claimed that Orvieto was the ancient Salpinum, or, again, identified it as the site of the *Fanum Voltumnae*, the most famous of the Etruscan sanctuaries. These last two theories have also lost popularity, and so the question of the Etruscan name of Orvieto remains unanswered.

The nearby Tiber contributed decisively to the city's prosperity. In ancient times it was undoubtedly navigable and so an extremely important route for trade and communications. There was easy communication by way of the river and its tributaries with the Faliscans to the south and the Umbrians and other Italic peoples to the north. An investigation of Archaic inscriptions in the cemeteries of Orvieto has shown that many of the dead had Italic names. This favoured class of foreigners, probably traders, often achieved leading positions in local aristocratic society.

From nearby Lake Bolsena, furthermore, good roads led to the wealthy coastal cities of Vulci, Cerveteri and Tarquinia. Trading relations with these towns are well documented

Orvieto. Tempio del Belvedere: figures from the terracotta relief. Orvieto, Museo Archeologico dell'Opera del Duomo

Opposite: Torre S. Severo (Orvieto). Details of the polychrome sarcophagus: Ulysses with the seer Tiresias, and Ulysses with the enchantress Circe. Orvieto, Museo Archeologico

Below: Orvieto. Plan of the Tempio del Belvedere

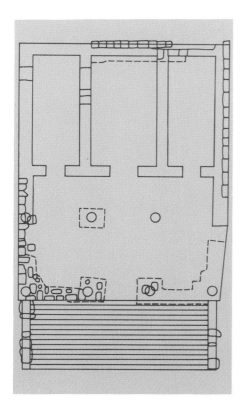

by the Greek black- and red-figure vases found in the cemeteries; these reached Etruria by sea and were then carried overland to Orvieto.

A few objects dating from the Bronze and Iron Ages have been found, showing that the site was inhabited in prehistoric times. The archaeological remains from the Etruscan period, on the other hand, are abundant and indicate the existence of a prosperous city, especially in the 6th and 5th centuries B.C.

A path cut in the rock near the present-day Porta Maggiore led up to the plateau, where there was formerly extensive evidence of the Etruscan settlement; unfortunately, little now remains. The many fragments of architectural terracotta facings which have been found suggest there were many temples in the city (as many as 17 buildings, it has been asserted, but that is surely an exaggeration; there may have been only six). There is nothing to show, as a rule, which deities were worshipped in them, but two conical cippi, one from Piazza del Duomo, the other from near the church of S. Giovanni, are inscribed with dedications to Tinia, the Etruscan chief of the gods, who had many features in common with the Greek Zeus and the Roman Jupiter.

The most interesting temple at Orvieto is certainly the Tempio del Belvedere, discovered near the Pozzo di S. Patrizio. Built on a high podium reached by a flight of steps, the building follows the plan typical of Etruscan temples, with three cellae at the end and columns in front. The many fragments of architectural terracottas from the temple attest the successive phases of its decoration, from the 5th to the 3rd century B.C. Particularly noteworthy are the figures in high relief depicting mythological characters, which must have decorated the rear pediment. Although clearly inspired by Greek art of the second half of the 5th century, they exhibit marked characteristics of authentic popular art.

Other exquisitely worked terracottas, from the temple in Via S. Leonardo, reflect the influence of post-Phidian Greek classical art.

The Etruscan cemeteries are, as usual, situated outside the city area, all around the base of the plateau. They are divided into two main groups: the Crocifisso del Tufo cemetery to the north and the Cannicella cemetery to the south.

There are other cemeteries farther away, along the hillside facing Orvieto to the south (at Settecamini and Castel Rubello).

Crocifisso del Tufo cemetery. The most striking feature of this cemetery is its planned layout, in clear imitation of an Etruscan city: the tombs are grouped into blocks, bordering long streets crossing at right angles. The tombs, built of large tufa blocks, are rectangular and often have a richly moulded cornice along the upper part of the façade; on top is a small tumulus of earth into which is set a *nenfro* cippus shaped like a ball or a pine-cone. Usually each tomb has a small vestibule and a burial chamber with two benches; the ceiling is built of courses of blocks progressively projecting to form a false vault. In rare cases the tombs have two chambers. The entrance was originally closed by a large tufa slab; the lintel bears an inscription, giving the name of the first person buried there.

The tombs, dating mainly from the 6th to 5th centuries B.C., were often used for both inhumation and cremation burials. There are obviously similarities to the cube-tombs of Cerveteri and the Archaic tombs of the region of the cliff cemeteries: the tombs have the same rectangular plan, moulded upper cornices and cippi on the tumulus, while in the cemeteries there is the same attempt at a regular layout.

Cannicella cemetery. This cemetery lies under the southern edge of the city plateau and contains both trench- and chamber-tombs, arranged on a series of terraces. The

Orvieto. Street of tombs in the Crocifisso del Tufo cemetery

chamber-tombs, either rock-cut or built up, line the dividing pathways. As in the Crocifisso del Tufo cemetery, inhumation and cremation burials both occur. There are many inscriptions on the lintels over the doorways and on the tomb cippi, which are either made of trachyte and phallic in shape, or rectangular blocks of green serpentine fixed on a small carved *nenfro* base. The Cannicella cemetery is slightly older than the one at Crocifisso del Tufo: the first tombs date from as early as the 7th century B.C.

On one terrace, almost in the centre of the cemetery, were found the remains of a building constructed with large blocks, four stone altars, a square basin, bronzes, votive and architectural terracottas, and finally a marble nude female statue dating from the 6th century B.C. On the site, which shows clear traces of destruction by fire, there stood a shrine dedicated to a deity, perhaps Aphrodite, if the female statue (one of the few marble sculptures found in Etruria) has been correctly identified.

In the outlying cemeteries of Orvieto three tombs containing wall paintings have been found, the first two (called the Tombe Golini I and II, after their discoverer) at Settecamini, the third (the Tomba degli Hescanas) not far away, at Castel Rubello. The paintings from the Tombe Golini have been removed to the Museo Archeologico at Florence.

Tomba Golini I (also known as the Tomba dei Velii) consists of a large rectangular room divided by a tufa partition which extends from the end wall half-way into the tomb. The paintings depict the arrival of the dead man in the underworld, where his ancestors await him at a banquet. The partition in fact separates the servants from the masters: the left-hand space shows the servants and cooks preparing for the banquet, to the cheering accompaniment of a flute-player, in the customary Etruscan manner. A realistic still-life element is the representation of the animals destined for the table, shown hanging from the rafters. The right-hand space shows the dead man in a horse-drawn chariot entering

Nenfro head of a warrior, from Orvieto. Florence, Museo Archeologico

Orvieto. Row of tombs in the Crocifisso del Tufo cemetery

the underworld where the lavish banquet is taking place, in the presence of Hades and Persephone.

Tomba Golini II (also known as the Tomba delle Due Bighe, 'Tomb of the Two Chariots') consists of a single rectangular chamber in a very ruinous state. The subject is the same as in Tomba Golini I: the arrival of the dead in the afterlife where the usual banquet is in progress, enlivened by players of trumpet and *lituus* (curved trumpet). The two deceased are shown on either side of the entrance. Both tombs can be dated to the final decades of the 4th century B.C. Despite the obvious influence of classical Greek art on the paintings, they have a somewhat provincial tone, but a spontaneous and truly Etruscan quality.

The third chamber-tomb, the Tomba degli Hescanas, has a gabled ceiling and a bench on which three sarcophagi and an urn were placed. Some of the decoration has survived, showing the usual banquet and a funeral procession of over twenty people, including demons and winged spirits. The style of the paintings and the tomb furnishings suggest that this tomb is later in date than the Tombe Golini.

Although, as we have seen, there are many remains of Etruscan Orvieto, very little survives from the Roman period, indicating that from the 3rd century B.C. the scale of life in the town was much reduced. Only in the Middle Ages did Orvieto again become a flourishing and well-populated city.

The 17th-century Palazzo dell'Opera del Duomo houses the archaeological museum of the same name. On view are many examples of tomb furnishings from the cemeteries of the city, including some fine Athenian black- and red-figure vases signed by well-known potters. In addition there are some particularly interesting items:

1. The group of architectural terracottas from the Belvedere and S. Leonardo temples.

2. The statue in Parian marble of a nude goddess known as the Venere della Cannicella.

3. A cippus of the 6th century B.C. from Crocifisso del Tufo, in the shape of the head of a helmeted warrior.

4. A *peperino* sarcophagus from Torre S. Severo, decorated with polychrome reliefs. The long sides depict the sacrifice of Trojan prisoners at the tomb of Patroclus and of Polyxena at that of Achilles. The short ends show Ulysses, first with the enchantress Circe, then with the seer Tiresias. The authenticity of the sarcophagus, believed to date from the 4th century B.C., has recently been questioned; it has been suggested that the chest itself may be ancient, but that it was originally smooth and was decorated in modern times by forgers.

5. The bronzes include an interesting bronze figurine of a female dancer holding castanets, which originally stood on top of a candelabrum of the 5th century B.C.

In the Palazzo Faina there is further archaeological material belonging to the private collection of the Counts Faina, which was presented to the Comune of Orvieto in 1954. The collection included objects of various origins, in addition to many excavated in the territory of Orvieto.

The museum's outstanding exhibit is the rich collection of painted Greek vases, mainly signed by or attributed to famous painters. There is also a fine collection of Roman coins, canopi from Chiusi, a large amount of bucchero ware, a group of the so-called 'silvered' vases produced at Bolsena, and an important collection of small bronzes from all periods.

Tbe Faliscan Teppitopy

The easternmost part of the Etruscan territory was under the cultural and political domination of Etruria in ancient times, although it remained ethnically and linguistically distinct from the rest of Etruria. Geographically it was bounded by the Tiber to the east, Lakes Vico and Bracciano to the west, the Monti Cimini to the north and the Monti Sabatini to the south. Its inhabitants spoke a local dialect of Latin, the Indo-European language of the Italic group which was originally spoken only in the neighbouring territory east of the Tiber, around the Alban Hills (*Latium vetus*, 'Ancient Latium'). The population of the region (the *Ager Faliscus*) are termed Falisci in literary tradition; they were regarded by ancient historians (Livy and Pliny) as an Etruscan people, perhaps because they always remained faithful to the Etruscan cause. There was, however, also a legend that they originally came from Greece, probably an attempt by tradition to explain their ethnic and linguistic independence.

The territory is volcanic in origin. The central area, where the region's chief city Falerii Veteres stood, forms an enormous tufa platform, geographically speaking, furrowed by many streams which to the south run into the Treia, a tributary of the Tiber. The deep gorges which erosion has produced, and is still producing, give the area its distinctively

Bronze shield, from the cemetery of Narce. Rome, Museo di Villa Giulia

Opposite: head of an old man, from the Tempio del Belvedere, and terracotta head of a barbarian deity, from the temple in Via S. Leonardo. Orvieto, Museo Archeologico dell'Opera del Duomo

picturesque appearance. In the south, near Monte Soratte (ancient Soracte) was Capena, the second major centre of the region (though strictly speaking not Faliscan), situated on Colle Civitucola, a broad tufa plateau which falls away steeply on three sides. There were other ancient settlements at Narce, in the Treia valley south of Falerii; at Nepi and Sutri, in the west of the Ager Faliscus on the communication route to Tarquinia; and at Vignanello and Corchiano, on the northern edge of the territory. In Roman times the Via Flaminia ran from south to north across the territory, following a course roughly parallel to that of the Tiber; the Via Amerina, branching off from the Via Cassia to the south, passed through Nepi (ancient Nepet) and, farther north, Falerii Novi; finally, the Via Cassia ran along the southwestern boundary of the region.

The earliest archaeological evidence of a single well-defined culture within the territory dates from the Iron Age (beginning of the 8th century B.C.). Elements from different periods and sources, both from Villanovan Etruria and from Latium and the Umbro-Sabine hinterland, nevertheless contributed to its development.

A distinctive feature of Archaic Faliscan culture is the more or less simultaneous appearance of pit-tombs for cremated remains and trench-tombs for inhumations. In the former we find the egg-shaped or spherical impasto urns typical of the Latial and particularly of the Umbro–Sabine culture. Villanovan influence on this type of grave is apparent, on the other hand, in the use of large *nenfro* containers akin to the jars of Tarquinia, and in the tomb furnishings, which included items (fibulae, vases, razors) similar to those found in the Etruscan cemeteries of the southern coastal strip.

The cities of coastal Etruria (Cerveteri, Tarquinia) also had a decisive influence on the development of Faliscan civilization at the beginning of the Orientalizing period. However, archaeological evidence from the 7th century B.C. reveals a number of increasingly original features over an area which includes Veii and Rome as well as the Faliscan towns.

Reconstruction of decoration of the temple at Lo Scasato, Falerii Veteres (Civita Castellana). Rome, Museo di Villa Giulia

One custom typical of the region, where the rite of inhumation was by now firmly established, was the use of large hollowed-out tree trunks to bury the dead. Equally characteristic, among the grave goods, is pottery in polished red impasto or imitation bucchero. The decoration (scratched, painted on, or executed by scraping away the clay around the figure) draws on the Orientalizing repertoire (fantastic animals, fish and birds), with additional decorative elements such as double spirals, rosettes and palmettes. The most common pottery shapes are jars, plates supported on feet, large stands for vases, and amphorae.

Capena. Plan of the archaeological zone

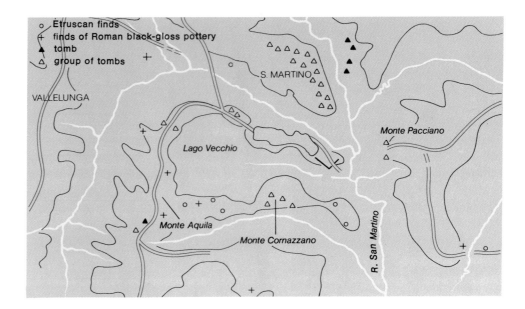

During the 6th and 5th centuries B.C. the Faliscan territory became associated economically and culturally with the Etruscan world, although it remained in a position of secondary importance. This was particularly true of the city of Falerii, which from this period emerged as the focal point for the area's cultural development. In the cemetery of Falerii a small amount of rather poor-quality imported Athenian pottery has been found, showing that even the leading Faliscan city was not among the foremost trading centres of central Italy: imported pottery reached it only after the great coastal cities of Etruria had taken their pick. In the same period the architectural terracottas for temple decoration, the production of which was a particularly flourishing industry at Falerii from the last decades of the 6th century B.C., show that the city came within the Etruscan cultural sphere. In style these terracottas are clearly influenced by the Ionian and Athenian artistic trends predominant in contemporary Etruscan art, although some distinctive local details reveal a certain independence of approach.

At the end of the 5th century B.C., the chief towns of the Faliscan territory were involved in the first armed clashes with Rome, alongside Etruscan Veii, which was struggling to prevent Rome gaining exclusive control of the lower reaches of the Tiber. However, in 396 B.C. Veii was forced to surrender and totally destroyed. Its fall was immediately followed by Roman reprisals against the Faliscan allies of Veii: Capena, Nepi and Sutri had to surrender and Rome thus gained possession of important strategic positions which until then had been entirely under Etruscan influence. In 383 B.C. two Roman *coloniae* were established at Nepi and Sutri. The Faliscan capital was besieged for a year (394 B.C.), but was able to resist because of its impregnable position, and a peace was arranged, apparently without any great disadvantage to Falerii, which continued to pursue its anti-Roman course, siding with Tarquinia in its first war against Rome in 358 B.C. Rome was again victorious and signed a treaty with the two cities, making them in effect politically dependent.

Falerii subsequently tried to rebel on two occasions. The Romans decided to destroy the city in 241 B.C., forcing the inhabitants to abandon it and settle on the plain not far away, where they founded Falerii Novi.

In spite of these upheavals, Faliscan culture apparently flourished in the final stages of its development and seems to be no longer totally dominated by Etruscan influence. The extensive production of architectural terracottas and, from the 4th century B.C., a wide range of red-figure vases made at Falerii show that the Faliscan territory, like the whole of central-southern Italy, was part of the general Hellenized culture which developed at this period, influenced chiefly by the city of Tarentum in Magna Graecia.

One of the finest examples of Faliscan pottery, now in the Museo di Villa Giulia in Rome, deserves special mention: an enormous volute krater (p. 296). The principal scene, delicately painted on the body of the vase, shows Aurora reclining in a chariot drawn by four white horses; she is embracing the young man Cephalus, whom she has seduced and who now lies at ease in her arms.

A calyx-krater in the same museum is painted with equally delightful scenes, perhaps by the same artist as the vase already described. It depicts the loves of two divine couples. On the left Leda opens her cloak to reveal her beautiful young body and receive (unknown to her) Zeus in the form of a swan; on the right Aphrodite embraces the risen Adonis.

The theme of love recurs on two cups, again in the Museo di Villa Giulia, inscribed with various light-hearted sayings in the Faliscan language. One runs *foied vino pipafo cra carefo* ('Today I'll drink wine, tomorrow I'll have none').

Civita Castellana

Falerii Veteres, the chief city of the Faliscan territory, was situated on the hill where the mediaeval and modern town of Civita Castellana now stands, 54.50 kilometres from Rome along the Via Flaminia. The long narrow hill, running east–west, is in places as much as 90 metres high; at its eastern end a low isthmus links it to a second hill, the Colle del Vignale, where the acropolis of the ancient city stood. The Maggiore, a tributary of the Treia, flows beside the steep slopes of the northern sides of both hills. The Treia itself flows to the south of the eastern hill, and the Filetto, another of its tributaries, flows past the southern slopes of the Colle di Civita Castellana. To the north of the city is a series of plateaux separated by short watercourses, all flowing into the Treia: these are the Celle, Montarano and Colonnette hills, where the oldest cemeteries (8th–7th centuries B.C.) of the Faliscan city were established. Finally, to the west of Civita Castellana is a broad low plateau, sloping gently towards the south, which was used for the later cemeteries (6th–3rd centuries B.C.).

Little remains of the ancient settlement, but there were many sacred buildings in and around the urban area, as is shown by remarkable discoveries, made during excavations carried out some time ago (1886–1925) in that area, of the rich terracotta decorations which covered their wooden structures. This material, now mainly in the Museo di Villa Giulia in Rome, covers a long period, from the end of the 6th to the 1st century B.C. This shows how long the city's sanctuaries were in use; some of them continued to exist even after the inhabitants had been moved to nearby Falerii Novi. During this period (6th–1st centuries B.C.) all these buildings had their architectural decorations renewed, at least to some extent, and they were all first built in the 6th or 5th century B.C., except for the temple at Lo Scasato, which dates only from the 4th century B.C.

One of the finest and most complete decorations of the Archaic period (6th century) comes from the Tempio ai Sassi Caduti, which stood at the foot of the high eastern cliff of the Colle di Colonnette. This includes a large fragment of the central acroterion (the group of figures which stood on the apex of the roof), depicting two armed warriors fighting: the well-preserved figure on the left, on one knee, is about to be overwhelmed by his

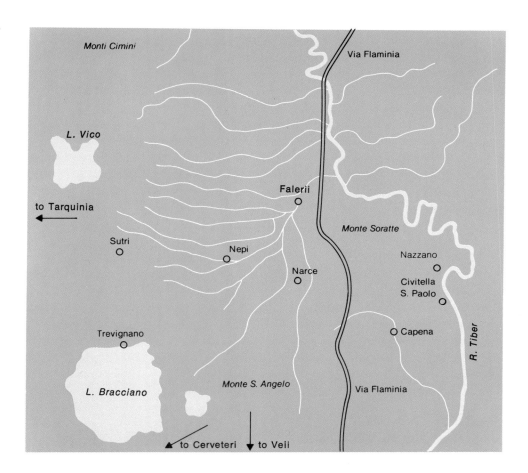

Map of the Faliscan territory and that of Capena

adversary; only the lower part of the body of the latter has survived. The relief, made in a mould and finished by hand, is remarkable for its bright colours. Similar skilled workmanship is found in the antefixes covering the tiles at the eaves on the long sides of the temple. Each shows a Silenus dragging away a maenad, in accordance with a design which occurs in other temples in Falerii, and especially in sacred buildings in Latium (Rome, Velletri, Lanuvium, Satricum). In each group the faces of the figures are characterized in a lively, varied and expressive manner.

A series of terracotta figures dating from the early Hellenistic period (end of the 4th–beginning of the 3rd century B.C.), which are among the most important examples of Italic sculpture of this time, come from a second temple that stood in the southeastern part of the Colle di Civita Castellana at Lo Scasato. The details of style and iconography show that local craftsmen imitated and elaborated Greek artistic achievements, under the influence of the great 4th-century sculptors (Scopas, Praxiteles and Lysippus). The statue of Apollo, which formed part of the temple's pedimental relief and was worked entirely by hand, resembles in style and conception the portrait of Alexander the Great by Lysippus. The lower part of the body is missing; the figure was perhaps shown as seated in the chariot of the sun. The head, with its long flowing locks of wavy hair, leans slightly to the left; the eyes look upwards with a melancholy expression. Two other heads, one male, one female, again from the pedimental decoration of the temple, reflect with great delicacy the style of Scopas and the tender art of Praxiteles, respectively.

The twelve antefixes of male and female heads from this building reveal the same qualities. A fine bearded head of Zeus, however, is inspired by the work of Phidias, and thus belongs to an earlier period (early 4th century B.C.). Although it was also found at Lo Scasato, it may have come from another sacred building in the area. The face has a very pronounced expression, achieved by making the eyes unusually large.

A third temple, at the foot of the Colle di Celle, is the only sacred building at Falerii with remains of its plan partly visible on the ground. It may have been a vast temple with three cellae, inside a large courtyard, but it has been suggested, more recently and more convincingly, that there was a sacred complex consisting of two buildings, each with three cellae, standing side by side on a single platform of blocks. Fragments of the architectural decoration from the latest stage of construction (4th–3rd centuries B.C.) include a fine torso of a woman wearing a mantle, clearly influenced by the work of Praxiteles.

Finally, two more temples stood on the Colle del Vignale; here a large number of terracottas have been found, both from the first temples constructed in the 6th and 5th centuries (antefixes with the head of a maenad, Silenus or a harpy) and from the later buildings of the Hellenistic period (head of Mercury). A considerable range of votive objects, including model heads, hands, feet, eyes, breasts and genital organs, come from the two deposits of offerings which must have been somewhere near the two buildings.

The remains of the public buildings of Falerii include some surviving stretches of the walls built round the city in the first half of the 4th century B.C. to reinforce its strong natural defences. The most notable remains are in the northern part of the Colle di Civita Castellana, east of the Ponte Clementino, where there is a section about 30 metres long and as many as seventeen courses high.

Just as little survives of the ancient town, so practically nothing remains of the vast burial-grounds which in time spread gradually from north to west on the heights opposite the northern and western sides of the hill on which the city itself stood. The oldest pit-, trench- and chamber-tombs, excavated during the 19th century, have now disappeared; only their furnishings are left, with their vases of black or polished red impasto, decorated with geometric or Orientalizing designs which are scratched, painted or scooped out on the sides of the vases. However, many 4th- and 3rd-century chamber-tombs cut into the slopes of the Celle, Colonnette and Terrano hills still survive. Usually they contain many niches cut along the inner walls, sometimes in as many as five rows one above the other on each side of the chamber.

Santa Maria di Falleri

The ruins of ancient Falerii Novi lie to the left of the modern road which leads from Civita Castellana to Fabrica di Roma. The ground here is level and open, bounded to the south by a narrow gorge which contains the Purgatorio, a sub-tributary of the Treia. As mentioned earlier, the town was founded when the inhabitants of Falerii Veteres were forced to leave their city by the Romans, against whom they had rebelled (241 B.C.). As an allied city, it immediately became an integral part of the Roman state; under the Gracchi it received a *colonia* of Roman citizens (*colonia Iunonia Faliscorum*); after the Social War (90–89 B.C.) it became a *municipium*. The city survived until the 11th century, when, since it was too obvious a target for constant barbarian raids, the inhabitants returned to the site of ancient Falerii, thus founding modern Civita Castellana. The ruins of the Romanesque church of S. Maria, with coloured marble mosaics by the Cosmati family, standing inside the city walls, date from this period.

Little remains of the Roman settlement except the imposing walls from the Republican age, which are clearly identifiable along their perimeter of roughly two kilometres. Built of squared blocks of tufaceous stone laid in horizontal courses, they are two metres thick and have survived to a height of at least five metres. They are strengthened by fifty rectangular towers, built in the same manner and jutting out from the walls at regular intervals. There are also a number of gateways, including the Porta di Giove in the west wall, which deserves special mention: the gate is so called after the head of Jupiter carved on the keystone of the arch, which is built of tufa blocks and framed by a fine relief cornice. In the south wall is the Porta del Bove ('Gate of the Ox'), which is similar and has a head of that animal carved on the keystone of its arch. Near this second gateway are the remains of the theatre, the only ruins visible inside the city. The street plan must have formed a regular network,

Opposite, above: fragment of the central acroterion of the Tempio ai Sassi Caduti, Falerii Veteres. Rome, Museo di Villa Giulia

Below, left: head of Zeus, from a temple at Lo Scasato, Falerii Veteres. Rome, Museo di Villa Giulia

Right: torso of Apollo, from a temple at Lo Scasato, Falerii Veteres. Rome, Museo di Villa Giulia

with the main roads, as usual, orientated north–south and east–west. Outside the inhabited area, near the north wall, are the remains of the amphitheatre and a mausoleum built in rubble concrete (*opus caementicium*).

Sutri

Sutri (ancient Sutrium) is situated on a fairly low tufa plateau between two short water-courses, 50 kilometres from Rome along the Via Cassia. In ancient times this was an important strategic position, on the borders of southern Etruria, the Faliscan territory and *Latium vetus*, and it was in order to acquire this position that the Romans conquered the city after the fall of Veii, settling one of their earliest *coloniae* there (383 B.C.) At the end of the 4th century, while Rome was engaged in the Second Samnite War, the Etruscans made an unsuccessful attempt to regain it, but Sutri remained a Roman possession and became a *municipium* after the Social War (90–89 B.C.).

In the Middle Ages, too, the history of the town is closely linked to its strategic position as an outpost of Rome: the donation of its castle by the Lombard king Liutprand to Pope Gregory II formed the nucleus of the Patrimony of St Peter (A.D. 728).

The remains of the ancient city are no earlier than the Roman conquest, except for some tombs of the 6th and 5th centuries B.C. One can still see some stretches of the walls, however, built of tufa blocks laid lengthwise and end-on, with two gates. One is known as the Porta Furia, in honour of the Roman conqueror of Sutri, Furius Camillus; it has an arched lintel made of a double row of blocks.

Santa Maria di Falleri (Falerii Novi). Porta di Giove

Below: Civita Castellana (Falerii Veteres). Plan of the archaeological zone

Bottom: Santa Maria di Falleri. Plan of the archaeological zone

Opposite: Sutri. Cemetery

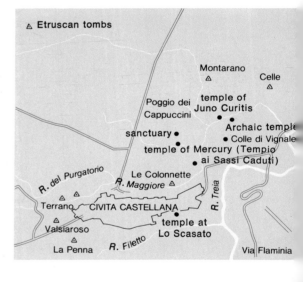

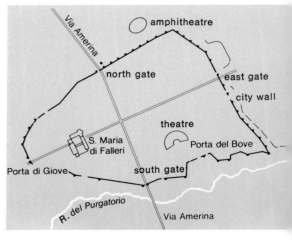

The most important monument is the amphitheatre (1st century B.C.), which is entirely rock-cut except for the entrances leading into the *cavea*, which are built of brick; the longer axis of the arena measures about 50 metres. Near the amphitheatre, finally, is an underground temple of Mithras of the 3rd century A.D., which was subsequently turned into a small Christian church dedicated to the Madonna del Parto; it is entirely rock-cut, consisting of a rectangular chamber divided by tufa pillars into a nave and two aisles.

Scorano

Near the modern town of Scorano, 18 kilometres along the Via Tiberina, excavations begun in 1952 have brought to light the ancient settlement of Lucus Feroniae. According to Livy, this was the site of an important ancient sanctuary dedicated to Feronia, an Italic

Sutri. Roman amphitheatre

goddess. Because of its favourable geographical position—between the Latin, Sabine, Etruscan and Faliscan territories, near the Tiber and near the beginning of routes of communication leading to the territory of the Picenes and the region of Teramo and L'Aquila—the cult centre was, as early as the period of the kings at Rome, an important meeting-place for those peoples, who attended a famous fair there every year. The sanctuary was sacked by Hannibal in 211 B.C. and all that has been found of it is a deposit of votive objects relating to fertility and abundance, characteristic attributes of the goddess.

Some important remains, dating from the Roman period, have been found of the settlement which grew up around the sanctuary. The town became a Roman *colonia* in Caesar's time (50 B.C.) and received a subsequent settlement of veterans under Augustus. It was at its most prosperous during the 1st century A.D., as is shown by the many honorary inscriptions found in the forum. This forum occupies a long rectangular area, bordered on its west side by a long portico behind which there is a row of shops interrupted in the centre by a wide paved road running east–west. The other side is bounded by a high wall in blocks set diamond-fashion (*opus reticulatum*), with a long narrow basin set against it on the side facing the forum. On the north side is a podium 2.20 metres high, built of limestone blocks, on top of which are traces of a rectangular building with columns. Two pillars at the sides of the podium, each bearing a dedication to Feronia, suggest that the unidentified building may have been the temple of that goddess, rebuilt after Hannibal had destroyed the earlier one. The high platform contained the *aerarium* which housed the funds of the *colonia*, public documents and military standards; it was closed off on the forum side by a shutter.

North of the forum there are the remains of a small Republican temple and of a large chamber with an apse, in which a series of headless statues wearing togas were found; they are now kept in the nearby Antiquarium. Further discoveries are a small amphitheatre, some stretches of road with houses, and a public lavatory against the end wall of the block to the northeast of the forum.

Museo Gregoriano Etrusco

The Museo Gregoriano Etrusco in the Vatican was founded on 2nd February, 1837 by Pope Gregory XVI and chiefly contained finds excavated between 1826 and 1836 in Etruria and Latium. A few months after the museum was founded, the rich furnishings of the Tomba Regolini-Galassi at Cerveteri were acquired; in 1900 the Falcioni di Viterbo collection was purchased; and finally in 1935 Marchese Guglielmi presented his collection, consisting chiefly of objects from the Vulci area, to Pius XI.

In Room I, which contains stone monuments, it is worth noting a pair of *nenfro* lions from Vulci; in a way characteristic of this city, they stood as symbolic guardians at the entrance of the tomb. A limestone sarcophagus, from the Tomba dei Sarcofagi at Cerveteri, has a lid with a reclining male figure wearing a crown, an armlet and a necklace; the figure is very finely carved, whereas the funeral procession carved in relief on the chest of the sarcophagus is pedestrian by comparison (late 5th–early 4th century B.C.).

Room II displays items found in the Tomba Regolini-Galassi in the Sorbo cemetery at Cerveteri. The rich tomb furnishings are the most significant instance of the high level of prosperity reached in Cerveteri during the Orientalizing period. Many precious objects were imported from the East, such as the silver cups, Cypriot silver-gilt bowls decorated with Egyptian-inspired motifs and the situla (metal vessel with handle) which has a wooden body decorated in sheet silver. There are others of local manufacture, the most outstanding of which are the magnificent examples of gold-work with decoration both by embossing and in the characteristic technique of granulation; this technique, probably Eastern in origin, widely used in the Greek world, and perfected by the Etruscans during the Orientalizing period, consisted of soldering minuscule spherical gold granules on to a smooth surface.

Among the most remarkable pieces is a sumptuous fibula (p. 17) which must have been used to fasten the cloak of the deceased at the shoulder; it is decorated with plant motifs (palmettes) and animals (little geese in the round and embossed lions). There was also a large gold pectoral that covered the dead man's breast, made of bronze covered with sheet gold ornamented with bands of embossed designs running round a little central shield; these decorations depict lions, panthers, sphinxes, chimaeras and the Mistress of Animals. Two bracelets, consisting of flat strips of gold (p. 161), are divided into rectangular panels, each decorated with three women holding hands. At the end of each bracelet are two similar scenes, repeated on the inside: the Mistress of Animals between two lions that are being stabbed in the back by a man. There is also a necklace made of gold mesh with three gold and amber pendants, each one having four lion's heads at the end.

The tomb also contained bronze objects including a chariot, a carriage, a throne, a couch and large shields, some decorated with geometric patterns, others with Orientalizing figures. There are also cauldrons with lion- and griffin-head handles and a fine stand, with two globes forming the stem and a conical base embossed with a series of fantastic animals: it is an example of Etruscan imitation of the Eastern products that were so widely imported into Etruria.

In the same room are the bucchero vases found in the Tomba Calabresi in the Sorbo cemetery at Cerveteri. The most remarkable is a zoomorphic vase with two long necks ending in horses' heads (p. 166, no. 2). A male figure stands on the back of the vase with its ribbon handle resting on his shoulders. The horses' mouths are pierced to make spouts and on their heads are two lotus-flower stoppers (7th century B.C.).

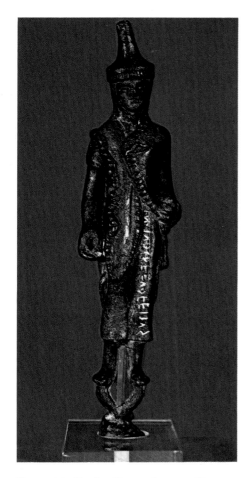

Bronze statuette of an Etruscan haruspex. Rome, Musei Vaticani

Globular vase with tall stem. Rome, Musei Vaticani

Overleaf: gold pectoral with embossed decoration, from the Tomba Regolini-Galassi, Cerveteri. Rome, Musei Vaticani

Room III houses the bronze collection: Villanovan cinerary urns, fibulae, mirrors, candelabra, tripods, statuettes etc.

There is an outstanding series of discs typical of the region of Tarquinia, with the head of a lion or of Acheloüs (a horned river-god) in the centre, and a statuette of a haruspex in his characteristic costume and tall hat. However, the most interesting object is undoubtedly a very large statue of the god Mars, found at Todi. The product of an Umbrian workshop, it wears a corslet of narrow plates; it once had on its head a helmet, which is now lost, and held a lance in its right hand. An Umbrian inscription is incised on the corslet. The statue dates from the first decades of the 4th century B.C. and shows obvious Greek influences, which the artist has not succeeded in combining into a harmonious whole.

Room IV contains a series of small stone urns dating from the Hellenistic period.

Room V displays the Guglielmi collection of bronzes, bucchero vases, and Etruscan and Greek painted vases.

Room VII (the terracotta collection): the first two cases contain valuable objects that once occupied the smaller room VI. The other material consists of a large number of terracotta objects: vases, sarcophagi, votive and architectural material. One of the finest vases is a typical product of the Faliscan region, with incised decoration, dating from the 7th century B.C. The vase is globular and shows a man between two horses kneeling to him. The incised parts were filled in with red impasto, of which traces still remain.

There are many architectural and votive terracottas from the region of Cerveteri. Among the finest is an antefix with a female head, dating from the 6th century B.C., and an acroterion in the shape of a winged horse, dating from the early 5th century B.C.

Room VIII contains the Roman Antiquarium, with decorative clay plaques from temples, a series of oil lamps, a group of glass objects, vases and bronze fragments of statues.

Room IX contains the Falcioni di Viterbo collection, of objects from different periods and sources (small bronzes, gold-work, oil lamps, votive objects, vases etc).

The remaining rooms and the Hemicycle contain an impressive collection of painted Etruscan, Greek and Italiote vases. There is an outstanding Laconian (Spartan) cup showing the torments of the Titans Prometheus and Atlas: on the left Atlas is depicted supporting the vault of the heavens, while on the right Prometheus, in chains, is attacked by the eagle which is feeding on his liver.

There is also a Caeretan hydria depicting Heracles and Alcyoneus; the latter led the revolt of the giants against the gods and was killed by Heracles. On the vase the hero is shown threatening the giant with his bow and club.

Among the Athenian black-figure vases is an amphora by Exekias: on one side Castor and Pollux are depicted with their parents Leda and Tyndareüs, and on the other Ajax and Achilles throwing dice. Similar to the style of Exekias is another amphora by the Painter of Vatican 350 with a woman weeping over the body of a warrior (which may be Eos mourning her son Memnon).

Outstanding among the red-figure Athenian vases are an amphora by the Kleophrades Painter showing Athene and Heracles on one side and an orgiastic scene on the other; also an amphora by the Berlin Painter with Apollo on a winged tripod, and an amphora by the Achilles Painter, found at Vulci, depicting Achilles with his favourite slave Briseis.

There are also many Italiote vases, the most important of which are three colossal Apulian volute-kraters, dating from the mid-4th century B.C.

3

1. Etruscan mirror depicting the abduction of
Cephalus by Eos, from Vulci
2. Bronze candelabrum, from Vulci
3. Bronze cauldron with lion heads, from
Cerveteri
4. Etruscan mirror depicting Calchas, from Vulci.
Rome, Musei Vaticani

4

Museo di Villa Giulia

The Villa Giulia was built for Pope Julius III between 1551 and 1553. The main body of the original building remains, with its rectilinear façade broken only by a small balcony. The interior is a hemicycle, with a splendid nymphaeum separated from the main part of the building by a colonnaded courtyard. Vignola, Ammannati, Vasari and Michelangelo collaborated in the design of the villa; it was acquired by the State in the 19th century and was given two additional rectilinear side wings.

In 1889 the palace became the home of the museum, founded to house pre-Roman finds from that area of Latium lying between the right bank of the Tiber, Umbria and Tuscany.

It was later enriched by the acquisition of the Barberini and Castellani private collections and by finds made during the excavations in the region that came under the jurisdiction of the Soprintendenza alle Antichità dell'Etruria Meridionale.

On the left, just inside the entrance, is a small room containing the most important discoveries from the excavations of the sanctuary at Pyrgi. On the entrance walls are excellent explanatory notices and illustrations. It is advisable to go round the room from left to right; the left-hand half of the room is dedicated to temple B (the older one) and the right-hand half to temple A.

Part of the left-hand side of the pediment from temple B has been reconstructed, with its painted terracotta decorations. The tiles form a high vertical parapet (*sima*) with an upper cornice which has a bean motif and a band painted in a diagonal pattern filled in with little squares and hooks. Three of the terracottas on show formed one of the sides of the enclosure in which the gold plaques were discovered. The lower slabs (casts) that covered the beams of the sloping roof have relief decorations of lotus flowers and palmettes. This reconstruction allows one to see the means used to fix these terracotta facing slabs to the wooden structure of the roof.

A case displays fragments of antefixes and acroteria from temple B; the most interesting of these are complete figures with heads of cocks, and the heads of Negroes and maenads in the middle of large shells with curly edges. On the end wall is a reconstruction of the terracotta cornice of one of the temple doors. A case on the same wall contains electrotype copies of the gold plaques (the originals are kept in a safe), the gold-headed nails that were found with them, and inscribed bronze plaques.

The right-hand part of the room is dedicated to temple A. The most interesting discovery is undoubtedly the mythological relief already described (pp. 176–177). A statue of a young man with a crown of ivy, coming from temple A but dating from the late classical period, should also be noted.

The first four rooms of the museum display material found in the Vulci area. The first contains the stone sculptures (a centaur, and a youth on a sea monster) described above (p. 222), and the other rooms contain tomb furnishings, displayed in chronological order.

Room 2 (at present in course of rearrangement) contains Villanovan and 7th-century material. This includes the fine bronze cinerary urn described on p. 219 (illustrated p. 14).

Room 3 contains tomb furnishings from the 7th and 6th centuries B.C. The Orientalizing period, or more precisely its final phase, is well represented by the furnishings from the Tomba del Pittore della Sfinge Barbata in the cemetery of Osteria (630–580 B.C.). Besides the imported pottery, such as Corinthian vases painted with the usual processions of animals, and Ionian cups with a black-gloss surface, except in a narrow band on a level with the handles (case 2), the collection includes much pottery of local manufacture.

Fragment of a terracotta acroterion, from the
Tempio ai Sassi Caduti, Falerii Veteres

Nenfro centaur, from Vulci. Rome, Museo di Villa
Giulia

There are some bucchero vases, including a fine kantharos (case 4) with incised decorations of deer, horses, sphinxes and lions with human legs hanging from their jaws (the last being a common theme in Etruscan representational art of the Orientalizing period). There are, finally, some Etruscan vases imitating the imported Corinthian ones, Vulci being one of the leading centres for the production of these; two (case 1, middle shelf; case 3) are by the Bearded Sphinx Painter who gives his name to the tomb. The difference in quality between the Corinthian vases and the Etruscan imitations is noteworthy: the drawing on the imitations is much more crude and careless, and the incised marks to show anatomical details are very few. Nevertheless, although the artist relied largely on Corinthian models, he shows a real originality in his choice of subjects, as for example in his preference for bearded sphinxes. A *nenfro* sphinx stood near the entrance to the tomb; this work, dating from the second half of the 6th century B.C., was obviously placed as a guardian of the tomb when it had already been sealed for several decades.

Room 4 contains furnishings from Vulci from the 6th to the 1st century B.C. The Tomba del Guerriero in the Osteria cemetery dates from the second half of the 6th century. A complete set of bronze armour—shield, helmet, greaves, sword and iron lance (case 1)— was found in it, also two bronze plaques, embossed with rosettes and a rectangular panel depicting the legend of Achilles and Troilus (Achilles is lying in wait behind a fountain, while the unsuspecting Trojan hero comes to water his horses). The furnishings include bucchero vases, bronze vases and domestic implements (colander, bucket: case 6) and Athenian black-figure pottery. A Panathenaic amphora (case 3), one of the large vases of pure olive oil that was given to the winners of the athletic contests held during the Panathenaean festival at Athens, is decorated on one side with a boxing-match, probably the sport for which the vase was given as a prize.

Room 5 contains various objects from the territory of Vulci, Bolsena, Bomarzo and Celleno. There is a stone capital from the Tomba Campanari at Vulci, decorated on each side with a female head crowned with a diadem, above rich plant decorations (4th or 3rd century B.C.). A large *nenfro* sarcophagus with Amazons in battle also comes from Vulci. The central cases contain, among other things, votive offerings found near the north gate at Vulci and at Tessennano. There are interesting little clay models of city buildings (a portico, a tower, a temple).

From room 5 a staircase leads down into a semi-basement room where there is a full-scale reconstruction of tomb no. 2 of the Tumulo Maroi in the Banditaccia cemetery at Cerveteri, with its furnishings laid out just as they were found.

Room 6 is devoted to material from Bisenzio, and contains grave goods from the cemetery of Olmo Bello, dating from the 8th–6th centuries B.C. In case 2 there are some very fine bronzes, including the incense-burner on wheels described on p. 268 and a situla, likewise decorated with human and animal figures in the round. On the lid is a chained bear round which armed and unarmed men seem to be performing a kind of dance; round the neck of the vase other groups of people are depicted, including a man driving an ox. The furnishings displayed in the central cruciform case (6) include numerous vases, made locally, in the Geometric style, with red-brown decoration on a white background. There are two outstanding askoi shaped like birds and another shaped like a small barrel, and a vase with, besides the usual geometric decoration, a scene representing three people in a rowing boat.

Room 7 contains material from the sanctuary of Portonaccio outside the city of Veii. In the centre is a magnificent gorgon-head antefix and also the famous statues attributed to Vulca that originally stood on the great central beam of the temple roof (pp. 230–231).

The artist depicts an episode in the twelve labours of Heracles, who is shown fighting with Apollo to win the Arcadian hind with the golden horns and hoofs. The two statues are placed facing each other, as they probably were in the original composition: Apollo faces to the left and Heracles, with the bound hind beneath his feet, faces right. The third statue is of a woman holding a child, perhaps the baby Apollo, who, in the arms of his mother Leto, killed the serpent Python sent by Hera to kill him. These sculptures are strongly influenced by Ionian art but show no trace of the affectation and mannerism sometimes associated with aspects of that art; these strong, massive bodies with their vigorously carved details are clearly the work of a truly original artist. In case 1 there is a wonderful head of Hermes and in case 4 the head of a boy, called the Malavolta head (catalogue no. 40777) after the man who discovered it; this sculpture shows the influence of the great Greek artist Polycletus (second half of the 5th century).

Rooms 8, 9 and 10 display objects from Cerveteri.

Room 8: the cases contain tomb furnishings and votive and architectural terracottas from temples in the city of Cerveteri. In the centre are two red pottery pithoi (jars), typical Caeretan products, and the fine Sarcofago dei Leoni, made of terracotta slabs with stamped decorations of lions; the lid is shaped like the gabled roof of a house, and on the top of this are four felines carved in the round (mid-6th century B.C.).

Room 9: the Sarcofago degli Sposi from Cerveteri (about 520 B.C.). The chest is made to resemble a wooden couch (kline) with turned legs and a mattress, and a man and wife are reclining on it. The woman is wearing a tunic and a cloak, the typical Etruscan head-covering (tutulus) and pointed shoes (calcei repandi). The man is bare-chested and his arm is affectionately laid on his wife's shoulders. Like the Sarcofago dei Leoni, this represents a stage in Etruscan art when the Ionian influence was most strongly felt: for example, in the soft fleshy surfaces, the faces with their pointed chins and noses, the drape of their clothes and the extreme accuracy of the details. It appears that both faces were made in the same mould, and only the details applied afterwards differentiate them.

Room 10 contains partial and complete tomb furnishings from the cemeteries of Cerveteri that provide evidence for Etruscan art of the period from the 7th to the 2nd or 1st century B.C. Some of the most interesting objects in this room are:

Case 3, lower shelf: a very fine East Greek hydria. It depicts the entrance of Heracles to Olympus; the hero is preceded by Iris (the messenger of the gods), Hermes, and his wife Hebe standing in a chariot.

Star case: arm 7. On the upper shelf are two Laconian cups. One shows the legend of Achilles and Troilus, the other the Harpies, who persecuted Phineus by defiling his food, being themselves in turn pursued and driven away by the sons of Boreas. On the lower shelf are two Caeretan hydriae: one depicts the blinding of Polyphemus and the fight between Heracles and the centaur Nessus, and the other one satyrs harvesting grapes. In arm 10 of the star case is an Athenian black-figure amphora, by Exekias or his school, depicting Heracles fighting Triton.

Case 11: on the upper shelf is a beautiful Athenian red-figure cup decorated with Heracles fighting Nereus, surrounded by fleeing Nereids; on the other side is a sacrificial procession.

Case 18, upper shelf: Athenian red-figure krater with satyrs and maenads dancing. On the middle shelf is an Athenian red-figure pelike showing Heracles and Old Age, personified by the emaciated and grotesque figure of an old man.

Case 20: on the lower shelf is a large Athenian red-figure krater by the Berlin Painter. On the body are warriors. On one side of the neck is the struggle between Heracles and the fearsome robber Cycnus, and on the other men wrestling.

A staircase leads from room 10 to the Antiquarium; this contains material either from the former Museo Kircheriano, or acquired by purchase or gift.

Rooms 11–14 are devoted to bronzes. There are many noteworthy examples of fibulae, statuettes, armour, domestic implements, mirrors, candelabra etc.

Room 15: in the centre of case 3 is an Athenian Geometric amphora (about 700 B.C.) decorated on the neck and handles with little serpents in relief. Besides the usual Geometric decoration, it is also painted with a line of women holding hands: on the body is a procession of warriors, some on foot and some in chariots. It is interesting to note the schematic way the figures are drawn: the eyes are the only facial features shown.

1. Terracotta statuette of a young man, from the sanctuary of Portonaccio (Veii)
2. Detail of the terracotta Sarcofago degli Sposi, from Cerveteri
3. Head of a boy (the Malavolta head), from the sanctuary of Portonaccio
4. Gold pectoral, from the Tomba Bernardini at Praeneste (Palestrina). Rome, Museo di Villa Giuli

1

3   4

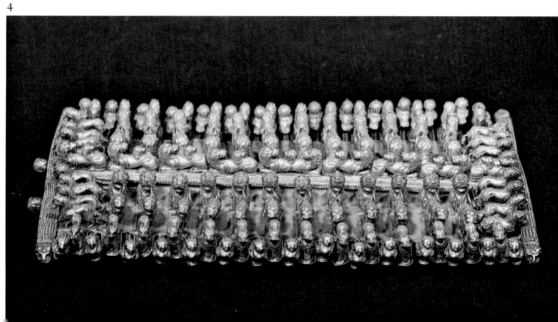

On the upper shelf of case 4 is one of the most characteristic examples of the so-called Protocorinthian vases, the Chigi olpe, found near Veii, which dates from 650–640 B.C. The body is divided into three bands with scenes painted in the miniaturistic style. On the top band are painted two groups of armed warriors about to engage in combat. The middle band depicts a lion hunt, a procession of riders and chariots, and also the first representation of the mythological scene that became a favourite subject of Greek vase-painting: the beauty contest between the three goddesses Hera, Athene and Aphrodite, submitted to the judgement of Paris. Parts of the inscription giving the names of the goddesses are still visible. The bottom band shows a hare hunt. This vase is without any doubt the finest example of the type of Protocorinthian pottery known as polychrome because several colours (including red, white, brown and yellow) were used in its decoration. Presumably the scenes illustrated, which are often highly complex, like the fighting warriors, were influenced by large-scale painting.

Included on the lower shelf of case 4 is a small bucchero amphora, also from the Veii area, with the Etruscan alphabet scratched on it.

Rooms 16 and 17 contain balsam jars, Athenian, Etruscan and Italiote pottery, votive offerings, architectural fragments, oil lamps, theatrical masks etc.

In case 2 in room 17 there is displayed a fine fragment of a calyx-krater signed by Assteas, a vase-painter from Paestum active between 360 and 330 B.C. It is painted with a parody of the mythological episode in which Ajax takes possession of Cassandra by dragging her from the image of Athene to which she clings.

Room 18 contains eight small terracotta urns of the Chiusine type, dating from the Hellenistic age, and three terracotta sarcophagi with the figure of the deceased recumbent on the lid.

Room 19 contains terracottas presented to the State by Augusto Castellani in 1919. Also part of the Castellani collection is an important series of gold-work which is not at present on display. For reasons of space, it is possible to describe only a few of the most interesting vases from this collection:

On the middle shelf of case 3 are two Caeretan hydriae. One depicts Europa on the bull, the other (p. 26, no. 1) Heracles, who has captured Cerberus and is preparing to put him in the wine-jar where the terrified Eurystheus has taken refuge.

On the middle shelf in case 4 is a very fine fragment of a vase signed by the painter Exekias. The Greek inscription 'Exekias made me' is still clearly legible. On the inside of the rim is a procession of war-ships.

In the centre of the lower shelf is a large Laconian krater decorated with alternating upright and inverted palmettes.

Case 8, middle shelf: two Athenian red-figure hydriae by the Kleophrades Painter. On one Heracles is shown fighting the Nemean lion, on the other are two male figures with a hare.

On the lower shelf is a red-figure Athenian vase showing Ulysses and his companions coming out of Polyphemus's cave hidden under the bellies of rams.

Case 10: on the middle shelf is a pelike by Hermonax, showing orgiastic scenes with satyrs and maenads.

Rooms 25, 26, 27 and 28 contain material from cemeteries belonging to settlements in the Faliscan territory. The most interesting of these finds are the following:

In room 25, case 1 contains a plate from Latium (first half of the 3rd century B.C.), found at Capena, decorated with a rather unusual subject, painted in colours over a black-gloss surface: a war elephant, followed by its baby, with a crenellated tower on its back and warriors leaning out of it. This is believed to represent one of Pyrrhus's elephants which so terrified the Romans, who had never seen such beasts, when they had to face them in 280 B.C.

In room 26, case 3, is a large series of dark impasto vases typical of Faliscan workshops. There are two large kantharoi with handles terminating at the top in double rams' heads, with incised decorations and applied triangles of amber, from a trench-tomb at Falerii

Below: Faliscan krater depicting the abduction of Cephalus, from Falerii Veteres (Civita Castellana). Rome, Museo di Villa Giulia

Opposite: the Chigi olpe, and Faliscan red-figure krater depicting scenes of the fall of Troy. Rome, Museo di Villa Giulia

dating from the 7th century B.C. There are also a large bronze belt-buckle, two swords and eighteen boat-shaped fibulae.

In the same case is an interesting sheet-bronze urn, in the form of a chest on high feet, with a lid shaped like a gabled roof, in imitation of a real architectural feature; it comes from a cremation tomb at Falerii.

Case 5 contains the large krater by the Aurora Painter described on p. 278, which is one of the finest examples of Faliscan red-figure pottery.

Room 29 contains some architectural terracottas from the numerous sacred buildings in Falerii.

On the gratings on the left wall nos. 14, 15 and 16 are two groups of pedimental terracottas from the temple at Lo Scasato (p. 276). They consist of a perforated cornice with a very intricate ribbon pattern, surmounted by palmettes; tiles with a band of bean-shaped decoration and another painted in a meander pattern; a torus decorated with leaves; and finally facing slabs covering the roof beams and decorated with relief palmettes, alternately upright and inverted. On grating no. 18 are the architectural terracottas from the sides of this temple: tiles from the eaves surmounted by antefixes and facing slabs similar to the above. Finally, on grating no. 22 are the figures that constituted the great pedimental relief, including a beautiful statue of Apollo (p. 281); in case 1 are numerous antefixes of male and female heads.

On the same wall in room 29 is a partial reconstruction of the architectural terracottas from the Tempio ai Sassi Caduti: the pedimental decoration belongs to the late Archaic period (5th century B.C.) and is on gratings nos. 5 and 6: the side decorations belong to the same period and are on grating no. 7. The terracotta figures are in case 3. Material from the latest period, including several door cornices consisting of rectangular slabs with relief decoration of intersecting bands and four-pointed stars, is displayed on gratings nos. 1, 3 and 4; the terracotta figures, including the lower half of a statue of Mercury, are in case 2.

Terracottas from the two temples on Colle del Vignale, in the shape of heads of a maenad and Silenus, are in case 4.

Of the decorations of the temple on Colle di Celle, the Archaic female figure in tufa (6th century B.C.) is particularly worth noting. It may represent the very ancient image of the Sabine goddess Juno Curitis, to whom the temple was dedicated (case 5).

Room 30 contains material from the temple of Diana at Nemi, one of the most venerated sanctuaries in ancient Latium, including an interesting little terracotta model of the roof of an Etrusco-Italic temple. It clearly shows all the structural elements of this part of the temple: one can distinguish the central beam (*columen*) and the two side beams which supported the roof; the facing slabs, decorated with figures in relief, that covered the ends of the beams at the front; and the little antefixes, inside the triangular cavity of the pediment, that covered the ends of the tile-gutters laid on the horizontal ceiling beams.

Room 32 contains material from Satricum, the ancient city of the Volsci, identified as a site northeast of Nettuno. It was famous for its temple dedicated to Mater Matuta, to which belonged the fine architectural terracottas in case 3; these include the heads of a warrior with an Athenian helmet and of another, dying warrior, who is shown with eyes and mouth half-open, his brow furrowed with pain. They formed part of the slab covering the end of the *columen* and date from the end of the 6th century B.C.

Room 33 contains objects comprising the furnishings of two large, rich tombs of the Orientalizing period, discovered at Praeneste (Palestrina). Among the many imports from Greece and the East is a large cauldron with a stand in bronze (case 1). There are also many precious objects manufactured in Etruria, such as the bronze tripod decorated with applied figures of humans and dogs; a basin on a tripod, also in embossed bronze; a gold clasp decorated with two rows of ten little lions; two gold pectorals; and two little ivory fan handles decorated with bands, one above the other, of real and fantastic animals.

Etruscan expansion

Bologna

Felsina (the Etruscan city on the site of Bologna) was the chief of the Etruscan settlements in the Po valley (Etruria Padana). Known to us from the impressive body of evidence which has survived, it provides a rare example of unbroken occupation from at least the late Bronze Age down to the present day. Its development falls into a number of distinct phases: Bologna I (Bronze Age), Bologna II (Iron Age), Bologna III (Etruscan period), Bologna IV (the period of the Gauls) and finally Bologna V (Roman period).

The earliest phase consisted of a series of small-scale, transient settlements scattered extensively around the site where the city eventually emerged, within a radius of some ten to fifteen kilometres from the Colle dell'Osservanza.

More is known about Villanovan Bologna, but an important question remains: was there a single settlement, on a scale unknown elsewhere in northern Italy at that time? or did a complex of independent nuclei gradually merge as they grew? or did one village slowly become more important than the others, relegating them to the role of satellites? Foundations of huts have been discovered in several parts of the city, and two clusters have been clearly identified, one to the east, between Via Castiglione and Via Farini, and one to the west, near Piazza Malpighi, Via del Pratello, Via S. Isaia and Via S. Felice, separated by the mediaeval course of the Aposa stream. Study of the burial-grounds, rather than of the few finds from the hut foundations, has made it possible to subdivide Villanovan culture into four phases, traditionally labelled Savena–S. Vitale, Benacci I, Benacci II and Arnoaldi, more or less contemporary with Villanovan I and II and the early and late Orientalizing periods in Etruria proper.

Already in the late 6th century, and particularly in the 5th and 4th centuries B.C., the Etruscan element was evident in both artistic production and inscriptions. This phase is known as the Certosa culture after an important cemetery near the former monastery of the Certosa.

Felsina, or Bologna III, developed on roughly the same site as the Villanovan settlement, on the Colle dell'Osservanza and the terrace which lies between the Aposa and the Ravone, but its exact boundaries can only be guessed at. Judging from finds around the former Villa Cassarini (now the University Faculty of Engineering), at Porta d'Azeglio and at the Palazzo Albergati, between Via Saragozza, Via Malpertuso and Viale Aldini, the Etruscan settlement stood on the rise behind the Faculty of Engineering, spreading north and east. Its exact extent cannot be determined because unbroken occupation of the site during ancient and mediaeval times, right up to the present day, has destroyed much evidence, especially in the southwestern part of Bologna. If, as at Marzabotto, dry-stone walling was used, obviously the walls would not have been able to survive the passage of time and the effect of later building activity. Some traces remain of the Etruscan road system in the road parallel to the Apennines, corresponding to Via Toscana, Via Murri,

Viale Gozzadini, Viale Panzacchi, Viale Aldini, Via Saragozza and Via Porrettana, with the cemetery in the public gardens; and the road roughly corresponding to Via S. Isaia and Via A. Costa, along which the western cemeteries were situated.

The Etruscan cemeteries, on the whole, extended to the west of the inhabited area, beyond the Villanovan burial-grounds of the former Arnoaldi estate. Etruscan tombs have also been discovered to the east, beyond the late Villanovan tombs at the Arsenale (now occupied by the Direzione d'Artiglieria and the ORMEC workshops), in the former Tamburini estate, and particularly in the region of the public gardens, on the slopes of the Colle di S. Michele in Bosco, and as far as Via del Cestello. Significantly, the Etruscan tombs follow the Villanovan tombs both chronologically and topographically, a further indication that Bologna II and Bologna III must have roughly coincided.

The Etruscan tombs are always of the trench type, sometimes lined with dry-stone walling; one exception is a tomb in the public gardens, built in *opus quadratum* of travertine blocks. In the western cemeteries, inhumation and cremation are mixed, while in the eastern ones inhumation predominates and the furnishings seem to be richer.

The use as markers of cippi and especially of stelae with carved figures and, somewhat later, inscriptions is a widespread custom. These sandstone carvings are typical of the Villanovan period and the subsequent Etruscan Certosa phase. The Villanovan stelae (also called proto-Felsinan, as forerunners of the Felsinan or Etruscan stelae) are characteristic of Bologna in both form and decoration. It has been suggested that their shape—a rectangle with a disc on top—is a schematic representation of the human body, or, less convincingly, a solar symbol. The most interesting themes depicted include the journey of the dead to the underworld, and the tree of life standing between two rampant animals, a very ancient subject of Eastern origin. The more characteristically Etruscan stelae of the 5th–4th centuries B.C. are of a distinctive horseshoe shape, not found outside Bologna: the circular part of the older stelae becomes the major element in these later ones, with the rectangular part now no more than a support, driven into the ground and so hidden from view. In style and decoration one can clearly see the influence of contemporary Etruscan art, with its pronounced Hellenizing elements.

The Certosa situla. Bologna, Museo Civico

The stelae are decorated by slightly carving away the background round the figures; internal details are drawn in, at least in most cases. The figures must originally have been coloured, although there is now no sign of it.

The furnishings of the Etruscan tombs are rich in Athenian black- and red-figure pottery; bronze objects such as candelabra, often with decorative figures on top of the central shaft, mirrors, fibulae and vases; glass vases and bottles; wooden and ivory stools (*diphroi*); personal ornaments in gold, faience or amber; weapons and ivory objects. These finds show that an oligarchy existed in the city, perhaps made up of the rich merchant and entrepreneurial class which must have dominated city life. A study of the finds reveals the extent of trade between Etruscan Bologna and Etruria proper, the Adriatic cultures, the Veneto and the Alpine regions. In particular, it raises the question of relations with Greece, since many workshops at Athens are known to have been almost exclusively occupied in making vases for export to Etruria Padana. The role of Spina, the great trading centre on the Adriatic, must have been crucial in this respect; Athenian pottery found in the two cities comes in fact from the same workshops. On the other hand, Felsina itself produced some types of goods for export on a large scale: for example the caskets with cord decoration found in central and northern Europe.

It was certainly the chief city of the Po region. Situated where the main trans-Apennine route reached the plain, at the centre from which trade routes radiated towards the north, Bologna more than any other city profited from the opening-up of a port at Spina. The trading relationship between the two cities was so close that Bologna to a certain extent took on the role of middleman in the distribution of Athenian products from the Adriatic coast inland.

The Latin *colonia* of Bononia was founded in 189 B.C., in close connection with the Via

Aemilia; since the city centre was built over a Villanovan settlement, one cannot hope to find signs of Felsina in the plan of the Roman settlement.

The museum, housed in the palace beside the Archiginnasio, was founded in 1881 and combined the collections of the University and the city, the latter consisting of the Palagi collection together with Villanovan and Etruscan finds from excavations during the last decades of the 19th century. Some grave goods are exhibited together as they were found, in exact reconstructions of the tombs.

One of the most remarkable items on display is the Certosa situla (early decades of the 5th century B.C.), which was found with a single Athenian vase of about 475 B.C. In the shape of a truncated cone, rounded at the shoulder, it consists of a single sheet of bronze worked in relief and joined at the edges with clinched nails. The decoration is divided into four zones and depicts, from top to bottom, a parade of warriors in hoplite armour and horsemen, a sacred procession, scenes of domestic and country life, and a row of animals. It is a fine object, both as a work of art and as a document of daily life and customs in the northern regions.

Spina

The settlement of Spina stood about six kilometres west of Comacchio, near the mouth of a branch of the Po called Padus Vetus on mediaeval maps (the name survives in Paviero); the riverbed is still discernible in the Canalazzo. The site was identified in 1922 when the Valle Trebba cemetery was discovered; before then it was known only from numerous literary sources, usually referring the close historical links between Spina and Greece to the distant mythological past, and speaking of Spina as a Greek city flourishing on Etruscan soil.

The city was a canal port, centred on a canal some 15–20 metres wide, which shows up clearly in aerial photography; with two smaller canals, it was supplied artificially from

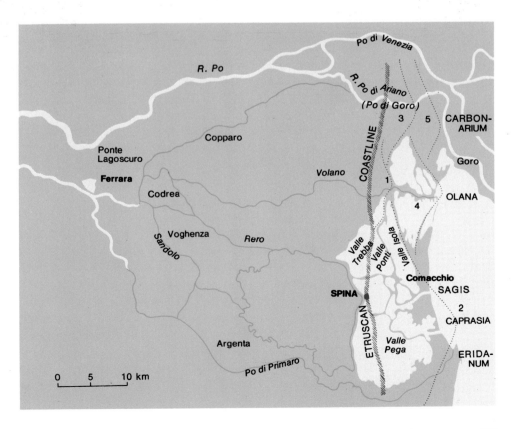

Spina and the surrounding region (1–5 = Roman and mediaeval coastlines)

the nearby Padus Vetus. Flowing at first in a northerly direction, in its final stretch it flows west–east in an almost straight line for about two kilometres. It was cut in order to keep open the link between the sea and the lagoon on which the city stood, since this tended to get silted up as the coastline gradually shifted. The population was scattered in a number of settlements some distance apart on what was in Etruscan times the sea shore. Two in Valle Pega seem to have been particularly important: one near the embankment of Borgazzi alla Paganella, the other on the Sabbioni sandbar. Standing on the banks of the artificial canal, both were built on a regular grid plan of canals separating more or less rectangular *insulae* (blocks). On the sandy ground between the canals, excavations have revealed the remains of the piles which were necessary in a lagoon to support the houses, consisting of stakes driven vertically into the ground; the section up to the junction with the horizontal stakes has been preserved, but the upper part and the horizontal stakes themselves have been destroyed in the course of time. The building material was usually wood.

The cemeteries lie north and northeast of the settlement, in the two lagoons of Valle Trebba and Valle Pega; both cemeteries are of the same date and have the same kind of tomb furnishings. The tombs are situated in the dunes along the ancient coastline, on either side of a former arm of the Po delta which corresponds to the modern road from Ostellato to Comacchio. They seem to have been divided into groups of various sizes, depending on the nature of the sandbars; in Etruscan times these were suitable sites for cemeteries, although today they are only slightly higher than the level of the surrounding countryside.

Excavations have been particularly difficult because they have had to be carried out about a metre below sea level; the presence of the water-table has made it exceedingly hard, especially in the past, for archaeologists to dig and to recover objects from the tombs. Wood or metal coffer-dams were therefore used to enclose the area being excavated, so that the water could be pumped away while a tomb was examined and its furnishings recovered.

The objects have obviously been affected by their long stay in very salt water, particularly those made of metal, bone, ivory and wood, which need special treatment for their recovery and conservation.

Most of the tombs had no external marker, although occasionally there was a stone, from the mouth of one of the Apennine rivers nearby, or, even less frequently, a little column, a cippus or a small stone or marble altar, all without inscriptions. The tombs were at ground level or of the trench type. The body was buried together with the grave goods, unprotected except perhaps for a sheet. Only in a small number of cases were wooden coffins, often made of large oak beams, used; the use of sarcophagi of Cycladic marble is exceptionally rare.

Both funeral rites occur, though inhumation is more frequent than cremation. The body of the deceased was laid out on a northwest–southeast alignment, often on a couch, of which traces have been found. In his right hand he often clutched a piece of cast bronze, believed to have been the coin for Charon, while the grave goods were placed parallel to the body, usually to the right, but sometimes to the left or on both sides. Children's tombs are easily recognizable, not only from the size of the skeletons, but also by the tiny objects found among the grave goods, often decorated with scenes of children's games, and the clay dolls representing a goddess suckling a baby.

In cremation tombs, the ashes and fragments of bone were placed in rough jars or, less frequently, in painted Greek vases, with no grave goods or very few. There is also an intermediate type of grave with objects arranged as in a inhumation grave, while the ashes and charred fragments of bone are placed to the left on the bare earth.

Spina. Aerial view

The style and dating of the tomb furnishings, and the Greek and Etruscan vase inscriptions help to build up a picture of this important centre of the northern Adriatic. It was the point of contact and fusion between the Etruscan and Italic cultural sphere and that of Greece and the East, and at the same time a centre for spreading cultural elements to the inland Po region and central Europe. Spina flourished between the last quarter of the 6th century and the 3rd century B.C., when life came to an end in consequence of the invasion of the Gauls. The bulk of Athenian imports date from 480 to 360 B.C.; as a result it has been possible to assemble at Ferrara, from the Greek pottery found at Spina, the most comprehensive collection of Athenian vases of this period.

The presence of this huge quantity of Greek pottery, of Etruscan bronzes, jewellery from Magna Graecia and Etruria, vases imported from Etruria proper and southern Italy or made in local workshops, terracottas, faience and amber, and the richness of the tombs all testify to the power and importance of the city as an extremely busy port, both as a destination and as a transit stage on trade routes.

Spina controlled the northern Adriatic, sharing with Adria a vital role with regard to the inland regions. Since the southern Adriatic was infested by Liburnian pirates from the Dalmatian coast, the protection of ships coming north had to depend on close collaboration and understanding between Greeks and Etruscans. The commercial interests of the two were in fact closely connected and complementary, as is shown by the fact that Spina built a treasury in the sanctuary at Delphi, containing a tithe of its trading profits. The Greeks at Delphi thus acknowledged the importance of Spina in commercial activities as a trading centre shared by Greeks and Etruscans.

Objects found during the excavations at Spina are now displayed in the Museo Archeologico at Ferrara, which was opened in 1935 in the palace of Ludovico il Moro, built by Biagio Rossetti, the greatest Renaissance architect of Emilia.

A visit to the museum tells much about Spina and its culture. The most striking feature is the large amount of Athenian pottery; of the many vase-painters represented, three 5th-century masters and their followers stand out: the Berlin Painter, the Penthesilea Painter and Polygnotos. The finds at Spina have made it possible to identify and, in many cases, to appreciate and study the stylistic traits and individual features of these artists, their pupils and the potters who worked with them in different workshops: their taste for mythological scenes or general subjects, for complicated compositions or single figures.

This provincial market, like Etruria itself, shows a marked predilection for large and elaborate vase-shapes, especially volute-kraters. As well as figure-painted vases, Spina imported black-gloss vases from Greece and from other workshops, particularly in northern Etruria. Then there are red-figure pottery of Etruscan and Italiote manufacture, bronze candelabra and tripods, Etruscan bronze vases with figures as handles, gold-work from Etruria and Magna Graecia, amber and other items, all making the Museo Archeologico at Ferrara one of the richest and most interesting in Italy.

The other great Adriatic port was Adria. To what extent this was an Etruscan city is still being debated. Finds to date show a marked Greek presence, as well as an Etruscan element evident in small bronzes, gold-work, Hellenistic pottery and Etruscan inscriptions on vases.

Marzabotto

Marzabotto, the only major city in the valley of the Reno in ancient times, flourished between the end of the 6th and the 4th century B.C.

It occupied the terrace called Pian di Misano and the adjacent height of Misanello, on the southern edge of modern Marzabotto. It has been suggested that its ancient name was Misa, but this is an unsubstantiated hypothesis; since literary sources do not mention it, all we know or can conjecture about the history and life of the city is based on archaeological evidence.

The circumference of the city is about 2,500 metres; at least a third of the terrace has been destroyed by erosion over a long period, caused by a change in the course of the Reno only recently halted by river-control works. The ground is fairly even, sloping down gently towards the river in the southern and eastern sectors. The marked difference in level between the inhabited area and the bed of the Reno provided a natural defence against possible enemy attack from the river.

Some signs of prehistoric settlement have been found, but the outstanding remains so far discovered by excavation are those of the Etruscan city, dating from the late 6th to the 4th century B.C.

The recent scientific and thorough excavations have revealed two phases of Etruscan settlement: the pre-urban phase (Marzabotto I), preceding perhaps only by a decade or so the next phase (Marzabotto II), with its grid plan of streets. The fragments of black-figure Greek pottery and bucchero-type vases, found during a trial excavation between the southern scarp and the railway tunnel, belong to the first period, as do a number of

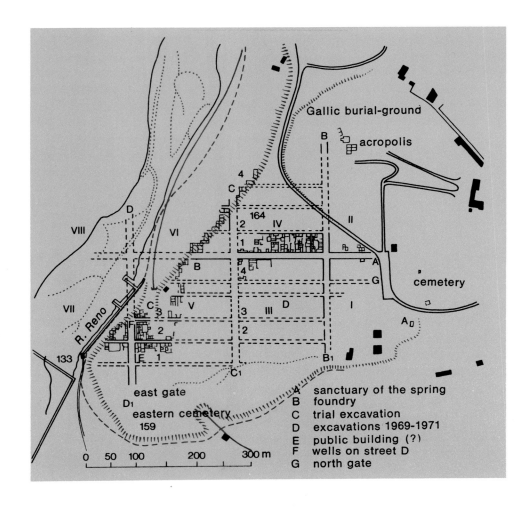

A sanctuary of the spring
B foundry
C trial excavation
D excavations 1969-1971
E public building (?)
F wells on street D
G north gate

buildings. One of the most interesting of these is a small sanctuary built round a spring in the northern part of the city, on the north edge of Pian di Misano, which stands out because it is on a different alignment from the later city. The spring, which in fact turns out to have no particular therapeutic qualities, is surrounded by a small stone building consisting of a paved room and a little courtyard with two basins and bases with mouldings in the Archaic style. This is the oldest stone building in Marzabotto, and indeed in the whole of northern Italy: pottery found during the excavations shows that it dates from the end of the 6th or the beginning of the 5th century B.C.

To the same pre-urban phase should be attributed a foundry on the main street crossing the city from north to south, part of the eastern cemetery and a number of small Archaic bronzes.

In the next period, from the early 5th century B.C. we find the city laid out on a strict grid plan, with one main street running north–south intersected at right angles by three more running east–west. These main streets are 15 metres wide, while other north–south streets are five metres wide, i.e. one-third the width of the main roads. This grid plan seems to be a combination of Greek concepts of town planning on a number of street axes with the Etruscan custom of dividing the city by just two main streets crossing at right angles.

The most northerly on the three main east–west streets probably led up to the acropolis, where the temples stood, facing south and aligned in exactly the same way as the city. The sacred buildings can be identified from what remains of their foundations, podia and internal stone walls. There is an interesting square altar, with a well in the centre, which rests on foundations six metres deep. The acropolis, which has no defensive role, illustrates the non-military nature of Marzabotto.

Two of the city gates are known and appear to have led to the cemeteries. One is in the southeastern corner of the surviving grid plan. The other lies to the north, at the end of the minor road which ran just east of the main north–south street; traces of wooden piles survive on the inside. At the gate, the street was reduced to half its width by the construction of a wall along the axis of the road, as if to restrict passage.

Recent excavations have revealed, along the main roads and at the intersections, large limestone boulders taken from the bed of one of the nearby watercourses and sunk into virgin ground. These provide evidence of operations in laying out roads: they are markers left by the land-surveyors measuring out the terrain and subsequently buried under the ballast of the road. They are seen as confirming the sacral nature of Etruscan surveying (*limitatio*) and the correspondence between marked-out space (*templum*) in the heavens and on earth. The stone found at the centre of the road system of Marzabotto, in particular, has two incisions at right angles on its top surface, orientated to the cardinal points. Here, most probably, the *groma* or a similar surveying instrument was placed at the beginning of the sequence of operations which determined the grid plan of the streets of Marzabotto. Once the axes marked by the stone markers were traced out, the main streets were created by allowing 25 Roman feet (7.50 metres) on either side of the axis. Ditches were then dug alongside the roads, making use of the natural gradients to drain away both rain-water and waste from the houses. They also separated public areas (i.e. the roads) from the *insulae*, which were private areas. The gradients were such that the south–north drains flowed into the west–east ones, which in turn flowed into the river. Finally dwellings were built inside the *insulae*, after marking off the ground into plots and making more east–west channels which subdivided the *insulae* across their width. The rectangularity of the entire city plan was thus reflected in the plan of the individual *insulae*.

Marzabotto. Ruins of a burial-ground

Inside the city there are areas (Regio III, *insulae* 2 and 3) with no buildings at all, although it is difficult to know why none was ever built there; they may have been free public areas for political and commercial activities.

Potters' workshops have been discovered in several places in the city. One of them (Regio II, *insula* 1) contains tanks for purifying and settling clay, an area for drying-out vases, covered by a roof which would have rested on wooden supports, and kilns with longitudinal cavities. This workshop may have had something to do with a room floored with brick, an unusual feature in Marzabotto, which was found to contain basins on stands still in position. The water supply was provided by an independent system.

There were other workshops, of metal-workers, in Regions III, IV and V, along the main north–south street; the working rooms were on the street side, while the actual living quarters were inside, arranged around an open central courtyard which was reached from the street by a long passage. Water was supplied by a well in the courtyard; waste was generally drained away by means of a drain running under the entrance passage. The siting of workshops inside the city seems to some extent to be a legacy from the pre-urban phase. The width of the main roads, with their pavements on either side five metres wide, is interesting, as it has recently been suggested that the pavement may have been used for the display of goods for sale.

Building materials used at Marzabotto were modest, and there is no evidence of monumental buildings. Some architectural terracottas decorated with painted reliefs have been found, coming from the acropolis and the city, but in general there seems to have been little artistic interest in building. The foundations are of river stones bound with mud, and the walls of partly-fired brick; the podia of the temples were faced with courses of travertine blocks. Recent excavations have found signs of the use of wood in construction. From the width of the load-bearing walls, on average 50 to 60 centimetres, their height can be calculated as three metres or a little more.

From archaeological evidence, Marzabotto was clearly a commercial and industrial city. Agriculture and stock-breeding (chiefly of pigs, as animal remains show) were not important factors in its life; the land is in fact still fairly unproductive today, and in the past

it must have been largely covered with forest. It was the pottery and metal industries which were the city's mainstay; there are deposits of clay all round the city and the workshops found indicate a fair level of vase-making activity which must have satisfied local demand. The high-quality and durable products of the brickworks were also exported to neighbouring towns: both flat tiles, sometimes exceptionally large, and curved tiles. In addition they made water pipes, well-curbs, cylindrical stands and unfired discs with three protuberances and Etruscan inscriptions, whose function is not clear.

Metal-work—iron and to a lesser extent bronze—must have been an important element of the city's economy. The location of the mineral deposits used is still uncertain. Since existing geological knowledge rules out the possibility of iron and copper mines in the Apennines, the metal was most probably imported from Etruria proper, which was one of the chief mining areas of ancient Italy.

Imports also included foodstuffs, painted pottery, ornaments (faience, ivory and goldwork) and a certain type of marble, used for funerary monuments.

Marzabotto's position in terms of communication routes was also vital to its economic life. It stood in the middle of the Reno valley, on the route linking Tuscany and Bologna, which joined the all-important road at the foot of the Apennines leading to the inland region of the Po valley and the Alps. The ridge road which today passes through Grizzana was also important; beside it stood the Monteguragazza sanctuary, the most significant relic of Etruscan culture in the Apennines.

The position and character of Marzabotto give the impression of a colonial city, founded as a complete unit on virtually virgin soil. It has been suggested that it was established to compete with Bologna and Spina as a foundation from inland northern Etruria, basically Chiusi, with which it evidently had links.

Marzabotto flourished until the Gauls occupied it in the 4th century B.C. The inhabited area then shrank, as is shown by discoveries of Gallic tombs among the Etruscan houses. By the beginning of the 3rd century B.C. the city seems to have been abandoned, although there are signs of life in Roman times in the form of a small farm.

The cemeteries lay to the north of the inhabited area, along an extension of the main south–north street, and to the east, at the end of the southernmost west–east axis. The tombs are chest-tombs, made of large travertine slabs and marked by stones, cippi or small columns; only one has a stele. The upper mouldings with spouts, interestingly, recall similar monuments from Perugia, Chiusi and the Fiesole area. Marzabotto was culturally quite distinct from Etruscan Bologna, only 25 kilometres away. Although for a time it came within the economic orbit of Felsina, its origins were quite independent, as is shown by the absence of stelae, the small amount of imported Greek pottery and the prevalent burial rite of cremation.

The fine Museo di Marzabotto was extensively damaged during World War II. Containing objects from the city and its cemetery, it was handed over to the State, together with the entire archaeological zone, by its owners, the Counts Aria. One of the most interesting items is a Greek marble head of 500 B.C. found in one of the ditches beside the main south–north street; it was unusual for Greek sculpture to be imported into Etruria, and this is the only example from north of the Apennines. The small bronzes include the famous armed warrior with a crested helmet, accompanied by a draped female figure holding out a cup in her right hand; in style it is similar to the votive deposit of bronzes found in the 19th century near Monte Falterona, and it was certainly imported from Etruria.

The small bronzes, architectural terracottas, cippi, pottery, bronze vases and furnishings, and barbarian objects found during the course of the many excavations, all show the level of artistic life in the city.

Casalecchio di Reno

Another Etruscan settlement developed where the Reno valley opens out into the plain,

on the road between Marzabotto and Bologna, about 2.50 kilometres from the rich
Etruscan cemetery of Certosa. The town, which corresponds to modern Casalecchio di
Reno, was continuously occupied from the Villanovan period until its occupation by the
Gallic Boii (late 3rd–early 2nd century B.C.) and was abandoned later than Marzabotto.

The buildings so far discovered are of river stones mixed with mud, as at Marzabotto,
but they are less carefully constructed and do not have deep foundations. The settlement
is laid out on a rectilinear grid, orientated north–northwest rather than north; drainage
apparently depended on the gradient of the ground down towards the Reno. Excavation
has not revealed a destruction level corresponding to the Gallic invasion in the first decade
of the 4th century B.C. The finds show that the town was an Etruscan settlement which
must have come within the economic and cultural orbit of Felsina.

Monteguragazza

In the Bologna area, on a ridge road leading to Marzabotto, there stood an Etruscan
sanctuary where an important votive deposit from the early 5th century B.C. has been
found. It included two bronze figures of worshippers whose style links them to Tyrrhenian
bronze-work and the modelled terracotta statues from Veii.

Much uncertainty still surrounds the extent and duration of Etruscan occupation and
influence north of the Apennines, apart from the area round Bologna and Spina. Literary
sources, the study of place-names, Etruscan inscriptions and isolated archaeological finds
provide some information. One particularly important discovery is the bronze model of a
sheep's liver found at Piacenza and now in the Museo Civico there. This was in all probability
a device used in divination: the haruspex would place it so that the pyramid-shaped lobe,
of crucial importance to the priests deriving omens from a liver, pointed north. The names
of sixteen Etruscan gods are inscribed in sixteen compartments round the edge; the rest
of the surface is also divided into compartments, although it is not quite clear how these
relate to those round the edge.

The model liver from Piacenza. Piacenza, Museo
Civico

This valuable object shows how Etruscan religion allotted the different regions of the
sky to different deities: the superior, favourable deities were to the east and northeast,
those of nature and the earth to the south, and the infernal and unfavourable deities to
the west and northwest. There was an exact correspondence between individual gods and
the position of visible phenomena (the flight of birds, lightning or prodigies) in the sky
or the appearance of the liver of a sacrificed animal.

The model liver of Piacenza was found by a peasant in 1877 at Ciavernasco di Settima
di Gossolengo, not far from the city. Count Caracciolo subsequently acquired it and
presented it to the museum. Unfortunately there were no associated finds to establish the
date of the liver and its context; although the purchaser made the peasant search for
several days in the area where it was found, all he discovered was part of an ancient wheel
rim and two Roman coins, of unknown date.

Capua

Capua (modern S. Maria Capua Vetere) was the chief city of Etruscan Campania. Built,
like many other towns in the region, on level ground, it was occupied continuously from
the early Iron Age to the late Empire, as is shown by finds from various parts of the city.
The Etruscans transformed an earlier Oscan settlement into a city, apparently in the second
half of the 6th century B.C. In the 5th century it was conquered by the Samnites and in
338 B.C. came within the Roman orbit.

Remains of buildings inside the city show that the street plan was more or less regular,
although not perfectly rectangular; in the southwestern quarter the layout is irregular,
perhaps because this was the area of the older settlement. The rectangular street plan
dates from after 312 B.C., when the Via Appia was built; the route of this road takes into
account the position of the city, which was clearly already in existence.

An important sanctuary of the 4th century B.C. has been discovered on the Patturelli estate, in the inner suburbs. The sanctuary of Diana on Monte Tifata was also connected with the city.

The oldest cemeteries lay to the north of Capua, at Tirone, and to the west, in the Fornaci area. Burials continued here uninterrupted from the 9th to the 5th century B.C. Tombs of the 6th and 5th centuries B.C. have been discovered to the north at Madonna dei Lupi, and to the west and south of the city. The Samnite tombs, with their remarkable painted decoration, are apparently clustered in several groups round the inhabited area to the southwest, northwest and north, while the Roman tombs were usually along the roads leading out of the city.

Study of the tomb furnishings reveals the different phases of Capua's existence. The earliest phase corresponds to the Villanovan period in Etruria and the region of Salerno. Early, middle and late Orientalizing periods followed, and finally came a period of classical influences. Typical finds from the early Iron Age include globular or biconical pots, often used as cinerary urns, bowls without handles, small 'Latial' amphorae and small sacrificial bowls. At first cremation was the only burial rite, but between the 9th and the 8th century inhumation appeared; by 720–710 this became the universal practice. In the 6th-century tombs cremation frequently reappeared, as well as instances of a rite, common in the Greek world, in which the *ustrinum* (the place where the body was cremated) was also used as the tomb.

In the period corresponding to the late Orientalizing phase (640 to 580/570 B.C.), relations with Etruria were so close that in artistic and material culture Capua was an Etruscan city. Etruscan Protocorinthian vases were made locally, as is shown by the presence of

Capua. Archaeological plan

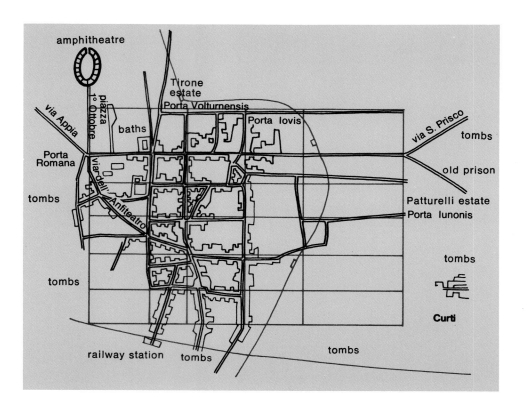

pottery wasters in the tombs; vases of thin-walled bucchero were imported. The fibulae are of the type with a knobbed catchplate. Between the last decades of the 7th century and the beginning of the 5th, bucchero was made locally, very similar in both form and decoration to the products of Etruria.

Protocorinthian, Cycladic and Athenian vases all appear among the imported pottery, and Athenian vases become increasingly frequent from the mid-6th century B.C.

Capua also produced black-figure pottery, closely resembling Etruscan work in style, one group of vases being decorated in an Atticizing style; architectural terracottas related to Peloponnesian and, later, East Greek models; bronzes, including the typical cauldrons with incised decoration and lids with moulded decoration; and votive statues.

One of the most important finds from Etruscan Capua is an inscribed tile, now in the Staatliche Museen zu Berlin; the second half of this is badly damaged. The 62 lines which survive, subdivided into 10 sections, refer to funerary rites performed in honour, it seems, of underworld deities. The text consists of short, roughly uniform phrases, which give directions about offerings with and without blood. The verb is in the imperative mood; a numeral states how many times the offering is to be repeated, while the name of the deity (Suri, Letham, Aphr-, Calu, Larun-, Tin, Uni, etc) is in the dative case. A number of terms refer to the sacred rite, the offering, and the officiating priests, but it is difficult to determine their exact meaning. It has been suggested that the text, intended as a calendar of rites, was connected with the sacrifices for salvation contained in the *Libri Acherontici*, religious writings of which we have only indirect knowledge.

Pompeii

Other Campanian cities also had an Etruscan phase, for example, Suessula, Nola, Acerra, Herculaneum and Pompeii. In the course of excavations under the temple of Apollo at Pompeii, in particular, fragments have been discovered of bucchero vases, probably made in Campania but with Etruscan graffiti. These provide important evidence of the presence of Etruscan-speaking individuals in Pompeii during the 6th century B.C.

Region of Salerno

In the region of Salerno, in particular along the coast, it is possible to identify a series of cultural phases parallel to those of Etruria itself.

Marcina

Recent finds of Archaic Greek pottery and heavy buccheri in the area between Vietri sul Mare and the beach have again raised the question of the identity of Marcina, an Etruscan city later occupied by the Samnites, to which the geographer Strabo refers (V, 4, 13-C 251). Although the finds, from a small number of tombs, do not provide incontrovertible evidence of a city as important as Marcina must have been, their distribution and chronology (they can be dated to the 6th century B.C.) tally with what we know of the city from classical sources and with the Etruscan occupation of the area in the 6th century B.C.

Pontecagnano

Near the small town of Pontecagnano extensive cemeteries have been discovered, belonging to an ancient settlement not far from the modern town, inland of the major road running down to Calabria (S.S. No. 18). The ancient name of the town is not known, but fragments of vases found in a well show that it dates back at least to the 7th century B.C. Some houses of the 4th century B.C. are also known; houses were built above them in the 1st and 2nd centuries A.D. The town had a harbour at Magazzeno, where rooms decorated with mosaics have been discovered.

Whereas during the Chalcolithic age the area had cultural links with settlements on the Adriatic side of Italy, in the early Iron Age only the more inland region maintained these links, while the coastal strip shows the diffusion of cremation, biconical urns and crescent-shaped razors. All in all, there is an obvious affinity with the Villanovan culture of coastal Etruria, combined with elements of the trench-tomb culture.

Both pit-tombs and receptacles were used for cremations, while for inhumations there were trenches covered with stones.

In the earliest period the biconical urn, with a crested helmet or a bowl as a lid, is found together with vases of various shapes, fibulae and razors. Later new vase-shapes and more complex fibulae are added, but the range of decorative elements is reduced. During a second phase, characterized by the presence of trench-tombs, new forms and decorations appear that are reminiscent of southern Etruria, particularly the Ager Faliscus, together with leech- and enlarged-bow fibulae.

In the Orientalizing period which followed, there are trench-tombs, with a covering of stones, and chest-tombs of travertine slabs. The pottery is very like that of southern Etruria, Latium and the Faliscan territory. From the last decade of the 8th century B.C. and increasingly during the early 7th century, the grave goods include imported Greek pottery and imitations of it.

Two tombs from the first half of the 7th century are similar in structure to the Tomba Bernardini at Palestrina and contained rich furnishings, including bronze and silver vases.

From the middle of the 6th century B.C. the tombs become poorer, but they flourish again in the 4th century when figured vases, particularly those made at Paestum, appear. The city appears to have had strong connections with the plain of the Sele and with Velia, a city whose coins are often found in tombs here.

Other Villanovan settlements have been found at Sala Consilina, in the Tanagro valley, and at Capodifiume, near Paestum, on the left bank of the Sele. At Capodifiume the cremation tombs consisted of heaps of stones forming a rectangular enclosure or a small tumulus; they chiefly contained roughly-made impasto vases. The cemetery of Sala Consilina dates from early historical times and contains rectangular or round pit-tombs and trench-tombs with a tumulus of stones. The grave goods, showing two distinct phases of settlement, are displayed in the museum that has been set up in the Certosa di S. Lorenzo monastery at Padula.

Bibliography

Chronological table

Glossary

Index

Bibliography

General works

K. O. MÜLLER – W. DEECKE, *Die Etrusker*, 2 vols (Stuttgart 1877; 2nd edn [reprint] Graz 1965)
G. DENNIS, *The Cities and Cemeteries of Etruria*, 2 vols (3rd edn London 1933)
A. SOLARI, *Topografia storica dell'Etruria*, I–IV (Pisa 1915–20)
P. DUCATI, *Etruria antica*, 2 vols (Turin 1927)
B. NOGARA, *Gli Etruschi e la loro civiltà* (Milan 1933)
Mostra dell'arte della civiltà etrusca (2nd edn Milan 1955)
A. BOETHIUS et al., *Etruscan Culture, Land and People* (New York – Malmö 1962)
J. HEURGON, *Daily Life of the Etruscans* (Eng. tr. London 1964)
E. RICHARDSON, *The Etruscans. Their Art and Civilization* (Chicago – London 1964)
G. A. MANSUELLI, *Etruria and Early Rome* (Eng. tr. London 1966)
H. H. SCULLARD, *The Etruscan Cities and Rome* (London 1967)
D. STRONG, *The Early Etruscans* (London 1968)
M. PALLOTTINO, *Civiltà artistica etrusco-italica* (Florence 1971)
M. PALLOTTINO, *Etruscologia* (7th edn Milan 1972; 3rd edn tr. as *The Etruscans*, Harmondsworth 1955, rev. tr. 1975)
E. MACNAMARA, *Everyday Life of the Etruscans* (London – New York 1973)
L. BANTI, *The Etruscan Cities and Their Culture* (Eng. tr. Berkeley 1973, London 1974)

Classical encyclopaedias
A. PAULY – G. WISSOWA, *Real-Encyclopädie der klassischen Altertumswissenschaft*, article 'Etrusker' in vol. VII
    (Stuttgart 1907) and articles on individual cities and people
Der kleine Pauly (Stuttgart 1964–   )
Oxford Classical Dictionary (2nd edn London 1970)

There are also articles on the Etruscans in general encyclopaedias, for instance:
Enciclopedia Italiana, XIV (Rome 1932), article 'Etruschi'; 2nd appendix (1948), I; 3rd appendix (1960), I
M. PALLOTTINO, 'Italic Peoples, Ancient' in *Encyclopædia Britannica*, Macropædia 9 (1974)

Studi Etruschi, specialist periodical published by the Istituto di Studi Etruschi ed Italici, Florence (1927–   )

Art

O. MONTELIUS, *La civilisation primitive en Italie*, I–II (Stockholm 1895–1910)
P. DUCATI, *Storia dell'arte etrusca*, 2 vols (Florence 1927)
G. Q. GIGLIOLI, *L'arte etrusca* (Milan 1935)
P. J. RIIS, *An Introduction to Etruscan Art* (Copenhagen 1953)
M. PALLOTTINO, *Art of the Etruscans* (London 1955)
T. DOHRN, *Grundzüge etruskischer Kunst* (Baden Baden 1958)
R. BIANCHI BANDINELLI – G. COLONNA, 'Etrusca arte' in *Enciclopedia dell'arte antica, classica e orientale*, III (1960)
M. PALLOTTINO, 'Etrusco-Italic art' in *Encyclopedia of World Art*, V (New York 1961) and 'Orientalizing style',
    ibid., X (1965)
M. MORETTI – G. MAETZKE, *The Art of the Etruscans* (London 1970)

Arte e civiltà degli Etruschi (catalogue; Turin 1967)
Nuovi tesori dell'antica Tuscia (exhibition catalogue; Viterbo 1970)

Architecture and architectural decoration

J. DURM, *Die Baukunst der Etrusker und Römer* (Stuttgart – Leipzig 1905)

Å. ÅKERSTRÖM, *Studien über die etruskischen Gräber* (Lund 1934)

A. ANDRÉN, *Architectural Terracottas from Etrusco-Italic Temples* (Lund 1939–40)

G. PATRONI, *Architettura preistorica generale ed italica. Architettura etrusca* (Bergamo 1946)

R. A. STACCIOLI, *Modelli di edifici etrusco-italici*, I: *Modelli votivi* (Florence 1968)

A. BOETHIUS – J. B. WARD PERKINS, *Etruscan and Roman Architecture* (Harmondsworth 1970)

Sculpture

H. BRUNN – G. KÖRTE, *I rilievi delle urne etrusche*, 3 vols (Rome–Berlin 1870–1916)

L. GOLDSCHEIDER, *Etruscan Sculpture* (London 1941)

P. J. RIIS, *Tyrrhenika. An Archaeological Study of Etruscan Sculpture in the Archaic and Classical Periods* (Copenhagen 1941)

O. VESSBERG, *Studien zur Kunstgeschichte der römischen Republik* (Lund 1941)

M. PALLOTTINO, *La scuola di Vulca* (Rome 1945)

R. HERBIG, *Die jüngeretruskischen Steinsarkophage* (Berlin 1952)

G. M. A. HANFMANN, *Etruskische Plastik* (Stuttgart 1956)

A. HUS, *Recherches sur la statuaire en pierre étrusque archaïque* (Paris 1961)

Painting

F. WEEGE, *Etruskische Malerei* (Halle 1921)

F. POULSEN, *Etruscan Tomb Paintings* (Oxford 1922)

F. MESSERSCHMIDT, *Beiträge zur Chronologie der etruskischen Wandmalerei*, I (Rome 1928)

M. PALLOTTINO, *Etruscan Painting* (Geneva 1952)

M. MORETTI, *Nuovi monumenti della pittura etrusca* (Milan 1966)

Pottery and minor arts

E. GERHARD – K. KLUGEMANN – H. KÖRTE, *Etruskische Spiegel*, 5 vols (Berlin 1840–97)

A. FURTWAENGLER, *Die antiken Gemmen*, 3 vols (Leipzig 1900)

J. D. BEAZLEY, *Etruscan Vase-Painting* (Oxford 1947)

G. BECATTI, *Oreficerie antiche* (Rome 1955)

Y. HULS, *Ivoires d'Étrurie* (Brussels–Rome 1957)

R. A. HIGGINS, *Greek and Roman Jewellery* (London 1961)

P. ZAZOFF, *Etruskische Skarabäen* (Mainz 1968)

P. G. GUZZO, *Le fibule in Etruria dal VI al I secolo a.C.* (Florence 1973)

Language

Corpus Inscriptionum Etruscarum, I, II.1 (fascicles 1–4), II.2 (fascicle 1) (Leipzig 1893–   )

G. BUONAMICI, *Epigrafia etrusca* (Florence 1932)

M. PALLOTTINO, *Elementi di lingua etrusca* (Florence 1936)

M. PALLOTTINO, *Testimonia Linguae Etruscae* (Florence 1954)

R. A. STACCIOLI, *La lingua degli Etruschi* (Rome 1971)

M. CRISTOFANI, *Introduzione allo studio dell'etrusco* (Florence 1973)

Fiesole

A. DE AGOSTINO, *Fiesole. La zona archeologica e il Museo* (Rome 1949)

G. MAETZKE, 'Il nuovo tempio tuscanico di Fiesole' in *Studi Etruschi*, 24 (1955–6), pp. 227 ff.

G. CAPUTO – G. MAETZKE, 'Presentazione del rilievo di Fiesole antica', *ibid.*, 27 (1959), pp. 41 ff.

P. BOCCI, 'Nuovi scavi del tempio di Fiesole', *ibid.*, 29 (1961), pp. 411 ff.

F. NICOSIA, 'Due nuovi cippi fiesolani', *ibid.*, 34 (1966), pp. 149 ff.

I. PECCHIAI, 'Catalogo dei buccheri nel Museo Civico di Fiesole', *ibid.*, 35 (1967), pp. 487 ff.

Quinto Fiorentino

G. CAPUTO, 'Gli "Athyrmata" orientali della Montagnola' in *Arte antica e moderna*, 17 (1962), pp. 58 ff.

G. CAPUTO, 'L'obelòs della Montagnola' in *Studi Etruschi*, 33 (1965), pp. 521 ff.

G. CAPUTO, 'La tholos della Mula in un nuovo rilievo', *ibid.*, 38 (1970), pp. 367 ff.

Artimino and Comeana

F. NICOSIA, 'Schedario topografico dell'archeologia dell'Agro fiorentino' in *Studi Etruschi*, 34 (1966), pp. 277 ff.

F. NICOSIA, *Il tumulo di Montefortini e la tomba dei Boschetti a Comeana* (Florence 1966)

F. NICOSIA, 'Nuovi centri abitati etruschi nell'agro Fiorentino' in *Atti del Convegno sulla città etrusca e italica preromana* (Bologna 1970), pp. 241 ff.

Arezzo

G. DEVOTO, 'Arezzo. Agli inizi della storia aretina' in *Atti Accademia Petrarca di Arezzo*, 34 (1947–8), pp. 60 ff.

G. MAETZKE, 'Terrecotte architettoniche etrusche scoperte ad Arezzo' in *Bollettino d'Arte*, 35 (1949), pp. 251 ff.

C. LAVIOSA, 'Torso arcaico del Museo di Arezzo', *ibid.*, 44 (1959), pp. 193 ff.

J. P. MOREL, 'Notes sur la céramique étrusco-campanienne. Vases à vernis noir de Sardaigne et d'Arezzo' in *Mélanges de l'École française de Rome*, 75.1 (1963), pp. 7 ff.

P. BOCCI, 'Crateri volterrani inediti del Museo di Arezzo' in *Studi Etruschi*, 32 (1964), pp. 89 ff.

On the red-gloss pottery:

H. DRAGENDORFF – C. WATZINGER, *Arretinische Relief-keramik mit Beschreibung der Sammlung in Tübingen* (Reutlingen 1948)

A. STENICO, *La ceramica arretina*, I: *Museo di Arezzo, Rasinius*, I (Milan–Varese 1960)

CHR. GOUDINEAU, *La céramique arétine lisse* (Paris 1968; supplement to *Mélanges de l'École Française de Rome*, no. 6: *Fouilles de l'École Française de Rome à Bolsena (Poggio Moscini) 1962–1967*)

Pieve Sócana

P. BOCCI in 'Rassegna degli scavi e delle scoperte', *Studi Etruschi*, 38 (1970), p. 254; 39 (1971), p. 304

Cortona

A. NEPPI MODONA, *Cortona etrusca e romana nella storia e nell'arte* (Florence 1925)

L. PERNIER, 'Tumulo con tombe monumentali al Sodo presso Cortona' in *Monumenti Antichi dell'Accademia dei Lincei*, 30 (1925), c. 89 ff.

R. BIANCHI BANDINELLI, 'Il putto cortonese nel Museo di Leida' in *Critica d'arte*, I (1935), pp. 90 ff.

E. FRANCHINI, 'Il Melone di Camucia' in *Studi Etruschi*, 20 (1948–9), pp. 17 ff.

A. MINTO, 'La tanella Angòri di Cortona' in *Palladio*, I (1951), pp. 60 ff.

E. PARIBENI, 'Un gruppo di frammenti attici a figure nere da Cortona' in *Studi Etruschi*, 40 (1972), p. 391

Chiusi

R. BIANCHI BANDINELLI, 'Clusium' in *Monumenti Antichi dell'Accademia dei Lincei*, 30 (1925), c. 210 ff.

D. LEVI, 'La tomba della Pellegrina a Chiusi' in *Rivista dell'Istituto Italiano di Archeologia e Storia dell'Arte*, IV (1933), pp. 40 ff.

D. LEVI, *Il Museo Civico di Chiusi* (Rome 1935)

M. PALLOTTINO, *Etruscan Painting* (Geneva 1952)

E. PARIBENI, 'Rilievi chiusini arcaici' in *Studi Etruschi*, 12 (1938), pp. 57 ff.; 13 (1939), pp. 179 ff.

J. THIMME, 'Chiusinische Aschenkisten und Sarkophage der hellenistischen Zeit', *ibid.*, 23 (1954), pp. 25 ff.; 25 (1957), pp. 87 ff.

L. DONATI, 'Vasi di bucchero decorati con testi plastiche umane (zona di Chiusi)', *ibid.*, 36 (1968), pp. 319 ff.

O. TERROSI ZANCO, 'Il fenomeno della scultura funeraria chiusina di arte cosiddetta severa' in *Arte antica e moderna* (1964), pp. 380 ff.

M. F. BRIGUET, 'La sculpture en pierre fétide de Chiusi au Musée du Louvre' in *Mélanges de l'École Française de Rome, Antiquité*, 84 (1972), pp. 847 ff.

M. CRISTOFANI, 'Sul più antico gruppo di canopi chiusini' in *Archeologia Classica*, 23 (1971), pp. 12 ff.

L. VLAD BORRELLI, 'Il canopo di Dolciano' in *Nuove letture di monumenti etruschi dopo il restauro* (Florence 1971), pp. 61 ff.

M. CRISTOFANI, 'La "Mater Matuta" di Chianciano', *ibid.*, pp. 87 ff.

M. CRISTOFANI, 'Le due pissidi della Pania', *ibid.*, pp. 67 ff.

M. CRISTOFANI, 'Per una nuova lettura della pisside della Pania' in *Studi Etruschi*, 39 (1971), pp. 63 ff.

Montepulciano

G. SECCHI TARUGI, 'La tradizione delle origini etrusche di Montepulciano' in *Studi Etruschi*, 28 (1960), pp. 339 ff.

Perugia

G. BELLUCCI, *Guida alle collezioni del Museo Etrusco-Romano in Perugia* (Perugia 1910)

A. PAOLETTI, *Studi su Perugia etrusca* (Perugia 1923)

P. J. RIIS, 'The Etruscan city gates in Perugia' in *Acta Archaeologica*, 5 (1934), pp. 65 ff.

V. CAMPELLI, 'La cinta murata di Perugia' in *Rivista dell'Istituto Italiano di Archeologia e Storia dell'Arte*, 5 (1935), pp. 7 ff.

L. BANTI, 'Contributo alla storia e alla topografia del territorio perugino' in *Studi Etruschi*, 10 (1936), pp. 97 ff.

A. VON GERKAN – F. MESSERSCHMIDT, 'Das Grab der Volumnier bei Perugia' in *Römische Mitteilungen*, 57 (1942), pp. 122 ff.

A. M. PIEROTTI – U. CALZONI, 'Ricerche su Perugia etrusca. La città e la necropoli urbana' in *Studi Etruschi*, 21 (1950–1), pp. 275 ff.

A. J. PFIFFIG, 'Untersuchungen zum Cippus Perusinus', *ibid.*, 29 (1961), pp. 111 ff.

G. DARDEGGI, *Urne del territorio perugino. Un gruppo inedito di cinerari etruschi ed etrusco-romani* (*Quaderni dell'Istituto di Archeologia dell'Università di Perugia*, 1; Rome 1972)

Volterra

H. BRUNN – G. KÖRTE, *I rilievi delle urne etrusche*, 3 vols (Rome–Berlin 1870–1916)

A. MINTO, 'Le stele arcaiche volterrane' in *Scritti in onore di B. Nogara* (Vatican City 1937), pp. 305 ff.

E. FIUMI, 'Gli scavi nella necropoli del Portone a Volterra negli anni 1873–74' in *Studi Etruschi*, 25 (1957), pp. 367 ff.

E. FIUMI, 'Materiali volterrani nel Museo Archaeologico di Firenze', *ibid.*, 25 (1957), pp. 463 ff.

E. FIUMI, 'Scoperta di due tombe etrusche e di una romana in località Poggio alle Croci, Volterra', *ibid.*, 27 (1959), pp. 251 ff.

E. FIUMI, 'Volterra. Scavi nell'area del teatro romano negli anni 1950–53' in *Notizie degli Scavi* (1955), pp. 114 ff.

A. DE AGOSTINO, 'Volterra, il teatro romano. Studio architettonico e ricostruzione', *ibid.* (1955), pp. 150 ff.

E. FIUMI, 'La facies arcaica del territorio volterrano' in *Studi Etruschi*, 29 (1961), pp. 253 ff.

M. MONTAGNA PASQUINUCCI, *Le kelebai volterrane* (Pisa 1968)

M. MONTAGNA PASQUINUCCI, 'La ceramica a vernice nera del Museo Guarnacci di Volterra' in *Mélanges de l'École Française de Rome, Antiquité*, 84.1 (1972), pp. 269 ff.

F. H. PAIRAULT, *Recherches sur quelques séries d'urnes de Volterra à représentations mythologiques* (Collection de l'École Française de Rome, 12; Rome 1972)

Siena

R. BIANCHI BANDINELLI, 'Siena' in *Enciclopedia dell'arte antica, classica e orientale*, 1970 supplement (Rome 1973), pp. 718 ff.

R. BIANCHI BANDINELLI, 'La tomba dei Calini Sepus presso Monteriggioni' in *Studi Etruschi*, 2 (1928), pp. 133 ff.

R. BIANCHI BANDINELLI, 'Materiali archeologici della Valdelsa' in *La Balzana*, 2 (1928)

A. DE AGOSTINO, 'Nuovi incrementi del Museo Archeologico' in *Studi Etruschi*, 21 (1950–1), pp. 332 ff.

K. M. PHILLIPS Jr, 'Relazione preliminare sugli scavi promossi dalla "Etruscan Foundation" di Detroit nella provincia di Siena durante il 1964' in *Notizie degli Scavi* (1965), pp. 5 ff.

Asciano

A. DE AGOSTINO in *Studi Etruschi*, 27 (1959), pp. 277 ff.

A. J. PFFIFIG, 'La genealogia della Famiglia Hepni', *ibid.*, 31 (1963), pp. 239 ff.

Murlo—Poggio Civitate

Poggio Civitate : the Archaic Etruscan Sanctuary (catalogue of 1970 exhibition) (Florence 1970)

M. CRISTOFANI – K. PHILLIPS, 'Ager Clusinus (Poggio Civitate, Murlo, Siena)' in *Studi Etruschi*, 38 (1970), pp. 288 ff.

K. M. PHILLIPS Jr, 'Bryn Mawr College excavations in Tuscany, 1972' in *American Journal of Archaeology*, 77 (1973), pp. 319 ff; 78 (1974)

Castellina in Chianti

L. PERNIER, 'Castellina in Chianti. Grande tumulo con ipogei paleoetruschi sul poggio di Montecalvario' in *Notizie degli Scavi* (1916), pp. 263 ff.

F. NICOSIA in *Studi Etruschi*, 35 (1967), pp. 280 ff.

Luni

L. BANTI, *Luni* (Florence 1937)

A. ANDRÉN, *Architectural Terracottas from Etrusco-Italic Temples* (Lund 1939–40), pp. 282 ff.

G. CAPUTO, 'Nuova testa fittile del tempio di Luni' in *Studi Etruschi*, 24 (1955–6), pp. 221 ff.

Castiglioncello

G. MAETZKE, 'Castiglioncello' in *Enciclopedia dell'arte antica, classica e orientale*, 1970 supplement (Rome 1973), pp. 188 ff.

Cecina

G. MAETZKE, 'Cecina' in *Enciclopedia dell'arte antica, classica e orientale*, 1970 supplement (Rome 1973), pp. 196–7

P. MINGAZZINI, 'La tomba a tholos di Casaglia' in *Studi Etruschi*, 8 (1934), pp. 58 ff.

Populonia

A. MINTO, *Populonia. La necropoli arcaica* (Florence 1922)

A. MINTO, *Populonia* (Florence 1943)

A. DE AGOSTINO, 'Nuovi contributi all'archeologia di Populonia' in *Studi Etruschi*, 24 (1955–6), pp. 255 ff.

A. DE AGOSTINO, 'La nuova tomba a edicola di Populonia', *ibid.*, 26 (1958–9), pp. 27 ff.

C. BATTISTI, 'Sul nome di Populonia', *ibid.*, 27 (1959), pp. 385 ff.

A. DE AGOSTINO, 'Populonia (Livorno). Scoperte archeologiche nella necropoli negli anni 1957–60' in *Notizie degli Scavi* (1961), pp. 63 ff.

A. DE AGOSTINO, 'La cinta fortificata di Populonia' in *Studi Etruschi*, 30 (1962), pp. 275 ff.

Massa Marittima

D. LEVI, 'La necropoli del lago dell'Accesa' in *Monumenti Antichi dell'Accademia dei Lincei*, 35 (1933), c. 5 ff.

G. MONACO, *Museo Civico. Collezioni archeologiche* (Empoli 1964)

R. GRIFONI CREMONESI, 'Revisione e studio dei materiali preistorici della Toscana' in *Atti della Società Toscana di Scienze Naturali, Memorie*, series A, 78 (1971), pp. 170 ff.

Vetulonia

I. FALCHI, *Vetulonia e la sua necropoli antichissima* (Florence 1891)

G. CAMPOREALE, 'Rapporti fra Tarquinia e Vetulonia in epoca villanoviana' in *Studi Etruschi*, 32 (1964), pp. 3 ff.

G. CAMPOREALE – G. UGGERI, 'Tumulo e fossa di Castelvecchio (Vetulonia)', *ibid.*, 34 (1966), pp. 273 ff.

A. TALOCCHINI – G. GIACOMELLI, 'Il nuovo alfabeto di Vetulonia', *ibid.*, 34 (1966), pp. 239 ff.

G. CAMPOREALE, *La tomba del Duce* (*Monumenti etruschi pubblicati dall'Istituto di Studi Etruschi ed Italici*, 1; Florence 1967)

G. CAMPOREALE, *I commerci di Vetulonia in età orientalizzante* (*Studi e materiali dell'Istituto di Etruscologia e Antichità Italiche dell'Università di Roma*, VII; Florence 1969)

Roselle

C. LAVIOSA, 'L'urbanistica delle città arcaiche e le strutture in mattoni crudi di Roselle' in *Atti del Convegno sulla città etrusca e italica preromana* (Bologna 1970), pp. 209 ff.

R. BIANCHI BANDINELLI, 'L'esplorazione di Roselle', *ibid.*, pp. 141 ff.

P. BOCCI, 'Correnti di commercio e influssi culturali a Roselle', *ibid.*, pp. 157 ff.

C. LAVIOSA, 'Roselle' in *Enciclopedia dell'arte antica, classica e orientale*, 1970 supplement (Rome 1973), pp. 676–7

Grosseto

A. MAZZOLAI, 'Materiali per un corpus di bronzetti etruschi. La collezione del Museo Archeologico di Grosseto' in *Studi Etruschi*, 26 (1958–9), pp. 193 ff.

A. MAZZOLAI – G. BARTOLONI, *Mostra del restauro archeologico. Etruria grossetana* (Grosseto 1970)

Talamone

A. ANDRÉN, *Architectural Terracottas from Etrusco-Italic Temples* (Lund 1939–40)

O. W. VON VACANO, 'Grosseto. Scavi sul Talamonaccio' in *Notizie degli Scavi* (1965), pp. 30 ff.; (1961), pp. 251 ff.

O. W. VON VACANO, 'Oedipus zwischen den Viergespannen. Studien zur Komposition der Giebelskulpturen von Telamon' in *Römische Mitteilungen*, 68 (1961), pp. 9 ff.

P. SOMMELLA, *Antichi campi di battaglia in Italia* (*Quaderni dell'Istituto di Topografica Antica dell'Università di Roma*, III; 1967), pp. 11 ff.

M. MARTELLI – F. NICOSIA in *Restauri archeologici* (Florence 1969), pp. 117–18

Orbetello

M. SANTANGELO, *L'Antiquarium di Orbetello* (Rome 1954)

G. MAETZKE, 'Orbetello. Trovamenti archeologici vari' in *Notizie degli Scavi* (1958), pp. 34 ff.

Cosa

F. E. BROWN, 'Cosa I: history and topography' in *Memoirs of the American Academy in Rome*, 20 (1951), pp. 7 ff.

F. CASTAGNOLI, 'La centurazione di Cosa', *ibid.*, 24 (1956), pp. 147 ff.

D. M. TAYLOR, 'Cosa: black-glaze pottery', *ibid.*, 25 (1957), pp. 65 ff.

F. E. BROWN – E. H. RICHARDSON – L. RICHARDSON, 'Cosa II: the temples of the Arx', *ibid.*, 26 (1960), pp. 1 ff.

Magliano

A. MINTO, 'Per la topografia di Heba etrusca' in *Studi Etruschi*, 9 (1935), pp. 11 ff.

A. MINTO, 'Magliano in Toscana. Scoperte archeologiche in località denominata le Sassaie' in *Notizie degli Scavi* (1943), pp. 15 ff.

G. MAETZKE, 'Tombe etrusche in località Poggio Bocchino', *ibid.* (1956), pp. 6 ff.

Marsiliana d'Albegna

A. MINTO, *Marsiliana d'Albegna* (Florence 1921)

G. CAMPOREALE, 'Su due placche bronzee da Marsiliana' in *Studi Etruschi*, 35 (1967), pp. 31 ff.

M. CRISTOFANI, 'Un'iscrizione arcaica da Marsiliana d'Albegna', *ibid.*, 37 (1969), pp. 283 ff.

M. CRISTOFANI – F. NICOSIA, 'Il restauro degli avori di Marsiliana d'Albegna', *ibid.*, 37 (1969), pp. 351 ff.

M. CRISTOFANI, 'Kotyle d'argento dal Circolo degli Avori di Marsiliana d'Albegna', *ibid.*, 38 (1970), pp. 271 ff.

M. CRISTOFANI, 'Il Circolo degli Avori di Marsiliana d'Albegna' in *Nuove letture di monumenti etruschi dopo il restauro* (Florence 1971), pp. 31 ff.

Saturnia

A. MINTO, 'Saturnia etrusca e romana' in *Monumenti Antichi dell'Accademia dei Lincei*, 30 (1925), pp. 1 ff.

Poggio Buco

G. MATTEUCIG, *Poggio Buco. The Necropolis of Statonia* (Berkeley–Los Angeles 1951)

G. BARTOLONI, *Le tombe da Poggio Buco nel Museo Archeologico di Firenze (Monumenti etruschi pubblicati a cura dell'Istituto di Studi Etruschi ed Italici*, 3; Florence 1972)

Pitigliano

R. BIANCHI BANDINELLI, *Sovana* (Florence 1929)

A. MAZZOLAI – G. BARTOLONI in *Mostra del restauro archeologico* (Grosseto 1970), pp. 72 ff.; pp. 100 ff.

Sovana

G. ROSI, 'Sepulchral architecture as illustrated by the rock-façades of central Etruria' in *Journal of Roman Studies*, 15 (1925), pp. 1 ff.; 17 (1927), pp. 59 ff.

R. BIANCHI BANDINELLI, *Sovana* (Florence 1929)

P. E. ARIAS – O. PANCRAZI – M. MONTAGNA PASQUINUCCI, 'Sovana (Grosseto). Scavi effettuati dal 1962 al 1964' in *Notizie degli Scavi* (1971), pp. 55 ff.

Sorano

R. BIANCHI BANDINELLI, *Sovana* (Florence 1929), *passim*

G. MAETZKE in *Notizie degli Scavi* (1957), pp. 53 ff.

The islands

M. BIZZARRI, 'Un ripostiglio eneo nell'isola del Giglio' in *Studi Etruschi*, 33 (1965), pp. 515 ff.

R. C. BRONSON – G. UGGERI, 'Isola del Giglio, isola di Giannutri, Monte Argentario, laguna di Orbetello', *ibid.*, 38 (1970), pp. 201 ff.

R. CREMONESI GRIFONI, 'Revisione e studio dei materiali preistorici della Toscana' in *Atti della Società Toscana di Scienze Naturali, Memorie*, series A, 78 (1971), pp. 170 ff.

Florence, Museo Archeologico

G. CAPUTO in *Enciclopedia dell'arte antica, classica e orientale*, 1970 supplement (1973), p. 335

A. MINTO, 'La tomba a camera di Casal Marittimo' in *Studi Etruschi*, 4 (1930), pp. 54 ff.

P. BOCCI, *Guida ai vasi etruschi* (Florence 1959)

P. BOCCI, 'Il sarcofago tarquiniese delle Amazzoni al Museo Archeologico di Firenze' in *Studi Etruschi*, 28 (1960), pp. 109 ff.

P. BOCCI, 'Alcuni vasi inediti del Museo di Firenze', *ibid.*, 29 (1961), pp. 89 ff.

C. LAVIOSA, *Guida alle stele arcaiche e al materiale volterrano* (Florence 1962)

F. NICOSIA, 'Il cinerario di Montescudaio' in *Studi Etruschi*, 37 (1969), pp. 367 ff.

M. CRISTOFANI, 'Prolegomena a un nuovo restauro del cratere François' in *Bollettino d'Arte*, series V.3–4 (1972) pp. 199 ff.

Cerveteri

R. MENGARELLI in *Studi Etruschi*, 1 (1927), pp. 145 ff.; 9 (1935), pp. 83 ff.; 10 (1936), pp. 67 ff.; 11 (1937), pp. 77 ff.

L. PARETI, *La tomba Regolini-Galassi* (Rome 1957)

B. PACE – R. VIGHI – G. RICCI – M. MORETTI, 'Caere, scavi di R. Mengarelli' in *Monumenti Antichi dell'Accademia dei Lincei*, 42 (1955)

M. PALLOTTINO, *La necropoli di Cerveteri* (Rome 1957; earlier edn tr. as *The Necropolis of Cerveteri*, Rome 1950)

I. POHL, 'The Iron Age necropolis of Sorbo at Cerveteri' in *Acta Instituti Romani Regni Sueciae*, XXXII (Stockholm 1972)

Pyrgi

G. COLONNA *et al.*, *Pyrgi, scavi nel santuario etrusco (1959–67)*, 2 vols (1973; supplement to *Notizie degli Scavi*, XXIV, 1970)

Le lamine di Pyrgi (Quaderni dell'Accademia dei Lincei, 147; Rome 1970, with biblio.)

Tarquinia

M. PALLOTTINO, 'Tarquinia' in *Monumenti Antichi dell'Accademia dei Lincei*, 36 (1937)

P. DUCATI – P. ROMANELLI – G. BECATTI – F. MAGI – M. CRISTOFANI, *Monumenti della pittura antica scoperti in Italia*, 4 fascicles (Rome 1937–71)

P. ROMANELLI, *Tarquinia, la necropoli e il museo* (*Itinerari dei Musei e Monumenti d'Italia*; Rome 1940)

P. ROMANELLI, 'Tarquinia. Scavi e ricerche nell'area della città', in *Notizie degli Scavi* (1948)

C. M. LERICI, *Prospezioni archeologiche a Tarquinia. La necropoli delle tombe dipinte* (Milan 1956)

R. BARTOCCINI – C. M. LERICI – M. MORETTI, *La tomba delle Olimpiadi* (Milan 1959)

M. MORETTI, *Nuovi monumenti della pittura etrusca* (Milan 1966)

H. HENCKEN, *Tarquinia, Villanovans and Early Etruscans*, 2 vols (Cambridge, Mass. 1968)

H. HENCKEN, *Tarquinia and Etruscan Origins* (London 1968)

Sanctuary at Punta della Vipera

M. TORELLI, 'Terza campagna di scavi a Punta della Vipera e scoperta di una laminetta plumbea inscritta' in *Archeologia Classica*, 18 (1966), pp. 283 ff.

M. TORELLI, 'Terza campagna di scavi a Punta della Vipera' in *Studi Etruschi*, 35 (1967), pp. 332 ff.

Porto Clementino

M. TORELLI – F. BOITANI, 'Gravisca. Scavi nella città etrusca e romana. Campagne 1969 e 1970' in *Notizie degli Scavi* (1971), pp. 195 ff.

M. TORELLI, 'Il santuario di Gravisca' in *La Parola del Passato* (1971), pp. 44 ff.

Vulci

ST. GSELL, *Fouilles dans la nécropole de Vulci* (Paris 1891)

F. MESSERSCHMIDT – A. VON GERKAN – K. RONCZEWSKI, *Nekropolen von Vulci* (Berlin 1930)

R. BARTOCCINI, 'Tre anni di scavi a Vulci (1956–1958)' in *Atti del VII Congresso Internazionale di Archeologia Classica*, II (Rome 1960)

R. BARTOCCINI, 'Il grande tempio di Vulci' in *Études Étrusco-Italiques* (Louvain 1963)

M. T. FALCONI AMORELLI, *La collezione Massimo* (Rome 1968)

A. HUS, *Vulci étrusque et étrusco-romaine* (Paris 1971)

M. TORELLI. 'Vulci' in *Enciclopedia dell'arte antica, classica e orientale*, 1970 supplement (Rome 1973)

Veii

J. B. WARD PERKINS, 'Veii, the historical topography of the ancient city' in *Papers of the British School at Rome*, 29 (1961), pp. 1 ff. (with biblio.)

A. KAHANE – L. M. THREIPLAND – J. B. WARD PERKINS, 'The Ager Veientanus north and east of Rome', *ibid.*, 36 (1968)

A. DE AGOSTINO, 'La tomba delle anatre a Veio' in *Archeologia Classica*, 15 (1963), pp. 219 ff.

L. BANTI, 'Le pitture della tomba Campana a Veii' in *Studi Etruschi*, 38 (1970), pp. 27 ff.

'Scavi nelle necropoli villanoviane in località "Quattro Fontanili"' in *Notizie degli Scavi* (1963), pp. 47 ff.; (1965), pp. 49 ff.; (1967), pp. 87 ff.; (1970), pp. 178 ff.; (1972), pp. 195 ff.

Monti della Tolfa

O. TOTI, *I monti Ceriti nell'età di Ferro* (Civitavecchia 1961)

O. TOTI, *Allumiere e il suo territorio* (Rome 1967)

M. A. DEL CHIARO, 'An archaeological-topographical study of the Tolfa–Allumiere district: preliminary report' in *American Journal of Archaeology*, 66 (1962), pp. 69 ff.

M. TORELLI, 'Tolfa' in *Enciclopedia dell'arte antica, classica e orientale*, VII (1966), pp. 904 ff.

Civitavecchia

S. BASTIANELLI, 'Civitavecchia. Scavi eseguiti nelle Terme Taurine o Traiane' in *Notizie degli Scavi* (1933)

S. BASTIANELLI, 'Civitavecchia. Nuove esplorazioni eseguite nelle Terme Taurine', *ibid.* (1942)

Region of the cliff cemeteries

G. ROSI, 'Sepulchral architecture as illustrated by the rock-façades of central Etruria' in *Journal of Roman Studies*, 15 (1925), pp. 1 ff.; 17 (1927), pp. 59 ff.

G. COLONNA, 'L'Etruria meridionale interna dal Villanoviano alle tombe rupestri' in *Studi Etruschi*, 35 (1967), pp. 3 ff.

S. Giuliano

A. GARGANA, 'La necropoli rupestre di S. Giuliano' in *Monumenti Antichi dell'Accademia dei Lincei*, 33 (1931), pp. 298 ff.

P. VILLA D'AMELIO, 'S. Giuliano, scavi e scoperte nella necropoli dal 1957 al 1959' in *Notizie degli Scavi* (1963), pp. 1 ff.

Blera

H. KOCH – E. VON MERCKLIN – C. WEICKERT – B. NOGARA, 'Bieda' in *Mitteilungen des Deutschen Archäologischen Instituts, Römische Abteilung* (1915), pp. 161 ff.

A. GARGANA – P. ROMANELLI in *Notizie degli Scavi* (1932), pp. 485 ff.

Norchia

A. GARGANA, 'Le sculture dei tempietti rupestri di Norchia' in *Bollettino Municipale di Viterbo* (1933)

A. GARGANA, 'Norchia, ritrovamento di tombe etrusche' in *Notizie degli Scavi* (1936), pp. 268 ff.

C. F. GIULIANI, 'Norchia (studi di urbanistica antica)' in *Quaderni dell'Istituto di Topografia Antica dell'Università di Roma*, II (1966), pp. 5 ff.

Castel d'Asso

E. COLONNA DI PAOLO – G. COLONNA, *Castel d'Asso* (*Le necropoli rupestri dell'Etruria meridionale*, I; Rome 1970)

S. Giovenale

E. BERGGREN – M. MORETTI, 'S. Giovenale' in *Notizie degli Scavi* (1960), pp. 1 ff.

K. HANELL in *Etruscan Culture, Land and People* (New York–Malmö 1962), pp. 279 ff.

Various authors, 'S. Giovenale' in *Acta Instituti Romani Regni Sueciae*, XXVI.1 (Stockholm 1972)

Luni sul Mignone

C. E. ÖSTENBERG, 'Luni sul Mignone e problemi della preistoria d'Italia' in *Acta Instituti Romani Regni Sueciae*, XXV (Lund 1967)

Tuscania

L. MARCHESE, *Il museo di Tuscania* (1964)

G. COLONNA, 'Tuscania, monumenti etruschi di epoca arcaica' in *Archeologia*, 6 (1967), pp. 87 ff.

S. QUILICI GIGLI, *Tuscania* (*Forma Italiae*, Regio VII, vol. II; Rome 1970)

Acquarossa

Gli Etruschi, nuove ricerche e scoperte (Viterbo 1972)

Ferento

L. ROSSI DANIELLI, *Gli Etruschi nel Viterbese*, I: *Ferento* (Viterbo 1960)

Volsinii and Lake Bolsena

French excavations: *Mélanges d'archéologie et d'histoire—École Française de Rome*, 59 (1947), pp. 9 ff.; 62 (1950), pp. 53 ff.; 67 (1954), pp. 49 ff.

G. COLONNA, 'L'Etruria meridionale interna dal Villanoviano alle tombe rupestri' in *Studi Etruschi*, 35 (1967), pp. 3 ff.

F. T. BUCHICCHIO, 'Note di topografia antica sulla Volsinii romana' in *Mitteilungen des Deutschen Archäologischen Instituts, Römische Abteilung*, 77 (1970), pp. 19 ff.

Orvieto

M. BIZZARRI, 'Orvieto' in *Enciclopedia dell'arte antica, classica e orientale*, V (1963), pp. 773 ff.

M. BIZZARRI, 'La necropoli di Crocifisso del Tufo in Orvieto' in *Studi Etruschi*, 30 (1962), pp. 1 ff.; 34 (1966), pp. 1 ff.

A. ANDRÉN, 'Il santuario della necropoli di Cannicella ad Orvieto', *ibid.*, 35 (1967), pp. 41 ff.

G. A. MANSUELLI, 'La necropoli orvietana di Crocifisso del Tufo: un documento di urbanistica etrusca', *ibid.*, 38 (1970), pp. 3 ff.

The Faliscan territory

W. DEECKE, *Die Falisker* (Strasbourg 1888)

L. A. HOLLAND, *The Faliscans in Prehistoric Times* (Rome 1925)

E. STEFANI, 'Civita Castellana. Tempio di Giunone Curite' in *Notizie degli Scavi* (1947), pp. 69 ff.

M. W. FREDERIKSEN – J. B. WARD PERKINS, 'The ancient road system of the central and northern Ager Faliscus' in *Papers of the British School at Rome*, 25 (1957)

G. DUNCAN, 'Sutri', *ibid.*, 26 (1958), pp. 63 ff.; 32 (1964), pp. 38 ff.

G. D. B. JONES, 'Capena and the Ager Capenas', *ibid.*, 30 (1962), pp. 116 ff.; 31 (1963), pp. 100 ff.

G. GIACOMELLI, *La lingua falisca* (Florence 1966)

Museo Gregoriano Etrusco

C. ALBIZZATI, *Vasi antichi dipinti del Vaticano*, I-VII (Vatican City 1924-37)

J. D. BEAZLEY – F. MAGI, *La raccolta B. Guglielmi nel Museo Gregoriano Etrusco*, I-II (Vatican City 1939-41)

A. D. TRENDALL, *Vasi italioti ed etruschi a figure rosse*, I-II (Vatican City 1953-5)

L. PARETI, *La tomba Regolini-Galassi* (Vatican City 1947)

W. HELBIG, *Führer durch die öffentlichen Sammlungen klassischer Altertümer in Rom*, I (Tübingen 1963), pp. 469 ff.

Museo di Villa Giulia

A. DELLA SETA, *Il museo di Villa Giulia* (Rome 1918)

M. MORETTI, *Museo di Villa Giulia* (Rome 1964)

W. HELBIG, *Führer durch die öffentlichen Sammlungen klassischer Altertümer in Rom*, III (Tübingen 1969)

Bologna

A. GRENIER, *Bologne villanovienne et étrusque* (Paris 1912)

P. DUCATI, *Storia di Bologna*, I: *I tempi antichi* (Bologna 1928)

G. A. MANSUELLI, 'La terza Bologna' in *Studi Etruschi*, 25 (1957), pp. 13 ff.

'Spina e l'Etruria padana' in *Atti del I Convegno di Studi Etruschi, Ferrara 1957* (supplement to *Studi Etruschi*, 25; 1959)

M. ZUFFA, 'La questione etrusca in Felsina' in *Civiltà del Ferro* (Bologna 1960), pp. 119 ff.

G. A. MANSUELLI, 'Quesiti e presupposti dell'urbanistica bolognese' in *Atti e Memorie della Deputazione di Storia Patria per le Province di Romagna*, new series, 12 (1960-3), pp. 301 ff.

G. A. MANSUELLI, 'Bologna etrusca' in *Mostra dell'Etruria padana e della città di Spina, Catalogo Mostra 1960*, I (Bologna 1960), pp. 145 ff.

C. MORIGO GOVI, 'Persistenze orientalizzanti nelle stele felsinee' in *Studi Etruschi*, 38 (1970), pp. 67 ff.

S. MAZZARINO, 'Intorno alla tradizione su Felsina *princeps Etruriae*' in *Atti del Convegno sulla città etrusca e italica preromana* (Bologna 1970), pp. 217 ff.

Spina

B. M. FELLETTI MAJ, 'La cronologia della necropoli di Spina e la ceramica alto-adriatica' in *Studi Etruschi*, 14 (1940), pp. 43 ff.

P. E. ARIAS – N. ALFIERI – M. HIRMER, *Spina* (Florence 1958)

Mostra dell'Etruria padana e della città di Spina, 2 vols. (Bologna 1960)

P. E. ARIAS – N. ALFIERI, *Spina. Il Museo Archeologico di Ferrara* (Florence 1960)

G. UGGERI – S. UGGERI PATITUCCI, 'Nuovi alfabetari dall'Etruria padana' in *Studi Etruschi*, 39 (1971), pp. 431 ff.

Adria

G. B. PELLEGRINI – G. FOGOLARI, 'Iscrizioni etrusche e venetiche di Adria' in *Studi Etruschi*, 26 (1958), pp. 103 ff.

G. FOGOLARI – B. M. SCARFÌ, *Adria antica* (Milan–Venice 1970)

Marzabotto

E. BRIZIO, *Guida alle antichità della villa e del Museo di Marzabotto* (2nd edn 1928)

P. E. ARIAS, 'Considerazioni sulla città etrusca a Pian di Misano (Marzabotto)' in *Atti e Memorie della Deputazione di Storia Patria per le Province di Romagna*, new series, 3 (1953)

G. A. MANSUELLI, *Guida alla città etrusca e al Museo di Marzabotto* (Bologna 1966)

R. A. STACCIOLI, 'Sulla struttura dei muri nelle case della città etrusca di Misano a Marzabotto' in *Studi Etruschi*, 35 (1967), pp. 113 ff.

C. SALETTI, 'Problemi artistici di Marzabotto' in *Atti del Convegno sulla città etrusca e italica preromana* (Bologna 1970), pp. 279 ff.

G. A. MANSUELLI, 'Marzabotto: dix années de fouilles et de recherches' in *Mélanges de l'Ecole Française de Rome, Antiquité*, 84.1 (1972), pp. 111 ff.

Casalecchio

CH. PEYRE, 'L'habitat étrusque de Casalecchio di Reno (Bologne)' in *Atti del Convegno sulla città etrusca e italica preromana* (Bologna 1970), pp. 253 ff.

F. H. PAIRAULT, 'L'habitat archaïque de Casalecchio di Reno près de Bologne. Structure planimétrique et technique de construction' in *Mélanges de l'École Française de Rome, Antiquité*, 84.1 (1972), pp. 145 ff.

Piacenza

M. PALLOTTINO, 'Deorum sedes' in *Studi in onore di A. Calderini e R. Paribeni*, III (Varese–Milan 1956)

F. ARISI, *Il Museo Civico di Piacenza* (Piacenza 1960), pp. 199 ff. no. 250, pp. 223 ff.

Capua

A. ADRIANI, 'Sculture in tufo' in *Cataloghi del Museo Provinciale Campano* (Rome 1939)

J. HEURGON, *Recherches sur l'histoire, la religion et la civilisation de Capoue préromaine* (Paris 1942)

M. PALLOTTINO, 'Sulla lettura e sul contenuto della grande iscrizione di Capua' in *Studi Etruschi*, 20 (1949), pp. 149 ff.

F. CASTAGNOLI, *Ippodamo di Mileto e l'urbanistica a pianta ortogonale* (Rome 1956)

W. JOHANNOWSKY, 'Problemi di classificazione e cronologia di alcune scoperte protostoriche a Capua e Cales' in *Studi Etruschi*, 33 (1965), pp. 685 ff.

W. JOHANNOWSKY, 'Problemi relativi alla precolonizzazione in Campania' in *Dialoghi di Archeologia*, 1 (1967), pp. 159 ff.

F. PARISE BADONI, *La ceramica campana a figure nere* (Florence 1968)

M. BONGHI JOVINO, *Capua preromana. Terrecotte votive*, I–II (Florence 1965–71)

Pompeii

A. SOGLIANO, *Pompei nel suo sviluppo storico*, I (1927)

A. BOETHIUS, 'Gli Etruschi in Pompei' in *Symbola Philologica O. A. Danielsson dicata* (Uppsala 1932)

A. MAIURI, 'Greci ed Etruschi a Pompei' in *Saggi di varie antichità* (Venice 1954), pp. 241 ff.

Marcina

B. D'AGOSTINO, 'Marcina?' in *Dialoghi di Archeologia*, 2 (1968), pp. 139 ff.

Salerno region

Catalogo della Mostra della Preistoria e Protostoria nel Salernitano (Salerno 1962)

A. VACCARO, 'La patera orientalizzante da Pontecagnano presso Salerno' in *Studi Etruschi*, 31 (1963), pp. 241 ff.

M. NAPOLI, 'Pontecagnano: problemi topografici e storici', *ibid.*, 33 (1965), pp. 661 ff.

B. D'AGOSTINO, 'Nuovi apporti della documentazione archeologica nell'Agro Picentino', *ibid.*, 33 (1965), pp. 671 ff.

B. D'AGOSTINO, 'Pontecagnano' in *Enciclopedia dell'arte antica classica e orientale*, 1970 supplement (Rome 1973), pp. 636 ff.

Ancient authors

Some of the ancient historians mentioned in the text survive only in fragments or quotations by later writers. Herodotus, Polybius, Dionysius of Halicarnassus, Cicero, Virgil, Livy, Strabo, Vitruvius, Pliny the Elder and Rutilius Namatianus, however, can all be found translated in the Loeb Classical Library series, with the Greek or Latin original text alongside (Rutilius Namatianus being in a volume entitled *Minor Latin Poets*). Several of these authors are also available in English translation, in the Penguin Classics and other series.

Chronological table

(Note: some dates, though given as exact years, may be found to differ by a year or so from those given elsewhere; this is usually the result of varying interpretations of ancient sources)

B.C.

?	Palaeolithic
c. 5000	Neolithic
	Chalcolithic
2000	
	Bronze Age: Terramara culture in northern Italy; Apennine culture in central and southern Italy
(c. 1400–	
c. 1100	Mycenaean Bronze Age culture in mainland Greece)
(c. 1200	'Peoples of the Sea' attack Egypt)
	Sub-Apennine culture
	(Protogeometric pottery in Greece)
1000	
	proto-Villanovan
	(Geometric pottery develops in Greece)
	Villanovan I
(814	Traditional date for foundation of Carthage by Phoenicians from Tyre)
800	
	Villanovan II
c. 770	Earliest Greek colony in Italy: Pithecusa, on island of Ischia
753	Traditional date for foundation of Rome by Romulus
c. 740	Greek colony of Cumae founded on Italian mainland
736	Earliest Greek colony in Sicily: Naxos (Protocorinthian pottery)
	Orientalizing period begins
700	
616–578	Traditional dates of reign of Tarquinius Priscus (Tarquin the Elder) at Rome
(c. 630	Corinthian pottery begins)
578–534	Reign of Servius Tullius at Rome
(c. 570	Athenian black-figure pottery begins)
(540s	Persians conquer kingdom of Lydia, advance to Aegean coast. East Greek cities of Ionia and elsewhere come under Persian rule)
c. 540	Greeks from Phocaea in Ionia settle at Alalia in Corsica, but are defeated at sea by joint fleets of Etruscans from Cerveteri and Carthaginians. Survivors settle at Velia in southern Italy
(c. 530	Athenian red-figure pottery begins)
534–510	Reign of Tarquinius Superbus (Tarquin the Proud) at Rome

524	Attack on Cumae by Etruscans and Umbrians repulsed by Cumaeans led by Aristodemos
510	Expulsion of the Tarquins from Rome
509	First year of the republic at Rome. Dedication of temple of Jupiter on Capitol
508	Supporting the exiled Tarquins, Porsenna of Chiusi attacks Rome
504	Etruscans, led by a son of Porsenna, defeated at Ariccia in Latium by Cumaeans under Aristodemos
499	Rome defeats Latins at Lake Regillus
(499–494	Unsuccessful revolt of Ionians against Persia
492–490,	
480–479	Graeco-Persian Wars)
483	Veii supports Fidenae against Rome
	(Classical style begins in Greece)
479	Raid from Veii on Janiculum hill (across Tiber from Rome). Clan of Fabii mounts own campaign against Veii from fort in Cremera valley
477	Fabii overwhelmingly defeated near the Cremera
474	Hieron of Syracuse defeats Etruscan fleet off Cumae. Peace treaty between Rome and Veii
453	Syracusan raid on Elba and Corsica
	Fidenae, supported by Veii, revolts against Rome, possibly more than once
425	Fidenae finally taken by Rome
424	Samnites from the mountains take Capua
421	Samnites take Cumae
(431–404	Peloponnesian War in Greece, including disastrous Athenian expedition against Syracuse (415–413))
? c. 400	Gauls invading from the north gradually settle in Po valley, raid repeatedly across Apennines
405–396	Siege of Veii by Romans, ending in its destruction
395	Capena submits to Rome
394	Unsuccessful siege of Falerii by Romans
391	Truce between Volsinii and Rome. Invading Gauls attack Chiusi, driven off by Etruscans and Romans
390	Rome sacked by Gauls

388	War between Rome and Tarquinia
384	Dionysios I of Syracuse raids Pyrgi
383	Romans establish *coloniae* at Nepi and Sutri
359–351	Wars between Tarquinia and Falerii, and Rome
353	Cerveteri (having supported Tarquinia and Falerii) makes peace with Rome
343–341	First Samnite War. Cities of Campania call on Rome for assistance against fresh invasions of Samnites from mountains
(323	Death of Alexander the Great. Beginning of Hellenistic age (to 30 B.C.))
311–310	Etruscans, intervening to support Samnites against Rome in Second Samnite War (326–304), make massive assault on Sutri. Fabius Rullianus crosses Monti Cimini and defeats Etruscans at Lake Vadimo near Volsinii
302	Roman intervention in civil strife at Arezzo
298–290	Third Samnite War. Samnites assisted by Gauls, Etruscans and other peoples of Italy. Roman victory at Sentinum (295)
294	Capture of Roselle. Etruscans make peace
283	Gauls, and Etruscans from Vulci and Volsinii, defeated at Lake Vadimo
(282–272	War in southern Italy between Romans and Pyrrhus, king of Epirus)
280	Surrender of Vulci, followed by Roman acquisition of its territory
273	Cerveteri submits to Rome. *Colonia* settled at Cosa
265–264	Destruction of Volsinii. Inhabitants resettled at Volsinii Novi
(264–241	First Punic War between Rome and Carthage, fought mainly in Sicily. Most of Sicily becomes first province of Roman empire)
241	Destruction of Falerii. Inhabitants resettled at Falerii Novi
225	Invading Gauls defeated by Romans and allies at Talamone
218–201	Second Punic War. Hannibal leads a Carthaginian army from Spain into Italy (218), ravaging Etruria and elsewhere and remaining in Italy until 204. Capua and other Campanian cities go over to him (216; Romans recapture Capua in 211). Romans counterattack in Spain and, from 204, in Africa under Scipio Africanus. (Victorious Romans are increasingly drawn into the Mediterranean world and into conflict with the Hellenistic kingdoms of the Seleucids (Syria and Asia Minor), Pergamum (Asia Minor), Macedonia and Egypt) Etruria, like most of Italy, suffers aftereffects of the war: the growth of large

	slave-worked estates, rural depopulation and urban unemployment. Symptoms of general unrest are revolts (in 196 in Etruria) of rural slaves, mainly former prisoners of war, and the growth of secret groups devoted to the orgiastic cult of Bacchus (the Roman Senate bans such groups in 186)
189	Latin *colonia* at Bologna, marking stage in gradual Roman conquest of Po valley (known as *Gallia Cisalpina*, Cisalpine Gaul, and not part of Italy until 42). Inhabitants of Latin *coloniae* had Latin status: not full Roman citizenship, but more rights than the Italian allies of Rome (the *socii*)
183	*Colonia* at Saturnia
177	*Colonia* at Luni, marking stage in Roman reduction of wild Ligurian tribes of northwest Italy
133	Tiberius Gracchus attempts to remedy agrarian problem by large-scale land grants, but is killed in a riot while seeking re-election as tribune
123–121	Tiberius's brother Gaius Gracchus, as tribune, introduces a wider programme, including new *coloniae* in Italy and outside it; killed in full-scale civil strife at Rome
91	Drusus, as tribune, proposes land reforms and granting Roman citizenship to the *socii*. His murder sparks off the Social War
90–89	Main fighting of Social War (Samnites continue resistance until 87). Citizenship granted by two laws: Lex Julia (90) grants it to Italian communities not in revolt, Lex Plautia Papiria (89) to individual applicants from other cities
88–82	Civil war (intermittent, and complicated by war in the East) between the conservative senatorial party, led by Sulla, and the populists, led by Marius (who dies in 86). After a final massacre, the victorious Sulla attempts conservative reform as dictator, but retires in 79
63–62	Catiline, unsuccessful candidate for consul, attempts a *coup d'état* at Rome, revolt in Etruria, but is killed in a skirmish near Pistoia
49–45	Civil war between Julius Caesar, and Pompey and the senatorial party. Caesar becomes dictator
44	Assassination of Caesar. His greatnephew C. Octavius takes the name C. Julius Caesar Octavianus (usually known as Octavian in English)
43	Antony (M. Antonius), Octavian and Lepidus appointed triumvirs (supreme commission of three). Sextus Pompeius (son of Pompey), appointed fleet commander by Senate, seizes Sicily, raids and blockades Italy

41–40	In Antony's absence abroad, his wife Fulvia and brother L. Antonius revolt against Octavian. L. Antonius besieged in Perugia, which is taken and sacked by Octavian	96–98	Nerva
		98–117	Trajan
		117–138	Hadrian
		138–161	Antoninus Pius
		161–180	Marcus Aurelius
39	Sextus Pompeius recognized as governor of Sicily, Sardinia and Corsica (until final defeat by Octavian's fleet in 36)	180–192	Commodus
		193–211	Septimius Severus
		211–217	Caracalla
(31–30)	Battle of Actium. Deaths of Antony and Cleopatra. Last Hellenistic kingdom, Egypt, taken over by Rome)		(The reigns of subsequent emperors are usually brief and violent, because of foreign invasions, army mutinies and other unrest)
27	Octavian takes title Augustus. Constitutional settlement makes him the first Roman emperor	284–305	Diocletian emperor; empire reorganized. Henceforward, division already existing usually recognized by appointment of two emperors, one for the East (capital Byzantium/Constantinople), one for the West

A.D.

14–68	Death of Augustus. Succession of other Julio-Claudian emperors: Tiberius (14–37), Caligula (37–41), Claudius (41–54) and Nero (54–68)	476	Deposition of Romulus Augustulus by the German Odoacer. End of Western Roman Empire
69–96	Flavian emperors: Vespasian (69–79), Titus (79–81) and Domitian (81–96)		

---

1 millimetre (mm) = 0·039 inches
1 centimetre (cm) = 0·394 inches (5 cm (= 50 mm) is just under 2 inches)
1 metre (m) = 3·281 feet (3 m is just under 10 feet)
1 kilometre (km) = 0·621 miles (8 km is just under 5 miles)
1 hectare (ha) = 2·471 acres

Glossary

a baule. Earrings made by bending a thin rectangular metal plate into an approximate cylinder and fitting little discs on the ends (Italian *baule*, 'travelling-bag', refers to the shape)

Acheloüs. God of the Greek river of that name; represented as bearded and horned (p. 209)

acropolis. Highest and best defended part of a city

acroterion. Ornament or statue placed on top of the pediment of a temple or other building (at the apex or at the ends of the gable)

aerarium. Treasury; public building containing a city's funds and other treasures

aes grave. Heavy cast bronze coinage of early Italy; earliest coinage of Rome

ala. Wing; corridor running alongside the cella of a temple; side room entered from the cella

alabastron. Small, almost cylindrical perfume jar

alberese. A form of limestone

amphora. Storage jar with two handles (p. 213)

anta. Pilaster terminating the side walls of a building projecting forward from the front wall

antefix. Plaque placed along the eaves at the side of a building to cover the end of a row of curved tiles (pp. 178, 265)

architrave. Lintel; the part of a colonnade that rests on top of the columns

arx. Citadel, usually on the acropolis of a city

askos. Pot with body resembling a wine-skin, and mouth (for filling) and spout (for pouring) on opposite sides at either end of central handle

barbarian. In this context, general term referring to the various invaders of Italy during the Dark and Middle Ages

basilica. Chief secular public building (usually a large rectangular hall) of a Roman town or city, used as law court and centre of local government

black-figure. Decoration of pottery in black gloss on the background of the natural reddish colour of the fired clay

bucchero. Pottery with a black-gloss surface (pp. 26, 166). There are two forms, **thin-walled** and **heavy**

caldarium. Room of a Roman bath-building with a hot steamy atmosphere

canopus. Urn with a human head (p. 44)

capitolium. Originally the Capitoline hill (Capitol) at Rome; a temple of Jupiter, Juno and Minerva (the **Capitoline triad**) at Rome or *coloniae*

cardo. In Roman cities built on a rectangular grid plan, street running north–south; the **cardo maximus** is the principal north–south street, in the centre of the city

cavea. Semicircular auditorium of a Roman theatre

cella. Principal room, behind the porch, of a temple, containing the cult object, usually a statue; small chamber in a tomb

chimaera. Monster, part lion, part goat, part snake (p. 43)

cippus. Small stone pillar, round or four-sided (pp. 24, 70)

cithara. Musical instrument resembling a lyre

colonia. Settlement of Roman citizens, planted in Italy or (later) outside it

columbarium. Cemetery consisting of niches in which cinerary urns were placed (pp. 234–235) (literally 'dovecot')

cornice. Horizontal moulded projection at the top of a wall

cube-tomb. Rock-cut tomb whose upper part consists of a monolithic free-standing block, more or less resembling a small building (pp. 260–261). Sometimes called die-tomb (*tomba a dado*)

curator. In the later Roman Empire, imperial official appointed to oversee the finances of a town

decumanus. Street running east–west (see **cardo**); the chief east–west street is the **decumanus maximus**

dentil. Raised rectangular architectural ornament, used in rows, forming part of the cornice

dictator. At Rome, originally a military commander with extraordinary powers; later an extraordinary supreme political office

dromos. Entrance corridor of a tomb

East Greek. Refers to the Greek settlements to the east of Greece proper, principally in coastal Asia Minor and its offshore islands

faience. Glazed terracotta (sometimes referred to as **glass paste**). Not to be confused with the Italian Renaissance ceramic of the same name

fibula. Large safety-pin, varying in shape; often highly decorative (p. 131)

foculus. Portable brazier; small rectangular pottery tray (p. 61)

frigidarium. Cold room of a Roman bath-building, usually containing or adjoining a cold plunge-bath

frons scaenae. Back wall of a Roman stage

gens. Clan. At Rome, a man's second name (a woman's first or sole name) gives the *gens* (e.g. C. Julius Caesar belongs to the *gens Julia*)

gorgon. Monstrous female with a terrifying expression, usually with snakes for hair (p. 231)

griffin. Monster with a lion's body and eagle's head and wings

groma. Roman surveying instrument, consisting of two bars at right angles with plumb lines at their ends

harpy. Monster with a woman's head and bust and a bird's body

haruspex. Priest skilled in divination, especially **haruspicy**, the derivation of omens from the appearance of the organs of sacrificed animals, particularly the liver (p. 287)

hawksbeak. Combination of convex and concave moulding resembling a hooked beak in profile

hoplite. Soldier in Greek heavy armour (p. 228)

hydria. Large water-jug, usually with handles on the body

hypocaust. Under-floor hot-air heating system of a Roman bath or house

impasto. In this context, unpurified clay used for early coarse pottery

Italic dialects. The group of Indo-European languages spoken in ancient Italy that includes Latin, Faliscan, Oscan and Umbrian

jar-tomb (*tomba a ziro*). Form of burial in which the urn is placed inside a large jar, and then buried

kantharos. Drinking cup with two tall handles and a foot

kline. Couch (used both for sleeping and for dining)

krater. Wide-mouthed vessel used for mixing wine and water. The handles of **column-kraters** are made of two rolled strips of clay; **volute-kraters** (p. 296) have handles curled into volutes on top; **calyx-kraters** (p. 297) are shaped rather like the trumpet of a daffodil

kylix. Shallow cup with handles and a foot (p. 210)

laconicum. Hot dry room of a Roman bath-building

Latins. Originally the inhabitants of Latium; later individuals and communities with the limited civil rights known as **Latin right** (*ius Latii*)

loculus. Rectangular niche

maenad. Female follower of Dionysus, usually represented dressed in skins and ecstatically drunk

magistrate. Official having judicial powers, often military authority as well

Magna Graecia. General term covering the Greek colonies in southern Italy, often including those in Sicily as well. Greeks from these colonies in Italy are sometimes termed **Italiotes**, from those in Sicily, **Siceliotes**

Mistress of Animals. Goddess, depicted as flanked by wild animals, worshipped in many cultures of the Near East, and known by many names; often identified by the Greeks with Artemis (p. 148)

municipium. Originally an Italian community in alliance with Rome; later a community of conquered people with a limited franchise; finally (from 1st century B.C.), any self-governing Italian town that was not a *colonia*

nenfro. A greyish tufa (p. 273)

Neo-Pythagoreanism. Greek philosophy, loosely related to the ideas of Pythagoras (late 6th century B.C.), who was particularly interested in numbers, cosmology and reincarnation

nuraghic. Belonging to the Bronze Age culture of Sardinia characterized by the building of stone towers (*nuraghi*)

nymphaeum. Room with fountains and statues

oinochoe. Wine-jug (p. 18; 'three-lobed' refers to the shape of the lip)

olpe. Oil-jug (p. 297)

opus caementicium. Rubble concrete

opus incertum. Concrete faced with irregularly-shaped stones

opus quadratum. Construction with rectangular blocks of stone

opus reticulatum. Concrete faced with square-based pyramidal blocks of stone set point inwards in a diamond pattern (p. 238)

opus signinum. Fine concrete containing crushed tile, often used for flooring

opus spicatum. Herringbone brickwork

orchestra. Space between stage and auditorium in a Greek of Roman theatre

Orphism. Greek religion, believed to have been founded by Orpheus, greatly interested in the fate of the soul after death

panchina. A brownish stone

patera. Shallow round dish, often with a raised boss in the centre, used for pouring ritual libations (p. 156)

pectoral. Large ornament covering the chest (pp. 288, 295)

pediment. Triangular space below a gabled roof

pelike. Wide-mouthed jar

peperino. A dark grey tufa from the Alban Hills

pietra fetida. A form of sandstone (p. 60)

pietra serena. A bluish sandstone

pithos. Large storage jar

pit-tomb (*tomba a pozzo*). Form of burial in which the urn is placed in a pit dug in the ground (pp. 166–167)

podium. Stone base of a building

polis. City, city-state

polychrome. Multi-coloured

polygonal work. Stonework using blocks of

different sizes and shapes carefully fitted together (p. 120)

praefurnium. Heated vestibule of a Roman bath

praetors. Originally the annually appointed chief magistrates and military commanders at Rome, later called **consuls**; later, the annual magistrates next in rank after the consuls

pronaos. Vestibule of a temple

proscenium. Raised stage of a Roman theatre

pyxis. Small box or box-like pot (p. 26)

red-figure. Decoration of pottery with the figures left in the natural reddish colour of the fired clay on a black-gloss background

satyr. Mythological being, part man, part animal (usually goat)

scarab. Beetle-shaped ornament or amulet

Scylla. Female sea monster, sometimes represented as a ferocious double-tailed mermaid

sea horse. In this context, fantastic animal, part horse, part fish (p. 300)

Silenus. Companion of Dionysus; represented as a fat, drunk old man with pointed ears (p. 178)

situla. Bucket; large wide-mouthed jar with no handles (pp. 185, 302)

skyphos. Drinking cup with two handles

sphinx. Monster with human head and lion's body. Graeco-Roman sphinxes are usually winged (p. 60) and female

stamnos. Wide-mouthed jar

stele. Stone slab, usually set upright in the ground to mark a tomb or commemorate an event (pp. 78, 300)

strigil. Instrument resembling a curved blunt knife, used for scraping off perspiration and excess oil after a bath

stylus. Pointed instrument for writing on waxed tablets

sudatorium. Hottest steam room of a Roman bath-building

tepidarium. Warm room of a Roman bath-building

tholos. Circular building; in this context, circular tomb with corbelled roof

torus. Convex moulding

trench-tomb (*tomba a fossa*). Tomb in which the body is buried in a long grave

tribunal. Raised platform; in a basilica, the place where the magistrates sat

tribune. Elected official, usually regarded as supporting the people against the Senate

tumulus. Mound of stones or earth over a tomb or tombs (p. 97)

tutulus. Roughly conical hat (p. 25); similar style of hairdressing

Typhon. Snake-footed giant (pp. 173, 201)

tyrant. Unconstitutional ruler (not necessarily a pejorative term in ancient times)

urn. Container for cremated remains; may be biconical (pp. 212–213), hut- (p. 184), jar- or chest-shaped (p. 258)

vase painters. The names of some of these are signed on their vases. Others are called after: potters whose vases they painted (e.g. Kleophrades Painter); museums (Berlin Painter) or collections; individual vases (Painter of Vatican 350) or vase-subjects (Aurora Painter); or stylistic pecularities (Bearded Sphinx Painter)

volute. Architectural or other ornament in the shape of a spiral coil

vomitorium. Doorway leading into a theatre or amphitheatre

wasters. Pots that went wrong in the firing, usually found near the place of manufacture (being unmarketable)